KOOP

KOOP

The Memoirs of
America's Family Doctor

C. Everett Koop, M.D.

RANDOM HOUSE   NEW YORK

Copyright © 1991 by C. Everett Koop and Allen V. Koop
All rights reserved under International and Pan-American Copyright Conventions. Published
in the United States by Random House, Inc., New York and simultaneously in Canada by
Random House of Canada Limited, Toronto.

Grateful acknowledgment is made to the following for permission to reprint previously
published material:

Dartmouth College: Excerpts from the Dartmouth Alma Mater. Copyright Trustees of
Dartmouth College, Hanover, New Hampshire.
Harcourt Brace Jovanovich, Inc., and Faber and Faber, Ltd.: Excerpt from "The Hollow
Men" from *Collected Poems,* 1909–1962 by T. S. Eliot. Copyright 1936 by Harcourt Brace
Jovanovich, Inc. Copyright © 1964, 1963 by T. S. Eliot. Rights throughout the world
excluding the United States of America are controlled by Faber and Faber, Ltd. Reprinted
by permission of Harcourt Brace Jovanovich, Inc., and Faber and Faber, Ltd.

Library of Congress Cataloging-in-Publication Data
Koop, C. Everett (Charles Everett), 1916–
Koop: the memoirs of America's family doctor

R154.K45A3 1991
610'.92—dc20
[B] 91-52671

Manufactured in the United States of America
24689753
First Edition

To my wife, Betty, our children, and theirs

Acknowledgments

So many have affected my life and thus the recounting of it that I am indebted to people, families, and institutions too numerous to cite.

I always knew I would someday write about surgery and the development of pediatric surgery as a specialty. From time to time, I wrote or dictated bits and pieces to be used later. One of my Children's Hospital secretaries, Eiko Ikeda, did the typing. Although I have thanked her many times, I am still grateful.

When I went to Washington I kept notes from time to time—not just about what happened but how I felt about it. Laura B. Lyons, another Children's Hospital secretary, but then retired, was the ideal person to type some of these. She was loyal, faithful, and trusted.

When I finally began putting it all down, the typing was begun by Veneda Dietrich and then taken up by Nancy Breckenridge, and finally by Nancy Rittmann, who fit so well into my life and endeavors that she became my assistant by the time the first draft was completed. From then on, she and two other remarkable women managed my life so I could complete the task. Mary Lee Geoghegan joined me the day I retired as Surgeon General, and with unusual competence has managed my professional life ever since. Diane Andrejkovics is the third. She grew in responsibilities by the day, making it possible to keep me productive. To fill gaps in my memory, find dates, and verify recollections, I am indebted to a long list of friends, new and old: Faye Abdellah, Ed Martin, Shirley Bonnem, Erna Goulding, Louise Schnaufer, James Martindale, Ron Davis, Matt Myers, Jim Brown, Sue Dahlman, Jan Aamodt, Sharon Smith, Walter Wimer, and Fran Fenn.

Ted Cron, who was my special assistant for my entire tenure as

Surgeon General, contributed in many ways to my understanding and articulation of issues. He'll remember the evolution of many efforts and recognize his contribution to much I have written.

Jim Dickson has been advisor and confidant for the past decade and has contributed more than he knows. Tim Johnson provided a quiet refuge to do some of the writing, was my first critic, and the only person who read the whole manuscript except my family. He was invaluable.

Owen Laster, my agent, and Peter Osnos, my publisher, provided the necessary discouraging criticism early on but the encouragement I needed to finish. I am grateful for their expertise, insight, and guiding hand. When I met Betsy Rapoport, my editor, I told her I wanted her to be that editor I always read about, "whose unbelievable skills and understanding made this book possible." She was all those things and more; she became a friend. John Whitman met tight deadlines and made good photos out of bad ones.

My family took up lots of slack and their considerate planning helped in many ways. My daughter, Betsy Thompson, helped enormously with collating and cataloging incidents and anecdotes and computerized them for ready access. As always, my wife, Betty, was counselor and guide, reader and proofreader, critic, advisor, and friend.

When it came to creative and innovative help, hard work, writing, and drudgery, my eldest son, Allen, must take the lion's share of credit for this book; without him it would not have appeared for years—if ever. As I began to write, his importance to the project grew, especially as other obligations with television, the lecture circuit, and professional obligations began to compete for book time. I will never be able to say thank you and feel that I have said it adequately.

Contents

CONTENTS

PART III: BECOMING SURGEON GENERAL

PART IV. GREAT ISSUES

PART V. THE SURGEON GENERAL REPORTS

KOOP

Introduction

On an ordinary day in August 1980, a call slipped through the screening system in my office at the Children's Hospital of Philadelphia.

"Don't you think it's time the Surgeon General was a surgeon?"

"Who is this?"

"It doesn't matter—don't you think it's time the Surgeon General was a surgeon?"

I didn't have a ready answer. In fact, like most Americans, I didn't think about the Surgeon General very much, if at all. But my caller urged me to consider the opportunity to serve a new Republican administration. The presidential election was still fifteen weeks away, and I was anything but a politician, but instinctively I decided to keep my options open. I said I might be available. I took the caller's name and number and tucked it under the corner of my desk blotter. He was Carl Anderson, administrative aide to North Carolina Senator Jesse Helms.

The next day the Heritage Foundation called.

"You've turned up in our memory bank as a conservative Republican, one who is pro-life with a credible experience in academia. How would you like to be Surgeon General?"

I repeated to the second caller—whose name I no longer remember—that yes, I might be available. A new name and number joined its predecessor under the corner of the blotter.

A few days later came the third call.

"Dr. Koop, this is John Condon. We met at Billy Graham's when you briefed him on some biomedical issues. I am now a headhunter for Reagan–Bush. How would you like to be the Surgeon General?"

"What makes you so sure they'll be elected?"

"Don't worry about that!"

"This is the third call I've had on this subject. Do you guys work together? Do you know what each other is doing? . . . You can say I might be available."

That name and number found its place with the others.

Stretching back in my desk chair, I wondered about the timing of the calls. I was entering the last year of my academic career. I would turn sixty-five the next calendar year, and it was customary at the University of Pennsylvania School of Medicine to retire in June of the year when the magic number sixty-five rolled around.

A member of the medical school faculty since 1942, I had climbed the academic ladder to hold two professorships. In addition, as a pediatric surgeon, my clinical interests and credentials had put me in the role of surgeon-in-chief of the Children's Hospital of Philadelphia—the first in the country—since 1948. My retirement had already been planned for April: a farewell party in combination with a scientific program to which some of my colleagues in pediatric surgery from around the world had been invited. Then I would be old Mr. Chips at the Children's Hospital, with my successor already in my office.

Over the next few weeks, the three telephone calls about the Surgeon General position crossed my mind only infrequently. My wife, Betty—I alone usually call her Liz—mentioned it occasionally, but the prospect never seemed very real to me.

After work on election day in November 1980, Betty and I drove down to Deerfield, New Jersey, about an hour away from our suburban Philadelphia home, to watch the election returns with our son Norman and his wife, Anne. As I say, I was not a political animal, my only involvement in politics being limited to membership on the Committee of 70, a political watchdog committee striving to keep voting honest on election day in Philadelphia—no small chore. I wanted to see a Republican victory in 1980 because I—like most of the electorate, as it turned out—was fretting about the apparent inability of our country to achieve its potential during the Carter administration. As we watched the Reagan landslide, I felt an optimism unlike anything I had previously felt on an election evening.

As we drove home, Betty, with her customary good sense, gave me a bit of advice that changed my life: As usual, she was filling her role as my most valued counselor. Over the years, her advice had repeatedly—and wisely—steered our course.

"You do know you're going to be miserable in the job you've chosen for yourself next year after you retire. Have you really thought what it would be like, after being chief for thirty-some years, to be floating around the hospital—operating, teaching, and so on, but with someone else at the helm? You will still be regarded by many as the boss, and they'll bring you all their dissatisfactions that come with a new regime—but you'll be powerless to do anything about it. You'll be miserable. Why don't you call those people about being Surgeon General?"

Driving along in the Pennsylvania darkness, I knew she was right. I didn't have a shred of enthusiasm as I looked at my future. So Wednesday morning, first thing, I found tucked under the leather border of my desk blotter the wrinkled scraps of paper with the three names and phone numbers.

Rather miraculously, I found the first two immediately at the other end of the line. John Condon called me back. I remember being surprised that his wife knew who I was. I said the same thing to each: "When we last spoke, I said in reference to the appointment of Surgeon General that I 'might be available.' I would like to change that now to 'enthusiastically seeking.' "

"Surgeon General" is a better-known title than it is a position. The job itself is just a little more than a hundred years old. In 1870 a legislative act placed the Public Health Service, which had been founded in President John Adams' day, under the direction of one medical doctor called the Supervising Surgeon, a title later changed to Surgeon General. After the creation of the Department of Health, Education and Welfare in the early fifties, the Surgeon General's position largely disappeared from sight, except for the landmark 1964 report on the hazards of smoking and the ensuing requirement to print a warning on every cigarette package and advertisement. In fact, by 1980 the Surgeon General's position had become essentially moribund. It had been left vacant under the Nixon presidency, and under Carter it had been combined with the job of assistant secretary of health in the Department of Health and Human Services (HHS). The Reagan plan called for reestablishing the position, placing it directly below the authority of the assistant secretary of health. I didn't know for certain what the Reagan people had in mind, but in hindsight it is clear they saw the Surgeon General's job primarily as a means of promoting their social agenda—especially pro-life and family issues.

At the time, though, I naively didn't realize that my nomination was a political issue and that my supporters had little idea of my medical background except for my pro-life position. As far as they were concerned, that was my only qualification. And they had based their opinion largely on a program of seminars, films, and books called

Whatever Happened to the Human Race? that I had made with theologian Francis Schaeffer to dramatize the issues of abortion, infanticide, and euthanasia. Those programs had become widely known in conservative political circles.

I saw the Surgeon General's job very differently. I saw it as a position of medical leadership, especially in the education of the public about the promotion of health and prevention of disease. And in that misunderstanding lay the origins of my complicated relationship with the people who brought me to Washington.

Once I had decided I wanted the position of Surgeon General, I found myself whipsawed between optimism and pessimism. After my name was announced as one of several possible candidates for Surgeon General, I began to receive newspaper editorials and copies of letters sent to congressmen urging my appointment. I didn't know if and when I would ever hear anything official from the Reagan people. Each day brought more reports, rumors, and suggestions that I was "in," only to be followed by similar signs and clues that could only mean I was "out."

When Richard Schweiker was appointed Secretary of Health and Human Services, the first of three with whom I would work, I saw that as a good sign. I had met Schweiker before and saw this as a good appointment. On Valentine's Day Schweiker told me that President Reagan had appointed me as deputy assistant secretary of health, with the promise that I would be nominated as Surgeon General and that shortly thereafter there would be a reorganization of HHS. No one ever said explicitly that the price of my job was to be the zealous pursuit of the pro-life agenda. I don't think even Schweiker fully understood this.

I was excited. And I was not at all concerned about one little technical problem. I was too old. Schweiker called me one night to say he had just learned that existing legislation mandated that the Surgeon General could be no more than sixty-four years and twenty-nine days old. I had been alive for about one hundred days longer than that. But, he assured me, the Senate, which by statute had to offer its "advice and consent" to the president regarding the appointment, could see that Congress changed the law. After all, the nation had just elected seventy-year-old Ronald Reagan as our oldest president. Certainly no one could imagine that a sixty-four-year-old would be barred from serving as Surgeon General.

So Betty and I tied up our affairs in Philadelphia and prepared to move to Washington, although for a while I would still supervise the care of about thirty recent patients to whom I felt a particular responsibility. As we drove down to Washington on March 8, 1981, I began to realize how little I knew about what I might be getting into. I said to Betty, "If I ever have to say anything I don't believe or feel shouldn't be said, or if I am forbidden to say what should be said, we'll go home."

Given the way the Reagan administration subsequently operated, it would prove almost miraculous that I was never put into that position. On my very first day in Washington, I sat down with Schweiker and told him, "Mr. Secretary, I think you should know it is not my intent to use my appointment as a pulpit from which to preach pro-life messages. I really think that I have said all that I need to say on abortion, infanticide, and euthanasia. I have written two books, I have made five motion pictures, and I have spoken across the length and breadth of the land and abroad on this issue. What more can I say?"

Dick probably saw what was coming, and he gave me some good advice: "Chick, keep your head down and your mouth shut."

But whether I liked it or not, the abortion issue was pivotal, because my opponents, who grew increasingly vicious, assumed the exact opposite of what I had told Schweiker that morning.

Betty and I were among the hundreds of new arrivals to the nation's capital at the dawn of the Reagan era. Our immediate problem was to find a place to live. For the first week, we stayed at a Quality Inn not far from the Capitol. One of my former surgical trainees, Marty Eichelberger, had assumed a pediatric surgical position at the National Children's Hospital Medical Center, and he and his wife, Nancy, invited Betty and me to live with them until I was confirmed. As things turned out, I imagine they are glad we stayed only a week, declining their further gracious hospitality. They would have had us as houseguests for nine months.

My first day on the job, March 9, 1981, I felt worse than when I was a little boy on the first day at a new school. I had received a letter to report to a room on the seventh floor of the Department of Health and Human Services' Humphrey Building, two blocks down the Mall from the Capitol. The little office was starkly empty except for a desk and a chair. Following instructions, I sat there and waited for someone to show up. And waited. I busied myself by cleaning the telephone. Through my window I could see the dome of the Capitol, the American flag crowning it flapping in the breeze. It was a stirring sight, and as I gazed out the window, I felt a sense of mission and purpose that I had not felt since that day early in 1946 when I had first walked into the Children's Hospital to begin my career in pediatric surgery. Now I stood on the brink of a new career. How could it possibly top the sense of accomplishment and joy that pediatric surgery had brought?

My sense of expectancy and enthusiasm diminished as the hours crept by. In the early afternoon, Charlie Miller, retiring deputy assistant secretary of health, took me to meet Ed Brandt, my new boss, who had recently been designated assistant secretary of health. A laconic Oklahoman apparently preoccupied by his own confirmation concerns, Ed simply told me I would have to be sworn in. He gave me no further explanations or instructions. Tom McFee, deputy assistant secretary of health (personnel) did the honors. I went back to my cheerless office with its uncluttered desk, looked again at the Capitol dome and the American flag, and wondered if my new role would ever make sense. My sense of isolation began to grow.

If ever I believed in the sovereignty of God, it was during those first lonely minutes in that vacant Washington office. I felt a great sense of God and country, of mission and opportunity. In spite of my misgivings that first day, I believed the only clouds on the horizon were small. There was that technical problem about my age, but I trusted the people who said it was nothing to worry about. Although I had seen a few articles in the press noting the dissatisfaction expressed by some pro-abortion groups about my appointment, it had not yet dawned on me what vicious opposition I would face from both them and other groups as I awaited confirmation.

I faced a long uphill climb against formidable foes. I would need to prove myself each day, each time I met someone. It was going to be just like my first days as a surgeon at the Children's Hospital of Philadelphia, when I had to prove myself to people who said I was not needed, who told me I was unwanted. It was going to be lonely and tough, just like my first days at PS 124 back in Brooklyn.

Part I

Becoming a Doctor

Chapter 1
Brooklyn Boy

I am a Brooklyn boy. I have never understood why people seem to enjoy making fun of Brooklyn—and Brooklyn boys. Most people in Brooklyn don't call the neighboring state "New Joisey," and they don't live somewhere near "Toidy-toid Street." I'm proud to have my roots in Brooklyn, and I have always been fascinated by this unique borough of New York City on the western tip of Long Island. When the Dodgers left Ebbets Field for Los Angeles, I felt sorry for them. At a recent banquet of the National Academy of Sciences, a gathering of eminent scientists with national and even international reputations, eight of the nine people at my table boasted Brooklyn origins. Although Brooklyn is no longer my home, I return often, and visit my old haunts with pleasant nostalgia. I walk by my grandfather's house, making sure it is still covered with that huge wisteria vine. I can smell the fragrance of shady streets I remember from my childhood. I see myself playing stickball on Fourteenth Street. I'm riding my bicycle down Rugby Road in Flatbush. I'm playing baseball with a sandlot team—the Conquerors—at the parade grounds near Prospect Park. I'm fishing for goldfish with a bent pin in a cemetery pond and for larger prey at the East River docks. I'm ice skating with my grandfather on the big lake in Prospect Park. I'm a wide-eyed adventurer at Coney Island. Brooklyn still seems much like it did when I moved away in 1941.

I was an only child. An older brother was stillborn; his difficult birth almost killed my mother, who was warned to avoid another pregnancy. But five years later, in 1916, I came along, like most in my generation born at home. Accounts of my birth always made me wince; it was a textbook case of unsafe obstetrics climaxed by a risky procedure almost certain to produce a brain-damaged child. My mother was in labor for ninety-two hours, but since my head never engaged, those long days of labor pains were futile. By then it was too late for a cesarean section, which should have been done three days sooner, so the obstetrician applied forceps to my floating head and somehow extracted me. I often wonder if my traumatic entry into the world had something to do with the path in life I chose.

I was named Charles Everett Koop. My father was John Everett. His brother Charles lived with us when I was born. I used to wonder if I might have been called Charles if he had lived elsewhere, as he soon did. I hated the name Everett. Except for my father, I was the only Everett I ever knew until I was grown. If people had known about identity crises back then, I should have had one. My father called me "Jim," one grandfather called me "kid," the other called me "boy." When I wasn't with either of them, I was simply "the kid" or "the boy."

Home was a three-story row house on Fourteenth Street in South Brooklyn between Fourth and Fifth Avenues. The house was brick, with a stoop climbing from just inside a wrought-iron gate to a huge door with a fanlight on the second floor. The first floor was about a foot below street level, and its windows were protected by vertical iron bars, each topped with a sharp finial. When one of my frequent childhood ear infections stretched me out on a couch in the lower room, I dreamed of taking one of those spears and riding off to battle as knights of old. I was a crusader even then.

Being an only child has both advantages and disadvantages. One advantage was the closeness I enjoyed with my father and mother. They, of course, had the most profound effect on my years as a child. My father, J. Everett Koop, was descended from Dutch settlers who, I am told, sailed to New Amsterdam in the seventeenth century. He was a handsome, warm man—I believe without an enemy or even an adversary. He had tremendous strength of character, but his outgoing, friendly manner made him very approachable. He also had guts. Once, when I was home from college for a weekend, my mother approached me in the pantry:

"What are we going to do about your father's smoking? He smokes almost three packs a day, coughs all the time, and I'm certain he's shortening his life."

I replied, "Forget it, Mom. Pop hasn't got the guts to stop smoking."

That was a stupid, sophomoric thing for me to say, because I was talking about a man who had once pulled out his own decayed teeth with pliers, without anesthetic. As I thoughtlessly dismissed Dad's ability to stop smoking, he quietly stepped into the room without my knowing it and overheard what I said. Without a word, he turned around, went upstairs, threw his cigarettes in the toilet, and wrapped up all of his smoking paraphernalia, never to smoke again in his life. He proved something health professionals learned only much later: the importance of a self-rewarding goal when you're trying to quit smoking—in Dad's case, his son's approval. With what I now know about nicotine addiction, how I wish I could tell him how proud I should have been of him then.

My father never finished high school, but no one would have guessed it. As assistant vice president of one of America's largest banks, he held his own not only in banking circles, but in other fields as well. Once, when I was in the fifth or sixth grade, I asked him what "sarcastic" meant. He opened for me a new window on his knowledge. He began reciting Shakespeare: Marc Antony's speech at Caesar's funeral. As Dad quoted the oft-repeated line, ". . . but Brutus was an honorable man," he never had to describe sarcasm; he acted it. I was impressed.

At his funeral, a woman told me she had been his secretary in his early days with the bank. She described how he had reacted to my unending questions when I was a small youngster. Whenever he could not readily answer what must frequently have been outlandish questions from his only child, he would skip lunch the next day, go to the New York Public Library, and dig out the answer to my question, which he would share with me that night when he returned from work. Suddenly, at his funeral, it all made very good sense. I well remembered Dad coming home and giving me a complete answer to a question I had already forgotten I had asked the previous day. But even without the library, he was superb.

Once, when I was very young, Dad asked me to go upstairs and get something from my grandfather, two floors above. I said I was afraid, and when my father asked why, I confessed, shamefully, that I was afraid of the dark.

"Come, son, let me show you why you shouldn't ever be afraid of the dark." He lit a candle and placed it in the center of the kitchen table. That was the sun. A tennis ball became the earth, and a small rubber jacks ball was the moon. As my father rotated the "earth," as he circled the table, illustrating the earth's orbit, I learned the rudiments of the solar system and the earth's rotation as well as the origin of moonlight. I walked up the two dark flights of stairs without any fear.

My mother, Helen Apel, grew up in a large Brooklyn family. She always described her childhood as idyllic, but spent her adult life covering up many insecurities and fears. Well read and intelligent, she entered the work force in a secretarial/managerial capacity when many women were excluded. She was a wonderfully kind and generous woman who adored me, doted on me, and felt I could do little wrong. She possessed an extremely strong personality. When my mother was in good spirits, the group around her became lively; when she was glum, conversation went flat and the party proved dull. We were very close during my growing-up years, and her high expectations of me are in part responsible for much of my striving for achievement.

My mother should have been a nurse or a doctor. She had all the compassion needed, and a good deal of know-how as well. In her earlier years—before I came along—she had administered anesthesia for surgeons who did certain operative procedures in the patient's home. I am amazed at the courage—but bothered by the failures—of surgeons who operated on kitchen tables with anesthetic assistance from anyone they could talk into the job. Many times I heard Mother's story about trying to give anesthesia to a neighbor's child while the doctor chiseled away his mastoid bone. She once held the head of her own maternal grandmother between two bed pillows while the famous ophthalmologic surgeon Dr. Willie Meyer removed a cataract from the old woman's eye. And, of course, my mother stood anesthetic watch over many a tonsillectomy. Indeed, I had my tonsils out at home, but at least my father had the good sense to require an anesthetist who held an M.D. My father was charged more for the services of the anesthetist—$75— than the family doctor charged for the tonsils. That was a lot of money in 1924.

Like many youngsters in those days, it was my privilege to grow up in a three-generation world. I am saddened to read that today only 9 percent of children in the United States live within walking distance of their grandparents. My father's parents, Grandma and Grandpa Koop, lived on the top floor of our house, while my parents and I lived on the lower two floors. When I was thirteen we moved from Fourteenth Street to a house on Rugby Road in the Flatbush section of Brooklyn, but we maintained the same living arrangements, with my grandparents upstairs. (My grandfather owned the first house, my father the second.)

As a child, I reveled in being surrounded by a large family. Five backyards down Fifteenth Street, I could see the house of my maternal grandfather, Grandpa Apel, a house that he had built for his bride (she died when I was six) and in which he maintained the seat of the patriarchy until he was in his late seventies, when he finally moved to Flatbush, a Brooklyn neighborhood to which by that time all of his children had migrated. Grandpa Apel never went to school a day in his life—not in the ten years he lived in Germany before sailing to New York, not after he arrived on these shores. Yet he employed his hard-earned, extensive vocabulary in speech that was free of grammatical errors, and, like that of many proud new American citizens, free of any trace of a German accent.

Grandpa Apel had transformed his apprenticeship as a tinsmith into the business of heating and ventilating—a precursor of air-condi-tioning—as well as roofing. As we drove around Brooklyn in his horse and wagon, he would point out to me all the Apel roofs that graced Brooklyn churches. He was a Christian and a craftsman more than a businessman; much of his labor came without charge, especially for indigent elderly folks. Grandpa Apel taught me the special responsibil-ity and pleasure of being generous, not only with money, but also with time.

As he made his rounds through Brooklyn, he often stopped by our house at midmorning to enjoy the coffee and coffee cake my mother prepared for him. Better still, sometimes he would take me off with him. I don't think my mother ever knew the precarious places to which he took me. Frequently he would sit me against the chimney on a roof and say, "Don't move until I come back!" Once, when I was only seven or eight, he perched me on a tiny ledge just below the pinnacle of the Woolworth Building. I was as exhilarated as I was frightened. As often as we climbed above ground, we descended below it, into dark cellar caverns where he tried to find ways to repair dilapidated heating sys-tems. We talked constantly. I knew everything about his German childhood, from the storks that had nested outside his garret window to the traveling circus his father had taken up and down the Rhineland. I lived and relived his becalmed six-week crossing of the Atlantic on a sailing vessel so that I could almost feel the hunger pangs from two weeks without food. I felt the sadness about his baby sister, Ocean, who was born at sea, died, then was buried at sea. Most important, I saw things and people through his eyes. I never tired of hearing about his boyhood encounter with Abraham Lincoln, his watching the launching of the *Monitor* in Brooklyn (he later fashioned a scale model out of tin for me), his nimble scamper across the catwalk hung from the single cable of the Brooklyn Bridge during its construction, or winning the breaststroke race from Hellgate to Bedloe's Island, later the home of the Statue of Liberty. Every story held a moral lesson. He had once declined a position on the Board of Education in New York City or Brooklyn (I don't remember which) because he did not think it was right for an uneducated man to accept. I remember saying, "Grandpa, you aren't uneducated; you just didn't go to school."

Until I became a doctor—and my own family's chief physician—my grandparents received more than their share of terrible medical advice. My other grandfather, Grandpa Koop, had developed chronic nosebleeds as a young man. Someplace along the line he was advised by a physician: "John, unless you get a job where you have a tremendous amount of exercise out of doors, you're going to die." My grandfather, thinking he was fighting for his life, decided the life of a letter carrier would provide constant exposure to the elements as well as nine or ten miles of walking daily, with hundreds of stairs thrown in for good measure. What this had to do with nosebleeds, I am at a loss to say. It may have kept him healthy, but it was not a job to employ his skills. Grandpa John had been an engraver on silver and gold. Most of all he enjoyed engraving pocket watches, until wristwatches became the style and brought his work to a sudden end. Nonetheless, he kept his skills sharp, because he never sat without doodling. First he would draw, freehand, an almost perfect circle—that was the watch case—and then ornament the perimeter with holly leaves or ivy. In the center of the circle he would sketch a dramatic scene: the *USS Maine* sinking into the sea, a gazebo with two lovers, a bumblebee in flight. Grandpa Koop was happiest with his hands in motion, creating something of intricate beauty.

I have often thought that having two grandfathers who were so facile with their hands shaped my desire to use my own hands as a surgeon. Perhaps I treasured the satisfaction such activities seemed to give them; perhaps it lay in the genes.

Brooklyn was made to explore. It was fascinating and a little dangerous. On one of my first expeditions, when I was a seven-year-old on my scooter, I was ambushed by two boys much larger than I. In no time at all, they had knocked me onto the ground, pinned me against an iron fence, and run off with my scooter. I later learned that the streets of Brooklyn held hazards far more perilous than scooter stealers. Once during the prohibition era I was caught in the crossfire of gang warfare on Fourteenth Street right in front of my house. I dropped to the ground. One of the gang dropped to the ground, too, but he was dead.

After scooters came roller skates, and with roller skates came my declaration of liberty. All of Brooklyn became my turf. Alone or with

friends similarly equipped, I roamed the length and breadth of Brooklyn. The best skates I could buy were $1.65 a pair, with replaceable
wheels. One day my father invited me to skate beside him as he walked
up Fourteenth Street to Prospect Park, then north to his dentist three
miles away. In great glee I skated next to him, around him, in front
of him, behind him. Then, while he subjected himself to the dentist,
I decided to circumnavigate Prospect Park, one of the largest municipal
parks in the country. Eight happy miles later, I rolled home, proudly
showing my grandfather that in one day on brand-new roller skates I
had worn out two wheels.

Roller skating in Brooklyn was rough business. The asphalt streets
were smooth, but unsafe because the speeding trucks and cars paid little
heed to small skaters. The sidewalks loomed as obstacle courses, with
pedestrians, vendors, and the large cracks formed by flagstones resting
in uneven juxtaposition. A clever skater knew how to jump over the
cracks without catching the front wheels of the skates and taking a
serious fall. I took my share of tumbles, frequently tearing away the
knees of my knickers and then the underlying skin.

I was the only kid I knew whose father was interested in polo. He
took me to polo games between society teams out in Westbury or the
Army teams at Fort Hamilton. Our interest had to be vicarious, since
we didn't have a horse. I found a substitute in bicycle polo, a game I
taught my friends. We used a softball and our mallets were homemade—quite rigid with no spring to them. The mayhem provided by
bicycle polo was even more serious than in our other dangerous game,
roller-skate street hockey squeezed in between passing cars. The damage to clothing and injuries to skin that resulted from falling on skates
were small compared to the expensive repair of broken front-wheel
spokes of bicycles, to say nothing of the extensive contusions that
resulted from going over the handlebars.

Fortunately, there was a place in Brooklyn that offered unending
thrills for a little boy with no actual threat to life or limb: Coney Island.
Even sixty years later, the mention of the name brings back the marvelous fragrance of five-cent Nathan's hot dogs roasting on griddles, of
corn boiling in cauldrons, the perfume of cotton candy—the smell of
Coney Island was all of those things put together, plus a little dirt and
sweat. Coney Island: masses of humanity crowded on the hot sand
trying to get some relief from overheated houses not yet graced with
air-conditioning, an amusement park unequaled in size and diversity,
a haven for sun-worshiping older folks basking on the boardwalk, a
residence for affluent urbanites living in the private enclave of Seagate,

and a place to rub shoulders with those that made it the honky-tonk
heaven it was for me as a child.

I've had a love affair with Coney Island all my life. First I went with
Grandpa Koop, who walked me along the boardwalk with its sleazy,
tempting sideshows—then called "freak shows." There was the Tat-
tooed Man, the Fat Lady, the Sword Swallower, the Snake Woman,
and the Two-Headed Calf and other farmyard congenital anomalies.
Then there were games of chance that were almost impossible to win,
such as throwing a hoop over a doll whose head was too big to permit
it, and pony races where the operator could decide the winner.
Grandpa Koop would point out a nondescript man in the crowd, the
"capper." We would follow him for several hours. The "capper" would
be the first to put his dime down to go see the freak show. Grandpa
and I would go around to the side door and watch him come out
immediately. We would then follow him over to the Kewpie doll
boardwalk game, where he'd win a prize easily; we'd follow him to the
back door to see him return it. He bought snake oil and boxes of
saltwater taffy, only to return it all on the sly. Naturally, he was always
the big winner at the pony races. I have frequently said that suspicion
is a necessary requirement for a surgeon: I learned it there. And I was
intrigued by Coney Island's unusual hospital exhibit: premature infants
in incubators. Often I would drag my older cousin Walter there to stare
at those babies, neither of us realizing the role premature babies would
play in my life.

People should not feel sorry for youngsters born in big cities. I never
felt deprived. Indeed, I felt privileged. An empty lot was like a state
park. And Prospect Park, and especially some of its wooded inner
reaches (known, I thought, only to my cousin Clinton ("Kinky") and
me) seemed miles away from the city world, a real wilderness. When
I hiked there on Saturdays with a full knapsack, I could have been
hiking on the northern frontier of Canada.

I also expanded my horizons by collecting—anything and everything. The nooks of my room were filled with Indian pottery and
arrowheads, cavalry swords from the Civil War, stamps of all sorts, and
a collection of teeth. Two molars came from the skull of a South
American Indian woman I had found in my high school science lab.
When I had asked the teacher if I could have one or two of the teeth,
he had said, "Go ahead. If you can get them out, they're yours." I
searched the lab for forceps, pliers, or even wire but found nothing I
could use to extract the teeth. So I simply seized the Indian's molar
between my own molars and pulled it out. Then I got another one out

the same way. When I told my mother how I did it, she shuddered, but then said that my method of extraction showed I would not shrink from any task surgery would require me to do. I put the molars on my shelf in a Swedish milk cup dated 1863, between one of Tommy Hitchcock's polo balls and an Italian stiletto.

Teenage summer work in hospitals provided new treasures. One day I came home with a gallon mayonnaise jar of formaldehyde containing an amputated foot from a diabetic patient. I fully intended to dissect it someday. But I never did, and when I left home to get married, my mother demanded that the foot leave with me. I didn't know what to do with it. I was afraid to toss it into the trash, thinking somebody would find it and cause all kinds of problems. So I took it in its container to an unbuilt part of Flatbush where sewers had already been installed and dropped it over a corner sewer grate, expecting that the glass would break and allow the foot to fall into the gaping sewer inlet. But instead the glass smashed and the foot stood resolutely on the grate, dripping formaldehyde solution. I drove away. I have no idea what happened, but I have always imagined the police found it, kicked it down the sewer, and were glad they didn't have to get involved.

(My life has always been strewn with stray pieces of anatomy. Years later, my children eventually found the left ear of my medical school cadaver, which I'd kept for some silly sentimental reason. I quickly explained it was a trophy from my sword fight with a Spanish pirate on the streets of Marseilles. I don't know how much of that they believed, but I know it wasn't for long. A few days later they told me solemnly that Marseilles was in France, and that the ear had probably come from Cornell Medical School.)

Holidays are part of growing up, and for me they bridged the gap between my relatively lonely life as an only child and the often frenzied atmosphere that prevailed in the more boisterous homes of my many cousins. Christmas in Brooklyn until I was twelve was a ritual that began on Thanksgiving morning, when my cousin Kinky and I, following a unique Brooklyn tradition, would dress up as ragamuffins and go from door to door asking rather pitifully, "Got anything for Thanksgiving?" We usually got fruit or candy, but enough people gave us coins so that we could go Christmas shopping the next day for each of the fourteen cousins expected at Grandpa Apel's Christmas party.

The Koop household (my parents, paternal grandparents, and I) did not acknowledge Christmas with any decorations until the afternoon of Christmas Eve. My mother hung the Christmas wreaths, made of fresh holly, in the four front windows at about 3:00 P.M. on December

24, and then, at long last, Christmas officially arrived. But it didn't last long. After a formal dinner, we exchanged gifts that evening, because in those days, for letter carriers like Grandpa Koop, Christmas morning was their busiest time because many people mailed their greeting cards to arrive then.

Later in the day we would leave one grandfather's home for another's to exchange gifts with all of my cousins and their parents. The Apels' house was beautifully decorated with coal fires in open grates, holly and laurel about the house, and a very festive air indeed. Their Christmas tree reached to the ceiling and was lit with candles to produce an effect never achieved by electric bulbs. My grandfather circled the tree constantly with a candle snuffer in his hand and a pocket full of new candles to stick into the melted bases of the old ones. He never took his eyes off the tree. Four buckets of water stood nearby in case of a fire. Christmas tree fires were not uncommon in those days, and in December the newspapers routinely carried tragic stories of houses burned down, children burned to death, and families destroyed. By the time I was ten, the candles had given way to electric lights, and Christmas never seemed the same again.

The other big holiday was New Year's Eve, a special holiday for us because it was also the celebration of my parents' wedding anniversary. About half the guests gathered at 11:00 P.M., and the rest didn't show up until about 12:30, having been to church for the Watchnight service. The church members testified to the goodness of the Lord throughout the previous year, and after a communion service at midnight, the new year was underway. This party went on until three or four in the morning. There was no alcohol at any of these family gatherings, and this close-knit family seemed to have a good time no matter how often they came together.

Brooklyn was important in shaping my young life, but the times spent away from the city on vacation did just as much to prepare me for later life. For a city boy, I was unusually privileged to experience the country life and to learn a variety of adult responsibilities early.

In Nova Scotia we stayed as boarders on a farm in Arcadia village, not far from Yarmouth. It took only a few hours to transform me from a Brooklyn boy into a tiny farmhand. In the Porters' farmhouse, there was the smell of baking bread every morning and after lunch the aroma of molasses or ginger cookies. Everything we ate was homemade, and the garden produce was either fresh off the farm that day or had been canned the previous season. The rich, creamy milk I poured onto my cereal in the morning came out of a pitcher shaped like a cow with the milk making its exit from the cow's mouth. I was so intrigued with this pitcher that my mother bought one, which I used until I was in high school.

In Nova Scotia I learned about the sea and those who wrest a livelihood from it. Grandpa Apel introduced me to the life around the sea in the north, just as Grandpa Koop had introduced me to life around the sea in Brooklyn and on Long Island. Our family had a romance with Nova Scotia. It had begun years before I was born, when Grandpa Apel missed the boat from Yarmouth to Boston. He had been singing for his supper with a double male quartet that had spent their vacation traveling around Nova Scotia. In those days the boat from Yarmouth to Boston made only one trip a week. Stranded, Grandpa was taken in by a Nova Scotian sea captain, which led eventually to a romance and then marriage between the captain's daughter and Grandpa's son Clinton, the future father of my cousin Kinky.

My grandfather had missed that boat because he had dallied too long entertaining a lighthouse keeper. Naturally, when I came along, two generations later he took me on a singing tour of lighthouses. We would drive a horse and buggy along the shores of the Bay of Fundy, stopping near an offshore lighthouse. After tethering the horse, my grandfather would play a fanfare on his cornet. At that signal, the lighthouse keeper would lower a dory and row through rough seas to pick us up and take us back to his lighthouse. There my grandfather spent the day entertaining the keeper, his wife, and their children in whatever way he could. In addition to his cornet, he always carried with him his five-string banjo and his concertina. He interspersed the music with his consummate story-telling about a legion of winsome characters even more engaging than the Muppets.

These Canadian vacations gave me my first excursions alone with my father, when we would paddle a canoe around the northern wilds. These were very special times for me.

On a vacation closer to home, but still far from the city, I grew up fast in the summer of 1928, when I was twelve. It was growth in responsibility, if not maturity—responsibility through necessity. My parents had rented a summer cottage on a peninsula at the end of West Meadow Beach in Stony Brook, about fifty miles from Brooklyn, on the north shore of Long Island. At that time Stony Brook was a sleepy little village; its years as a university community lay decades in the future. Living at the tip of the peninsula, we had a choice of a long walk through sand from the end of the road to our house on the beach or—more convenient—we could take a boat across the creek to the

"mainland." Talk about high adventure—it was like living on an island.
I was captain of our small rowboat. There were tides to contend with
as well as the rapid Long Island Sound currents that filled and then
drained the creek behind our house.

There were fish to be caught, three kinds of clams to be dug, eels
to be speared, groceries to be bought, and a car to be driven. None of
these could be accomplished without a boat to be rowed, a canoe to
be paddled, or an outboard to be started. I learned how to do all this
more or less on my own. I suddenly became the man of the house, since
my father continued to work in Manhattan, joining Mother and me
on weekends and for one week a month from June through September.
There was a period of an hour or so on both sides of dead low tide when
the low water allowed me to walk across the creek, a distance of about
fifty yards. I occasionally transported my commuting father, dressed in
a business suit and a straw hat, piggyback to the mainland from whence
he made his way to the railroad and to New York City. Even though
I was bigger and stronger than most twelve-year-olds, I think my father
got a tremendous kick out of knowing his son could carry him piggyback across a creek—without getting him wet.

Each morning Mother would give me the fish order for the day. The
choices all involved trust, discovery, and responsibility for me—steamer
clams (wait for low tide, walk a mile, dig for them in deep mud);
littleneck clams (row up the bay with the incoming tide, dive into eight
feet of water and dig the clams from gravel with my hands, wait out
the change of tide and row home on the ebb); chowder clams or
quahogs (a half-mile walk, low tide, use a clam rake); fish (snappers and
flounder from an anchored boat, porgies from a dock, trolling for
bluefish from an outboard); and eels, speared in the creek. It was not
Robinson Crusoe, but it seemed pretty close.

I also learned to shoot, although this additional skill was not in the
line of duty or survival. As the tide began to go out, I would place six
bottles on a board, launch it in the creek, and set it adrift. By the time
I ran to the porch on the opposite side of the house and got set with
a .22 rifle, the board had rounded the peninsula and was going at a fast
clip left to right past the front of the house out into Long Island Sound.
I had time to shoot the six bottles before the board got out of range.
The shattered glass went to the bottom of the channel, where, local
legend claimed, it provided the floor for the home of a sea monster of
the Loch Ness genre and seen as infrequently.

The next year, when I was thirteen, we began years of summers a
few miles east of Stony Brook, at a beach cottage just thirty yards from

Long Island Sound near Mount Sinai. This was my summer home from ninth grade until my final year in medical school. I continued to prowl the beaches and tidal flats of Long Island, fascinated by the rich variety of marine life I found nestled in a bewildering variety of environments. For a budding biologist, it was all a magic laboratory. In nearby Port Jefferson there was something even more appealing to me: a hospital, even two hospitals. From the time I was seventeen until I was twenty-three, my beach prowling and swimming had to wait for the evening hours. Days I worked, without pay, at Mather Memorial Hospital and St. Charles Hospital for Crippled Children in Port Jefferson. Because I always wanted to be a doctor.

I can't remember a time when I didn't want to be a doctor. The doctors I knew as a very young child must have helped to plant the desire in me, when I was as young as age five or six. One homeopathic physician, Dr. Justice Gage Wright, was a great model. (Homeopathy is an almost abandoned school of medical thought in the United States in which symptoms are treated by minute quantities of drugs that produce those same symptoms. Like other physicians, homeopathic doctors in those days also used the few basic drugs that had proven pharmacological effect, such as morphine, digitalis, and quinine.)

Dr. Wright was a diminutive man, compact, brusque, with an iron-gray mustache and neatly pressed clothing. When he made a house call on me or a member of the family, from the moment he stepped out of his blue Buick parked at the curb, he was a presence. When he entered the home my family spoke more softly, as though a normal sound would break the spell. When he set down his large black bag on a chair in the bedroom, healing had already begun. When he took my pulse, I knew I was in the proper hands. And when he hauled out of his vest pocket an enormous gold watch, pressed the stem, and popped open the cover, I was on the road to recovery.

Dr. Wright had the biggest doctor's bag I've ever seen—then or since. It contained literally hundreds of corked glass vials three inches high and less than three-quarter inch in diameter, containing fluids ranging from clear to amber. To each was affixed an adhesive label inscribed in Latin. The preparation of the patient's medication and the directions that followed were also part of the healing process.

After his examination, Dr. Wright always said the same thing: "Get me two tumblers, two-thirds filled with cold water, two butter chips, and a teaspoon." Soon my family knew to keep these already prepared in the kitchen and they were produced forthwith, usually by my grandmother or grandfather. Dr. Wright would drip into each glass three to five drops of two or three ingredients, stir each with the teaspoon, place the butter chips on top of the glasses to prevent evaporation, and then lay the spoon across them as they stood on the bedside table side by side, towering symbols of the magic of medicine.

The instructions never varied: "Take two teaspoonsful alternately every two hours." The bowl of the spoon, resting on one butter chip or the other, indicated the next dose. Waiting for the successive hours to roll around was also part of the healing process: The entire family participated.

Office visits ended with the same ritual except that the drops of magic potion were dribbled over tiny sugar pills the size of BB shot in small vials. Dr. Wright labeled the corks "1" and "2," and you took those pills alternately, two pills every hour. Even then I wondered and questioned just a little. Such homeopathic wet pills were more concentrated at the bottom of the vial, while those at the top contained hardly any medication at all. Even as a young boy it seemed to me that you should get the most medication in the beginning when you were the sickest, then taper off toward the end.

Although today few believe in the underlying precepts of homeopathy, few doubt the psychological benefit of the "therapy." It was not a placebo effect. It was satisfaction with and confidence in the hands-on attention paid to the patient, still a potent adjunct to healing.

Another ritual that I presume came from Dr. Wright was the "purification" of my liver, which took place every four to six weeks, more often in the winter than the summer. I was given ten $\frac{1}{10}$-grain tablets of calomel (mercurous chloride), which I would take one every fifteen minutes until they were gone. I'm sure I derived no benefit from these tablets, but because the pills were thought to be poisonous, I was given a powerful purgative of citrate of magnesia, which ruined every Saturday on which I took it. Even though I had a healthy skepticism toward his remedies and rituals, I knew I wanted to be at least somewhat like Dr. Wright.

Dr. Strong was an osteopathic physician to whom our family went for orthopedic problems. (Maybe my family didn't know that osteopathy and orthopedics were not synonymous.) Dr. Strong could take an injured arm, hand, or foot in his two most gentle hands with the largest fingers I think I ever saw, and without hurting could make it "all better," as he said. I wanted his gentleness when I became a doctor.

There was another old physician who influenced me, though largely through the opinion others had of him. He was my grandfather's cousin, Uncle Henry Risch. Uncle Henry had come to this country from Germany a few years before my grandfather but had never lost his accent. He wore his hair in a wild halo like Einstein, but his face was much more cherubic.

Every morning, summer and winter, Uncle Henry would jump on his bicycle at his home in Brooklyn Heights and peddle five miles to Coney Island, where he would park his bicycle in the sand, kick off his sandals, and wade into the ocean, still clad in the white linen suit he always favored. Emerging from the water, he'd jump onto his brown leather saddle and pedal five more miles to my grandmother's home, where he would have homemade coffee cake and coffee for breakfast. The five miles of wet white linen on old scuffed brown leather produced a brown stain on the seat of Uncle Henry's pants that would never come out in the wash, and I was sometimes embarrassed when the folks in my neighborhood heard me call him "Uncle." In spite of his eccentricities, everybody I knew referred to Uncle Henry as a "genius," and I heard that people came from far and wide to avail themselves of his care.

Fifteen years after these childhood recollections, when I was a senior in medical school and Uncle Henry had been dead several years, I asked my mother if she knew why he had had such fame as a physician. Her reply was simple: "He cured people of pernicious anemia."

"That's not possible, Mother. The cause and treatment of pernicious anemia are relatively new discoveries. By any chance, do you know what Uncle Henry's treatment might have been?"

"After Uncle Henry had his breakfast at Mama's every morning, he would get on his bicycle and go to the slaughterhouses, where he picked up fresh liver. This he ground and packed into sausages in his own basement and delivered to his patients on his bicycle."

"Mother, they gave the Nobel Prize for that discovery in 1934." Uncle Henry was decades ahead of his time. I knew I wanted some of the genius of Uncle Henry.

Yet none of these men were surgeons, and I *knew* I wanted to be a surgeon. The idea of using my mind, then my hands, to heal someone simply fascinated me. My parents had made me aware of operations, and I knew people who had been deathly ill and then became hale and hearty again after an operation. But I found it hard to understand how they got better after someone had cut into their tummies. As a boy, I didn't realize that surgical incisions healed. When my grandmother's friend had her gallbladder removed, I pictured her with a perpetual hole in her side. I thought her corset held her organs in place.

When I was about seven or eight years old, my parents took me to a movie depicting the struggles and sacrifice of an immigrant family living on the Lower East Side of New York who put their son through medical school. I was deeply moved by the extraordinary pride his parents had in him when he became a doctor.

I think my natural impatience had something to do with my desire to become a surgeon. Wanting results yesterday instead of next year has always been one of my personality traits. Surgery requires quick decisions, and it yields quick results.

Even as a young boy, I was certain that I wanted to become a surgeon, so I began my training early: I would spend hours cutting pictures out of magazines with my left hand as well as my right hand, to train both hands to make delicate, precise, intricate maneuvers. I never became ambidextrous, but I was able to use both hands in surgery better than some. Later I tried to perfect my skills in tying one-handed knots in small corners. I did this by stapling a thread to the bottom of a small wooden matchbox and then tying single knot after single knot with my right hand, snugging them up on the taut thread held in my left.

I decided I could not wait until medical school to see some surgery, so I cajoled my father into asking a bank customer who was a surgeon to let me watch him operate. He accommodated me almost too well. He took me right into the operating room with him while he was doing a submucosal resection of deformed bones in a patient's nose. It was bloody and I was very close—and very queasy. Somehow I stuck it out.

Soon thereafter, I found easy access to the operating theaters at the Columbia Presbyterian Medical Center. By the time I was fourteen, my size and apparent maturity permitted me to masquerade as a medical student. Paul Strong had shown me how. Paul Strong and his family lived next to us when we summered at Mount Sinai on Long Island Sound. When I first met him, he was a medical student, and we have been friends ever since. Paul taught me how to see all the surgery I desired. I would get up early on Saturday mornings, take the subway from Brooklyn to upper Manhattan, and enter the side door of Columbia's Presbyterian Hospital without being questioned; security was unnecessary in those days. As though I had every right to do so, I would take the elevator up to the bacteriology labs where Paul worked, grab a white coat, don it quickly and go back to the elevator, up to the gallery looking over the multiple operating theaters. There I could watch surgery to my heart's content. Few, if any, other observers were in the galleries on Saturday morning, and it was not unusual for a surgeon to look up, see an inquiring face, and reward it with a description of what he was doing or the dilemma he was facing. I wasn't only in the gallery—I was in seventh heaven.

After I had seen a fair amount of surgery on those Saturdays, I began to try my hand at it at home. My father and grandfather Koop had built me a lab of sorts in the basement. Here I played with my chemistry set and later did more advanced experiments I learned from a science teacher at the Flatbush School. Eventually, I had white rabbits, and too many white rats, all properly housed in cages I had built.

Some of these I anesthetized and operated upon, removing duplicate organs or segments of intestine. My mother was my willing assistant. We would place the animal to be anesthetized in a new, clean garbage pail with an ether-saturated piece of cotton. When the animal was asleep, we would put it on the operating table and my mother would maintain anesthesia in a style I later learned was pretty proficient. She certainly had no problem in anesthetizing a rat, a rabbit, or indeed a stray cat.

As I have told this story over the years, people have had one of two predictable reactions. Most have been intrigued by my adolescent surgery, but some have been concerned about the animals. I, too, always shared that concern. Like those kitchen surgeons of yesteryear, I was remarkably successful. I don't remember losing a single patient. And since I usually removed one ovary from these stray and abandoned cats, I figured I was leaving all their essential organs, but perhaps cutting in half (I didn't know any better) the likelihood that they would contribute to Brooklyn's stray cat problem.

My first summer job in a hospital, when I was sixteen, put me into the laboratory at Mather Memorial Hospital in Port Jefferson. I started off by slicing pathologic sections on a microtome and then mounting them for the pathologist to read. Before long I was doing urinalyses and the blood counts on the wards. One day I decided I had discovered the eggs of a parasitic worm in the stool specimens I examined. An older, experienced, and very understanding doctor let me know I was looking at the blueberry seeds from last night's blueberry pie.

I seemed to hit it off well with the pathologist at Mather Memorial, and soon he started to bring me the pathology specimens from Pilgrim State Hospital, a six-thousand-bed institution for the mentally ill. I realized he was taking advantage of me, but I kept up with the increased workload. Sometimes I became so sleepy that I would take a nap on the autopsy table, the head block serving as my pillow. By the end of the summer I had moved up to assisting the pathologist in the actual autopsies, and I even did the mechanics of the autopsy, removing the organs on my own. He, of course, did all the diagnostics.

In summers while I was in college, Long Island surgeon Dr. Frank S. Childs invited me to observe him operate, and then he allowed me actually to assist him in surgery. I spent most of my time at the St. Charles Hospital for Crippled Children, where I had to change the dressings of the osteomyelitis patients once a week. This bone infection, which used to be the nemesis of orthopedic endeavors, is now almost unknown because of antibiotics. It took me from Monday morning at eight o'clock until Saturday noon to get through all of the patients' dressings once. It gave me a remarkable insight into medicine before sulfonamides were available and penicillin was discovered. Maggots, which developed from eggs laid by flies on soiled bandages, did a lot of the cleaning up of dead tissue for us; we even inserted clean maggots into wounds ourselves for the same purpose.

One day in the summer before my senior year at college, at age nineteen, I was about to assist Dr. Childs in doing an amputation of a patient's left leg. I took my usual position on the right side of the table when he said to me: "Koopie, you've seen me do enough of these so that you ought to be able to do one if I help you. Come on over here."

Each day of my youth, whether playing or working, I felt directed toward my eventual career as a surgeon. I thought about it every day in school, except perhaps for those early days when getting home in one piece was all I could think about.

My grade school, P.S. 124, was on the corner of Fourteenth Street and Fourth Avenue in South Brooklyn. At the time I went there the neighborhood was largely Italian and Polish, although a few Irish families still lived on Park Slope, and of course my extended family was there, scattered on adjacent streets. P.S. 124 was a white stone building with a sunken play yard. It smelled unmistakably of stale urine. It smelled that way when I was in kindergarten, and it smelled that way when I left the school at the end of the sixth grade to go to P.S. 40. I was afraid to go to P.S. 40. Although only a few blocks away, it was in a rougher neighborhood, and even the tough boys from P.S. 124 looked with some trepidation on going there.

Fortunately, or perhaps unfortunately, there was an escape route. Brooklyn had four "junior high schools," rapid advancement sections housed in regular grade schools. Rapid advancement meant that you took the seventh, eighth, and ninth grades in two years and entered the second year of high school. I was chosen to join this experimental program and rose to the occasion. I couldn't believe I was going to a school that had a name instead of a number: Dewey Junior High School.

But Dewey was eight miles from my new home in Flatbush, forcing me to take a long trolley ride each day with a mile to walk at the start and a half mile at the end. Dewey was in another Italian–Polish neighborhood. The rapid advancement classes were almost all Jewish. I was the oddball, no matter how you looked at it. When the school day ended, my Jewish friends went off in groups to Hebrew school, and I was left to fend for myself as I walked to the trolley through the tough neighborhood. Although I never did anything to antagonize the older boys who hung out on the street corners, I was beaten up just about every afternoon before I got to the trolley car.

I wasn't much of a fighter, especially when I was outnumbered six, eight, or ten to one. I used to get my allowance changed into nickels so that I could go into phone booths and make telephone calls, hoping my antagonists would tire of waiting for me. I don't know how I got through that year, but somehow I did. But I didn't know how I would survive the next year before getting into high school. I was sure to run out of nickels and get beaten to a pulp.

Fortunately, I made an unexpectedly rapid exit from Dewey Junior High School, thanks to a sadistic art teacher. One afternoon we had just gathered together and were sitting in the timeworn stupid posture of clasping our hands in front of us on our desks when Miss Hamilton said, "I have to leave the room and I don't want anyone to make a sound."

I was sitting in the front row. Of course, as soon as she made her exit, there was a roar as spitballs, paper airplanes, and other things flew through the air. All of a sudden, Miss Hamilton reappeared to an immediate hush. She asked anyone who was making noise to stand up. I alone, foolishly honest, rose, assuming that all my fellow culprits would join me. How Miss Hamilton could think I was responsible for all the noise she had heard, I don't know. However, she walked up to me, and without warning hauled off and hit my left cheek with the flat of her hand hard enough to make me stagger. I went home as slowly as I could, but when I got there the welts were still visible and my mother saw them. I had made great efforts all the previous year not to admit that my clothes had been torn in fights or that my bruises had come from fighting. Now I didn't care whether my mother knew or not, because I just wanted something to happen to get me out of Dewey.

My father was at a banking convention in Boston, and my mother, timid though she was, took matters into her own hands. The following morning she enrolled me in the Flatbush School, probably the smallest country day school in the nation; it certainly was the smallest one in Brooklyn.

The tiny school, on Newkirk Avenue between Sixteenth and Seventeenth streets, consisted of a number of old-fashioned Flatbush frame houses joined together by walkways and skyways. The layout of many of the houses was just like the one I lived in, so it was like taking algebra in my mother's bedroom or geometry in my grandfather's study. Compared to Dewey, it was wonderful.

Dwight R. Little was the principal, and Mary Ames was the dean. Miss Ames was a very large woman—we were known as "the little school with big aims"—and she was a gem. She appeared gruff and tough, but she had a real concern for children. She knew how to handle their troubles, how to put them at ease. She listened to my story, my mother's account of Dewey, and said, "Everything will be fine here for Everett. We will put him in the college preparatory section and in his senior year we will stiff-gate him into college." I had no idea what that meant but it didn't sound good. I later realized she was saying that they would "certificate" me into college. That meant I would not have to take the college entrance exams because this school had a sufficiently high rating academically that it could place a student into college, even an Ivy League college. At that time, I didn't know what Ivy League meant.

At the Flatbush School I made some close friends, especially Ralph Spritzer and Frank Young. Frank became my roommate the first year at Dartmouth, and thirty years later Ralph and I found ourselves on the faculty of the same university.

I was a timid youngster when I entered high school. I recall going to the junior prom and standing in the stag line for about an hour before getting up the courage to walk out on the dance floor. It wasn't to tap a classmate on the shoulder and dance with his partner—I was just getting up my courage to walk across the dance floor and go out the exit into the school yard, over the fence, and home.

But the small Flatbush School helped me lose my timidity and gain self-confidence. The teachers encouraged me to try new things. I loved the athletic opportunities, especially football. Although the tiny school could barely field a football eleven in my senior year our team remained unbeaten, untied, and even unscored-upon in our division in New York City thanks to several ringers. I also joined the wrestling team but made the terrible mistake of pinning the coach. After 1933 I never saw him again until 1988, when I gave the commencement address to the graduates of Harvard Medical School. There was Fred Bruchs, age ninety-four, in the audience. At the suggestion of the Harvard Dean, we had a joyous reunion on the platform—and rekindled an old friendship that would last until his death two years later.

At the Flatbush School I played baseball and I played at basketball. Off the playing fields, I joined the debate team, became editor-in-chief of the school paper, and enjoyed my only effort in politics before I was plunged into national politics as the controversial nominee for Surgeon General in 1981. Student elections at the Flatbush school took place on national election day, and we ran campaigns for president with all the hoopla of the Republicans and Democrats. In 1932 I was able to capitalize on the national election, as I ran for student president with the slogan:

A Double O should have your vote on November 8th—

ᕼOOᐯER,

ᴋOOᴘ,

ʀOOsᴇᴠᴇʟᴛ.

I won, probably because I also passed out pencil erasers to every kid in school that were printed, "Make no error—vote for Koop."

After my mother died in 1974 at the age of eighty-six, I found among her treasured papers an autobiographical essay I had written in January 1933, the year I graduated from the Flatbush School. Its final paragraph distilled the essence of my childhood:

Now at sixteen I picture myself a great surgeon being consulted by other surgeons no less great. Nothing, it seems, would give me a bigger thrill and would please me more than to operate on a human being from an altruistic viewpoint of relieving his ills, or from the scientific viewpoint of giving to science some information unknown to it.

If my plans take form during the next few years, I will attend Dartmouth College in Hanover, New Hampshire. . . .

As I write this, I am in a quiet and fateful mood. My closing hope and prayer is that these plans will take shape and be lived during my life, yet I place my petty problems in the hands of One whose infinite wisdom guides our lives for the best.

Chapter 2

The Still North,
The Hill Winds

On a cloudy September day in 1933, I gazed out the window of the family car with intense excitement as my parents and I drove the narrow road winding through the pine-covered New Hampshire hills to the little village of Hanover. In a way, I was still somewhat surprised that I was headed for Dartmouth College. The family roots went deep in Brooklyn, and most of my relatives and friends expected me to attend college not far from home. My only relative who seemed to know anything about the collegiate world had steered me in the direction of Princeton in nearby New Jersey. But I had chosen Dartmouth mainly because Princeton did not have a medical school and Dartmouth did. It also had a program that covered four years of college and two of medical school in five years. It was the wrong reason for my choice, but it was the right choice. My four years at Dartmouth were among the best of my life; they shaped what happened to me and my family. Much of what I was to accomplish as a surgeon, as Surgeon General, as a person, stems from decisions I made or from what I learned while I was at Dartmouth.

At Dartmouth I fell in love. I fell in love with the rugged hills and serene valleys of New Hampshire. I fell in love with skiing. I fell in love with learning. And I fell in love with Betty.

At first it seemed all so very new, inviting, and yet intimidating. I was a city boy about to settle down in the wilds of New Hampshire. I had graduated from a tiny school with only fifteen youngsters in the senior class, and now I was at a college of more than two thousand young men, among them 670 freshmen, each eager to show what he could do. I would be younger than most, only sixteen when I matriculated. I felt enthusiastic and proud to be part of it all, determined to get the absolute last drop out of this experience away from home. As we drove up the hill to the campus, the stately beauty of the brick Georgian buildings, the elm-ringed green, and the gleaming white buildings of Dartmouth Row gave me a thrill. They still do.

I can't imagine that any incoming Dartmouth freshman prepared with greater enthusiasm than I did. I had spent the summer listening to a ten-inch record that a Hanover store had mailed as an advertising gimmick, and I knew every Dartmouth song as well as those of the other Ivy League schools. My mother heard me sing them so often— sometimes she chimed in with her lovely soprano voice—that she could still get through the words thirty years later when her grandchildren enrolled at Dartmouth.

Right away Dartmouth changed my name. The fellows I met decided that my unusual last name required an appropriate nickname, so I became "Chick" Koop. Years later, when I began my medical career in Philadelphia, I thought an aspiring young surgeon should not be known as "Chick," so I decided to drop my nickname. But the first person I bumped into in Philadelphia happened to be a friend from Dartmouth, who promptly introduced me to everyone as "Chick." That's who I've been ever since.

Dartmouth offered an inviting variety of extracurricular activities, but I decided to concentrate on my studies. And football. I have always said that good surgeons are suspicious people. And I have always said that the field of surgery attracts people who are by nature suspicious and compulsive. But I didn't show any of those tendencies my first week at Dartmouth. Instead of realizing how important it would be not to be late for the first football practice, I went off instead with my mother and father for a drive through the White Mountains, about fifty miles north of Hanover. Our outing took much longer than anticipated, and I missed football practice completely. I later learned that because of my high school record my name had been called out for the position of center on the first team but since I had missed the first practice, I was never able to regain that coveted slot.

But when spring practice rolled around, something happened that changed my life. In the twenties and thirties, Ivy League football played a much more important role in national sports than people reading the sports pages today might imagine. But Dartmouth had not enjoyed an outstanding season for several years. Therefore, when a new head coach, Earl Blaik, arrived in Hanover from West Point, bringing with him his coterie of assistant coaches, it made quite a stir in the north country and in Ivy League circles in the sports world.

In those days, each player played both offense and defense; offensive centers played defense by stepping into the backfield, the so-called "roving center," where they might intercept passes in the flat, just beyond the line of scrimmage. On the second or third day of spring practice, when Blaik was choosing the first and second squads, I was engaged in an exercise of running at right angles to the trajectory of a short pass and trying to intercept it. A bunch of other guys were trying out for the same position. Before I got up for my next shot at a pass, one of the managers approached me and said, "Coach Blaik wants to see you."

Could this mean that my blunder of missing that first day of fall practice was going to be offset by actually being noticed by the great Earl Blaik? Did he like what he saw? I certainly didn't know, but I jogged over to Blaik and said the customary:

"Yes, sir!"

"What's your name?"

"Chick Koop."

"Do you know you run like Buckler? I haven't seen anybody run like that since I left the Point."

Later that day, when the first team roster was posted, my name was listed as center. Within twenty minutes after people had a chance to read those typed columns, my life changed. Now, suddenly, there was a certain deference in the way people spoke to me. People who hadn't looked my way as we passed on the stairs of my dormitory now knew my name and seemed anxious to befriend me.

One night during the second week of spring practice I walked down Main Street to get my usual toasted cheese sandwich and chocolate milk shake. As I approached Allen's Drug Store, Blaik and three of his assistant coaches were walking toward me four abreast. I was with my roommate and several friends from the dormitory, and when Blaik's "Hello, Chick!" was echoed by each of the assistant coaches, I was in seventh heaven. I think my friends would have been willing to carry me home on their shoulders if I had asked them.

A few days later we had a scrimmage, the first team against the second team. On defense I was playing roving center, and the opportunity came to intercept a short pass, just as Blaik had seen me practice. I snagged the pass, found a hole in the line, and must have run about ten yards before I was hit by two very vicious tacklers. I was knocked out cold. I don't really know how long it was, but my friends told me I was on the ground for several minutes. When I tried to walk to the sidelines I realized that my shoulder was extraordinarily sore. More disturbing, something strange had happened to my vision. I was seeing two of everything, a second image superimposed on the first, somewhat to the right and above it.

Nobody seemed too concerned about my double vision or my intense headache. At first Blaik was solicitous. He advised me to come to practice and walk through the plays, but not to suit up and risk further injury. I did this for the rest of the week, receiving the same fawning treatment when I passed the coaches on Main Street.

The double vision was strange. When I woke up in the morning, it was very severe, and the two images were separated widely. By sheer effort of concentration, I could pull the two images together and hold them there, a feat I later learned I was able to do by tightening the six extraocular muscles around each eye. Throughout the day, as I got more and more tired, it became harder and harder to hold the images together, especially when reading. By the time I was ready for bed, the two images were as widely separated as they were when I awoke in the morning.

When the weekend came, and my eyes and headache were getting no better, I decided I would go to the Dartmouth Eye Clinic for a consultation with Professor Bielschowsky, perhaps the most knowledgeable person in the world at that time regarding the function of the extraocular muscles of the eye. He addressed me in moderately accented English after a very complete examination.

"What will be your major?" was his first question.

"I'm premed."

"You're premed and you play this foolish game of football? Let me see your hands." I showed them to him, fingers outstretched, palms down and then palms up.

"They're beautiful. They're surgeon's hands. So you not only risk your sight and maybe your life, but your hands and your career. Such foolishness."

He then told me in no uncertain terms and in rather scathing language that being a football hero offered at best a very limited benefit, and I was risking permanent disaster if I suffered another head injury. He explained that I had probably had a tiny hemorrhage in or very close to the nucleus of the fourth cranial nerve that supplied one of the extraocular muscles, that it would probably never improve, but that with eyeglasses I could live with it perfectly well. On the other hand, if the area became more damaged, I would place a surgical career in jeopardy.

He made sense and I knew it. But I had to decide if I were mature enough to give up all that big-man-on-campus attention for the much less glamorous life of an anonymous premedical student. I made the decision and went to see Earl Blaik the next morning in the field house. I told him about my conversation with Bielschowsky and said that after a very painful deliberation I had made the reluctant decision that I should drop out of football if I valued my tremendous ambition to be a surgeon.

Blaik tried to change my mind, arguing that many men had played football and then gone on to be doctors. I don't know how I was strong enough to resist his persuasive tactics, but I was. His next comment destroyed the man in my sight forever, no matter how many bronze plaques commemorate his coaching years at Dartmouth and West Point. He looked at me and said, "So, in other words, you're a coward."

That night when I passed the four coaches on Main Street, they looked the other way.

Within a few days, as it became known that I had dropped out of football, the pedestal on which I had been balancing toppled. No longer was I the injured football hero, no longer did people envy my relationship with the new coaching staff, no longer did I eat at the training table, no longer did upperclassmen athletes pay the same attention to me.

I don't think Dartmouth football suffered much from my absence. Instead, Dartmouth got a very fine center, Carl "Mutt" Ray, who inspired the team for the next three years, especially when in 1936 Dartmouth finally broke the "Yale jinx" to pull off the great football victory during my college career.

Meanwhile, I was fitted with special eyeglasses, and a new series of problems began. When I woke in the morning and put my glasses on, they seemed to make my vision worse. I could not leave my room until I used my eye muscles to bring the two images together, a difficult exercise that could take as long as thirty minutes. I learned that the reason for this was that my eye muscle paralysis was not total, and it varied throughout the day. Therefore, the prisms I was using were the average that I would require throughout the day. That made them "strong" early in the morning. Gradually that half hour of adjustment dwindled, but even now, when I put my glasses on, I see double for a fleeting two or three seconds, and when I take them off the same thing happens. My wife thinks it's quite humorous that I managed to be such a successful pediatric surgeon and had the confidence of so many patients' parents for so many years, when all the time I had double vision. As she has frequently said: "Isn't it good your patients' parents never knew!"

Giving up football was one of the hardest and wisest choices I made at Dartmouth. Not only had I acted wisely to save my surgical ambitions, but I also moved into a different social world, choosing a quieter path that would bring me close friendships with other premed students. For my last three years I roomed with Mike Petti, another premed student from Brockton, Massachusetts. We became good friends with two other premeds, Ed McGrath, from Milton, Massachusetts, and Dan Barker from Niantic, Connecticut. Two of us came from metropolitan areas, one from a small city, and one from a very small town. Two of us were Protestant and two Roman Catholic. We all shared similar family values, but there was a sufficient diversity to permit arguments long into the night. We couldn't have had more different personalities, but fortunately we all had a good sense of humor.

When I look back on my college years, I bring to mind all the usual hijinks, but most of my time at Dartmouth I studied. There were times it took all the discipline I could muster, as when the shouts and laughter of fellows playing baseball on the green echoed in the chemistry lab where I was fighting quantitative analysis, carefully making sure my experiments came out correctly by using a tiny camel hair brush to remove dust particles from the weights and scales. I had decided early on that recreation did not always fit into the schedule of a premed student or a surgeon.

My zoology major kept me busy, offering me intellectual stimulation and career preparation as well as employment. The college lost interest in giving me a scholarship as soon as I left the football team, so I sought out a variety of jobs to help my father finance my education, although he did not request it. I washed dishes, sold saddle shoes, ran a laundry service, tutored, and finally served as a research assistant in the zoology department. I thrived on work that allowed me to be on the brink of scientific discovery by using not only my mind, but also my hands.

One of my professors, Bill Ballard, was experimenting on lens transplants in the eyes of the *Amblystoma notatum,* a strange little five-inch long amphibious vertebrate. After the professor had taken the infinitesimally small lens from one eye of a newborn (½ inch long) and inserted it into the other, my job was to see that the little creatures maintained their nutrition. I did this by feeding them chopped newt liver, which I diced up into pieces small enough to pick up on the end of a needle inserted into a lollypop stick. I would then tease the recovering *Amblystoma* into opening its mouth so that I could scrape a tiny piece of liver onto the tip of the upper jaw. This was painstaking work. I didn't know it at the time, but the *Amblystoma* liver lunches would be part of the training of the future pediatric surgeon. Another job, not as interesting, was to label with India ink all the zoology specimens in the college museum; forty years later I saw my labels still in place.

When the operating season on *Amblystomae* was over, I found other work to do under Professor Norman Arnold. It was from Norm that I learned embryology, but it was also from Norm that I learned how to teach. In his soft, persuasive, unhurried manner, he went to all lengths to explain the very complicated field of embryology. While he talked to the class, he used modeling clay to make three-dimensional embryology come to life. Although I could not foresee it at that time, my surgical career would be devoted to correcting the defects that occur in the unfolding of embryology in preborn children. What I learned in embryology became so deep a part of my understanding that I have to think it was all part of God's sovereign plan that made me an innovative pediatric surgeon.

Norm was also a true esthete, and it was he who fanned my budding interest in English literature, art, and music. He was the consummate teacher who took great pleasure in introducing me to everything from varieties of Vermont ferns to different types of cheeses. We worked together, we talked together, we skied together, we climbed mountains together. Norm quickly became my closest friend at Dartmouth. By my junior year, I had spent more time with him than with any student friend, and our friendship lasted for decades.

When I first enrolled at Dartmouth, I had planned to take advantage of the special curriculum that allowed certain students to take their first year of medical school as the fourth year of college. But in my junior year I decided against accelerating my education; instead I would use my senior year to gain greater academic and social maturity before entering medical school. I was also attracted to the opportunities zoology presented in my senior year, when I would be able to have my own little lab, my own equipment, and my own projects. This produced the only wavering of my lifelong desire to be a surgeon. I was the recipient of so much of my professors' teaching and convivial largesse that I wondered if perhaps I wouldn't be happy in a similar role. Again, it was Norm Arnold who straightened out my thinking on that. As he so aptly pointed out, if I went on to medical school and surgical training, I could always return to the academic world to do what he did, but if I prepared myself to be what he was, I could never do the other.

During those brief weeks of my freshman year when I seemed destined to be a football star, I never would have guessed that in my senior year I would be happy to spend Saturday afternoons looking at a shrimp. My zoology research had taken me into the fascinating life cycle of a tiny crustacean called the fairy shrimp, genus *Eubranchipus.* When full grown this little pink creature was not quite half an inch long, and under the microscope it looked like a shell being rowed by a well-disciplined crew. The legs would shoot out, stroke in unison from forward to back, and propel the fairy shrimp through the water in fits and starts.

In the process of studying *Eubranchipus,* I discovered a new species of shrimp. My mentors told me I could have the little shrimp named for me and suggested I stay on as a teaching assistant in the Department of Zoology. I decided that even being immortalized by *Eubranchipus koopii* wasn't sufficiently enticing to postpone medical school another year.

In another lasting contribution to my life, Dartmouth nourished my love of the outdoors. From my first visit to Dartmouth, I was enchanted by the beauty of the surrounding countryside. In later life, my work would take me all over the globe, to some of the earth's most spectacular scenery, but nothing could replace the special love I developed for the hills and valleys of northern New England.

In the winter I skied. In 1934 skiing in the United States was still in its infancy, and Dartmouth skiers played a major role in the development of the sport. It was while I was in college that the first ski tow in New England began to operate in nearby Woodstock, Vermont. Of course, it was all very new to a boy from Brooklyn.

My first skiing experience was in the light of a waning moon on the hills of the Hanover golf course. One of the greatest thrills of my life was to feel myself start down that very gentle slope with silence all around me, dark spruce trees stark against the white snow, bitter frost in the air, and the unbelievable thrill of gliding with no effort across the hard-packed snow. I became a devotee immediately; every minute that I could spare from my studies went to skiing. I think I skied almost every winter day of my four years at Dartmouth. My favorite outing was the triple moonrise. I would ski up to the top of Oak Hill, a small mountain about a mile north of Hanover, until the moon came up in the east, then I would schuss down Oak Hill, losing the moon, do cross-country skiing westward, and wait for the moon to rise again over

Oak Hill. Then I would descend into the deep valley by the river—a tricky business at night—and wait down there until the moon rose once again. I never tired of the thrill of that triple moonrise.

Perhaps because I had learned how to maintain my balance while roller-skating on cracked Brooklyn sidewalks, I became a fairly decent skier and got to the point where I was at least fearless, if not temperate, and had the temerity to ski the headwall of Tuckerman Ravine, which was in those days a feat usually reserved for experts. Skiing was not only a source of great fun, it was also, at least for me, a risky business. I had more than my share of accidents.

As Dartmouth's famed Winter Carnival approached in my sopho-more year, it was bitterly cold and there was plenty of snow—except on top of the tall ski jump, where the wind had blown it away. So a few of us in the Outing Club volunteered to pack snow onto the ramp of the jump. It was hard, slow work: hoisting the snow to the top of the jump with the help of a horse, rope, pulley, and trash can. I waited on the top of the jump to empty the buckets of snow the horse-and-pulley operation had pulled up. It was so cold up there that my hands and feet were numb. I lost my balance, fell, and started down the ski jump on my back, feet first. My screams alerted the crew preparing the lip of the takeoff at the bottom of the jump, and they caught me. Otherwise, I could have suffered a serious injury, hurtling off the jump onto the landing hill on my back.

The next day I had another near mishap when I was assisting in the fourteen-kilometer cross-country ski race. My assignment was to place the flags in the snow between the sixth and seventh kilometers to mark the course. Then I was to remain at the seven-kilometer mark as the turnaround checkpoint. If a competitor did not circle my flag and have his number checked off by me, he would be disqualified.

I was to be in place one hour before the start of the race at two o'clock. The ski out was routine but very cold. I planted my flags and put three at the turnaround point. Within ten minutes I knew I was in big trouble. I was going to freeze to death if I carried out my assignment. The temperature was forty degrees below zero, and the wind was swirling down from the north. (About twenty years later, when I was telling this story to a group of North Carolina cattlemen, one of my listeners challenged me on the temperature. We checked it out in *The Farmer's Almanac*, which recorded the temperature on that day in Lebanon, New Hampshire, a few miles away, as −40°. And they didn't calculate wind chill in those days!)

Sweat was beginning to freeze in some places under my clothes, and the ski mask I was wearing was a solid block of ice. When I inhaled, the sides of my nose would stick to my nasal septum, and sometimes when I blinked my eyes I could feel the lashes freeze together. I was in a tough spot—abandon the checkpoint (which meant leaving some skiers unattended) or possibly die.

The snow was about four inches of powder on a crust with several feet of snow under that. I took my skis off and used one of them to break through the crust. I enlarged that hole to about three feet in diameter and jumped in. By stamping the snow down, I created a foxhole inside which I could crouch and be completely out of the wind.

After an hour, only about half of the skiers on my list had come by. I learned later they had dropped out because of the cold. After no one had come by for half an hour, I thought it was safe to leave. But I couldn't get out of my hole in the snow. Every time I leaned on the crust to push myself over the edge, the crust broke. I was in the same predicament as someone who has fallen through the ice on a pond. I was now in a panic. I tried everything I could think of to get out. Nothing worked.

I wondered when—if ever—someone would come looking for me. I decided that would not happen before I died. I was getting sleepy. I prayed. One last effort and then I didn't think I would care any more. I began to convert my round hole into a long rectangle by deliberately breaking the crust off at the edges and stamping it down with my feet. When I had a rectangle about thirty feet long and the bottom of the cavity was as hard as I could get it, I put my skis and gear on the south rim of the hole, went to the north end, and rested. I then ran as fast as my bulky clothes would allow, dived upward without touching the edge of the crust, and rolled away. I was out—the crust held.

I don't have much recollection of the ski home. I met no one until I came to the place where I would cross the main road about a mile from Hanover. Almost in disbelief, I saw my family's car. My ordeal had made me forget that I had invited my mother and father for Carnival that weekend. I skied up to the driver's side of the car, but my own father didn't know me. The moisture in my breath had frozen on my ski mask. Except for my eyes, my face was once again encased in ice. Worse, I had come close to frostbite on my hands, once again risking my planned career as a surgeon.

My enthusiasm for skiing allowed me to get talked into representing my fraternity in the intramural ski-jumping competition. Since I had never jumped on skis, I began to practice. I would get up before my usual hour and attack the smaller practice ski jump at dawn. My routine never varied. I tried the landing hill first to assess its speed and then made three jumps. The limit of that jump was ninety feet, which may not seem much by Olympic standards, but for a boy from Brooklyn who had been on skis but two years, it was the closest thing to flying I would ever do.

On the day of the competition I had a lab and didn't get out until the sun had gone down behind the tall pines at the top of the jump. As soon as that happened, the slushy takeoff hill froze into ice. Because I was late and a little embarrassed to appear timid, I did not test the speed of the landing hill first. That was mistake number one.

Mistake number two was that instead of starting ten or fifteen feet down from the top of the takeoff hill, which was permissible, I went to the top. My third mistake was that instead of standing relatively straight up to brake my speed and slow my takeoff, I crouched. My fourth mistake was to jump when I should have just slipped off the lip of the jump.

All of these mistakes combined to make me rocket off the jump much faster than ever before, and I suddenly realized that I was higher than I had ever been, as high as the top branches of the surrounding pine trees. I had no idea what to do, and I don't pretend to say that I thought it out. But I attempted a kind of somersault to slow my speed and get down as fast as I could. I managed to get halfway around, landed on my back, and slid to the base of the hill, feeling as though I had been hit by a truck.

My friends took me on a toboggan to the college infirmary. No one did much for me, and I lay in bed in quiet panic, because I was partially paralyzed. I could move my arms and legs only with great difficulty. No one discussed my condition with me. I plunged into a deep depression, feeling for sure that surgical aspirations and perhaps even a normal life were no longer in my future. Only much later did I figure out that I had suffered a spinal concussion, from which I began to recover after three or four days. This was the first time I had ever been hospitalized. My case was poorly managed, and that made a lasting impression on me. I learned what it was like to lie alone and afraid in a hospital bed, not knowing what the future held, afraid to find out, more afraid not to know. I resolved that when I finally became a doctor, I would not let my own patients lie in fear caused by an inattentive physician.

A small part of my ski-jumping injury remained hidden at the time, for I had also sustained a very fine fracture in my neck. That would eventually catch up with me in the eighth decade of my life, nearly bringing to a quadriplegic conclusion my tenure as Surgeon General.

•

Despite my mishaps, skiing was one of the best things about college. But best of all, Dartmouth brought me Betty.

Before the Christmas break in my junior year, I was chatting with Dan Barker and told him I thought it was a shame that he was now in his senior year and had never invited a girl up for Winter Carnival. I knew that Dan had a longtime steady girlfriend at home, and that it was a foregone conclusion that he would eventually marry her. But I also knew that in the previous summer he had met Betty Flanagan, a girl who planned to enter Vassar in September and whose family summered in the Connecticut shore town where he lived.

I said, "Dan, I feel so strongly about this that I would be delighted to invite you and your girl as my guests at our fraternity, and you will be free to enjoy all the privileges that go with membership in that fraternity for the weekend." I still wonder what was in the depths of my mind as I made this offer.

"That might make a difference. But I don't know which one to ask," he said, looking at two 8 × 10 portraits on either end of his bureau. "Invite that one," I said, pointing to Betty.

We returned from Christmas break, got through the awful month of January, preparing for final exams in the last week of that month, and then there was nothing ahead but Carnival. There was a very special something in the air in Hanover as Carnival approached. Each fraternity and dormitory prepared a snow-and-ice sculpture, and the Dartmouth Outing Club constructed a huge snow statue in the center of the campus. The social events centered around formal dances with white tie and tails on Friday and Saturday nights and a tea dance (so called) after the athletic events on Saturday afternoon. Carnival itself consisted of an outdoor evening on Friday night, a gala affair often featuring an Olympic skating star, stunt skiing, and marvelous fireworks that illuminated the dark pine trees against the sparkling snow. The athletic events featured downhill, slalom, and cross-country skiing races, ski-joring (skiers pulled by horses around a race course), ice hockey, basketball, and ski jumping as the grand finale.

On Friday afternoon, I had just returned to the dorm from a skiing outing and was relaxing in Dan's room, when he walked in and introduced me to Betty. I was dressed only in my skiing long johns. It was an unusual beginning to a long relationship.

My date for the weekend was a girl I had known from home, an attractive, popular girl attending Duke who had little time for me once she saw the other Dartmouth men. After the ski jumping on Saturday afternoon, I returned to the fraternity house and, as was the custom, took off my ski boots so I could be ready to dance, if the occasion arose, in my ski socks. As usual, my date disappeared, but soon the front door opened, and in walked Betty.

"Where's Dan?" I asked.

"He's gone to take a nap," said she, "and he thought I should do the same."

"Do you feel like a nap?"

"Not at all."

"Why don't you go freshen up and come down, and I'll take care of you."

Although I might not have admitted it at the time, my romance with Betty Flanagan began that afternoon. Our first deep conversation was wide-ranging and fascinating for each of us. Later we often recalled that it had a prophetic quality. Among the many subjects we discussed was the difficulty medical students faced because of the unfair, albeit unspoken, prohibition against marriage for medical students. Little did we realize that afternoon that together we would break that barrier, the first of many.

A week later I sent Betty a valentine, unsigned, but obviously from Hanover. At the time I did not know that I had begun a chain of valentines that would extend for more than half a century.

In a strange way, I subconsciously furthered the casual relationship between Betty and Dan. Why did I intercept Betty's thank-you letter to Dan after Carnival, rub it well with Yardley's after-shave talc, and then slide it through the letter slot into his room? When I told the other fellows that Dan had received a perfumed letter, I was secretly pleased when Dan, unwittingly confessing his distance from Betty, said, "It smells just like her."

Winter Carnival receded, and springtime of 1936 came to Hanover as spring usually does there, quite explosively after the bleak mud season. I was unusually content as April gave way to May, as the first leaves burst out on the trees on campus. I felt good about my decision not to accelerate my education, to spend my final undergraduate year at Dartmouth, to focus on my research in zoology. I was simply delighted with everything.

I had no plans to have a date for the Green Key Weekend, Dartmouth's spring house party, in early May. So when one of my fraternity brothers was called home to a funeral, I accepted his invitation to drive to New York City with him. I spent Tuesday evening and all day

Wednesday with my family and met my friend to return to Hanover early Thursday morning.

As we drove slowly north through upper Manhattan and the Bronx, I suddenly proposed, "It's a gorgeous day, and we've just driven down the Connecticut Valley. Let's go back to Hanover up the Hudson Valley." I don't think I had a conscious ulterior motive in suggesting the change in route, although Betty insists I did. As we went up the Taconic Parkway, I said, "We have so much time, let's stop off in Poughkeepsie, find Vassar College, and visit Dan Barker's girl for a few minutes."

It took some effort to find Betty Flanagan. We were told she was not in her dormitory, but that she would be along from class if we cared to wait. Betty doesn't like me to describe the way she looked when she arrived from the library. She looked pretty bedraggled in an old polo coat, the lining of which drooped below the hemline on one side. It didn't matter to me.

I don't know why my friend had the good sense to become occupied with some other endeavor, but Betty and I took a stroll around the lake alone, reminiscing on things we had done and talked about during Winter Carnival, and I realized I was developing an unreasonable attachment to this girl, who had already come to mind many times between February and May. When we got halfway around the lake I stopped and said, "This is spring weekend at Dartmouth. Why don't you drive up with us, and Dan and I will squire you around?" A clear invitation, but sufficiently vague.

I have to admit to some immediate trepidation about having made that remark. First of all, I wasn't at all clear about the relationship between Dan and Betty, but I assumed it was tenuous. However, I also knew enough about Dan to know that he would not jump at the opportunity of sharing his girl with me for the weekend. Then there was a histology exam I had to take as soon as I returned. It was very important to my future, but as that thought went through my mind, I shoved it aside.

Betty said she couldn't possibly do it, and I coaxed. She softened a little, I pushed harder, and she accepted. But a problem remained. In those days a Vassar girl needed family permission to visit a men's college campus for the weekend. Betty phoned, finding only her grandmother at home. When her grandmother gave her permission, she unknowingly forged a bond between us that we both cherished for the rest of her life.

My friend reappeared, and the three of us were off, up the Hudson Valley to Rutland, Vermont, and across the Green Mountains to Hanover. I put off thinking about my histology exam. I also put off thinking about how I was going to explain all this to Dan, something that was going to be increasingly difficult because the ride up had convinced me that this was the girl for me.

Even all those chemistry courses in my premed curriculum would not allow a thorough analysis of the chemistry that flourished so quickly between Betty and me. She was an attractive girl, exquisitely feminine, but neither frail nor fragile. She was a girl who played well in men's sports, but who was not masculine. There was no froth or fluff to Betty. She was solid, genuine.

Betty's father, George Flanagan, the son of an Irish immigrant (his mother died when George was two), had worked in a factory to make enough money to put himself through medical school. As a family practitioner in New Britain, Connecticut, his compassion and profound sense of obligation to his patients had earned him the title of "beloved physician." Betty's mother, Ethel Swartwood, was descended from Dutch stock (Van Benschotens, Swartwoods, and Lents) who first set foot in New Amsterdam in 1659 and then moved up the Hudson Valley to live in upstate New York. With a flair for music and drama, Ethel graduated from Emerson College, where she wrote its alma mater, and then taught English at Syracuse University until she married Dr. George.

Among her many contributions to Betty and me was her standard of selfless devotion to her husband's practice of medicine, so that he could do what needed to be done for his patients. She passed this on to Betty, who would nurture it and improve upon it, making possible all I—or, I should say, we—accomplished as a surgeon and as Surgeon General. The rest of Betty's family showed the same sense of devotion and compassion. Her younger brother George, later to be my longtime sailing companion—before, during and after his career as an internist and then nuclear radiologist—was as well educated as anyone I have known (Milton–Harvard–MIT–Penn), but what impressed everyone about him was his down-to-earth care of and devotion to his patients. And Betty's grandmother Swartwood, one of the world's truly wise and gentle souls, would pay me a great compliment while I was only an intern when she insisted that I alone be the doctor to attend her as she died. All in all, Betty's background would make her the ideal wife for me. Our families held the same values, and there seemed to be few differences of philosophy to be reconciled. (One didn't take long. Like many college women in the thirties, Betty was toying with the idea of taking up smoking. In the course of our first conversation I happened to say that I would never be interested in any girl who smoked. After hearing that, she never took a puff. Little did I know then how many people I would eventually warn about smoking.)

Of course, all this lay ahead of me and unknown to me on that long (but all too short for me) ride from Poughkeepsie to Hanover. What I did know on that ride, as much by intuition as by observation, was that I was in the presence of honesty, loyalty, sensitivity, and understanding. Best of all, Betty had a great sense of humor and not a smidgen of the bane of my other encounters with women: tedium. I saw a lot in Betty, and I appreciated all I saw.

What I could not have known then, as the car wound its way along Vermont streams, was the extent of her steadfastness and willingness to sacrifice herself for me and my career. And I had not yet been guided by the wisdom and sense of balance that Betty would use to keep me on track through the years. Nor could I have foreseen then what it was that would keep us together and content for over half a century: a true meeting of the minds. And, as her eyes said as they sparkled that May day, "There's more!" That has been the priceless ingredient: There has always been more to come.

It was Thursday, and since the great influx of Dartmouth dates for the weekend did not begin until Friday, I was able to find a cheap room for Betty up on the third floor of the old Hanover Inn. It was *verboten* for the male students to go upstairs to rooms occupied by young ladies, so I left Betty in the lobby, promising I would be back as soon as I could, after I did some studying for my exam, and that then maybe we could have something to eat. I was nervous about meeting Dan. My attempt at a breezy introduction of the situation to him fell extraordinarily flat. I could tell by the tightening muscles in his jaw that he was angry, and in all fairness to him I have to say that I was so vague he could not possibly have known what my plans were. I was more than nervous—I was scared.

I was falling in love, and I knew it. I walked back into my room, closed the door, and went through the motions of cramming for the next morning's exam. The pages before me were a blur. I had no interest in the cellular structure of the liver or the microscopic intricacies of striated muscle. After a ridiculous hour, I threw in the towel, faced reality for the first time that day, and decided to go back to the inn to take Betty to dinner.

I called Betty's room from the lobby and got no answer. It never occurred to me that she might have gone out. I told the manager that I had called and gotten no answer and wondered if he could send somebody up to the room to see if she was all right. He looked at me as though I were out of my mind, but nevertheless complied and returned to tell me that the room was indeed empty.

If love is irrational, disappointment in love is more so. I had absolutely no claim on this girl. I knew deep down that even my close friends would not like what I had done. I had told Betty I was bringing her up for a shared weekend with Dan. I had given her no specific plans for the evening. Yet here I not only had an inexplicable emptiness in the middle of my belly, I was unreasonably hurt.

I tore back to my room in the dormitory. I went across the hall and found Ed McGrath, Dan's roommate, sitting at his desk looking very stern. When I inquired where Dan was, Ed said that he had left the room in some anger, muttering something about ". . . at least I'll take her to dinner." Then Ed let me know in no uncertain terms that what I had done was something between highly foolish and unkind. He might have also said insensitive and stupid. He reminded me that in Dartmouth lingo, the definition of someone who took a friend's girl was a "snake." Ed had a high sense of honor. We were, for the first time, on different wavelengths. How could he know how I felt, and wasn't all fair in love and war? I had a definite feeling I now had both on my hands.

I went across the hall, closed myself in my room, and seethed. Again, the histology text before me was a blur. When I heard Dan come in and close his door, I took off for the inn. Knowing it was against the rules but unreasonably angry with Betty, I walked up the main stairs that left the lobby in full view of the registration desk, found her room on the third floor, and knocked on the door.

When Betty answered, I suppressed all the surging warm and tender emotions that were once again aroused by seeing her. Instead I stepped inside and said in my anger, "Get your clothes packed. I'm driving you to Rutland. You can take a train to Poughkeepsie."

There was never any more sincere consternation than Betty displayed. If I had told her she was responsible for the rumors of the gathering clouds of World War II, she could not have been more startled.

"Why? What did I do?"

"You had dinner with Dan."

"Why shouldn't I? He told me you had sent him to take me to dinner because you had to study."

It was all so very reasonable, so very logical. But I was not. I had foolishly allowed my image of this wonderful girl to crumble over the past hour. I don't recall clearly what turned me back on the right track, but I began to rebuild the image with Betty's reasonable explanation.

As we talked, we rapidly recaptured the magic spirit of our short time together at the Carnival tea dance. We were back to talking about medical students being married. I never asked her to marry me, but I knew she was going to and she knew it, too.

In those few hours, a great many things in my life changed. Couples have been through this experience since the beginning of time. They fall in love, go together for a while, get to know each other, build a base on which to form an abiding faith and love with a lifetime commitment. The unusual thing about us was that we compressed all that into the hours between 10:00 P.M. and dawn. Betty often has said, "Chick works with dispatch!"

Dawn made its presence known by the light around the window shade. I couldn't believe the speed with which time had passed or the predicament I was in. Not only was I in a forbidden place; I had been there all night. If I had been caught, I could have been expelled. It was another time my medical career hung by a thread.

I said good-bye as though for the last time and started downstairs looking for an alternate route of escape. There was none. When the registration desk came into view, the clerk was obviously asleep. I sat down on the stairs, took off my shoes, and crept out the front door in stocking feet, unnoticed. Once on the porch of the inn, I put my shoes on and, breathing in the crisp New Hampshire dawn, sprinted back to my room. It was about 6:00. I was able to study until about 8:00. I took the exam, proving that from the start life with Betty would be productive. I got an "A."

By the end of Green Key Weekend, Betty and I knew we were headed for life together. After I placed her on the train back to Vassar, I called home.

"Mother, guess what! I'm engaged."

There was a long silence. My mother later told Betty, "My legs turned to jelly, but I managed to say, 'That's wonderful, Buddy.' "

I didn't see much of my Dartmouth friends the rest of that weekend, but in time things worked out. Ed came around and grew very fond of Betty. Dan and I remained cool for the rest of the spring term, but he needed my notes for two courses he was taking, and that kept things civil.

When Betty's letters began to arrive daily, including special deliveries on Sundays, Dan recognized and accepted the situation for what it was—overpowering and eventually out of his control. Our friendship resumed, we enjoyed cordial visits through the years thereafter, and he occasionally referred patients to me. He married the other girl whose picture stood on his bureau.

My senior year at Dartmouth was my best, as I reveled in the academic excitement of my major, prowled the countryside with Norm Arnold on foot, on skis, and in his old Ford, and went to see Betty whenever I could. In the summers she and I were on opposite shores of Long Island Sound and would use the Port Jefferson–Bridgeport ferry to visit at each other's homes. But during the school year we found that travel between Poughkeepsie and Hanover was difficult.

In 1937 I would hop on the midnight train in White River Junction, Vermont, get off in New York at dawn, take the subway to Brooklyn, borrow the family car, and drive to Vassar. Then, at the end of the weekend, Betty and I would drive back to New York together, return the car, and get on separate trains to return to our colleges. We managed to get together about every six weeks between autumn and my graduation in June 1937.

More than fifty years later, in June 1989, when we had to squeeze into one weekend Betty's fiftieth reunion at Vassar and my receiving an honorary degree at Dartmouth's commencement, we faced a familiar problem: It was *still* hard to get from Poughkeepsie to Hanover.

Dartmouth shaped my life in ways I am still discovering, and many things that have happened to me and my family can be traced to my decision to attend "the college on the hill." I have already mentioned some: education, close friends, my wife. There would be many green threads woven through my life. My love for the Hanover hills would lead me to spend summers there with my wife and children. That, in turn, would call a second and then a third Koop generation to attend Dartmouth. Our family's attraction to the White Mountains, for both work and play, also reflected my love of Dartmouth. My varied connections with Dartmouth gave me some of my happiest moments, and my greatest sorrow would come with the death of a Dartmouth boy.

There was something very special about Dartmouth. Many of us felt that at an isolated, all-male college, the depth of friendships was greater than on a coed campus, where social success with women can supersede male companionship. (However, having two Dartmouth granddaughters has let me see the Dartmouth experience in a new light.) Over the years, the class of '37 enjoyed what I like to think was a special camaraderie, perhaps because our college years were a brief parenthesis between the worst of the Depression and the war that claimed too many of us.

And there is a special claim that the isolated New Hampshire setting has upon the men—and now women—of Dartmouth:

> They have the still north in their hearts,
> The hill winds in their breath,
> And the granite of New Hampshire,
> Is made part of them 'til death.

Chapter 3

New York to Philadelphia

As I prepared for my career as a doctor, there was one thing I knew for sure. I would attend medical school at Columbia University's College of Physicians and Surgeons. Paul Strong was the reason. Older than I and a role model of sorts, Paul had been a medical student at Columbia when I was a young teenager. When I went to Columbia for my admissions interview in the fall of my senior year at Dartmouth, I felt very much at home in the familiar corridors where Paul had helped me masquerade as a medical student years before. It was inconceivable that I would not be admitted. My discussion with the admissions panel seemed to go well until one of them asked me, "Do you ever expect to make any major discoveries in medicine?"

It was a stupid question then; it is a stupid question now.

I responded, "Well, sir, from what little experience I have in reading about discoveries in the field of medicine, I rather think that those who make them are building upon the efforts of many who preceded them, but did not do the final thing that achieved success and fame. I would like to be one who makes a major discovery, but I will be content to contribute to the process."

Good answer then; good answer now.

"We don't think you've got the stuff we are looking for at the College of Physicians and Surgeons!"

I was devastated. My image of my medical career lay shattered. I was convinced that whatever happened now, it could be only second best. Little did I know. (Recently, while making some TV shows at Columbia, I told the president of the medical center that if Columbia had admitted me in 1937, I might have made something of myself. He agreed.)

Soon after my discouraging interview at Columbia, I went for my interview at the only other school I had considered, Cornell University Medical College, downtown on the other side of Manhattan Island. As soon as I walked into the main entrance, I sensed a convivial atmosphere. The dean's secretary greeted me warmly: "Good afternoon, Mr. Koop, we're so glad you're here."

When I returned to the dean's office, after spending several hours in interviews in New York Hospital, the Dean said graciously, "Mr. Koop, if you will accept it, Cornell would like to offer you a place in next year's entering class."

I loved every minute of it. I even loved the course in anatomy, always advertised as the toughest experience in medical school. Cornell was unusual in that we had only two students per cadaver, instead of the usual four. My cadaver's name was Ira Posey. I knew only that he had lived in Manhattan and had died of tuberculosis. I frequently pondered the life he must have led that had brought him to his destitute death. Even in death, Ira was one of the most important people in my life, and he contributed unknowingly to much that I accomplished as a surgeon. His was that ear I kept in my bureau drawer as a memento of our close association.

I survived anatomy—and the rest of the first year of medical school—only with the help of my teachers, my friends, and my family. Yet another skiing accident—this time a broken leg—during my Christmas vacation incapacitated me for months. Skiing was still a new sport in 1937, and skiing injuries were not as commonplace as they later became. The bone had to be refractured and reset as I hobbled around in a series of plaster casts, with crutches, then with a brace, and finally with a cane. It was eighteen months before I could walk without assistance. It took fifty-two years for my new walk to destroy my right knee.

I realized that if I had attended Columbia, I probably would never have graduated, would probably never have become a doctor. The arrogant, competitive atmosphere of Columbia's College of Physicians and Surgeons in those days would have weeded out a medical student who could not walk around, one who was dependent on other students, one who was stupid enough to break a leg. But at Cornell Medical School, the faculty and my fellow students rallied around me. My father's help was the most vital. I moved back to my parents' home in

Brooklyn while recuperating, and my father drove me to school each day, several hours before his job started, and then home again, several hours after he normally finished. Our time together in the car became precious to me as I formed a closer bond with my father, not only the bond of father and son, but that of the closest of friends. His death years later would leave a void that time would never quite fill.

The broken leg taught me a new method of study and retention. Walking around on my crutches, dragging a heavy cast, and standing balanced on those crutches for long laboratory periods made me extremely tired. I learned to take a couple of short ten-minute naps during the evening, and I also learned to wake up without feeling groggy. I slowly developed a new attitude toward lectures. I concentrated as hard as I could on what was being said. If it made sense, I made no notes. If it didn't make sense, I would write it down, check it out at the library, and record it in a black leather loose-leaf notebook that I carried in my white laboratory coat pocket. This "cold dope book" became the repository for the information I considered critical to review before exams. The system worked well for me then; it still does now.

The academic intensity of medical school leaves little time for anything but studies. It is almost like going through life with blinders on. Later, when my children would ask me, for instance, about world events leading to the Second World War, I would have to struggle to lift my memory out of the confines of my medical textbooks and courses. But this was a period of my life that showed the importance of the strong bonds of family love. My father and mother helped me overcome the ordeal of the broken leg and got me through the first year of medical school, while Betty got me through the next three. And the half century since.

During that difficult first year, Betty came down from Vassar on weekends whenever she could, and we spent much of the summer of 1938 trying to find a way to get married. We had two problems. We had no money, and Betty's father was in ill health, so it seemed unlikely that he could attend a wedding. But we were able to convince our families—as many couples have done—that two could live together on less than two can live apart. Our families were extraordinarily understanding, especially in a day when it was thought that married medical students would certainly fail. In great faith, we had wedding announcements engraved, leaving blank the date and place. Less than a week before medical school was to resume classes for my second year, Betty's mother reported that she thought Betty's father would be well enough to travel from Connecticut to Vassar College in Poughkeepsie for a wedding on Monday, September 19, just four days away. It was a small family wedding: four parents, four grandparents, Betty's brother George, and two attendants. Betty and I walked out, married, into an unusually heavy rainstorm. As the wind howled around us, I opened an umbrella. It showered confetti all over us, which stuck to our wet clothing like sequins. We couldn't hide being newlyweds. At the time, we could not have known how foolish it was to attempt a brief wedding trip motoring through New England in that weather. In the years since, we have celebrated our wedding anniversary with recollections of the infamous hurricane of '38.

Betty's friends had told her that four years at Vassar wouldn't prepare her for much in the world of business, and she discovered that three years did even less. She went to secretarial school, then landed a job in the office of the Social Service Department at New York Hospital. From then until I graduated, we were employed in the same building and could walk to work together. Even though I was always swamped with work, we were home together at night in our tiny apartment, and even in those days she was my sounding board and my confidante.

From the start, Betty made my career our career. In the first summer of our marriage we lived in Port Jefferson, Long Island, where I had a nonpaying job working in two hospitals. She commuted into New York City on the hot and sooty trains of the Long Island Railroad for six hours each day; on Saturdays she commuted six hours for three hours of work.

During the school year, Betty always joined me and the other students for lunch. Then and in the following fifty years, she picked up a lot of medical knowledge. I'm positive that she knows more than many doctors. For years, friends and family have come to her for medical advice. And she's usually right.

Although I've had my share of drudgery and some seemingly unrewarding endeavors in my life, in general, I have always thoroughly enjoyed everything that I did. Medical school was no exception, but the fact that I was married made it ever so much more enjoyable.

I have often viewed my life as a tapestry woven of many threads, its ultimate design and purpose determined by the sovereignty of God. So often in my career He had me in the right place at the right time. In the summer before my final year of medical school, my summer plans had just collapsed, and I was walking by the Dean's office when his secretary called to me.

"Mr. Koop, do you have any knowledge of any student who would be available to take a wonderful job that has just turned up across the street at Memorial Hospital?"

"It just so happens I do know one and here he is."

I ran up the street and put on better clothes and went down to Memorial Hospital (now Sloan-Kettering). There I was interviewed by Hayes Martin, a pleasant, no-nonsense kind of a man whom I grew to admire tremendously. He told me that he was onto a new and good thing. He was convinced that raw brewer's yeast, which contains large amounts of vitamin B, could help prevent the development of precancerous lesions in the mouth, and, indeed, might even slow the progress of those that had already formed. He wanted somebody to undertake a controlled study of a group of people with cancer or precancerous lesions to test his theory. I was delighted with the opportunity and readily undertook it. Dr. Martin was right, and we coauthored my first scientific paper.

When I reported my findings to the hospital director, Dr. James Ewing, a pioneer in the field of cancer, he said, "In other words, you are telling me that with trauma such as smoking or holding a pipe in your lips for years, in the absence of vitamin B, you have a better chance of developing cancer."

I replied that I thought that was true.

Ewing tested me, "Then why is it that horses, with the trauma of a bit in their mouths, don't develop more cancer?"

"Well," I said, "my grandfather's horse did die of cancer of the mouth, but then, on the other hand, I've known only two horses intimately."

"That's fifty percent! Not a bad series!"

The outstanding experience of my fourth year of medical school was obstetrics, primarily because I spent two weeks living in Harlem and delivering babies at the Berwind Free Maternity Clinic on West 116th Street. Four students were assigned there at a time. Of my team, only I had ever seen a delivery. None of us had ever participated in one. My first delivery was born before I arrived. After stepping over a huge dead rat, I found the mother kneeling on a coal pile, the baby and placenta lying between her legs.

I learned fast, delivering fourteen babies in fourteen days, and had practically every complication in the book. Some were due to the peculiar habits (if I may call them that) of my patients—such as the time I arrived to find my obstetrical patient trying to have intercourse with her boyfriend, even though she was already in labor and delivered two hours later. I could hardly be blamed for that infection. My initial experience in obstetrics was an eye-opening exposure to the need for adequate medical care in the poverty-stricken neighborhoods of American cities. I tried to do all I could for these neglected patients.

On one call, it had taken me too long to find the house, a condemned structure under the Triborough Bridge, where I found a woman about to deliver a baby through a birth canal so big that it was my impression that the baby could have crawled out on its hands and knees. A previous birth, or several, had torn the poor woman so much that her vagina and rectum were one and the same. When I arrived she was having active contractions, and I had barely gotten my gown and gloves on and the room set up for delivery when she gave what seemed to me to be two short coughs, and suddenly the baby was lying on the sheet between her legs.

I tied off the infant's umbilical cord, gave the baby to one of a large number of observing relatives, put them all out of the room, and contemplated what I should do next. I was alone. The resident who was on call to provide backup for me in this kind of an emergency had instead sent me off with the large bag that was essentially a small operating room. He was never supposed to let it out of his sight, but this resident, a rather lazy fellow, had not wanted to tote the heavy bag, so he had sent the portable hospital with me. I was angry with the resident who had shirked his duty and left me literally holding the bag. I had to make a spot decision about what to do next. This woman was in desperate need of surgery, yet I knew that the chances of her ever coming to the hospital for an operation were slim to none. I couldn't imagine how she could live out her life in her present condition.

The surgeon in me began to surface. I decided to fix that woman's problem right then and there. Although I had seen enough surgery to know what to do I didn't know then that the danger of infection was so high and the woman's tissues so stretched that the operation would put her at risk. Today, even in a modern hospital, an obstetrician would wait weeks or months before attempting to repair that problem. I believed then that it was now or never. I started right in, gave the woman a nerve block for anesthesia, and by the time I was finished, the delighted woman had, for the first time in years, a rectum and vagina that each would function as intended.

On my way back to the clinic, I began to realize my precarious position. At the least I could get decked by the resident, at worst I could be expelled from medical school. But since the resident had sent me alone, he had to cover for me. I visited my grateful patient as often as

I could, as pleased as she was that she healed completely without infection.

Sometimes while studying late at night, when I didn't think I could cram one more fact into a tiring brain, I would take a walk halfway across the Queensborough Bridge over the East River at 59th Street and then return home for another couple of hours of work before going to bed in the wee hours of the morning. I'd gaze at the lights of Manhattan from the Queensborough Bridge and realize how much I enjoyed learning to be a doctor and how I looked forward to what I hoped to accomplish. I often felt an overwhelming sense of thanksgiving.

They were tough days living in New York with no money, but they were days I wouldn't give up for anything. Our children hate to hear us talk about it, but Betty and I did manage to live on five dollars a week for food if we had three weekend meals with my family in Brooklyn. We had little time and no money for relaxation or entertainment.

In June 1941 I graduated from Cornell University Medical College. We all stood to sing the Cornell alma mater, "Far Above Cayuga's Waters"; but since few of us had attended the undergraduate college in Ithaca, most knew only the first four words. I had taken the Hippocratic Oath a few minutes before. I was an M.D. My mother and father joined Betty and me for dinner in Chinatown. The bright June days that followed were the last of total freedom that I remember. On the last day of June 1941, I reported for duty as an intern at the Pennsylvania Hospital in Philadelphia, the first and oldest in the United States.

A pattern for my life was developing, although at the time I did not see it. As with medical school, my quest for an internship brought first bitter disappointment, then something far better.

I had always assumed that after I finished my medical training, I would settle down as a doctor in Brooklyn, practicing in an office in a brownstone, being the kind of family doctor that would make all my relatives proud of me. I think if I had asked my cousins and uncles and aunts in 1940 if they would rather have me practice family medicine from a Brooklyn brownstone or become the Surgeon General, they would have chosen Brooklyn.

The expectations of my extended family had limited my own vision and had certainly lowered my horizon. I reasoned that if I were going to practice in Brooklyn, it made very good sense that I should intern in the New York metropolitan area. There were four or five outstanding two-year rotating internships on the East Coast, two of which were in

Brooklyn: the Brooklyn Hospital and the Methodist Episcopal Hospital. The purpose of this rotating internship was to allow the young doctor to rotate through several medical areas, adding experience to knowledge, and to sample all the medical specialties before entering general practice or selecting a residency in the field of his choice. Even though marriage and medical school had worked out extraordinarily well for me, I still had to contend with widespread misgivings—or outright prejudice—from my profession about mixing marriage and medical training. I was extraordinarily angered by my two interviews at the Brooklyn and Methodist Hospitals. Both interviewers were adamant that you could not be a good intern if you were married.

If they were right, medicine is in dire trouble today, because 14 percent of medical students are married before matriculation and 35 percent by graduation. Even more marry during their years of clinical training. Was it just Brooklyn that was closed to me as an intern, or would I find the same prejudice elsewhere?

At the same time as I explored internships, I probed the more distant future, looking into various options for surgical residencies after the completion of my internship.

My application to the training program at Vanderbilt University in Nashville brought a brief reply from Barney Brooks, professor of surgery: "Dear Koop, you didn't say whether or not you are married. If you are, don't answer this letter."

Discouraged, I turned to a former mentor, researcher Dr. Hayes Martin, who suggested I try the Jersey City Medical Center, a hospital in the news more for its political shenanigans than for its scientific breakthroughs. But when I requested a reference from Dr. C. P. "Dusty" Rhoades, medical director at Memorial Hospital where I had done some summer research during medical school, he opened my eyes to something I should have seen before. In America, he said, there were two kinds of medicine. There was academic medicine—medicine attached to the teaching program of a university medical school—and there was the rest of medicine. As he put it, academic medicine was in a special league, other medicine was out of the league. A doctor in academic medicine could leave the league any time he wanted, but once you were out of the league it was extraordinarily difficult to get back in.

I was grateful to Rhoades for making this clear to me, and I followed his advice. I set my sights on the top and applied to the best academic medicine residency programs on the East Coast. When I traveled to Philadelphia for my interview at the University of Pennsylvania, I took the precaution of removing my wedding ring. (The subject of marriage never came up.) I was interviewed by I. S. Ravdin, professor of surgery and director of the Harrison Department of Surgical Research, a man with a reputation as both a brilliant surgeon and a bear who was tough on his residents.

Ravdin told me, "If you work for me, you have got to do three jobs together. You have to be a Harrison Fellow in Research Surgery, a resident in surgery at the University Hospital, and an instructor in surgery in the School of Medicine. Do you think you can do that?"

How did I know?

I said, "Does anybody else manage that combination of assignments?"

"Yes, of course. At the present time, Dr. Frazier and Dr. Royster do it very well."

So I said, "If they can do it, so can I."

Ravdin was not one to waste time.

"Okay, you can get yourself an internship down at the Pennsylvania Hospital. At the end of those two years, I'll have you operate in the dog lab for two years. And then you can start the five-year Harrison Fellowship in surgery."

I quickly totaled up nine years of training before I would be a surgeon on my own. Although I realized how much I would learn there, I felt very depressed about leaving New York for the steamy summer climate of Philadelphia. Besides, Betty and I had a lease until October on our tiny New York City apartment and couldn't afford rent in two cities, which meant that Betty would have to stay in her New York Hospital job while I moved to Philadelphia. It was our first real separation, and we didn't relish it. I lived at the hospital until autumn, when we moved into our Philadelphia apartment.

Following the established ritual, my first day of duty was July 1, 1941. Every July 1, American medicine changes teams as a new staff of somewhat experienced residents and totally green interns arrives at each hospital. I have always hoped I would never have to be hospitalized in the first week of July.

One day of sweltering in the Philadelphia summer heat and unpacking in my cramped, lonely living quarters made me determined to find a way to get back to New York and Betty. Then I received a call from my roommate, Francis Jacobs, who was in the emergency room. He had an unusual patient, a man of Malaysian origin complaining of a stuffy nose. Something about the patient's face recalled textbook photos he had seen in med school. Francis realized where he had seen a face like that before and he confirmed his diagnosis with a microscopic study of the man's nasal discharge. It was leprosy.

My opinion of Philadelphia and the Pennsylvania Hospital changed in a second. If this hospital could, on the first day of my new internship, provide a patient who walked in off the street with leprosy, it had a lot to teach me. I was right. The year flew by, and it was loaded with marvelous experiences.

Pennsylvania Hospital claimed to be the oldest in the nation; Benjamin Franklin and Benjamin Rush had played a role in its founding. Brass plates engraved with the names of every house officer from the beginning adorned the wall, board meetings started at 2:00 P.M. by the pocket watch of the oldest member present. True to its Quaker heritage, the hospital maintained an old tradition of providing a bed, blanket, and bowl of soup for anyone who showed up at its door claiming to be tired, cold, and hungry. Even today, in the Pennsylvania Hospital's modern building, space is set aside in the cafeteria for indigent elderly folks from the immediate neighborhood. I hope no young manager or aggressive board member ever changes that policy.

Each day of my internship at Pennsylvania Hospital, and later of my residency at the University of Pennsylvania Hospital, I realized that these two Philadelphia hospitals were among the best providers of medical care in this country. I felt privileged to have joined them. Both institutions awarded me an unusual degree of independence and authority, and both made me appreciate everything that was good in medicine.

Very quickly I surprised myself by feeling at home in Philadelphia. It was different from New York. The first time I rode the Paoli local, the commuter train serving the Main Line suburbs, I was prepared to behave like a New Yorker as I boarded the train: turn my shoulder forward and push, because that's the only way you can get onto the New York subway. As I assumed the posture of a football fullback, I was astonished when several gentlemen wearing unpressed seersucker suits and panama hats motioned me toward the door and said, "After you, sir." The charm of the Philadelphia suburbs worked in combination with the hospital's exciting surgery to keep me a Philadelphian until the call came to serve in Washington forty years later. Betty and I felt blessed to be able to raise our family in suburban Penn Valley, and the place still has a hold on me. Years after I moved to Washington, I would sometimes mistakenly say "Philadelphia" when I spoke about going home. I still do.

We all had our lives changed by the coming of the Second World

War. I completed my training as a civilian physician during the war, and the shortage of doctors during the conflict intensified the scope of my surgical experience. I was called upon to perform operations usually reserved for surgeons with much more experience. It was nerve-racking at times, but exhilarating. The few surgeons left behind at the University of Pennsylvania Hospital during the war jokingly said we fought in the Battle of Spruce Street. We were thankful to spend the war years where we were, even though we were under constant stress and got little sleep. It wasn't combat, thank God, but even so, lives hung in the balance every day.

My career in Philadelphia was saved because Betty went for a Coke the day after the attack on Pearl Harbor. As she stood in the hospital snack bar, sipping her soda, she happened to overhear Dr. Ravdin confide in an associate that he planned to fly that night to Pearl Harbor to try a new drug, sulfanilamide, on some of the sailors' war wounds. She called me immediately and said, "If Dr. Ravdin goes out there tonight, who knows when he might return? Your future is very much up in the air."

I didn't really know what to do, but I had to do something. Dr. Ravdin's office was full of people racing around, so I went to wait by his car. The December dusk grew colder as I sat on the running board. Suddenly Ravdin appeared. He was a short man, probably no more than five feet, five inches tall, and he was wearing, as most men did in those days, a fedora hat. In the shadows he looked like Fiorello La Guardia, mayor of New York. I asked him if I might drive downtown with him, and he told me to hop in. After a few minutes, I spoke.

"Dr. Ravdin, I know you are going to leave for Pearl Harbor tonight, and before you go I thought we should have a discussion about what plans you have for me in reference to my surgical training now that there are so many factors to be considered."

Ravdin held his breath in his characteristic way before answering me. I like to think that what went through his mind was a consideration of how I knew he was going to Pearl Harbor. Either I was well connected or I had supernatural powers. In either case, I was a force to be reckoned with.

When he finally exhaled, in a very few words he set the stage for the rest of my life.

"Don't sign any papers. Before I leave for Pearl Harbor I will declare you essential to the University of Pennsylvania for the duration of the war. You will start as a Harrison Fellow on the first of July."

My training, already shortened by war when my two-year internship was cut to one year, had just been further curtailed by the elimination of a two-year stint in the dog lab.

In the next five years I crammed in a decade of surgical experience. With Ravdin away for the duration of the war, the surgical service was in the capable hands of Dr. Jonathan Rhoads. A tall, Lincolnesque man with a low-pitched voice and a laconic sense of humor, Jonathan Rhoads was a master surgeon and a master teacher. His judgment and diagnosis were superb. His research background was well regarded, and he was universally admired and respected in the field of surgery. I couldn't have had a better mentor.

Jonathan Rhoads was also gentle and generous. He was generous with the number of patients he assigned to me for surgery and with the time he took to teach me. He was generous in inviting Betty and me to his home for a roast beef dinner in the meatless days of World War II. He was generous with his car for a Sunday drive when he knew we hadn't stirred from our apartment for months. He was generous with his summer home in New Hampshire, which he let us have after we had gone three years without a vacation. Jonathan became a treasured friend. Although I am officially listed as a Ravdin trainee, I actually was the first surgeon Jonathan Rhoads trained from start to finish. I'm proud of that, and I think he is too.

Years later, after I had become Surgeon General, he took great delight in telling me how he had been standing on a street corner in Tokyo, wearing a conference badge on his lapel that said "Jonathan E. Rhoads—Philadelphia." A Japanese man, considerably shorter than Jonathan's six feet, four inches, scrutinized the badge, bowed, and said, "You very lucky man to live in same city as Dr. Koop."

In the last year of my tenure as Surgeon General, more than forty years after Jonathan Rhoads had trained me, I returned to the University of Pennsylvania Hospital to give a lecture. I met Jonathan in the elevator.

"How are things going, Jonathan?" I asked.

Jonathan, then eighty-one years old, replied, "Quite well, although my practice is falling off a little bit." I would have been perfectly happy to have this octogenarian master surgeon operate upon me right then if the need had arisen.

As I began my surgical training as a Harrison Fellow, I was in seventh heaven. I was, at last, an operating surgeon, and I loved every minute of it. A strange surgical case allowed me to assume a position with extraordinary responsibility for a first-year resident. An elderly woman patient was suffering from a serious skin disease known as exfoliative dermatitis; the outer layer of her skin kept sloughing off and falling away. Dr. C. H. Perry Pepper, distinguished professor of medicine, had determined that the dermatitis was being prolonged because of an infection in her gallbladder, but operating to remove the gallbladder would be tricky, in those pre-antibiotic days, because the open abdomen had to be protected from the infection on the skin. Improvising with sterilized cellophane (from a factory that made Henrietta cigars) and rubber cement, I was able to prepare the patient's abdomen so that Jonathan Rhoads could operate on her safely. (Little did I know that twenty-five years later this technique would become standard procedure for some abdominal operations.)

In early August 1942 I had been a surgical resident at the Hospital of the University of Pennsylvania for only five weeks. Jonathan, detained by another complicated operation, sent word that I should start the gallbladder case. I opened the woman's abdomen, as I had watched Jonathan do a number of times, and it was then my intent to wait until he arrived to remove the gallbladder.

But to my great surprise, the woman's gallbladder was right on top, instead of being in its usual place, buried in the liver. It seemed unusually easy to remove, so I performed the operation just as I had seen Jonathan do it. He arrived as I was putting in the last skin stitch. He said nothing but meticulously took out all the stitches I had just placed in the skin, muscle, and peritoneum in order to inspect my ligation of the cystic artery and duct. Then he replaced the drains exactly where I had them and closed the wound even as I had done a few minutes before. He never said a word, but I think he was impressed.

Two days later I was in his office when he took a telephone call, turned to me, and said, "Chick, there is a patient who has just come into the emergency room with a perforated, bleeding gastric ulcer. Would you go down and work him up and get him operated upon as soon as possible? You go ahead and do it. Call me only if you need me."

I was astounded and elated. In just five weeks I had graduated to surgery usually reserved for a resident in his third year. That early start, combined with the scarcity of surgeons because of the war and the tremendous number of patients we had for the next four years, gave me an operative experience as a resident that few (if any) had before and none have had since.

I could never describe adequately the passing days, months, and years of my surgical training—the joy and ecstacy of surgical success, the depression and sadness of surgical failure, the dedication and devotion of the men and women who worked with me, often all through the night, the understanding and patience of my patients.

If Jonathan Rhoads was my surgical mentor, the senior resident, Harold Zintel, taught me the essence of surgical patient care. Harold shared with me the secret of making rounds: They never end. We would start on the seventh floor at one end of the building and work our way down to the first floor at the opposite end of the building, a city block away, checking in on as many as a hundred surgical patients. Then, unless interrupted by scheduled or emergency surgery, we would start all over again. As a result of his guidance I developed a sense of necessary intimacy with the problems of my patients, and I never lost it.

In later years, surgical residents would enjoy adequate salaries and duty schedules allowing them time at home. But when I was a resident at the University Hospital, I was, well, a resident. I literally lived there, sometimes coming home only once every three days. I was always on call, without a day off in the first two years. It was a busy life, and a frugal one. In those days interns were paid nothing, but did have laundry and eating privileges at the hospital. As a Harrison Fellow I took home $1,000 a year for the first three years and $1,200 for the last two.

I gave myself to the job completely. My dedication to my surgery was matched only by Betty's dedication to my career. She never complained about the long hours, the claim my work made on my time. She knew the life of a doctor—and a doctor's family—was one of sacrifice.

Some times were tougher than others. It never entered anyone's mind that I should take time off. Who would cover for me? The combination of overwork, tension, and lack of sleep finally gave me a peptic ulcer. After it failed to respond to medication, I decided to treat it myself. I taped a broomstick to the headboard of our double bed, then hung a burette with a long rubber tube on the broomstick. Each night I filled it with a quart of milk. Then I passed a rubber tube up my nose and down my throat into my stomach, attached it to the gadget on the bed, and let the milk drip into my stomach all night long. Far too frequently the tube would get blocked, the milk would drip onto the bed, and Betty and I would wake up in a puddle of sour milk. We would get up, remake the bed, and try to get some sleep. This was on the nights when I was able to sleep at home. Other nights I dozed off on an operating table or gurney.

But I faced each day with enthusiasm. I couldn't wait to get to work. I reveled in the challenge of diagnosing a specific problem from a general complaint. My happiest hours were those in the operating room. I felt called to live on the edge of the life-and-death decisions that need to be made there.

The greatest continuing success story of the Ravdin surgical service was the proficiency of its gallbladder surgery. This service had not lost a patient following simple removal of the gallbladder for many years, and the number of such patients successfully treated climbed into the thousands. Each surgeon feared he might be the first one to lose a gallbladder patient.

As it turned out, I was the one who broke the successful series. But as has happened so often in my life, the tragedy also became a triumph—at least for a while.

One evening I walked up to the beside of a woman whose gallbladder I had removed two days previously. Suddenly she grabbed her throat, tried to say something, and died before my eyes—I believe she just had a pulmonary embolism.

I don't know where I got either the courage or the knowledge to do what I did, but in rapid succession I yelled for someone to get the elevator, gave the woman a shot of papaverine directly through the chest wall into her heart, and then ran toward the elevator, dragging the patient's bed behind me. One wheel of the bed fell off and tumbled down the elevator shaft. One floor up, I raced down the operating room corridor with the crippled bed, and we rolled the lifeless patient into an anesthesia room adjacent to an operating room. Without proper sterile clothing, I barged into an operating room—an operation by Dr. Eldridge L. Eliason, chief of Surgery, was about to begin—grabbed the astonished surgeon's instrument tray, pulled it back into the anesthesia room, and opened my patient's chest. (This was like rushing into the Oval Office and grabbing a pen out of the president's hand.) I had never before opened a chest, so I didn't do it properly, but I got in there. Somehow I located the blocked pulmonary artery, slit it open, and extracted a blood clot over nine inches long, in the shape of a Y. The vertical stem of the Y was as thick as a broomstick, while the two branches were about half that diameter. Then I slapped the heart, and it began to beat.

By this time a nurse-anesthetist was giving the patient oxygen, and to my amazement and joy, she began to stir. I closed the hole in the pulmonary artery with silk thread much heavier than that eventually used for vascular surgery. It might not have been the right choice, but it stopped the bleeding. My patient was alive, she was breathing on her own, her heart was beating, and I was trembling.

By this time other surgeons had gathered at the door, simply staring in. Jonathan Rhoads had been called, and he too simply stared. I decided to take one more step, which proved to be a fatal gilding of the lily. Since I had opened the patient's chest without sterile precautions, I was concerned about the very high possibility of infection. In the refrigerator in our lab, Harold Zintel and I kept Philadelphia's only supply of a new drug: penicillin. This was the new "miracle drug," and we overestimated what it could do. I thought that spraying penicillin over the now properly beating heart would prevent any infection. I remember squirting the golden solution over the beating heart with a sense of deep satisfaction that I was adding one more factor of safety for my patient. To my amazement—and horror—the heart stopped immediately. I did not know about the high concentration of potassium in penicillin—enough to stop any heart. By squeezing the heart I got it beating again, but it was really only fibrillating, not forcefully contracting. These were the days before electric defibrillators; I might have saved the patient with one. So my patient, who had already "died" and been brought back to life by somewhat daring surgery, had died again.

Her family had been informed about what was happening, and although saddened by her death, they remained grateful for the extra effort we had made. They appreciated that we had almost pulled her through a usually irreversible and fatal pulmonary embolism.

I wrote Dr. Ravdin, who was stationed in India, to tell him what I had done to save the patient's life—and his gallbladder series—complete with drawings and photos of the embolism. He was very kind and understanding in his reply. Several times in subsequent years I heard him tell about the night his bold resident tried the impossible and succeeded in extracting a pulmonary embolism from the pulmonary artery, and had done so successfully until he tried to gild the lily.

There were other times when my boldness could have gotten me canned. One day, after the war ended, Ravdin, now the John Rhea Barton Professor of Surgery and the surgeon-in-chief of the Hospital of the University of Pennsylvania, paraded through on rounds, followed by an entourage of over fifty persons, all eager to learn something from the master. They clustered around the bed of one of my patients, an elderly man who had a cancer of the colon. After presenting my patient's problem to Ravdin and his followers, I concluded my remarks by saying, "It is possible on rectal examination to feel the outlines of this tumor."

After Rav looked at the X ray of the tumor, which showed it to be at least sixteen inches above the place where a finger in the rectum could possibly feel it, he saw the chance to put me in my place. In his most professorial tone he addressed the multitude.

"Although we all know that Dr. Koop is a competent young surgeon and an excellent diagnostician, we also know that there is no way that even he can feel a tumor which is a foot away from the anus. This is an example of a young man feeling something because he knows it's there."

As Rav ranted on, I talked with my patient and asked his help. With my right index finger in his rectum and my left arm about his shoulders, I asked the elderly gentleman to strain as though he wanted to move his bowels. The tumor descended. When I could feel its lower edge, without any pain to him, I broke off a piece, pulled it out, and held it out to Ravdin in the center of my bloody gloved hand. Rav stopped talking. There was complete—and uncomfortable—silence.

Rav's face flushed. He looked me in the eye and said loud enough for at least the front two rows to hear, "Boy, someday you will push me too far." He left rounds. The next day he behaved as though it had never happened. We never discussed it.

Rav could be a bear in the operating room, but he never carried that behavior outside. During long operations I watched him berate and criticize his first assistant, then the senior resident, then the junior resident, and then any medical students who happened to get into the crossfire. Even though the surgery might have been a great success, everyone in the operating room would be in utter dejection. And then Rav would walk into the doctors' locker room, kick off his shoes, pull off his gown, and say, "Well, Chick, things certainly went well this morning, didn't they?"

That was Ravdin.

The high-quality medical care provided at the Pennsylvania Hospital and the Hospital of the University of Pennsylvania stemmed from the excellent professional cooperation between the physicians and the nursing staff. I learned very early that the best surgery would accomplish little without proper postoperative care. I was able to develop a special rapport with some of the nurses. Betty and I had no money to buy furniture, so I decided to make some in the Pennsylvania Hospital carpentry shop. I discovered that the yard behind the carpentry shop was separated from the backyard of the nurses' residence by only a low fence. So when the student nurses failed to make their 10:00 P.M. curfew (a common restriction in 1941–42), they would knock on the carpentry shop door. I would put out the lights, open the door, then lead them through the maze of machinery and lumber, out the back door and to the back of the yard, and give them a lift over the fence. They were home free.

On the night of their spring dance in 1942, the nurses were unhappy because they would not finish their twelve-hour day until nearly 8:00 P.M., but after the dance had to be back in their residence before the extended, but still unreasonable deadline of midnight. So, with the authority that seemed to have been vested in me by the departure of the senior staff for the war, I dismissed all the nurses on my ward at six o'clock and told them that I would take care of their duties and give the night report to the next shift.

Not everyone appreciated my alliance with the nurses. The World War I nursing veteran who ran herd on the student nurses complained to the Board of Managers at their monthly meeting: "There is entirely too much levity in the Pennsylvania Hospital since that Koop boy came down from New York." As far as I could tell, the Board of Managers did not act on her complaint. But the appreciative nurses put me through a capping ceremony complete with Florence Nightingale's symbolic lamp, declaring me an honorary nurse. Years later I would be pleased that one of my first acts as Surgeon General would be to appoint as Deputy Surgeon General Dr. Faye Abdellah, the highest-ranking nurse in the Public Health Service and the first nurse to serve as Deputy Surgeon General.

Even though there was more than enough clinical surgery to keep me busy, I became involved in a medical research project made necessary by the war. The ferocious combat made it clear that the armed services would need blood or blood plasma in quantities that far exceeded the supply. So the National Research Council assigned to various universities the challenge of finding a plasma substitute. The University of Pennsylvania investigated the possibility that a blood plasma substitute could be found in gelatin made by hydrolyzing sun-bleached bones brought from India to the Knox Gelatin Company, just across the river in Camden, New Jersey. I had the assignment of first testing the toxicity of the gelatin, then testing its efficacy in blood loss, first in dogs, then in patients. The assignment brought with it a commission with the grade of second lieutenant in the OSRD—the Office of Scientific Research Development.

I often wish that animal rights activists could have seen the relationship we had with the dogs upon which I did my experiments. When I walked into the animal rooms and called to my dogs, they greeted me with real enthusiasm. When I let them out of their cages, I never had to use a leash or a collar, because they trotted after me, playfully jumping up and pawing me until we got to the operating room, where, without any prodding, each of them would jump up on an operating table and lie paws up waiting to be restrained. Our studies were invasive in that we used needles in the dogs' arteries and veins and catheters in their bladders, but these procedures would never dampen the enthusiasm of the dogs when we met a week later.

All of us talked to our animals as though they were children. On one occasion I remember somebody working at an adjacent table who got so frustrated with a piece of equipment that he growled at the dog, only to be severely reprimanded by Ravdin's special nurse who supervised the dog lab.

I, too, was a subject of the gelatin experiments. I probably had more repeated exposure to gelatin than any other human being. After being bled the equivalent of one and a half donations of blood for transfusion, I replaced the lost blood with gelatin and measured the effects of gelatin on my cardiac output and vital signs. In spite of my lowered hemoglobin levels, I always felt perfectly able to carry on with my work.

We concluded that gelatin was an effective replacement for plasma, and that it controlled shock and hemorrhage extraordinarily well. But its viscosity made it congeal at cooler temperatures, so it was judged impractical for combat situations. However, by working with it I learned a tremendous amount about physiology and human nature, and I did get my second earned doctorate, a Doctor of Medical Science— Sc.D. (Med)—a degree for medical scientists pioneered by the University of Pennsylvania, then equivalent to a Ph.D. for those in medical pursuits. Years later, while traveling in Egypt as Surgeon General, I discovered an Egyptian physician, working in the shadow of the great pyramids, who was using gelatin as a plasma substitute. She showed me my papers, written decades earlier.

In addition to my surgical and research responsibilities, I added those of fatherhood, as Betty and I decided that at last we could afford to start a family. Our first son, Allen, arrived in January 1944.

He was tiny, had a slow start with jaundice, and kept us up nights— but what a joy! It was the beginning of another set of tensions in my life. I already had all too little time for Betty and now for Allen, too. The effort to balance family and clinical obligations grew with the arrivals of Norman in 1946, David in 1947, and Betsy in 1951.

Everyone who lived through the end of the war has a personal memory of that special day in August 1945. I remember the two burned children. They had gone to an automobile graveyard and found that by dropping lighted matches into the empty gas tanks they were sometimes rewarded with a pop. Unfortunately, they dropped a match into a tank that was partially filled with gasoline. It exploded, covering them with flaming liquid and they were admitted with almost 100 percent third-degree burns. I nursed those two children by living between their two beds in a small room, leaving only to go to the bathroom. I ate my meals standing up, and I frequently dozed off in the same position. One youngster died in thirty-six hours and the other in forty-eight, and I went home to bed. Betty, with our young son, Allen, who was nineteen months old, was visiting her mother in Connecticut. I had been awake for most of the past forty-eight hours and felt desperate to get some real sleep. As soon as I pulled the shade down, the city erupted with blowing horns, whistles, bells, and shouts in the street. It was VJ-day. The war with Japan was over, and no one no matter how tired, could sleep. Four of us who were residents went out to a small restaurant not far from the campus. I squandered a week's food money on a black market steak and then collapsed, asleep at the table. Somehow my friends walked me home and tucked me in bed.

With the end of the war, the end of my residency was in sight. As I contemplated my future, I realized that I was at best only halfhearted about my planned return to New York. In many ways I had grown fond of Philadelphia, but then after four years of nothing but hospital corridors and city streets, I longed for a change of scenery. Naturally my thoughts turned to those marvelous four years at Dartmouth. I had not lost touch with the people or the place. In late 1945, I made the familiar trip to New Hampshire with business as well as pleasure on my mind. I talked with the chief of surgery at the Dartmouth Medical School and learned that they would find a place for me if I wished to return there at the end of my residency. On the train back to Philadelphia I enjoyed a sense of peaceful anticipation of a move back to Dartmouth. Two days later my door burst open at 5:00 A.M., and in strode I. S. Ravdin, resplendent in his Army uniform, fresh from the Asian conflict.

As usual, he got right to the point.

"Chick, what do you plan to do with your life?"

I had just come back from New Hampshire, where I thought I had arranged my future. So I don't know why I answered as I did. But I said, "Well, Dr. Ravdin, I have grown very fond of the University of Pennsylvania. I also have invested a lot of my life in your surgical service. I'd like to stay here. There is one very weak spot in your program and that's the tumor clinic. Give that to me, and I'll make it sing for you."

But Ravdin had another idea, one that would change my life. "How would you like to be surgeon-in-chief of the Children's Hospital instead?" he asked.

Part II

Becoming a Surgeon

Chapter 4
Medicine and Faith

For my entire professional life, until I was called to Washington in 1980, I assumed my contribution to medicine would be in the developing specialty of pediatric surgery. The surgical care of newborns now seems so routine that it is hard to believe it did not exist in 1946, when I started work at Children's Hospital of Philadelphia. But for the next thirty-five years, I was devoted to a new course in the care of infants and disabled children. Everything I did was dedicated to saving the lives of children, many of whom had been previously considered beyond help. In a relatively few years, we in this new specialty were able to make pediatricians and parents realize that some of the most deadly congenital problems that had taken the lives of countless infants and children over the centuries could be corrected at last. After making anesthesia safe for newborns, we turned our attention to correcting their usually fatal congenital defects. When I first encountered these problems, the mortality rate was 95 to 100 percent. When I left pediatric surgery, the former mortality rate of 95 percent had become the survival rate for all but one of the five most serious problems in newborns. My belief that all life is precious became the basis of this intense focus on saving the lives of infants.

The offer Dr. Ravdin had made to me involved several stages. First, I would spend three months at the Children's Hospital of Philadelphia, then go on to the Boston Children's Hospital for a year to work with William E. Ladd, who was the only person in the United States at that time known as a "child surgeon" and who also had a teaching service. At the end of that training period I would return to Philadelphia, perform surgery on children exclusively, become the surgeon-in-chief of the Children's Hospital, where I was expected to establish the best possible academic service. I was told by Dr. Ravdin to discuss the plan with no one except my wife and parents. Although I had some doubts about limiting myself to children's surgery after training for so long to be a general surgeon, from the beginning Betty thought it was a great opportunity, and my father wisely counseled that if for some reason it did not work out, performing surgery on small children and infants could only make me a better surgeon, technically.

My mind was flooded with doubts. I was about to become a "child surgeon"—soon I would say "pediatric surgeon"—and eventually not only a professor of pediatric surgery but also a professor of pediatrics. But pediatrics had been almost completely omitted from my medical training; I had attended only six lectures on the subject, which covered little more than the feeding of infants. Then, when wartime pressures cut my internship from two years to one, pediatrics was one of the rotations left out. Then I had found myself in a surgical residency that did almost nothing with children. At the Hospital of the University of Pennsylvania, the children's ward for general surgical patients was tiny, only six beds, and they were for urgent operations only: appendectomy, hernia repair, or splenectomy. During my entire residency at the University of Pennsylvania, I knew of only three operations on newborns, and one of these had been botched.

The chief reason surgeons avoided children was the primitive state of anesthesia. Doctors were afraid to put children to sleep, because they weren't sure they could wake them up. So even though in all my training I had seen very few surgical procedures done on children, I knew kids were not getting a fair shake. And I wanted to change that.

But while most general surgeons avoided children, they saw no reason for anyone to specialize in surgery on children. And for years they actually opposed me and those of us attempting to get recognition for pediatric surgery as a separate specialty. In the late forties, many surgeons did not like what was happening in surgery. The large field of "general surgery" was being splintered into many subspecialties, since wartime surgery had spurred great advances in areas such as plastic surgery, burn management, and orthopedic surgery. General surgeons were forced to yield to specialists, which meant they suffered a loss of patients and income, not to mention a loss of freedom and a loss of the challenge they had enjoyed before the rise of surgical specialties.

So when this twenty-nine-year-old upstart came along one of only a handful talking about still another new field of specialty—"pediatric

surgery"—the general surgeons dug in their heels. This alleged insult
to general surgery took a long time to heal, and it was years before the
antagonism was overcome and pediatric surgeons were accepted into
the surgical fold. Ironically, within a short thirty-five years, pediatric
surgery itself would splinter into pediatric urology, pediatric neurosur-
gery, pediatric cardiac surgery, and so on. Young men and women
entering pediatric surgery today know nothing of the obstacles we had
to overcome, the hostility we had to subdue, or the struggles we endured. The real winners were the children. And eventually surgery itself
was enhanced and all of medicine could be proud of the newcomer.

Of course, I could foresee none of this on my first trolley ride to
Children's Hospital. I hopped off the trolley, walked down the sidewalk
on Bainbridge Street, and across the Children's Hospital courtyard,
which was paved with cobblestones so that the horses drawing ambulances of days gone by could have enough traction. When I opened the
oak-framed glass door and stepped into the tiled lobby of the hospital,
I was greeted by a young woman who told me she was the chief medical
resident.

"Why don't you go back where you came from? You're not needed
here, you're not wanted here, and you put four good surgeons out of
work."

I was taken aback, and it would take me several years to piece
together the entire story that explained why Ravdin had asked me to
go to Children's.

This, the oldest children's hospital in America, had become dilapidated and languishing, even though it had seen some remarkable research. Its chief pediatrician, Joseph Stokes, was known for a number
of accomplishments in pediatrics and for his wartime work with hepatitis in Italy, where more American soldiers were suffering from that
disease than from wounds suffered in combat.

The incident that prompted Ravdin to look for a chief surgeon at
Children's Hospital had taken place early in 1945. A child with abdominal pain had arrived at the hospital's emergency room. The medical
residents diagnosed an intussusception, in which the bowel telescopes
into itself, causing intestinal obstruction. Without a simple operation,
the child was in mortal danger of perforation of the bowel, peritonitis,
and death. There was only one treatment at the time: immediate
surgery. The resident telephoned the surgeon on call and explained the
situation. The surgeon should have operated immediately, but four
hours later, he had not even arrived at the hospital. They called him
again. After eight hours they called him again. This went on for about

two days. The patient died before a surgeon ever got there: a terrible
case of malpractice and negligence.

After this tragedy, the director of nursing, a woman who had worked
at Children's Hospital in Boston, gave Dr. Stokes an ultimatum: She
would give him one year to establish a service for child surgery so that
this sort of thing would never happen again. She told him if he didn't
offer services like those at the Boston Children's Hospital, she would
leave, taking every nurse in the hospital with her. Stokes called the
University of Pennsylvania's vice president for medical affairs, who
called Ravdin and gave him his mandate.

Apparently I had not been Ravdin's first choice. He had approached
the four general surgeons who were then doing surgery at Children's
as a sideline or as a very reluctant obligation. None of them was willing
to take any further training in surgery on children, and none of them
was willing to give up surgery on adults. The honor of becoming a
pioneer in the new specialty fell to me by default.

I explained to the angry medical resident that those four surgeons had
turned down the job, so I was there to do it. The resident's discouraging
welcome was no fluke. It quickly became clear that the pediatricians
who worked at the hospital already felt they knew everything about
children. How could a stupid surgeon who made his living by doing
things with his hands be welcome in that environment? With growing
trepidation I walked up to the fifth floor to introduce myself to Joseph
Stokes, Jr.

Dr. Stokes informed me that any patient that I treated would have
to be admitted on his service. He would make the diagnosis. Only when
he thought the child was ready to be operated on would he call me,
and after the operation had been completed, the patient would go back
on his service, where Stokes would manage the child's postoperative
care. My reply surprised him.

"That was the procedure until today, Dr. Stokes. The reason I am
here is so that will change. I am a surgeon who will soon take the
examination of the American Board of Surgery. When I take that
examination I must sign a statement affirming that I will be responsible
for my patient insofar as diagnosis, treatment, postoperative care, and
follow-up are concerned."

Stokes gruffly said, "I'll see about that!" and telephoned Dr. Ravdin.
I could hear only Stokes' side of the conversation, but obviously Ravdin
was laying down the rules in no uncertain terms. When Stokes put the
telephone down, it was the first victory for pediatric surgery in Philadel-

phia and maybe a victory for pediatric surgery in the whole country.

As the years went on, Stokes and I developed a mutual respect for each other, and by the time he retired, we were good friends—to the point that he was even taking the credit for bringing me to the Children's Hospital! But in the beginning we were definitely adversaries.

I found further evidence of my frosty welcome when I saw my "office": a table in the hospital library. I, the future surgeon-in-chief, would spend many dreary days just sitting there; the staff often would not bother to call me to consult on surgical problems that had come into the hospital. As I was being frozen out, several children with surgical problems that were correctable died on the wards. Years later, this would all come back to me vividly as I sat alone in my empty Washington office during those bitter days preceding my confirmation as Surgeon General, while problems that I might have corrected went unaddressed. After the planned three-month trial period, Betty and I, our two-year-old son, Allen, and our two-week-old son, Norman, set off as planned for a year's training session at Boston Children's Hospital.

Although in my later years, many people referred to me as the father of pediatric surgery in the United States, that honor belongs to Dr. Robert E. Gross of Boston Children's Hospital. But neither Gross nor I—nor any other pioneer pediatric surgeon—could have succeeded without the earlier vision and spadework of William E. Ladd. Although I learned pediatric surgical technique from Gross, I learned about the art and philosophy of pediatric surgery from Ladd. Following his retirement from his position as surgeon-in-chief of the Boston Children's Hospital, Ladd did not give up his contact with children. After eating his lunch at the Harvard Club, he would wander over to the Children's Hospital and walk through the wards, hoping to find a resident or an intern with whom he could have a conversation. I always tried to be there when he arrived. We would often just sit and talk, Ladd dangling his long legs over the side of an empty crib. It was from Ladd that I learned that children are just not small adults and that you cannot control their physiology and pharmacology by mere fractions of adult numbers. Although I never saw Ladd operate, I learned from him the delicacy of pediatric tissues, especially in newborns, and how easily they are traumatized.

For example, he gave me some pointers about pyloric stenosis, one of the first problems of infancy to be corrected by surgery. The condition, in which the muscular valve at the lower end of the stomach goes into spasm, usually affects babies about six weeks after birth and causes violent vomiting. A practiced finger gently touching a child's abdomen can actually feel this muscular valve, which is the size and shape of a tiny olive. Ladd taught me that infants' abdominal organs were so delicate that even feeling the "olive" with too heavy a hand could injure it, causing the child to vomit for several days, even after a successful operation. Thereafter, if I was scheduled to operate on a baby with pyloric stenosis and saw that the child had been examined by too many overeager residents, interns, medical students, or even senior physicians, I would post a "hands off" order for a day or two before going ahead with the operation so the infant could recuperate more quickly and comfortably. Ladd's lesson was simple, but invaluable.

There was another way William Ladd shaped my surgery. One day a group of us were standing around a crib while Ladd shared his insight. One of the surgical fellows recalled the way Dr. Ladd had performed an extremely complicated operation in a child's neck without any apparent trepidation and with consummate skill. Dr. Ladd listened to him intently, cocked his head to one side, and said, "Son, have you ever come home late at night and, after unlocking the door, walked across the floor without putting on the lights because you didn't want to disturb anyone? I do it all the time and I never bump into the furniture because I know where everything is. That's how I feel when I operate in the neck." I never forgot that statement. If a surgeon *knows* anatomy, much of his hesitancy during surgery will disappear.

Although my months in Boston were not easy, my problems couldn't compare to the difficulties Betty endured during that time, mainly because of our housing. Our problem, like that of many young couples, was a lack of money. Betty had her hands full at home with two small children, and I was still living on less than $2,000 a year. Before leaving for Boston, I had told Dr. Ravdin I could not afford to let my apartment in Philadelphia go. In the first year following World War II, housing was still in short supply, and rents were high. I needed an additional $50.00 a month to keep that apartment secured. Ravdin agreed to increase my income by $50.00 a month. The extra money came for two months and then stopped. When I wrote him about it, Ravdin replied: "Dear Chick, If I were you I wouldn't worry about $50.00 a month." It was signed "Rav," the first time he used his nickname with me. Familiarity did not placate my fury. I replied: "Dear Rav, I wouldn't worry about $50.00 if I were you" and signed it "Chick." I don't know what he thought about my reply; no additional money came my way.

The only place we could find in Boston within our budget was a Somerville house that had been abandoned seventeen years earlier.

Once an ornate frame house, 15 Adams Street was falling in on itself, and the overgrown yard had become a gathering place for every feline in town. We picked our way up the broken steps to the door, brushed aside the cobwebs and filth, and entered the kitchen, the floor still strewn with papers dated 1929. The former owner's false teeth sat in a glass on the bedside table. Our newborn son, Norman, was hungry and cold. (We had been told—erroneously—that he was allergic to cow's milk, so before we set out from Philadelphia to Boston in a borrowed car, I had stretched my limited funds to buy as much canned goat's milk as I could find. My attempts to heat a bottle on the engine block somewhere along the Merritt Parkway in Connecticut had been less than successful, and it had curdled.) The furnace lay on the cellar floor in a pile of rust and iron fragments. The lead pipes in the plumbing system were so corroded that when we flushed the toilet, no water could be obtained from any faucet on the first floor for at least ten minutes. Boston is cold in April, and the house was dank and damp. We put Norman in a very small bassinet behind the kitchen coal range that became our sole source of heat until Boston warmed up for the summer.

But even the pleasant summer weather posed a problem. Our kitchen refrigeration depended on an ancient hotel-type icebox with six doors. Ice was delivered every other day by a man who thought he had found a bonanza. We bought three of the large commercial cakes of ice from him every week, and even then the refrigerator wasn't cold. We later realized we could have purchased the best of modern refrigerators for less than the money we spent on ice that summer. As we walked around the house and jarred the floor, pictures occasionally fell off the wall as their rusty wires snapped. One night, when Betty was alone, the chimney collapsed and spilled itself through a fireplace onto the floor of the dining room.

When Betty's mother first came to visit us in Somerville, she took a taxi from South Station. There was no number on our house, so the taxi driver went past it two or three times until my mother-in-law said, "That has to be it." He replied, "It couldn't be, lady, nobody would live there."

But live there we did, as Betty struggled with the medieval inconveniences and I attempted to pack in as much knowledge of pediatric surgery as I could. I jumped at every opportunity that came along, no matter how menial. One of the medical interns assigned to the surgical service was called for government work and I took his place as the lowest of the low on the surgical totem pole. It might have been degrading in a sense, but I learned firsthand everything a doctor or nurse would have to do for a hospitalized infant. Over the years, when I was back at the Children's Hospital of Philadelphia, I was always grateful that I never had to ask anyone to do something for me that I couldn't do myself.

When I returned to the Children's Hospital of Philadelphia in November 1946, I hoped to find a more receptive atmosphere, but I suppose I should have known better. The hostility still existed, the senior staff was no more eager to have their hidebound, comfortable way of professional life altered by a young kid starting a new speciality, no matter how much it might improve the lot of children.

Some things cried out for immediate attention. I was astounded when I realized that the private practice in Children's Hospital was for white patients only. Most of the patients on the wards were black because the hospital was in the black ghetto. When I first admitted a black patient to the private floor of the hospital, one of the nurses resigned. That is how bad racism was in Philadelphia in 1947. At least I changed that at the hospital, and quickly.

Eventually, making progress some days, slipping back on others, I was able to carve a place for pediatric surgery and then to have the pleasure of helping it grow. Some days brought more triumph than others.

On the top floor of the Children's Hospital, ruling all beneath them, were the offices of the senior medical staff, most of whom stood firmly in opposition to me. Among them was a giant of a man in more ways than one: Dr. Milton Rappaport. Unmarried, he had given himself to the hospital and served as confidant to the house staff and resident philosopher. "Rap" never forgot anything; he was a walking compendium of medical and scientific knowledge.

But Rap didn't know surgery, and one day we came into sharp dispute on the management of a little boy who had pus in his chest following a bout with pneumonia. I wanted to drain the enclosed cavity surgically. Rap wanted to take out the pus with a needle and inject penicillin into the cavity. I knew that Rap's suggestion often had been unsuccessful in practice and was wrong in theory in spite of the advent of penicillin.

It was decided that the case would be presented at the Friday conference, where perplexing pediatric cases were adjudicated. Philadelphia pediatricians packed the auditorium and filled the aisles. There was no better place for a doctor to succeed—and no worse place to fail.

I had been warned by friends that Rap had said if I held out against him, he would ask the Board of Managers for my dismissal. That was disturbing, but about as farfetched as Governor Hunt of North Carolina asking for my impeachment as Surgeon General forty years later because I pointed out the health hazards of cigarette smoking. For two days before the conference, Rap and I, who were no longer speaking to each other, sat on opposite sides of a table in the tiny hospital library, mustering our ammunition.

The conference day came. Rap presented the case as a simple one of empyema, a condition in which pus fills the lower half of the cavity in which the lung resides, pushing a partially collapsed lung upward. Rap stated the empyema was caused by pneumonia at the very bottom of the lung. He had not changed his mind in the least about the cause of or cure for the little boy's woes.

Then it was my turn. I walked up to the X-ray view boxes, where about twelve films of the youngster's chest were on display. The audience leaned forward, eager for gladiatorial combat. Rap, the "good ole boy," erudite, knowledgeable, the house officer's role model, font of all knowledge, weighed in at more than three hundred pounds. I, the young upstart, unproven disrupter of limited horizons, a surgeon who wanted to lay claim to half the hospital beds, weighed in at a mere two hundred pounds.

I looked at the X rays carefully, recalling an identical case I had seen at the autopsy of an adult several years before. "I think Dr. Rappaport and his colleagues have been extraordinarily fortunate that they have not had a tragic complication from removing the pus in this chest with a needle."

That was certainly unexpected.

"If you look carefully at the edge of the opaque shadow here which he called empyema, you will note that there is a fine rim of air-bearing lung tissue between the opaque pus and the ribcage. This child does not have empyema; he has developed an abscess in a congenital cyst of the lung, and the rim of lung tissue, which probably completely surrounds the cyst, proves it."

Old Dr. Bromer, the radiologist, squinted at the films. "By George, Rap, Koop is right. I missed it."

Now surprise had turned to consternation. Rap nodded assent but said nothing. I continued.

"The reason I said Dr. Rappaport had been very lucky is that this variety of congenital cyst of the lung is an embryologic effort to form a separate additional lobe of the lung. The cyst therefore has the same blood supply as a lobe of the lung, with a large artery coming directly off the aorta and a vein or two returning blood directly to the superior vena cava. The cyst is lined with vessels of prodigious size. Had his multiple sticks with a needle punctured one of them—or worse yet, torn one of them—you could have had anything from a bad bleed to a fatal hemorrhage. If the infected cyst had been surgically drained as empyema should be, the drain almost certainly would have eroded a vein, and a fatal hemorrhage would have followed." (That's what had happened in the autopsy I had seen years before.)

"This youngster needs immediate surgery to excise the infected cyst. He should recover without sequelae. If you refer him to my service, I'll talk with the family and operate at nine o'clock on Monday."

Something happened that day. No fireworks went off, but I noticed a change in attitude of the other physicians. Many in the audience would become my referring pediatricians. A victory was won that Friday afternoon—at the conference, in the hospital, in the university, indeed in all of Philadelphia—a victory for pediatric surgery. It was an important thread in the tapestry of my life.

The changes in my professional life, as big as they were, were not as far-reaching as the change in my personal beliefs, which happened at the same time. I had always thought of myself as a Christian, and I had been raised in a churchgoing home. My parents had met at church, and much of the family social life had centered around church activities. I had been a member of the Sunday School from the cradle roll, I had belonged to the Mission Band, I had marched in the annual Brooklyn Sunday School Union's Anniversary Parade each May. But I didn't have a clue about who I was spiritually, where I had been, or where I was going. When my family moved to Flatbush and joined the Baptist Church of the Redeemer, I didn't know what a redeemer was and it never crossed my mind to find out. I must have felt a spiritual yearning because in 1948, during our summer visit to my parents' cabin on Maine's Vinalhaven Island, I sat on the rocks amid the splashing surf and read through the New Testament twice. But no new light dawned. Yet gradually that year, I realized what it meant to be a Christian. As a person whose training and experiences put full faith in science, I came to see an even higher truth. From then on, I saw a coexistence between science and God.

It was Erna Goulding, a valued friend and a nurse at Children's Hospital, who sensed that I was searching for spiritual meaning. One evening, as Betty and I left our apartment to attend the musical program that attracted many to the First Baptist Church in center city

Philadelphia, Erna suggested we walk a block beyond the Baptist Church and go to the evening service of the Tenth Presbyterian Church. She thought I would appreciate the intellectual approach to Christianity offered by its minister, Donald Grey Barnhouse. But we did not take her suggestion.

The next Sunday, however, I finished grand rounds early, and I found my feet taking me to the Tenth Presbyterian Church, just a few blocks north of the hospital. I entered the back door and quietly slipped up to the balcony. I was just going to observe. I liked what I saw, and I was fascinated by what I heard. I saw the congregation respond willingly and generously to social needs; this was no empty religion. I heard teaching from one of the most learned men I ever knew, a true scholar who also possessed a gift of illustrating the complexity—and simplicity—of Christian doctrine by remarkable and incisive stories and similes. I was interested enough to go back the next Sunday morning. And then just a few hours later I returned for the evening service. I did that each Sunday for two years, and except when I was out of town I never missed a morning or evening service. Since I was a busy surgeon, the only pediatric surgeon on the East Coast south of Boston, going two years without a compelling Sunday morning or evening emergency seemed to me almost miraculous.

After about seven months, I realized that I had become a participant and not just an observer; what made sense to that congregation made sense to me as well. And it was new to me. I wasn't just shifting gears from my parents' faith to one of my own.

It was not until I sat in that Philadelphia church balcony that I really understood the basics of the Christian gospel: that we all are sinners, unable to satisfy God's standard of righteousness and justice, no matter how hard we try. I learned that "sin" did not mean just the big bad things we do, or even the little bad things we do, but anything we do that falls short of the righteousness of God. I learned that the word the Bible often uses for "sin" was also applied to archery, and it meant to miss the mark. We all miss the mark of God's righteousness, no matter how hard we try. Like many other nominal Christians, I suppose I had been trying to live as correctly as I could, but like them, I knew in the depths of my heart that my nature, like everyone else's, was sinful, and my efforts to reform myself were to no avail. I knew that, like it or not, we are all immortal, and we must spend eternal life someplace when this life is over. Over those several months, sitting in the balcony at the Tenth Presbyterian Church, the preaching from the pulpit made it all clear: that the essence of Christianity was not what we did, but what

Christ had done for us. I understood the meaning of the crucifixion, I understood the meaning of Christ's sacrifice, I understood the meaning of divine forgiveness. I realized that either my sins were on my shoulders, or they were on the shoulders of Jesus Christ. I saw how the atonement of Jesus Christ was necessary to reconcile us to God.

Most of all, I understood the love of God. Like many new Christians—and many old Christians—I found the most meaningful verse in the Bible to be John 3:16:

> For God so loved the world that he gave his only begotten Son, that whoever believes in him should not perish, but have eternal life.

I was a believer.

Betty became one, too. She shared with me in our newfound faith, as I would come home from Church—with the birth of our third son, David, she had her hands full with three small boys—and share enthusiastically all I had learned. We grew as Christians together, and we grew together as Christians. It was one of the most heady times of our lives, with a thousand unanswered questions. Most are answered by now, but it is still heady and still exciting.

It was out of those beginnings that I acknowledged the Lord Jesus Christ in my life and rested in my abiding faith in the sovereignty of God. I came to realize that my life wasn't just a series of dilemmas followed by happy coincidences. I knew there was a plan for my life, and this brought me an assurance I had never known.

No matter what else I did in life, I would be a Christian. I soon discovered that people were not content when I told them that I was a Christian; they wanted to know what kind of Christian, what adjective, what denomination. After I became Surgeon General, the press often referred to me as a "fundamentalist" Christian. In one sense that is right, because I affirm the fundamental doctrines of Christianity. But fundamentalism has taken on a negative connotation: Fundamentalists are known more for what they are against than what they are for. That label never fit me. I always called myself an evangelical Christian. "Evangelist" means "messenger," bearer of news. An evangelical Christian carries to others the good news of the mercy of Christ. Throughout my life I've been a messenger, the bearer of news. Like any surgeon, I brought both good news and bad news to my patients. As Surgeon General, I brought good news some days and certainly my share of warnings on other days. But the most important news I have ever brought to anyone is the news of God's love for us through Jesus Christ.

This spiritual awakening had a profound effect on my life and influenced everything that happened thereafter. As an evangelical Christian, I attempted to evaluate everything in the light of Scripture, and in the Bible I found my guide for faith and conduct, always tempered by God's grace and forgiveness.

Faced with the pain and suffering of my patients and their parents, I needed the assurance that there was some greater plan—both for them and for myself. Anyone who lived with me in those days would understand why I was pro-life. My concern about the *un*born followed as the night the day my concern about the *newly* born. How could I ever accept the destruction of the unborn after a career devoted to the repair of imperfect newborns, knowing the joy and fulfillment they brought to their families? I had watched hundreds of them grow up to be innovative and creative human beings even though they were not always pristine in form and function.

I was a convert, and an enthusiastic one. I wanted to share my new faith with everyone I knew, colleagues and patients alike. At first I'm sure I was labeled by some as too zealous, but others, by the grace of God, sought to share my experience and faith. Although my partners and staff together would represent many—or in some cases no—religions, those around me who shared my Christian faith knit with me a close and treasured spiritual bond. Jim Martindale, who started out as my secretary and went on to become the business manager of the surgical clinic, has for decades served as a model of an exemplary Christian faith and life.

Of course, not all my patients saw eye to eye with me on religion. But just as it has so often been said that there are few atheists in foxholes, I found that there were few atheists among parents of critically ill children. There were times when sharing with them my faith in Christ and the sovereignty of God provided great comfort and strength for all of us.

Each time I operated, after I was gowned and gloved, after the patient was draped, right before I made the first incision, there was always the moment—not ritualized, but nevertheless subconsciously acknowledged—when I established an emotional distance between the patient and me. I don't know how many surgeons have articulated this moment, but for me, it made my judgment and perhaps even my technique as free as possible of emotional constraints. Surgeons who have operated upon close members of their families—as I once did—know the emotional concern is overpowering, and in a tight spot could be dangerous, devastating to the patient and to the surgeon. Many times when I operated I was dead tired, although I don't believe fatigue altered my judgment, and I tried never to let my emotions cloud my surgical performance.

Furthermore, believing as I do in a sovereign God, I realized that for all I might do with my hands and mind, all healing comes from God. Several reporters have portrayed me as a surgeon who prayed with every patient before each operation. It didn't happen that way. Prayer with a patient and the family is a very intimate moment and of invaluable benefit. I did it whenever I was asked, but it was never routine. Nor did I pray in private before each operation. My faith was bigger than that. I considered myself and my patient to be in God's hands; I trusted that the skills the Lord had given me would be available in time of need without my repetitious plea.

I had to learn some very tough lessons as I attempted to find a working relationship between faith and practice, and early in my newly awakened Christian life I made a serious mistake in judgment in the tension between family needs and spiritual obligations. Members of the Christian Medical Society from the various Philadelphia medical schools asked permission of the Philadelphia County Medical Society to act in Christian compassion in any way they could to the men on skid row—the equivalent of today's homeless people. I accepted the supervision of these young men and women on request and presumed it would be a chore easy to share with the seventy or so graduate members of the Christian Medical Society in Philadelphia. That did not prove to be the case, and I found that I was almost always the only available hands-on supervisor.

Every Sunday afternoon for several years, I left home immediately after dinner and went into the city to supervise and teach the students at the Wayside Gospel Mission. That took us well into the early evening. My second stint with the students began at the Twelfth Street Gospel Hall, where we fed 1,200 men at nine o'clock and ran a clinic until we finished, treating all who needed our limited medical help. We never finished before 11:00 and sometimes not until 1:00 A.M. My mistake was that I did not spend as much time with my family as I did with the homeless. Sunday afternoons were really the only time I was likely to be able to be home uninterrupted, except by emergencies. I now believe it would have been more important for me to spend at least half that time with my family. If Betty had not been so uncomplaining and had not taken great pains to be sure that the children understood that I was doing a service for other people, I think our children could have let my absence lead to resentment or worse.

As in so much else in my life, my success in the early days of pediatric surgery depended on Betty's support. She continued as my confidante and primary sounding board, just as she had during medical school, internship, and residency, just as she would during my years as Surgeon General. But now there was a family to raise: Allen, Norman, David, and now a daughter, Betsy. Best of all, our family and our new faith arrived in the same years, so we could raise the kids as Christians. Betty maintained that no matter how busy we were, it was easier to go to church every Sunday than to choose which Sundays to go.

The tension between obligation to family and obligation to profession is constant if you want to be a good doctor and a good father and husband. I took all those roles seriously, but I had the added burden of trying to develop not only a surgical practice, but also an academic service in a hostile environment. And after the first few years, I was absorbed in establishing pediatric surgery as a surgical specialty internationally, not only in the United States. I felt like a juggler with too many balls in the air. And, of course, I made lots of mistakes.

Betty and I were spared one common problem. Unlike many couples, we never bickered about money. At first, and for many years, we had almost no money. Eventually we had enough. But it didn't seem to matter one way or another. In almost sixty years together, Betty and I have never had an argument about finances.

The lessons Betty learned from her mother—more by observation and participation than by instruction—became precept. The deep satisfaction we feel about our children and the longevity of our marriage are due in large part to Betty's understanding of what I was trying to accomplish and her willingness to take second place to what I saw as my professional obligation. She understood that I would have preferred it to be otherwise, and she knew my striving was not for money or power or position, but to save the lives of children, to improve the lives of my diminutive patients, and to offer the blessings of pediatric surgery to as many children as possible, both here and abroad. My wife has always said to me, "Your profession comes first, I understand that. I'd like the time left over." My sorting of priorities was never easy, but two things made it bearable. Betty always said, "If you're happy, I'm happy." And after he was grown, Allen put a blanket of assurance over many years of tensions among obligations by saying—I hope for his siblings as well—"Although Dad was away a lot, Mom never let us feel he was absent from us."

That's the secret: the children's perception of their mother's sense of satisfaction. All too often I have seen it go the other way in physicians' families. When husband and wife are not on the same wavelength about priorities, resentment builds, resentment and anger are readily transmitted to children, and there follows a loosening of family bonds, loss of respect, loss of trust, followed by family members' quests to fill a perceived emptiness in life. Tragedies of all sort follow. Betty kept our family from this danger. She kept our family close. Although I became the public speaker in the family, sometimes giving as many as a hundred speeches in a year, I never saw a speaker as warmly appreciated as Betty after she would share her experiences and insights with young doctors and their spouses.

One of my colleagues, whose wife had much the same outlook as Betty did, had a son who unknowingly demonstrated what she and I tried to convey to our children and to other families in the same situation. The little fellow and a group of his friends were at the movies, watching *Bambi*. At the emotional climax in the film when Bambi's father bounds away, perhaps forever, the surgeon's young son blurted out, loud enough for the entire theater to hear, "He's going to the hospital to see a sick baby."

My family understood my work schedule because they realized the importance of my surgery, and they also knew something about it. While other families might enjoy slide shows of the trip to Disneyland, our kids were treated to slides I brought home showing the latest from the operating room: cleft palate repair, cleft lip surgery, abdominal operations.

One of the ways I tried to compensate for my professional life away from the family was to try to get home for family dinner. Unless an absolute emergency precluded it, I would make it home for the family meal, even if it meant going back to the hospital to tie up the loose ends of the day's work or to operate at 9 P.M. instead of 7 P.M. The eighteen-mile round trip between the hospital and our home in suburban Penn Valley was well worth it.

I was never happy about leaving the family when a surgical emergency called, and I was always planning ways to do something special with the four kids, individually or collectively. What I really wanted was to share with them something like my own childhood activities. It was an unrealistic expectation because I had been doted on by two grandfathers and a father, none of whom had any of my professional obligations. As a boy I had played for hours with the lead soldiers my grandfathers and I had created. I remembered the magic of melting the lead, skimming the scum off the molten surface, coating the insides of the molds with carbon black from a smoking candle, and pouring the lead into the molds. So, hoping to do for my children what had been done for me, I bought some molds to make lead soldiers, a cauldron to melt the lead, and a ladle.

I told my six-year-old son Allen that we would try to make lead soldiers together on the first rainy Saturday. Meanwhile he scouted around and found some lead to melt. A succession of sunny Saturdays and surgical emergencies kept postponing the lead soldiers. Now Allen still has waiting in the secret compartment of his bureau—long since passed on to one of his college-age daughters—the molding equipment, some of my old lead soldiers, and a supply of lead pipe he collected forty years ago. From time to time, we still joke about making lead soldiers on the next rainy Saturday.

No matter how busy life was most of the time, I did set aside four or five weeks in the summer for the family to be together, away from Philadelphia and its many demands. Our first family vacations took us to join my parents in a picturesque shack on Vinalhaven, an island off the Maine coast. It was a beautiful spot: pasture and spruce forest sloping down to the rocky shore, two little islands close enough to walk to in low tide. The day I discovered that the place was for sale, I decided to buy it. That night, as Betty and my mother were cleaning up after a great lobster feed cooked on the wood-burning stove, my father and I sat on the steps of the porch, watching the thick fog roll in. At bedtime I carried three-year-old Norman to his bunk and was startled to see a circle of bright red blood on the seat of his pajamas. As a pediatric surgeon, few things struck as much terror to my heart as seeing bright red blood coming from the rectum of a child, because the consequences can be so dire and so rapid in their evolution. I examined Norman immediately, and to my great relief, he was bleeding from either a pimple or a mosquito bite that he had scratched to the point of abrading the skin. But for the next three days, as the island was fogbound, with no boats coming or going, I wondered what I would have done had the bleeding been as serious as I had feared. Right then I made the decision that we would vacation near medical help that would not be impeded by isolation or fog.

So, no surprise, I returned once again to my favorite place, Hanover,

New Hampshire, where in a matter of days I had found an abandoned farm on the side of Moose Mountain. The place had been empty for several years, avoided by superstitious purchasers because of a murder that had been committed there. The Tobins—Flossie and Will—had lived there. Ironically, I had met them years before when I was a student at Dartmouth. Flossie had worked as a cleaning woman in my fraternity house, and once I had joined a student work crew that helped Will get in some firewood. One September evening Will had come in from his chores, and Flossie had shot him. Apparently she hadn't liked him for some time. Flossie slept in the house that night, then turned herself in the next day. The house had lain vacant for several years until the morning I bought it.

The land was beautiful, over two hundred acres of field and forest. But the house was so dirty that I wouldn't let Betty see it until the next year, after I had slapped a coat of paint on every surface, inside and out. The best thing about our summer cottage was what it lacked. With only two bedrooms (one a bunkroom for the kids), it lacked room for any overnight guests, so when the family went there, we were together and alone. Better still, it had no phone, no radio, no television. Each year the month on Moose Mountain bonded us together. Even now Betty and I know of no parents closer than we are to our children. Seven grandchildren have enlarged the family circle, but it remains as close as ever.

The children developed an attachment to New Hampshire, especially the White Mountains. Years later, Allen would work for several summers at the Lakes of the Clouds hut on Mount Washington, while the other three kids worked on the Mount Washington Cog Railroad, Betsy in the base station restaurant, Norman as a steam-engine engineer, David as his brakeman. In one way or another Allen, Norman, and David would all end up within a few miles of Moose Mountain. And Betsy, after she moved to Georgia, would always look forward to an autumn package of brightly colored northern maple leaves, mailed south by a brother in New Hampshire or Vermont.

From the time Betty was pregnant with Betsy until all the kids had gone to college, the best part of the year was the time from the last Friday in July until Labor Day, when we could enjoy one another and the little house on Moose Mountain. It was one more way Betty supported my career, this time by working harder while the rest of us had a vacation. The house didn't have all the conveniences of home, and she spent many an hour washing diapers and clothes first by hand, then in the old washing machine that too often pinched her fingers in the wringer.

I pitched in with the shopping, and the kids did breakfast. We puttered around the property, swam in a nearby lake, climbed mountains, picked berries, watched the wildlife, read to each other in the evenings, and cemented the love of family that would take us through so much. I cherished those weeks in New Hampshire with the family, when at last I was not torn between professional and parental concerns.

When the kids were injured, however, surgery and parenting went together. Kitchen-table surgery provided some of our most exciting family gatherings, although there may be something to the persistent rumor that doctors' kids don't get the best in medical attention. I often had to stitch up the many cuts my active children accumulated, but I rarely had a surgical kit at home. Betty's small sewing kit had to provide what we needed.

Our children enjoyed subjecting their injured friends to our family medicine. When a visiting little girl failed to negotiate our steep curving driveway on her bicycle and crashed into the house instead, Betty telephoned the child's mother: "Don't worry. Your daughter has a nasty cut, but Betsy's father is coming home from work soon, and he'll sew her up." There was a long pause, and the mother replied, "Is Betsy's father a doctor?"

One Saturday when I happened to be home, Betsy ran to ask me to look at her next-door playmate, about ten years of age, who was sitting on the ground crying, nursing an obviously broken arm. I had nothing suitable for a splint, so I improvised with some elastic bandages and two pieces of discarded board, one painted green, the other just dirty. The splint did the job, but it looked more like a child's construction project than a splint. At the local emergency room, the intern—who had probably rotated through my lectures the year before—laughed at the splinting job and asked mockingly, "What Boy Scout put this thing together?" Betsy knew enough not to reveal the handiwork of the surgeon-in-chief of the Children's Hospital.

These, then, are the three elements of my life: my work in the treatment of critically ill children, my religious faith, and my family. Sometimes, when surgery cannot save a young life, surgeon and family must cope with the death of a child. No one sets out to become an expert in this, but understanding my own family and having a religious faith enabled me to reach out to people in this most heartbreaking of situations. A pediatric surgeon learns early that there are different types of grieving parents. Those who lose a child who has suffered an illness from the moment of birth face a special grief compounded by a feeling of unreality. Their newborn child had to be taken from them for intensive care before they could adjust to being parents. They never even had a chance to bond to their own baby. Those who lose their child in a sudden accident have their own kind of grief. Those whose children die in mid-childhood of chronic diseases like cancer also have a special kind of grief, because they lose children who have become little people, after they have developed personalities. There is a special pain in knowing that the future of that child, that small person, will never be permitted to unfold. Some of these parents seem to lose their children twice—first when the hopeless diagnosis is made, again when the child dies. The real death is sometimes easier to bear, because it brings a sense of release and relief. But sometimes the period between diagnosis and death is long and extraordinarily difficult. I wanted to do for grieving parents what I did for parents coping with children with long-term physical or mental disabilities. So, about forty years ago, I began to bring grieving parents together, so they could talk to the only other people who could come close to understanding their pain.

I could manage the disappointment and grief brought by the loss of a baby better when I was alone than when I was with their families. Somewhere along the line some mentor told me that doctors should never cry with parents of pediatric patients. Well, I have to admit there were times I cried with mine, and I learned that instead of seeing this as a sign of weakness in their physician, parents saw it as a sign of empathy and support.

Then empathy became all too easy—or all too difficult—for me. As a surgeon of the newborn and children with cancer, I had developed a certain "expertise" in dealing with the parents of dying children. I remember vividly the first time I had to tell parents that I would not be able to save their child's life. It was a day when I was torn between joy and sorrow: the day my first son, Allen, was born and the day I had to tell a family that they were going to lose theirs. Later on, at a surgical conference in 1967 I was asked in the closing five minutes, "What do you tell the parents of a dying child?" Someone with a tape recorder captured my remarks, which soon appeared in several medical journals. In February 1968 *Reader's Digest* printed them as an article, "What I Tell the Parents of a Dying Child."

Among the Children's Hospital's many nationally recognized specialists were four doctors who, strangely enough, had children afflicted with the same rare problem for which they had established medical expertise. One day those four doctors and I were talking about this, and I wondered: "What is it for which I am well known?" I almost shuddered when I realized that my new "specialty" had become dealing with the loss of a child.

I began to have disturbing thoughts that I would lose a child. On Good Friday, 1968, I felt it had happened. Our son Norman was five hours overdue driving from Boston to Philadelphia. When the telephone rang, I was certain it would be the police with grim news. Instead, it was Norman, cheerful as ever, wondering why we were so upset, insisting that he had told us not when he would *arrive* at a friend's home in Philadelphia, but when he would *leave* Boston. A wave of relief swept over me, and I stopped brooding that one of my children would die. They were all safe: Betsy and Norman living at home while they attended high school and college, Allen in graduate school living a mile away, David a junior at Dartmouth College.

However, my feeling of relief was short-lived. A few weeks later, the most devastating event of our lives occurred. After an uneventful Sunday, the phone rang at about nine in the evening. Since we were expecting a call from David, both Betty and I picked up the phone on different extensions. It was the dean of Dartmouth College, telling us that David had been killed while rock climbing on Cannon Mountain in New Hampshire.

Roped to his climbing companion, Charlie, David was hammering a piton into the rock when a large section of the cliff sheared off from the mountain face, carrying him with it. Bound to his tether, he crashed into the face of the cliff like a swinging pendulum. Charlie managed to maneuver David onto a ledge and climbed down to make a desperate attempt to save his life. David was semiconscious and bleeding from a severed artery in his knee. Charlie attempted to stop the bleeding with a tourniquet, but it was too late. Within ten minutes, David was dead. Charlie tried mouth-to-mouth resuscitation, but to no avail.

Words are inadequate to describe the depth of our shock, hurt, and loss. Losing a child brings a poignant and tender grief unlike any other. We clung together as a family, and the support we received from our many friends and our own faith was enormous. David's death affected each family member deeply and uniquely. It would take another book to tell the whole story, and indeed, we eventually wrote one about our experience—hoping that *Sometimes Mountains Move* might be of some comfort and help to others who had lost a child.

We have been simply astounded by the large number of people who have written to thank us for writing *Sometimes Mountains Move.* Nothing changed our lives—and the lives of our surviving children— like the death of our son David.

I thought that now I might be better able to help parents of dying children, but for quite a while I felt less able, too emotionally involved. And from that time on, I could rarely discuss the death of a child without tears welling up into my eyes.

Chapter 5

Surgery and Children

As a physician, I have always been at least a crusader, at best a pioneer. I loved taking on difficult problems, even if there was only a remote chance of success. When parents brought newborns with congenital defects to me, I tackled problems that other physicians dismissed: "We just let those die—we can't fix them." I tried to do everything I could for afflicted youngsters, and because of that aggressiveness I learned a lot. Each day of those early years in pediatric surgery I felt I was on the cutting edge. Some of the surgical problems that landed on the operating table at Children's had not even been named. Many of the operations I performed had never been done before. It was an exuberant feeling, but also a little scary. At times I was troubled by fears that I wasn't doing things the right way, that I would have regrets, or that someone else had performed a certain procedure successfully but had never bothered to write it up for the medical journals, or if they had I couldn't find it.

There is a principle in surgery that you should never perform a purely experimental operation on a human being until you have first tried it on a laboratory animal. Many of the difficult problems presented to me for surgical correction in those early years were things no one had ever seen before and no one had expected. They might not be seen again for years, and time was of the essence. So we often had to tackle new problems by combining universal surgical principles and a little courage to chart new courses.

Above all, I soon realized that advances in pediatric surgery would have to await advances in pediatric anesthesiology. When I first arrived at Children's, I was horrified by what passed for anesthesia. A nurse-anesthetist would start a tonsillectomy patient under anesthesia with open-drop ether, hook the child to a machine that delivered ether vapor through a curved tube into the side of his or her mouth, then *leave that patient alone* to start another. It was only a little short of miraculous that there were not more misadventures. But at the time that was standard operating procedure at even the best of children's hospitals.

It was no better than that in much of the world when years later I was asked to demonstrate some pediatric surgical procedures in Germany. As I began my lunch, I suggested to the nurse-anesthetist that she start anesthetizing my patient. She shocked me by saying that the baby had been put to sleep forty-five minutes earlier and that she had attached the anesthetized infant to a machine so she could eat her lunch.

As I toured hospitals both at home and abroad, I realized that too many children had died on the operating table not because of the surgery they underwent, but because of inadequate anesthetic techniques. I needed to find someone who would dedicate himself or herself to pediatric anesthesia the same way I tried to dedicate myself to pediatric surgery. I found that person in Margo Deming, who had been senior resident in anesthesia when I was a senior resident in surgery at the Hospital of the University of Pennsylvania. I knew her as someone who would willingly stay all night in the hospital for the sake of her patients.

Margo and I began to develop techniques that made it possible to control anesthesia in small children. In the process, we also learned about how infants respond to drugs, which helped us develop better preoperative medication. We began to experiment with endotracheal anesthesia in infants, in whom it had not previously been successful. That involved running a small tube from the source of anesthetic through the child's nose and passing it down through the vocal cords and into the windpipe. By squeezing a bag that was interposed between the supply of anesthetic and the baby, we were able to control the amount of anesthetic and oxygen the baby received. The technique not only helped us regulate the amount of anesthesia but also prevented the baby's tongue from falling back into its throat, obstructing the airway.

As far as we knew no one had ever performed this procedure successfully in tiny infants, so we had to make our own equipment. We took ordinary rubber catheters, cut them to a proper length, and beveled the edges with sandpaper to prevent injury to the lining of the infant's windpipe. We then inserted a wire into the tubing, bent it and the surrounding tube to the proper curve, boiled it all in water, removed the wire, and hoped the rubber curve would retain its "memory." Many younger doctors practicing medicine today don't appreciate what a tremendous revolution took place in surgery when plastic tubing came onto the scene.

In the first several years we used these homemade endotracheal anesthesia techniques on twelve hundred small babies, and we never lost one. We had our share of scares, though, and there were many nights when Margo Deming and I sat up with a small infant whose windpipe had been traumatized, just in case the developing croup might call for a tracheostomy (cutting an emergency hole in the windpipe). Fortunately, in all those early experimental procedures, we never had to do one.

Although we experienced great success with our anesthesia, we were afraid to publish our results because we feared other physicians who might not take the precautions we did would be tempted to try the procedure. Yet that sort of success spread through the pediatric surgical community by word of mouth, eventually producing a body of literature. Today no one would operate on a child without an endotracheal tube in place.

I love surgery because I have always had an abiding reverence for the human body, reverence for the ways its anatomical details allow it to function: tendons running through tiny pulleys, nerves buried in tunnels to protect them from trauma, the ribcage protecting the liver and spleen, kidneys hidden away in the depths of the renal fossa and shielded by pads of perirenal fat—reverence for the tissues themselves, especially the delicate ones of infants.

As we were developing the specialty of pediatric surgery, one cardinal rule emerged: You cannot treat children simply as small adults. They require special treatment and special procedures. Before pediatric surgeons developed techniques for surgery and postoperative care, the way children suffered under surgery was almost criminal. When I was a resident, a simple inguinal hernia operation on a four-year-old child would start out with an incision three to four inches long, when one and a quarter inches would do. The old procedure produced a large, heavily sutured scar that made the poor child look like a toy football with thick laces. After the operation, the youngster would be mummified in a muslin girdle, which was erroneously believed to provide extra support; confined to a hospital bed for seven to ten days (an eternity to a child); and then sent home gingerly, with instructions that he could not laugh, sneeze, cough, or lift anything for six more weeks. It was barbaric surgery.

It took pediatric surgery pioneers like Robert Gross and William Ladd to change all that. It was Bob Gross who taught me the hidden or subcuticular stitch, which was placed in but not through the skin. When you used such stitches, you didn't even need to put a bandage on a child—just cover the wound with a protective liquid plastic, which dried on the skin. No one likes surgical scars, and parents are especially bothered by surgical scars on their young children. They would be delighted when their youngster came home from, for example, a hernia operation, after only one night in the hospital—later reduced to a matter of hours—with no visible scar or stitches and with no restriction on activity.

I was grateful that the parents of our little patients appreciated what we were trying to do, and I seldom had trouble with them about financial matters. I didn't charge high fees, and because I felt that a family that had gone to the expense of establishing insurance protection shouldn't get socked with an additional bill, I always tried to keep fees low. I did have one memorable argument with an obstinate father. I knew he could well afford to pay my modest bill of $125, and as much as he tried to knock the price down, I stuck to my guns. Finally I said, "Take as long as you want to pay it, but I'll not lower the price." He was smarter than I thought. He bought me $125 worth of United States savings bonds, and I had to wait ten years to collect my fee.

In many ways it was more difficult to bring local pediatricians around to our cause. They were wary even of my postoperative instructions to parents: "I have just operated on your child. Everything went smoothly. The operation is over. He has no stitches or bandages. His activity need not be limited in any way. That means you can take him home now, and if he wants to get on his tricycle and take off, let him do so. Give him a bath, feed him the way you normally do, and if anything happens, do what you would have done yesterday. If he falls down the stairs, do what you would have done yesterday. If he has diarrhea, do what you would have done yesterday. If he bangs his head, do what you would have done yesterday. But if anything bothers you, call me."

I never tired of doing those simple inguinal hernias, the most common operation in general pediatric surgery. I performed seventeen thousand of them, and in the latter half of my surgical career I don't think I ever took longer than six minutes. Most of those youngsters had slept in their own beds the night before their operation and would be home by early afternoon, with no restrictions on their activity.

After hernias, my second most common operation was the repair of an undescended testicle, a common congenital problem in young boys. I performed over seven thousand of these orchidopexies. One day, at a pediatric surgical meeting in Chicago, I rose to criticize a "new" operation for the repair of undescended testicle, which seemed to me to be inordinately complicated. I was nearly apoplectic when the surgeon presenting the paper said, ". . . and it only takes an hour and a quarter to do." I admit I got a little emotional during my discussion of his paper and ended by saying, ". . . and besides, the operation I have done several thousand times takes only seventeen minutes." I had never really timed myself, and my surgical colleagues challenged my statement. I returned to Philadelphia and asked the chief of anesthesiology to time me on the next ten orchidopexies I performed. The average was seventeen minutes; some things just work out.

I never tired of performing surgical procedures. No matter how relatively minor an operation might seem to me, however, I always knew that to the parents of my patients it was a monumental episode, and I realized that surgery requires more than just good hands. Judgment—when to do which procedure, when to do nothing—is what brings success. I loved the technical challenge of surgery when it could repair what nature had failed to complete, and I enjoyed the challenge of dealing with inflammatory tissue. I never tired of doing something as routine as an appendectomy, especially one where the child's appendix was inflamed, swollen, turgid, and perhaps surrounded by a wad of omentum, the large pad of fat that is nature's attempt to seal off the inflammatory process from the rest of the abdominal cavity.

Today, in the era of antibiotics, rupturing an appendix while removing it from the abdomen is not the tragic situation it was when I first started in surgery, before penicillin had made its appearance and we had only sulfonamides to ward off infection. In those days, a surgeon who ruptured an appendix could bring on peritonitis, which could ravage, even kill the patient. I delighted in being able to slip a probing finger into the abdomen of a child through a tiny incision, find the appendix, take stock of how inflamed and turgid it was, then blindly deliver it, unruptured. This is the closest a surgeon ever comes to defusing a bomb, although of course it is the patient who is at risk, not the explosives expert. The bombs in infants and small children were no less explosive.

Another breakthrough came when we put in the first shunt for hydrocephalus (water on the brain), to drain the excessive cerebrospinal fluid damaging the brain into the peritoneal cavity and prevent the head from enlarging. When word of this successful surgery spread, children with untreated hydrocephalus came from far and wide. There were days when I would arrive in the hospital courtyard to find a house trailer parked there, driven across the country by a family with a hydrocephalic child. The heads of some of these children were huge, as large as big pumpkins. Some of the children's conditions were so far advanced that they couldn't benefit from surgery—and their frustrated families became the core of one of our early self-help groups—but we were able to relieve the suffering and disfigurement of many.

We made exhilarating advances, but I have to admit there were times in the operating room when I was terrified. My greatest fear, which I think is shared by most surgeons, is a rapid, uncontrollable hemorrhage. When a friable blood vessel is ruptured, the bleeding can be so voluminous that it sounds like water rushing from a faucet. That sound is never so frightening as when it comes from the delicate body of a small child. After assuming my position as Surgeon General and realizing I would never go back to the operating room, I had the secret pleasure of knowing I would never again have to hear that terrifying sound.

I was fortunate to have Doris Bender, my first surgical resident, beside me in the operating room during those first tough years. I had met Dottie when she was an intern rotating through the surgical service at the Hospital of the University of Pennsylvania. I admired her surgical thinking and her technical ability, especially her digital dexterity. She endured those early years of hostility with me, objected to them mightily, but gave me two years of valiant service, especially while I was in Boston. She married one of the surgical residents and set up a surgical practice with him elsewhere in Pennsylvania.

Among the many people who helped me build the new field of pediatric surgery, I have to give special credit to the nurses, dedicated women whose skills I admired and whose loyalty to our mission I cherished. It is difficult to name any without naming all, because I would not want to leave anyone out. But certainly at the top of the list is Erna Goulding, a nurse of unusual dedication and competence who did everything to make my dream of an unsurpassed pediatric surgical service come true. Starting as our baby-sitter, she became a de facto member of our family. The operating room nurses all made remarkable contributions to my personal comfort and to the success of many surgical procedures. I have to mention Kitty Bell, who was a companion, confidante, absolutely superb scrub nurse, supervisor of my operating room for years, and the woman I most liked to dance with (except for my wife). Kitty was followed by Winnie Betsch, who was also invaluable to me. She believed everything I ever told her, except that she would die if she continued to smoke as excessively as she did. She succumbed to lung cancer as a very young woman.

Nothing in surgery is as satisfying as working with a skilled operating room nurse who knows the way you think, as well as the way you operate. You're like dancing partners who know each other's every move; no words need to be spoken in a synchronized duet. Each Christmas I took a page from Flo Ziegfeld's book when I hung a long sign over the door to the operating rooms that said, "Through these portals pass the most beautiful girls in the world." The nurses knew I wasn't talking about superficial physical attraction; they knew that I appreciated the beauty of all the things they did to make possible our successes in the operating room.

But I needed more than top-notch operating room nurses. Pediatric surgery also depends upon the quality of postoperative nursing care. Great technical surgical skill would come to nothing without the complete dedication of the nurses charged with the care of our tiny, fragile patients. In 1956, after many years of searching for funds, I was able to found the nation's first neonatal surgical intensive care unit. At first with only three incubators, eventually with twenty, the neonatal unit worked not only because of the high-tech equipment but also because of the dedication of the nurses who gave all their time to those patients. In just a few years I found it necessary to recognize the ICU nurses as I had the OR nurses, so signs then appeared in two places at Christmas: "Through these portals pass the most beautiful girls in the world."

Most people don't realize the tremendous burden we place on a young nurse in an intensive care unit. She may have to monitor heartbeat, respiration, venous pressure, and arterial pressure for three premature babies who together don't weigh ten pounds. In the neonatal ICU, monitors are constantly buzzing with warning signals, oxygen levels and temperature have to be continually adjusted, and the ultraviolet light has to be of the right intensity. To keep all these balls in the air at one time requires unusual skill and concentration. The ICU nurses always amazed me with their stamina, skill, and, yes, love.

You might expect an intensive care unit to be a sterile, scientific place, but over the years we saw among all the tubes, monitors, and high-tech gadgets a growing parade of sterilized teddy bears, placed in incubators next to babies half their size. Brightly colored mobiles would suddenly appear above bassinets or incubators. And the nurses would chip in to buy rocking chairs so the mothers could come to the neonatal unit to rock their babies. Most touching, at least once a year a nurse would ask to see me after hours and then timidly but firmly ask me, "Will you help me adopt the baby I'm caring for?" Many of these nurses developed a compelling love for the infants they cared for, and several did adopt youngsters who had been abandoned.

American medicine must go a long way to understand the burden borne by nurses, especially the grieving process nurses have to endure when a child whom they have nurtured for months finally succumbs to its disease and dies. In a children's hospital in Spain, when such a child dies, the nurse who has been responsible for its daily bedside care is given time off for grieving for a period of two to three weeks in order to get back on her feet before she returns and begins to care for other youngsters. We should provide similar emotional support for our nurses when needed, with pay.

The dedication at the Children's Hospital certainly wasn't limited to the nurses. Charlie Wilson was an operating room orderly when I first arrived at Children's. His grandfather, whom he remembered clearly, had been a slave. Charlie had often worked by cutting, splitting, and stacking firewood for twenty-five cents a cord. He asked little from life and gave much. I was one of the recipients of his concern and care as soon as he saw that he and I felt the same about protecting children. He brought the patients to the operating room, always comforting the older children as he wheeled them along. He ran the IVs; he mopped my brow in the non-air-conditioned operating theater on those hot Philadelphia days when I operated in shorts with an ice collar around my neck; he sharpened needles; he kept the instruments repaired; he made certain we never ran out of supplies; he counted the sponges on the floor and in the buckets during surgery; and when my back was in a knot from leaning over a small baby for hours on end, he massaged the pain away. Charlie appreciated me before anyone else at the hospital did. I appreciated Charlie, and I loved him.

One Saturday morning, after I had removed a huge tumor from a small child's abdomen and had only to mop up and close, Charlie whispered in my ear, asking permission to leave early for a doctor's appointment. Twenty minutes later, a nurse opened the operating room door and said, "Charlie Wilson has been shot in the street by a policeman."

I left my resident to close. Charlie had been two blocks from the hospital when a child ran out from a house ahead of him, pursued by a policeman holding his pistol and shouting obscenities at the boy. When the cop caught the child, he began to beat him over the head with the pistol. Charlie stepped in and said, "Here, here. You can't do that" and was shot in the chest for his concern. By the time I learned this, Charlie was in the emergency room of the old Graduate Hospital, several blocks away.

Still in my scrub suit, I jumped into my car (parked in the hospital courtyard) and arrived at the Graduate Hospital emergency room five minutes later. Charlie was lying in a bed, completely unresponsive. His usual *café au lait* skin color now blended with the gray sheets. He had undoubtedly lost a lot of blood, yet I saw only saline solution going into his arm vein. Two doctors lounged down the hall, one with his feet on the desk reading the newspaper, the other telling jokes to two nurses. I was initially polite, but when I found out that they had not typed his blood and that their plasma supply was not only low but also contaminated, my anger made up for the authority I lacked in that hospital.

I took apart those two disgraces to the medical profession, and finished with "If you are very smart in the next few minutes, you might still work here tomorrow. Get me a new IV for plasma. Get this man admitted. Call the chief of the thoracic service and tell him I want him in here now. Alert the operating room for a thoracotomy. Give Charlie a quarter grain of morphine, and move!"

They moved—not as fast as I would have liked, but they were probably out of practice. Meanwhile I got on the phone to my own hospital and told the chief medical resident, Joseph Rudolph, a good friend, "Joe, I'm coming through the hospital courtyard in about seven to ten minutes in a black Plymouth. Be at the front door with a boxful of bottles of plasma. I need it for Charlie Wilson, who is bleeding to death in the Graduate Hospital emergency room."

I started the new IV on Charlie, then drove off to the Children's Hospital. Waiting in the courtyard was good old Joe with a cardboard carton with about fifty bottles of plasma of the small 100-cc size we used for children. He put the box in the front seat of the car, and I roared back to the other hospital.

As soon as I got to Charlie's bedside, I ripped off the tops of six or seven bottles and filled the IV reservoir, opened the clamp wide, and watched as the life-giving plasma flowed into Charlie's vein. His blood pressure began to rise, his rapid pulse fell, and soon the bullet was extracted from just above his heart. This frightening episode concluded with Charlie's eventual recovery and the policeman's dismissal from the force.

While I was packing up the unused plasma to return to my hospital, I noticed the word "pertussis" on each of the bottles. In his haste and excitement Joe Rudolph had taken from the refrigerator not plasma, but instead bottles of hyperimmune pertussis serum, manufactured for pregnant women with whooping cough to prevent them from losing their babies from the spasmodic coughing that accompanies that awful disease.

The serum I gave Charlie was just as good for him as plasma was— indeed, it is almost the same. However, it was much more expensive. I calculated that I had given Charlie $8,600 worth of whooping cough immune serum. Later I told Charlie that he was well worth it, but if he ever so much as coughed again in his whole life, he and I were through.

Not everyone on the staff possessed Charlie's loyalty and honesty. One hot summer in the fifties, the day-by-day management of the Children's Hospital sank so low that essential materials were missing on the wards. On the day I could not find a pair of sterile scissors to take out the sutures in an appendectomy incision, I blew my stack. I couldn't accept that the gains we had fought so hard for were being jeopardized by loose management and light-fingered employees. Without any real authority, I called a meeting of the Board of Managers of the Children's Hospital. I can't imagine why they responded, but they did. I convened the meeting in one of the hot, non-air-conditioned rooms. I opened the meeting by reading the definition of trustee out of Webster's Dictionary. I then told them that, insofar as I had been able to ascertain thus far, they were a responsive body of men when costs actually touched children, and something had to be done about the supplies problem. The board assigned member John Williams and me to settle the issue. John Williams was Philadelphia's quintessential Philadelphia lawyer—a man so persuasive that his cases seldom came to court. We set up a plan to put those employees on notice that they would no longer get away with stealing.

One afternoon, without fanfare, John and I secured all of the exits from the hospital complex except the front door and one courtyard gate. We closed the remaining gate so that only one person at a time could pass through. When five o'clock came and the employees began to pour out of the building, John and I took our positions on either side of the narrow space in the gate.

The hospital's help filed toward us, each one waddling under the weight of at least one large, heavy shopping bag in each hand. We corralled the first eight or ten employees and announced that we were going to examine their bundles. The others beat a hasty retreat back into the building and returned empty-handed.

Our inspection of the packages turned up whole hams, sides of bacon, turkeys, and assorted kitchen utensils. (I had not been aware of the drain on the commissary.) In other bundles we found packages of sheets and pillowcases, mattress pads, hospital scrub suits, dozens of surgical scissors, and sundry items—in short, anything that could be removed from stockrooms, supply rooms, refrigerators, and the mail room. The thievery stopped. Supplies began to build up; indeed, there was a surplus. John Williams and I did two more spot checks. The word was out. You could no longer get away with rifling the Children's Hospital.

With the pilfering issue resolved, I was happy to be able to concentrate fully on surgery again. The most common congenital defects I saw that were life-threatening but correctable were esophageal atresia (in which the esophagus and stomach are not connected); omphalocele (when a baby is born with its abdominal organs protruding from a very much enlarged umbilical cord); imperforate anus (when a baby is born without a rectum); various forms of intestinal obstruction; and diaphragmatic hernias (when the abdominal organs end up in the baby's chest cavity because of a hole in the diaphragm).

In the most common form of esophageal atresia, the lower part of the esophagus, which should be connected to the upper part, looks like an elbow on a stovepipe and is attached to the back of the windpipe. This is called esophageal atresia with tracheo-esophageal fistula, a congenital defect that must be corrected surgically if the child is to survive.

When I started in pediatric surgery, the mortality for this condition was essentially 100 percent. By the end of my thirty-five years at the Children's Hospital of Philadelphia, my colleagues and I had performed over 475 of these operations, and I hadn't lost a full-term baby after this operation for eight years. The survival rate for low-birthweight infants—who sometimes weighed less than two pounds—was 88 percent: a wonderful testimony to what the advances in pediatric surgery and anesthesia had done for our children.

I started the operation for correction of atresia of the esophagus by opening the chest on the right side, with the baby lying on its left side facing away from me. I would cut across the side of the chest so that the skin incision fell between two ribs (when operating on females, I would make sure the front end of the incision was low enough so that it wouldn't deform the breast when it developed later). After I had opened the muscles down to the infinitesimally thin membrane that lines the lung cavity, I would slowly push the membrane away from the chest wall, very delicately, to avoid tearing it. After I had pushed the membrane far enough away so that I could see down into the very center of the chest, wherein lie the great blood vessels, esophagus, and trachea, I would search for the blind pouch of the esophagus above and the stovepipe connection below. Then I would separate the curved stovepipe from the trachea and sew the hole in the trachea closed. Then at last I could sew together the two open ends of the esophagus. I have described this procedure as sewing together two pieces of wet spaghetti in the bottom of an ice cream cone.

One night, as I was operating on a premature baby with esophageal atresia, I discovered a strange variation of the defect. X rays had shown no air in the baby's intestine. When most babies with this defect breathe, the air goes down the trachea through the esophageal fistula into the stomach and bowel, where it shows up on an X ray. But this baby had an airless abdomen. When I opened the baby up, I saw why: It had no lower esophagus.

Inside this tiny baby, the distance between the upper part of the esophagus and the stomach was about three to four inches—too far to stretch the truncated esophagus down or the stomach up to connect the two. So right then and there I opened up the baby's abdomen, removed a section of the right colon (keeping the blood supply intact), and sewed one end to the short upper esophagus and the other to the stomach. As far as I knew, it was the first time anyone had replaced a missing esophagus with part of the colon. That baby, born premature with pneumonia in both lungs, did not survive, but the second one on whom I did such an operation did. After earning a Ph.D. in physiology, she went on to graduate from Harvard Medical School. A revolutionary step that night, forged out of necessity and perfected in the years ahead, a colon interposition eventually became a standard procedure, saving many babies. No wonder I became so concerned as Surgeon General three decades later when Baby Doe, the ill-starred newborn who would spark a revolution in the treatment of handicapped infants, died of an untreated esophageal atresia with tracheo-esophageal fistula, just because his misinformed parents and a Bloomington, Indiana, judge forbade the lifesaving operation I had done so often.

The first year I was in practice I saw my first—and largest—omphalocele on a little girl. Within an hour of her birth, I had her transferred to the Children's Hospital, where I operated on her. She not only survived but also eventually supervised my intermediate intensive care unit after she graduated from nursing school.

I'll never forget my most spectacular diaphragmatic hernia. A garbled telephone call from a nearby hospital described what could only be a dying newborn with a diaphragmatic hernia. Once again I sprinted down to my car in the cobblestone courtyard, raced eleven blocks to the other hospital, parked my car on the sidewalk, and rushed into the lobby, only to find the elevators were not running. So I ran up to the ninth floor, wrapped the baby in a blanket, ran down the same nine floors and placed the baby on the floor of my car by the heater. Back at the Children's Hospital, I ran up two flights to the operating room and laid the baby on the operating table. By now the little fellow was dark blue and apparently lifeless. Without taking any sterile precautions, I slashed an incision across the left side of his chest, inserted my fingers, and pulled out the abdominal organs that had made their way up into the chest, thereby relieving the pressure on the lungs and the heart. Then I began to massage his tiny heart with one finger. It began to beat, and—a great sign—the edges of the wound began to bleed. We cleaned the wound as much as we could, inserted an endotracheal tube into the baby, and I completed the operation. I made the incision when the infant was only fifty-five minutes old. He remains my youngest patient.

About twenty-five years later, my secretary ushered into my office a young man about 6'4" tall who stood somewhat embarrassedly before me and said, "My father thought you'd like to meet me. You operated on me when I was fifty-five minutes old." I ran around the desk and hugged him.

Intestinal obstructions were a particularly challenging operation. We became so successful at them that I was honored with a most unusual patient. Early one morning my resident started, a little hesitantly it seemed to me, to tell me about a newborn with intestinal obstruction, probably at the upper level of the small bowel, and after giving a complete history—but no information from X rays—he said, "The only thing unusual about this patient is—it's an orangutan."

This baby orangutan from the Philadelphia Zoo, which weighed a little over two pounds, had been the third offspring of its mother, Christina, whose two previous babies had died after she had abandoned them. A young veterinarian took the baby orangutan home with her and nursed it with a bottle in her own bed where she kept it warm, only to find that it could keep nothing down. In desperation, she called a friend who was the secretary in our neonatal intensive care unit. That's how the orangutan got into the Children's Hospital. I was concerned that at some future time a parent might assume that the very presence of the orangutan in the hospital could be a source of some rare disease, so I instructed my staff to get the baby orangutan back to the zoo as fast as possible. My instructions provoked an argument within the house staff, some seeing my point, others determined to operate on the dying orangutan. At that moment a stranger walked over to me, introducing himself as the chief veterinarian at the zoo. He said, "We know a lot about animals, Dr. Koop, but we know nothing about newborns. That's where you're the expert. Please take care of our orangutan." I agreed, but I would do it only at the hospital at the University of Pennsylvania School of Veterinary Medicine.

It didn't take long for us to take a shine to our purple-bottomed patient. We soon learned that the skin of a newborn orangutan is about as tough as shoe leather. Nevertheless, we operated, we reoperated, we succeeded, and we made some people at the zoo—and the hospital— very happy. They had wanted to name the orangutan "Chick" after me, but since it was a female they settled for "Chickie." When I last heard, she was being courted by a young male orangutan at the Memphis Zoo.

Were there surgical failures? Of course there were. There were some children who didn't make it, but fortunately their number diminished over the years. Techniques improved over time, risks were reduced, cosmetic appearances were improved, and rehabilitation became a science of its own.

Yet, there are times when I contemplate the failures and have to wonder why. Take the Siamese twins, for example. Ironically, some of my greatest surgical successes became strange failures. My colleagues and I operated on over ten pairs of Siamese twins while I was at Children's Hospital, but three pairs became well known.

First there were the girls joined at the pelvis who came to me in the fifties from a New York suburb. I was elated at last to have the opportunity to separate conjoined twins. Dr. Louise Schnaufer, who would play an important role in two later separations, was my resident. The babies, scrubbed and draped, presented an odd picture from the rear: four legs rather symmetrically placed around two buttocks. The night before the surgery I had a nightmare about making the incision so that each child ended up with one leg of the other.

The operation was eminently successful, and for seven years we had two normal, growing, intelligent girls. Doctors and parents were delighted. Eventually the smaller of the twins required open-heart surgery to correct a congenital defect. Her operation went smoothly, but on the fifth postoperative day, as she was sitting up in bed eating breakfast, she inexplicably died. An autopsy provided no reason. At the surviving twin's wedding, only her parents, her husband, my wife, and I knew her medical history.

Then there were Clara and Alta Rodríguez, Siamese twins who were sent to me from the Dominican Republic. It was after separating these twins that I first received national attention from the press and public. Probably that was because I operated on Alta and Clara when they were fourteen months old, little girls with personalities, not tiny newborns.

The mother of Clara and Alta had gone into labor in a little village of about fourteen families, Los Ayomas, some twenty miles from the town of San José de Ocoa over a road impassable except by jeep. When her labor stalled, she was transported those terrible miles to town, where she delivered by cesarean section Siamese twin girls joined at the pelvis, but with complicated internal anatomy; they shared one liver and one colon, had four vaginas, and their urinary tracts were intertwined.

The twins were transported to the Children's Hospital in the capital, Santo Domingo, where the father was told it was not possible to separate them. A photo of Mr. Rodríguez holding his conjoined children after that news is the epitome of utter dejection. A year later a Philadelphia woman called me and asked what I knew about Siamese twins. She then told me about the Rodríguez girls; her maid was the twins' aunt. I arranged for free surgery, anesthesia, and hospital care for the girls, and the women from the American Embassy in Santo Domingo held a cake sale to raise the money for the flight to Philadelphia.

The press took an immediate shine to the cute little girls, especially Donald Drake, the science reporter for *The Philadelphia Inquirer*. He latched onto us, and we included him in our blackboard chalk talk where the surgical team met daily to figure out exactly how we would tackle this extraordinarily complicated problem. Louise Schnaufer, by this time my associate, worked with me to figure out every possible detail and snag before the operation began, as did the anesthesiologists and the OR nurses.

The fourteen-month-old twins had two distinct personalities and actually fought with each other, punching and scratching, but without being able to get away from each other. Yet after separation, I saw a poignant gesture as one separated twin reached out—for the first time across an expanse of bedsheet—to touch the hand of her sister.

The separation of these twins was perhaps the emotional highlight of my surgical career. After we had arranged the complicated surgery so that each part of it was done by the person on my team most expert at the task, we ended up with two normal girls. Four months later, Louise and I then took them back to the Dominican Republic, where our arrival was treated as a national event. We were feted by every possible authority from President Balaguer to the local politicians and dignitaries.

The only people who did not join in the celebration were the staff of the Children's Hospital, who had branded as "impossible" my claim that we could separate the twins successfully. When the press had reported to them that I had kept my word, they had said, "We don't believe it." But the continuing care of the little girls could be monitored by Louis Quinn, a Canadian priest who had spent his life in the Dominican Republic, and the Sisters of the Hospitaliers of Saint Joseph, especially Cecilia Smith.

Two years later Alta was playing with some beans on the porch of her home in the Dominican Republic. She popped one into her mouth, inhaled, lodging the bean between her vocal chords, and choked to death on the spot. If she had done that even in a hospital, we would have had trouble saving her. Clara grew to become a beautiful and charming young woman.

My most dramatic case of Siamese twins involved newborns who shared one heart. Their chests were one, and the ribs from one child came around from the left and joined the edges of the ribs of the right side of the other. We knew a lot about these twins because of autopsy findings on others born with the same condition. The twins had one six-chambered heart, which was failing because it could not support the life of the two growing children. In order for one twin to survive, the other would have to be sacrificed. This was an extraordinarily unusual and difficult situation.

Religious issues made it even more difficult. Both of the grandfathers were Hasidic rabbis, and they insisted on a seven-day Talmudic argument on the ethical issues involved. I was just as concerned, but I wasn't sure the children would survive the long argument.

Eventually we all came to the same position: One twin, the smaller, was essentially a parasite on the other. It was clear we had no choice about which twin would have to be sacrificed. Meanwhile, a friend warned me that my pro-life position had made me some enemies, and I might be taken to court in a civil suit in Pennsylvania if I deliberately brought about the end of the life of one twin. I therefore demanded a court order to do the separation. The judges questioned me about a possible malpractice suit, and I told them that my relationship with the family assured me that I had no reason to fear that. However, I did fear the civil suit and would not operate without their order. They gave it to me.

The operation was very tense. I assembled a team of experts to assist me, and then I made the incision in such a way that I could work with an ample chest cavity to contain the six-chambered heart. I profited by the mistakes of other surgeons who had attempted a similar procedure and failed. I would not let anyone else participate in the tying off of the second carotid artery, which spelled death for one twin. For a few moments there was absolute silence in the operating room. After producing the death of one twin it took me a little time to separate the body from that of the survivor. I then tenderly wrapped the body in a sheet and carried it to the door of the operating room, where I was told a rabbi would be waiting to take the body for burial. When I opened the door, I found an old friend, Rabbi Mandelbaum, whose presence somehow made me feel better about the whole affair. I had operated on many of his innumerable children.

No one had ever successfully separated conjoined twins with one heart. Although we all felt a great sadness about the death of one child, we rejoiced that we had succeeded in saving the other. The surviving infant had problems, including a six-chambered heart that eventually would probably require some sort of repair, but her future looked promising. Sadly, she never made it. Forty-seven days after separation she died from hepatitis, probably from a transfusion.

Three successful—and difficult—separations of Siamese twins, three strange failures, two living children out of six.

I never forget the failures, but thank God, the successes outnumbered them by far. The beautiful and extraordinarily talented young woman who graduated from Harvard Medical School after earning a

Ph.D. told me when she was a senior in college, "If it hadn't been for all of the surgical procedures I had, how would I ever have known I wanted to be a pediatric surgeon?"

Some youngsters stand out among thousands of patients because of the sense of relief and joy they brought me at the successful conclusion of the challenges they presented. Linda came to me as a five-day-old baby, brought by her very depressed parents. Her mother's striking beauty made the baby's appearance especially tragic. Little Linda had the largest tongue I have ever seen. It protruded from her tiny mouth, looking more like a fillet of beef than a child's tongue. Because it had been protruding from her mouth for several months before she was born, her upper and lower jaws were somewhat deformed. The poor child's appearance was grotesque.

We embarked on a series of operations that I completed over the next three years to reduce the thickness and length of Linda's tongue. Linda became one of those patients with whom Margo Deming and I took turns sitting up all night until the postoperative swelling went down and we were assured that she had an adequate airway. When Linda was three I undertook the final operation to remove the width of her tongue. I fashioned as well as I could a tip of the tongue, primarily for cosmetic purposes. I had no precedent in the literature to go on in those days, and I was essentially flying by the seat of my pants, trying to give a little girl the best possible chance for a normal childhood and a productive life.

But I had taken tremendous chances with the blood supply to her tongue. As the scars from the third operation began to contract, the remnant of Linda's tongue grew smaller and smaller, eventually becoming such a tiny nub on the floor of her mouth that I did not know how she would ever speak again.

I was terribly depressed about it. I couldn't wait for Linda's three-month follow-up visit, yet I dreaded it. What could I ever do with a child who couldn't speak clearly because of a surgical procedure I had performed?

The day for her follow-up visit came at last. I sat behind my desk, as far away from the door as I could get. The door opened. Linda came in first; her parents stood behind her, expressionless. My heart sank. Then Linda said, with just the slightest lisp, "Merry Christmas, Dr. Koop." Linda's parents beamed. I wept.

Jeff was a little boy who came to me because he was a Phillies fan. Jeff was sitting with his mother in the bleachers, watching the ball game while chewing an enormous wad of gum, when a man sitting next to him made some friendly remark about all that chewing gum Jeff was working on. The youngster's mother, defending her son, explained to the gentleman that the boy was only following doctor's orders, chewing gum constantly to get rid of a lump in his parotid gland.

The stranger said: "That is very interesting. Would you mind if I felt the lump in his cheek? I am a doctor, a radiologist. I know something about lumps in the parotid gland, and I'd sure like to feel it."

After this cursory examination in the ballpark, the doctor turned to Jeff's mother and said: "On the basis of everything I know, I can tell you that my best advice would be to get your son to see Dr. Koop at the Children's Hospital as soon as you possibly can and do whatever he tells you."

Jeff and his mother were in my office the next morning. The lump in the parotid, one of the salivary glands, had become no smaller on the chewing gum treatment, and to me it felt like a malignant tumor because it was stony hard.

This would be a touchy situation. All facial expressions, the ability to close one's eyes tightly, and the ability to whistle, are controlled by a pair of facial nerves that exit the skull just in front of the ear and spread out over and through the parotid gland like the fingers of a hand. Surgery on the parotid gland is fraught with the danger of cutting one or more branches of the facial nerve and thereby paralyzing the muscles supplied by that branch. Cutting the upper branch might conceivably affect just the closure of the eyelids; cutting the lower branch might produce a crooked smile. Cutting the entire nerve would produce total paralysis of that side of the face.

I operated the next day, and after a seven-hour procedure, I had removed the tumor and thought I had preserved every branch of the facial nerve. I was jubilant, but cautious enough to warn Jeff's parents about the possibility of recurrence. That recurrence took place far more quickly than I would ever have anticipated, and two weeks later we were back in the operating room, this time with a different task. Because the tumor was so malignant, because it had recurred in such a short time, and because our first objective was to save Jeff's life, I decided to do a radical removal of the entire parotid gland. This would mean deliberately severing all branches of Jeff's facial nerve except the one that closed the right eye. Jubilation had turned to frustration and depression.

The operation went well. It required nowhere near the skill of the previous one, and I did it radically enough to ensure, to the best of my ability, total removal of any malignant cells. Postoperatively, Jeff could close his eye, but he had no other power in his facial muscles. His smile was completely cockeyed. He could no longer whistle, and this seven-year-old boy had been a whistler.

But I had a plan for Jeff, one that could never have been accomplished without two parents, especially a mother, dedicated to achieving the best they could for their son. I told them that I could not guarantee what I was proposing, but it was worth the effort. There are occasions when branches of the fifth cranial nerve, the trigeminal, take over the function of the severed seventh cranial nerve, the facial. So I instructed Jeff's mother to stand behind him as they both looked into a mirror. She was to smile, laugh, bare her teeth, grimace, elevate her lips, puff out her cheeks—make any facial motion she could think of—and Jeff was to try to imitate her.

To Jeff's father I assigned the task of teaching Jeff how to whistle again. I suggested that Jeff and his father sit opposite each other at a narrow table, and every time the father lit a candle, Jeff would have the pleasure of blowing it out. Initially, he couldn't even make the flame waver, but perseverance on the part of all three members of this team eventually paid off.

One day Jeff and his parents stepped into my office. Jeff stepped forward, pursed his lips, and whistled, in its entirety, "Hello, Dolly." Once again I could only weep. I had grown close enough to this family to invite them to our daughter Betsy's wedding. When the orchestra played "Hello, Dolly," Jeff's mother asked me to dance with her to "our song."

Two patients were especially close to my heart: Andy and Paul, little boys who each posed a unique surgical problem and who opened up deep and lasting friendships between their families and mine, friendships Betty and I count among the great blessings of our lives.

Andy was a child we call a prune belly, which means he had an abdominal wall consisting only of skin with none of the fat and muscle layers of a normal child. When he contracted pneumonia almost immediately after birth, he had no muscles to produce a real cough to clear the mucus from his windpipe. I watched him go steadily downhill in spite of all the "high-tech" advantages we possessed by that time. I finally resorted to surgery—and won. I made him a "keel" from stem to stern by rolling all the redundant skin of his abdomen together and attaching one end to his pubis at the lower end of his abdomen and the other end to the base of his breastbone. At last Andy had something to cough against, and he cleared his chest. Although the little fellow required several more operations, he was a joy to his family and us and survived for eight years, only to die of an unrelated kidney infection. Andy's death was devastating. I tried to help the family when they needed me, took Andy's clothes to the undertaker, stayed close to the family before, during, and after the memorial service. They did these same things for us six months later when our David died. The bond that was forged has never been strained. Today Andy's family are among the closest of our friends. His sister Stephanie, who was a toddler when Andy was born, became my personal assistant for some very crucial years during my tenure as Surgeon General.

Paul's multiple congenital problems were overwhelming, not only to his family, but also to those who could help him. They were so overwhelming in their number and complexity, that several surgeons who first saw him decided nothing could be done for him. But doing nothing would lead to newborn Paul's death, a death with the excruciating pain of intestinal obstruction. True, Paul's problems were numerous and complex. But I knew they were amenable to surgical correction, one at a time. Tackling his problems one at a time took years, and we had to deal with complications along the way, sometimes operating on one problem twice to get the right result. Little Paul thrived through it all and became an admirable and affable young man with a sense of purpose and a sense of humor, even after more than fifty operations. He also became my friend. I admired his family. They coped with great difficulties and managed magnificently. Once Paul's mother was asked what the worst thing life had brought her was. She answered without hesitation: "Having Paul born with all those defects." Then she was asked what the best thing life had brought her was. Again, without hesitation: "Having Paul born with all those defects."

It was, of course, the patients with severe and complicated surgical problems whom I got to know the best. It was their families who became my friends under so many different circumstances. Sometimes the first operation would be dramatically lifesaving, but it would not correct the problem for the long term, making a second operation necessary later. In other instances, as with correcting an imperforate anus, it might take a child seven years or more to establish rectal continence—ample time for me to see the remarkable ways families cope with adversity.

I learned very soon that nothing makes a woman out of a girl faster than coping with a congenital defect in her child. Nothing in humanity is more encouraging than seeing the way parents manage with a child who is less than perfect. As outsiders look at the situation, they see the child's physical defects and mental deficiencies as a difficult, even unbearable burden. But the bond between a physically or mentally retarded child and his loving parents is a wonder to behold. Before we had the remarkable self-help movements of today, it was my custom to put parents in touch with other parents who had been through that same circumstance, veterans who could act as mentors and support those who were just starting out. It worked, and it worked beautifully.

Next to surgery, I loved to teach. When I began at the Children's Hospital, the University of Pennsylvania School of Medicine offered no instruction in pediatric surgery. But with the help of my former mentors, Ravdin and Rhoads, I worked pediatric surgery into the curriculum so that at one point, it was taught in all four years of medical school. Then, victim of curricular changes and medical school politics, we were squeezed off the board little by little until during the last seven or eight years of my tenure at Penn, pediatric surgery had been reduced to an elective course except for a mere eight lectures to the junior class given by members of my staff in rotation.

No matter; the core of any surgical teaching is not in the lecture hall, but in the operating room and at the bedside. My experiences with the parents of sick and dying children taught me that a pediatric surgeon needs to learn more than innovative surgical techniques: he or she must also learn how to give parents the emotional support they need under often mystifying or terrifying circumstances. Medical school, then and now, does a good job of teaching the science of medicine, but there seem to be few teaching the art of medicine. Then and now, few teach a young resident to be the kind of doctor the public wants, a doctor who not only can master the science of medicine, but also share the milk of human kindness with distressed patients.

As a professor at Penn, I tried to impart this blend of art and medicine. After visiting the various wards, I would choose an appropriate patient for final discussion and then withdraw to the nurse's station for a wrap-up with the medical students, residents, and anyone else in attendance. It was on these occasions that I tried to impress on my students that in pediatrics you never have just one patient. You have many: the child, the parents, the grandparents, the siblings, and occasionally the uncles and aunts.

I might start off by saying: "Have you ever wondered what the mother of this thirty-six-hour-old baby girl thinks of us? For about eight months she and her husband looked forward to the arrival of a bouncing baby. It never crossed their minds that their little one would be anything other than perfect. They envisioned holding in their arms a baby like the one on the Gerber baby food jar.

"Then came the delivery. The father was present, but there was a strange silence after the baby was delivered. After an explanation that was probably inadequate, the obstetrician and/or the pediatrician told the parents that this youngster had been born with a rare defect that was incompatible with life, but could be corrected—but not in that hospital in rural Pennsylvania. They would have to send the baby to Philadelphia.

"Perhaps the family saw the baby; perhaps they didn't. What do you think the mother thought when she woke up this morning with no baby in her arms, indeed no baby down the hall in a bassinet, as a matter of fact, no baby in the town in which she lived? Where was her baby? In the hands of total strangers. She wasn't even certain what the doctor said last night, whether he said the *survival* rate was 90 percent, or whether he said the *mortality* rate was 90 percent. We who have her baby are faceless people. We are people for whom she feels no affection, and to whom she has no allegiance.

"How are we going to correct that and include the parents in our understanding of what is going on with their baby?"

Then I would push the hold button on the telephone on the nurse's desk and hand the phone to one of my residents or to a medical student and say: "You have just called the father. He's at work. He has a little shop in town where he knocks dents out of fenders. He has no health insurance. His wife's mother has had a stroke and lives with them. The roof leaks. The refrigerator door doesn't stay shut. He has been up all night and has just gone to work. Tell him what happened to his child since she was admitted.

"And tell him in such a way that he will be so impressed with your kindness, with the comprehensive care provided by this hospital, with your thoughtfulness in calling to include him in the circle of knowledge about his baby that if he ever strikes it rich, he'll leave this hospital a million bucks!"

That kind of an experience in front of his peers could make a man out of a boy in a very short time.

Parents aren't the only ones who need emotional support. One of our goals in the early years of pediatric surgery was to get both the medical profession and the public to come to terms with cancer in children. In the late forties and early fifties, many pediatricians wanted to deny the existence of cancer in children. Some didn't even want to say the word. In 1948, when I was asked to discuss pediatric surgery on a radio show, the hostess warned me not to say "cancer." I said it anyway, because I had learned what a large, ignored problem cancer was for children and their families. Denial was part of the problem. People could not cope with a child dying from what was considered a disease of old age. At times, I have seen small communities actually become hostile toward the hospital and the surgical staff because they could not save a child from cancer.

As my surgical practice grew, I saw more and more children with tumors. Although we could save many, childhood cancer often brings death to the hospital ward, with an emotionally wrenching impact. Frequently, after a heartbreaking death, the student nurse on the case would lean on the staff nurse for emotional support, the staff nurse would lean on the supervising nurse, and so on until there was no one to lean on but me. We started a self-help group for grieving pediatric care providers. We met regularly, but also spontaneously when the pain became overwhelming. Today, a far cry from the old days of cancer denial, hospital groups meet routinely with the hospital chaplain to talk out their feelings.

Doctors are not supposed to be emotionally affected by the death of their patients, but just as the nurses developed a tremendous attachment to certain babies, so did I. It was especially hard when a child died after I had performed a new operation on it for the first time or had taken a risk to save its life.

It was my dream as early as 1948 to get under the roof of the Children's Hospital of Philadelphia the most comprehensive group of pediatric surgeons anywhere in the world. It took me thirty-three years to do it, and in 1979 I invited the hospital's Board of Managers to a dinner where I explained the dream it had taken over three decades to fulfill. I announced that at last I had twenty-seven partners, all either full-time in the Children's Hospital or sharing time in the adjacent Hospital of the University of Pennsylvania, who were bona fide pediatric surgical specialists in the eight subdivisions of surgery.

One important transition made it easier to fulfill that dream. In 1974 the Children's Hospital of Philadelphia moved from its ancient and dilapidated buildings in South Philadelphia to a magnificent new building, then the most expensive structure in Pennsylvania, on the campus of the University of Pennsylvania in West Philadelphia.

Moving a hospital is a tricky business. The logistics, especially concerning the transfer of patients, required months of planning. When the big moving day came, we relied on voluntary ambulance services from the surrounding suburbs in Pennsylvania and New Jersey and the cooperation of the Philadelphia police department. I watched it all from the roof of the old Children's Hospital, where I was equipped with a walkie-talkie that kept me in touch with several people along the route. Patients were carried out on stretchers or wheeled out in wheelchairs, then lifted into the waiting ambulances that shuttled back and forth between the old and new hospitals.

As the last ambulance pulled out of the cobblestone courtyard, past the heavy iron gates, I realized I was the only person in the old Children's Hospital except for the security guard. I took a last tour through every room in the old hospital and its adjacent outbuildings before I walked out the front door for the last time. I stood in the room where my own children had been patients. I stood in the tiny area that had been the first surgical neonatal intensive care unit in the country. I stood in the auditorium, where we had tried to inspire the wealthy of Philadelphia to espouse the cause of the Children's Hospital. I stood in the X-ray department, where I had spent many hours with my beloved friend, John Hope, not long dead from cancer. I stood in the room that had been the 125-seat amphitheater that served as the only operating room when I arrived there. It was modeled after the famed Allgemeine Krankenhaus in Vienna. I stood in the new operating suite, calculating briefly what it might have cost to build that facility in terms of service per patient and concluding that it was well worth it. I stood in the operating room where I had first separated Siamese twins. I stood in my old office, where I had spoken, counseled, laughed, cried, and prayed with so many doctors, nurses, patients, and families over the years.

It was difficult to select a resident from those who applied for a position in my training program. Early on, choices were few, but soon pediatric surgery began to attract many very bright and competent young men and women. I didn't care whether an applicant was Phi Beta Kappa (or Alpha Omega Alpha, the medical school equivalent), nor whether he or she came from one of the Ivy League medical schools. I felt that anyone who had finished the prerequisite arduous general surgical training and was willing to put in the extra two years certainly was sincere. He or she was certainly not doing it for money, because pediatric surgery is not a lucrative specialty. In the early days, there were no entitlement programs to cover children's illnesses, and later our entitlement compensation did not always cover expenses. Ultimately, I chose the people whom I thought it would be fun to teach, who were sensitive and caring people, fond of children.

The young men and women I trained formed a vital part of my life and a lasting contribution to surgery as their skills multiplied. My first trainee to enter academic surgery was Bill Kiesewetter whom I had trained for a year in the middle of his general surgery residency at Yale. After a few years with me he became the first surgeon-in-chief at the Children's Hospital at the University of Pittsburgh. The associate who spent the longest time with me was Harry Bishop. I didn't train him, but Bob Gross had done that superbly. Harry could be counted on to support me, substitute for me, and protect our new specialty when necessary—but he never tried to supplant me. I owe him much. Charlie Minor came to me from the Boston Children's Hospital, and after he spent a year and a half as a trainee with me, I asked him to stay on. Charlie was one of the most gentle surgical souls I have ever met. His loyalty and faithfulness enriched everything I was trying to accomplish. He left to become the senior pediatric surgeon in Wilmington, Delaware, about forty minutes south of Philadelphia, but he maintained his academic affiliation with us. Arie Verhagen, whose family Betty and I sponsored as Dutch immigrants, filled a special place as a surgeon and as a committed Christian. Our families grew close, and after many years with me he went to the Children's Hospital in Dayton, Ohio, to do pediatric surgery there. R. W. Paul Mellish came from the University of London hospital system, bringing the perspective of the United Kingdom to our growing surgical establishment. An affable, competent surgeon, Paul left us to become the chief of pediatric surgery at the University of Vermont, where he rose to a position of respect and influence. And of course there was Louise Schnaufer, whom I trained, whose long association with me spanned much of my surgical career, and whose skill, support, and spiritual empathy require too many words to describe adequately. I frequently told her I could never have done it without her, and that's true. Two other trainees eventually became partners, John Templeton and Mori Ziegler. John took charge of the trauma unit at Children's Hospital; Mori became the surgeon-in-chief at the Cincinnati Children's Hospital.

Regulations prevented my graduating more than one pediatric surgical resident each year. Early on their term of training was a year, later eighteen months, then two years. Over my lifetime at Children's Hospital, I graduated thirty-five residents and about fourteen foreign fellows. Many went on to become professors of pediatric surgery, directors of divisions of pediatric surgery, and surgeons-in-chief of children's hospitals. Just as I owed so much to my first resident, Dr. Doris Bender, I owed a lot to the last ones, Martin Eichelberger and Victor Garcia. Not only were they the last two on whom I would leave my personal imprint, but—ironically—each would end up in Washington, D.C., at about the same time I did, Marty on the surgical staff at the National Children's Medical Center and Vic at Walter Reed Army Medical Center. Washington gained two outstanding pediatric surgeons and I gained two surrogate sons who had much to do with getting me through my first difficult years on the Washington scene.

Except for family relationships, I don't think I've ever had more intimate and collegial times with anyone as I had with my senior residents—especially in the early years when we felt we stood against the world. I demanded a tremendous amount from them. I know they were under the same kind of stress that I was. I also know how difficult it was for their families; they had already gone through five to seven years of general surgical training, and just when most of their colleagues were ready to step out into the actual practice of surgery, they had chosen to sign on for two more years of perhaps the most grueling training of their experience. This could produce tremendous tensions in their families. Betty was always a great help to me—and to them—as she applied her special wisdom to the strains that pediatric surgery can place on the family of a resident.

As I call my patients to memory, I see an almost endless parade going by. I see all the things we did to help them: to repair simple hernias, to make deformed limbs right, to try tricky operations to make up for missing fingers, to replace absent feet with paratrooper boots, to remove birthmarks, to separate webbed fingers, to pin back lop ears, to repair cleft lips and palates, to close spina bifida and treat hydrocephalus, to correct heart defects, to repair the cosmetic but also physiological deformity of a funnel chest, to remove tumors, and above all to operate on "congenital defects incompatible with life, but amenable to surgical correction."

I have not performed surgery for more than a decade, and still each week brings one or more letters to my home from a grateful patient who may never have known me because he or she was too young when we first met, or from grateful parents and grandparents. Nothing gives me greater satisfaction. Above all I thank God for giving me the opportunity and privilege to prolong life and health for so many children. Today, as I travel so much, I don't count a trip complete unless some young adult stops me and says, "You don't remember me, but when I was four days old . . ."

I knew my last operation would be a difficult time for me, so I wanted it to be an operation that would present no unusual problems. I wanted no fuss made by my colleagues, standing around watching the last procedure of the retiring surgeon-in-chief. At a few minutes after 1:00 P.M. on March 6, 1981, I made the incision for a right inguinal hernia. Six minutes later, when that was closed, I made the left incision and was finished six minutes after that. My closest associate, Louise Schnaufer, wandered in at the end of the procedure, as she frequently did. No one said anything special, but the realization dawned on me that operative surgery, which had been the most exciting part of my career for nearly thirty-nine years, had now come to an end.

I put the dressing on the infant's two small incisions, waited until it dried, took off my gown and gloves, and walked over to the window separating the operating room from the scrub sinks. I dipped my finger into some soap, then wrote on the window the closing lines from T. S. Eliot's "The Hollow Men":

> This is the way the world ends,
> This is the way the world ends,
> This is the way the world ends,
> Not with a bang but a whimper.

The soapy writing stayed on the window until the fall, when one of the janitors, not knowing its significance, washed it away. With it went my last link to the operating rooms of the Children's Hospital of Philadelphia. But my bond with all those thousands of little patients will last at least a lifetime.

Part III

Becoming
Surgeon General

Chapter 6

Confirmation

Becoming Surgeon General was agonizing, a form of political and personal harassment unlike anything I had experienced in my life. My main supporters, with the significant exception of Secretary Dick Schweiker, seemed to be interested only in how aggressively I would put the pro-life agenda forward. The opposition, therefore, saw my appointment only in terms of the threat the Reagan administration posed to legalized abortion. Those were the outlines of the conflict, and I was caught somewhat haplessly in the middle. After thirty-five years at Children's Hospital espousing the cause of the disenfranchised and fighting for a fairer deal for children, I wanted to enter a larger arena and fight on behalf of a broader constituency.

Medicine and politics became entwined early in American history and have remained so ever since. President John Adams started it all. While he was American ambassador to the Netherlands, Adams boarded in his home a young American, Benjamin Waterhouse, who was studying medicine in Amsterdam. Later, as president, Adams chaired a meeting of the American Academy of Arts and Sciences, where Dr. Waterhouse discussed the revolutionary new practice of vaccination. President Adams was impressed with the report, as was his vice president, Thomas Jefferson. But although Adams' interest in health matters led him in 1798 to establish the Marine Hospital plan to stop the spread of infectious diseases brought to our shores from foreign ports, he did not support Dr. Waterhouse and the cause of vaccination because Waterhouse's approval of the practice had made him a controversial figure.

A few years later, President Jefferson, less afraid of controversial figures, appointed Dr. Waterhouse as director of the new Boston Marine Hospital. Waterhouse set one precedent after another. He established the first outpatient service, radically expanding the range of federal medical care. He also wrote the first regulations governing the way federal medicine should be dispensed, who should provide it, and who would be eligible to receive it. As a faculty member at Harvard, Waterhouse set up small clinics within the Marine Hospital, established the system of student internships, and in effect turned the Boston Marine Hospital into this country's first teaching hospital. Even though his brilliance might have made him seem abrasive to some, Benjamin Waterhouse was safe during Jefferson's two terms. But in 1809 our fourth president, James Madison, bowed to the arguments of a more conservative medical establishment and fired Waterhouse— whose position was a prototype of the Surgeon General—from government service.

Ever since the example set by Benjamin Waterhouse, the role of federal medicine has been to lead, not merely to follow. Some Surgeons General have been up to the task, others have not. Sometimes their colleagues in private practice have supported them, sometimes they have engaged them in sharp conflict.

It is probably impossible to dissect the anatomy of any political appointment. In my case, as perhaps with most, two forces worked together. First, there were the unsolicited efforts of those who sought my appointment for their own reasons. There were those first three callers, from Senator Jesse Helms' office, the Heritage Foundation, and the Reagan–Bush headhunters, as well as others, most of whom remain unknown to me. From time to time I heard about some of them, such as my longtime friend Billy Graham, who had a pre-election conversation with Reagan in which he mentioned me as someone Reagan might think about for the post of secretary of Health and Human Services.

Second, there were my own efforts. On the morning after election day, once I had made up my mind that I really wanted the Surgeon General's job, I decided there was no point in not pursuing it aggressively. I spent a good deal of my time in the next few weeks lining up people who could help me secure the appointment. I was told to use as many channels as I could find to get to Reagan and his transition team in order to make known my availability, qualifications, and willingness to serve. Some of my "connections" were tenuous: Nancy Reagan's half brother, Dr. Richard Davis, and I were members of the same department of surgery at the University of Pennsylvania, but he told me he had as many difficulties as anyone else in getting to Reagan and suggested I work through someone on the transition team. I spoke on the telephone with Dick Schweiker, who then seemed to have the inside track for the job as secretary of the Department of Health and Human Services.

I had met Schweiker when he attended a speech I delivered in one of the Capitol caucus rooms to the American Family Institute. Many of the people who would champion my cause attended that meeting and seemed pleased with my remarks about the management of handicapped children and their families. Schweiker complimented me on my speech, especially my position that children born with serious handicaps should be covered by catastrophic insurance. I told him that having never worked for an immediate supervisor during my surgical career, I couldn't think of any boss I would rather have than him. We came from similar backgrounds and held many of the same ideals. I respected his integrity and told him I hoped we might work together. Schweiker would play a key role in my eventual confirmation.

Six weeks after the election, I began to catch hints of problems. A pediatric colleague in California had learned from a friend on the transition team that a transition committee had told Reagan—this was pretty indirect information—that they were not sure I had sufficient standing in the medical community to be Surgeon General. Ironically, they were concerned that I might be so conservative that liberals would not be able to work with me.

Reagan, I was told, responded unusually to the concerns. He apparently asked his pastor, Don Moomaw, if some of the physicians in his congregation could check on me. The next week I began to receive calls from friends in various parts of the country who told me somebody had called to ask them about my standing within the medical profession. The messages to me were all the same: "The president is interested in you."

The next step was a trip to Washington at the invitation of Senator Orrin Hatch, who had arranged for me to meet a number of senators. Hatch had just become chair of the Senate Committee on Labor and Human Resources, which dealt with health issues (and my confirmation). I had not met him previously. Strom Thurmond told me, "You look like a doctor. There were nine doctors in my family. I hope to see you around here in the future." Paul Laxalt indicated that he would talk to Secretary Schweiker about me. Daniel Patrick Moynihan, a Democrat and a liberal, remembered having read my book *The Right to Live: The Right to Die,* and Joe Biden from Delaware, who had lost a wife and child in an accident, credited the Children's Hospital at Philadelphia, my home base, for helping his surviving children.

I then turned to the medical community to see if they would stand with me. When I asked the executive director of the American College of Surgeons, with whom I had enjoyed a cordial relationship since 1948, if he would be willing to endorse me as Surgeon General, I could tell that my request gave him some trouble. He said he would have to take it to the college's Board of Regents. My former mentor Jonathan Rhoads, for a considerable portion of his career the most respected surgeon in North America, stepped into the breach. Although the American College of Surgeons declined to support any candidate, from that time forward until the stirring speech he gave on my behalf before the Senate committee debating my confirmation nine months later, Jonathan was an outstanding supporter and went the extra mile for me on many occasions.

My interview with the Reagan transition team on December 18 seemed to go well, and I was told that after their screening process had been completed, they would submit three names to Schweiker, who would then decide which person the president would appoint.

Then a dark cloud appeared. On the day before Christmas Eve, a well-meaning group of Pentecostal Christians purchased time on a Washington television station to show eighty-seven minutes of the five movies from the series *Whatever Happened to the Human Race?* that I had made years earlier with Francis Schaeffer. Because these movies reflected my opposition to abortion, infanticide, and euthanasia, they stirred up the first antagonism from the public. Planned Parenthood, the National Organization for Women, and the National Abortion Rights Action League began to line up against me, and the first of what would be many negative articles about me appeared in *The Washington Post* and *The Washington Star.*

The days passed slowly, with little purpose, and for the next several weeks I seemed to be sure of less and less. I was told that the field of possible candidates for Surgeon General was growing. But my real problem had become the American Medical Association. I knew the AMA had opposed Dick Schweiker's appointment as secretary of HHS, and they were not thrilled with Schweiker's choice of David Swoap for undersecretary as well as the nominee to run the Health Care Finance Administration. Now they were refusing to back my appointment as well; in fact, they fought it. I began to wonder if Schweiker might sacrifice his desire to have me as Surgeon General in order to salvage his relationship with the AMA.

I decided to tackle this problem personally, so I called the executive vice president of the AMA, Jim Sammons. I asked Sammons why he was opposing my appointment as Surgeon General. I had been faithful to the American Medical Association over the years; I had been a member since I started my internship; I had kept the entire surgical service at the Children's Hospital active in the affairs of the AMA, as opposed to many other university departments that stood in opposition to its policies. Sammons replied that they were not opposing me but had their own candidate. I didn't really believe that, nor did I know for how many physicians Sammons was speaking. It was not until more than a year later that Sammons told me privately that it was my position on abortion that had turned the AMA against me. Most people suspected that all along, but that was the first time it was ever officially acknowledged. The AMA had only recently reversed its long-held anti-abortion position. Like any new convert, it wanted to make the most of its new position.

Rumors grew that the Surgeon General's position would go to a wealthy campaign contributor. I began to believe the system was so capricious and self-seeking that I wasn't sure I really belonged in government.

During the annual Washington pro-life march and rally in January, a selected group visited the White House to press my cause with the president. Many of them said the most important thing they had to discuss was the appointment of the Surgeon General, and the person they would most like to see in the job was Koop. I have to be grateful to all these people who spoke so well of me, even though some of them could not walk the whole distance with me during my years as Surgeon General.

One of those in the group, congressman Henry Hyde (Rep.-Ill.) reported, "The only thing that I could have done that I did not do was to take a spray paint can and paint Koop's name on the wall of the Oval Office. If I had had one, I would have." Later, as I thanked him for his efforts on my behalf, he said the president had told him that everything he had heard about me from other sources had confirmed that I would be the right person for Surgeon General. I wondered if it were rumor or reality?

Through its lobbyists the AMA continued to fight hard against me. The newest AMA choice for the job was former Indiana governor Dr.

Otis Bowen. Carl Anderson told me that if Bowen were indeed a candidate, I didn't have much of a chance. Bowen was a Republican, a physician, a superb administrator, had been a governor, and would have the support of the two Republican senators from Indiana. Bowen, as it turned out, was not interested, although later he would serve as secretary of Health and Human Services and we would get along famously. As time would tell, I would owe much of my success to Otis Bowen.

The web became even more tangled as the question of my appointment became mired in a variety of schemes to reorganize the Department of Health and Human Services. Shuffling around the positions of undersecretary for health, assistant secretary for health, and Surgeon General. Meanwhile the AMA had advanced a new name for Surgeon General and assistant secretary for health: Dr. Edward Brandt of the University of Texas. Finally, in response to more pressures and people than I can imagine, it was decided to split the only recently joined position of assistant secretary and Surgeon General. Brandt was nominated as assistant secretary, while I would be named Surgeon General. There was one little wrinkle: The Surgeon General would drop down one echelon in the hierarchy and would now report to the assistant secretary. All this mattered little to me at the time, and I understood it even less. I was simply relieved that I would, after all, become the Surgeon General. The story that began with those three long-ago telephone calls seemed to be coming to an end.

Or so I thought. But the opposition was gathering its forces, becoming vitriolic. The American Public Health Association (which had supported abortion on demand even before *Roe* v. *Wade*) began a vigorous campaign to block my nomination, trumpeting that I was "almost uniquely unqualified" to be Surgeon General. They claimed, among other things, that I had no experience in public health. Several supposedly reliable informers told me that Planned Parenthood had spent $100,000 to block my nomination. Who knows? A series of articles appeared in the local press, portraying me as nothing more than an anti-abortion religious zealot. It did not take long for me to feel abused by the press. I was disillusioned to see what passed for "investigative reporting" about the Koop case. It usually amounted to a reporter reading a hostile article about me in some newspaper and then writing a similar article for publication in his or her own paper. Months went by before any reporter asked *me* anything.

Occasionally I had to wonder if this were all a conspiracy. Did the whole world really feel that I was incompetent? How could people not see that as a pioneer in pediatric surgery many of my innovations amounted to measures in public health? Was my thirty-five-year record as chief surgeon and professor indicative of someone who would flub the job as Surgeon General?

The hubbub spread beyond the Beltway. *The New York Times* ran an editorial about me—"Dr. Unqualified"—insisting that my nomination as Surgeon General was "an affront to the public health profession and to the public." The same charges were parroted in *The Washington Star.* In Philadelphia, *The Bulletin,* hitherto a good friend, printed a large cartoon portraying me as a two-headed monster. Across town, *The Philadelphia Inquirer* pleaded with the Senate to reject my nomination. One columnist called me "Dr. Kook"; many others took it up.

Among the many false labels pinned on me in those early hostile days was that of "chauvinist." I have never been sure exactly what that meant. When one critic added the adjective "medieval," I was even more bemused. Some people refined the charge by calling me "anti-women." A strange label, I thought, to apply to someone who had trained more female pediatric surgeons than anyone else in America.

One day I decided to have lunch in the Humphrey Building cafeteria. As I walked into the dining room itself, I heard someone say, "Here he comes." By the time I reached my intended table at the far end of the room, the usual hum and clatter had subsided and a hush had fallen over the entire room. As I walked to my seat, I was absolutely astounded to see how many forks were poised in midair between plate and mouth as this unbelievable two-headed monster, the most unqualified Surgeon General appointee in history, prepared to eat his lunch.

My sense of isolation grew even worse. It was really more like solitary confinement. I had been on the job as deputy assistant secretary for several weeks, and I still had no job assignment, no obligations to perform. I had lost any sense of purpose, except perhaps my desire to be confirmed one day. The wheels of the political machinery ground on around me, but I was never privy to any of the process. While I was still doing very little, I was introduced to Ted Cron in the Public Health Service Office of Public Affairs, who said he would serve as my speechwriter. I told him I had always written my own speeches and didn't need his services. But Ted insisted—prophetically—that eventually I would be too busy to write my own speeches, and furthermore, I would need someone as a speechwriter who could protect me, someone who knew the history and workings of the department, someone who knew where the land mines were.

Ted Cron was right in everything he said. He became one of my closest associates, a valued advisor. Our differing political perspectives did not seem to matter much because we shared a quest for fairness, for justice, for protection of those people in our society who needed help. I count Ted Cron as one of the great assets of my time in Washington, a person who not only aided me in my mission, but also taught me a great deal.

There was one other person to whom I turned frequently in the dismay that began to grip me in those first weeks: Carl Anderson, the administrative aide to Jesse Helms who had first called me about the Surgeon General position, back in August. I had come to Washington unschooled and naive about the convoluted political and bureaucratic process that gets things done—or not done—in government. I must have called Carl several times each day during my first years in Washington for advice in navigating the bureaucratic shoals or just to hear a friendly voice. More than anyone else, Carl Anderson cleared the way for my initial appointment, giving me the knowledge to proceed and the courage to fight on. I would have loved to share with him that sweet sense of victory that eventually was mine. My gratitude to him is still broad and deep, and I have been sorry that his aversion to homosexuals and sex education was so intense that he severed our friendship in 1986 after I had included the telephone number of a homosexual resource center and mentioned condoms in my report on AIDS.

Woody Kessel, a pediatrician serving in the Commissioned Corps of the Public Health Service, stopped by my empty office and explained that much of the opposition to me was what he termed "theater," reminding me that when someone like Ted Kennedy blasted off about me in public, he was campaigning for the women in Massachusetts he expected to vote for him. I believe it now more than I did then, but I still cannot condone character assassination as a stepping-stone to public office. Woody was invaluable during that first awful year. And then there was the support of Faye Abdellah—but more about her later.

Gradually the flow of visitors to my office increased, and I welcomed the opportunity to communicate one-on-one with people with whom I hoped eventually to work. So when someone like Bob Graham, the director of one of the agencies of the Public Health Service, or John Kelso, his deputy, or Vince Hutchins, the director of the Bureau of Maternal and Child Health, or Bill Foegge, the director of the Centers for Disease Control, came by, I had a chance to say: "Let me tell you a little bit about who I am, what I've been doing for the past forty years, and what my hopes and aspirations are if I am ever confirmed as Surgeon General."

I shared with these visitors my long-cherished ambition to find ways to avoid overlap and duplication of services for handicapped children and their families, to provide computerized information banks to help physicians and nurses find proper care for defective newborns, and to enable their families to ferret out the resources that communities made available for their upbringing, education, and support.

In retrospect, these became some of my most important weeks in Washington. The delay in my confirmation, as trying as it was, gave me the chance to establish my credibility with these folks and many others in and out of government, and also helped me slowly and deliberately develop an agenda of the things I wanted to accomplish. Some of the things that I had in mind were issues usually beyond the purview of the Surgeon General. I was able to move in these directions only because of the rapport and confidence I established with the people I met in those first weeks, the people whose assistance I later needed, whose budgets I later spent, and whose support and cooperation were absolutely essential to all the things that are accredited to me as accomplishments during my tenure in two terms as Surgeon General. They share the credit and should share the sense of achievement.

In addition to my confirmation woes, I found myself, the new kid on the block, increasingly frustrated by my ignorance of Washington acronyms. The insiders love to use them, and of course it is easier to say "NICHD" than recite the whole nine yards of The National Institute of Child Health and Human Development. But it takes time to make sense of the alphabet soup. I began to get panicky when I couldn't tell an ASPE (assistant secretary for planning and evaluation) from an ASPER (assistant secretary for personnel). CDC for the Centers for Disease Control, NIH for the National Institutes of Health, and FDA for the Food and Drug Administration are easy, but when you get into NAID, ADAMHA, UCH, CPOD, you can lose your way, if not your mind.

In the early days I would frequently lose track during a report at a meeting because I was trying to figure out the acronyms. Finally the panicky feeling I got when I heard a new acronym disappeared one Sunday when Betty and I were driving back to Washington after spending the weekend in Philadelphia. (It was getting increasingly depressing to face the new week in Washington.) Most of the cars on I-95 had Maryland or Virginia license plates starting with three letters.

I found myself trying to make up an agency, a title, a bureau, or a division for every GBL, XLY, FGS, BGY that passed me. I think the absurdity of it all suddenly got to me, and from that time on I felt comfortable with acronyms.

For weeks I had been battling titans—the AMA, the press, the pro-abortion groups—yet my confirmation was almost derailed by devious political shenanigans. When the issue of my technically being too old for the position of Surgeon General surfaced, Senator Jesse Helms decided to deal with it quickly by the customary legislative maneuver of attaching a nongermane amendment to a bill before the Senate. In this case, his amendment, which would change the Public Health legislation restricting the age of Surgeon General appointees, was attached by the Senate to a humdrum bill dealing with credit cards. Normally a bill like this, which had already been passed by the House before receiving the Helms amendment, would, after leaving the Senate, be approved by the House or sent to a conference committee. But in this case Democratic Speaker of the House Thomas ("Tip") O'Neill found a way to fight back against Helms (as well as the president and me) by resorting to an old House rule (last used in 1951) to keep the issue in the House of Representatives, where Henry Waxman's Subcommittee on Environment and Health could bottle it up, even though the House has no jurisdiction over presidential appointments. An archaic law discriminating against me because of my age was being used against me by the Speaker of the House, who was four years older than I.

O'Neill knew that Waxman would do all he could to stop my nomination. Waxman had already been quoted in the press as saying, "I've never met Dr. Koop, but from what I've heard about Dr. Koop, he scares me."

The Democratic House leadership was plainly irritated with Senator Helms' attempt to resolve the age problem in what seemed to them a slippery maneuver. The entire House—which was controlled by Democrats—saw a chance to win a skirmish with a Senate controlled by Republicans. The pro-abortion forces sniffed victory in my defeat.

So, the victim of prejudicial decisions about my qualifications, I saw my nomination held up as the sixty-eight-year-old Speaker allowed age discrimination to stand against a sixty-four-year-old, and a congressional subcommittee that had no jurisdiction over the appointment of the Surgeon General now held me and my appointment hostage.

Henry Waxman, Democratic Congressman from Los Angeles, an outspoken advocate of abortion, became my chief antagonist. At the behest of Speaker O'Neill, his Subcommittee on Health and the Envi-

ronment announced a hearing on the bill changing the age requirement. I was asked to testify, but was advised by my small coterie of
friends and supporters that by so doing the Senate might assume I
thought the House had a role in my confirmation process, which it does
not. Some senators might think I did not understand the confirmation
process, and I might alienate those who were already on my side.

Senators got touchy, I was told, about procedural etiquette. So I was
advised to ignore the first invitation to appear before the House Committee, and when the second one came, Secretary Schweiker sent me
out of town so that I could not be called to testify. Although it would
have been a breach of protocol for me to appear, I had a natural urge
to defend myself. Instead, I had to read the transcript of the hearing
in which I was denounced and defamed by representatives from the
American Public Health Association (APHA), the National Gay
Health Coalition, and the United Mine Workers. The subcommittee,
it seemed, was not as interested in the age question as in harassing the
Reagan administration and me because of philosophical differences on
the issue of abortion.

The bizarre parliamentary maneuvering had produced a stalemate.
Washington insiders agreed that my cause would prevail on the floor
of the House, where the combination of Republicans and pro-life
Democrats would yield the necessary majority to pass the Senate bill
enabling my nomination as Surgeon General. But Waxman, it was
clear, would not release the bill from committee.

As all this dragged on, Betty and I had to find a place to live. We
were going to be in Washington too long to live in a motel, but—if
confirmation did not come—too briefly to move into a house. So Betty
looked around, finally settling on a nice little one-room apartment in
Georgetown. We felt we had come full circle, after forty years together
back in a one-room apartment like the one in which we had lived when
we were first married. Rents, however, had changed. The Georgetown
apartment cost us $1,000 a month, while our first apartment in New
York City in 1938 had set us back $48 a month. And even then the
landlord had thrown in a new mattress. Still unaccustomed to Washington housing prices, I tolerated the steep rental only because I figured
that in a month or two I would either be confirmed and in permanent
housing, or gone. Nine months later we were still there, waiting, pray-
ing, and paying.

But those months in Georgetown were very special for Betty and me.
She often said that those were the worst of times, but the best of times
in our marriage. It was a time when we needed each other because we

had no one else. It was a time when we needed each other because we were the only ones who understood the problems we both faced. I had never realized how hard it can be on the family of someone whom the press criticizes day after day, repeating false allegations, defaming character. My worst day in Washington was sometime in late April when I came home from work and opened the door to our top-floor apartment to see Betty silhouetted against the partially drawn venetian blinds with tears rolling down her cheeks as she read *The Washington Post*'s opinion of her husband.

It was also tough on the children. One of my sons would find articles from magazines or editorials from *The New York Times* circled in red grease pencil shoved under his office door.

It seemed impossible for me to get a fair hearing in the press, much less an article in my favor. One day I gave an interview to Mary Hager of *Newsweek,* who assured me her reporting would be accurate. But when *Newsweek* devoted its entire medical section to "The Koop Controversy," the article was nothing more than a rehash of the same old quotations by Waxman and the APHA. I later found out that Hager's editor had written the article even while she was doing the interview with me, and he refused to change it, ignoring the new information she had brought to him. Hager wrote other things about me over the years—always solid, truthful reporting.

On several occasions, if it had not been for my conviction that the Lord had put me in Washington for some specific reason, I would have succumbed to the temptation to say, "I don't need this kind of life, this kind of treatment, this kind of tension, and there must be something else to do." It also helped when Betty would remind me that I was otherwise unemployed.

And, just when things seemed the darkest, I would see a ray of light. Just when it all seemed senseless, I would be given assurance of purpose. Often this came as Betty and I did our morning Bible reading together after breakfast. There was that time—during some especially discouraging days—when we reviewed the life of the Hebrew patriarch, Abraham, and then read from 1 Peter in the New Testament. Certain things leapt off the page. Abraham had been wrenched from his home in order to follow the lead of God. I felt very much wrenched from my home, but also very much under the lead of God. Then I realized I couldn't quit because there were hundreds of thousands, maybe millions, of Christians and pro-life people for whom I had become a symbol. I couldn't let them down. I had to be patient. As I read the book of Genesis about God's promise of a son to Abraham, I calculated that between the promise and the eventual birth of Isaac were thirteen or even fifteen long years. If Abraham could wait, so could I. When I also read that even Abraham questioned whether or not he was acting in God's will, I realized doubts in Abraham's time were no different than in mine.

Our reading in 1 Peter equipped me for those lonely mornings when I went back into the office to face the vituperation and vilification of those aligned against me. First, I was reminded once again that my Christian faith was greater than any earthly problem. Second, as I read about submitting oneself to authority, I felt that I had tried to do that, even if those to whom I was submitting seemed incompetent, ungracious, and insensitive. And finally I was reassured when I read, "But how is it to your credit if you receive a beating for doing wrong and endure it? But if you suffer for doing good and you endure it, this is commendable before God." I felt that I certainly was suffering for doing good, that my problems stemmed from my defense of the sanctity of human life and my Christian confession. As has often been the case in my life, I felt the Lord's assurance when I needed it most.

It was difficult for me to adjust to the role of a passive pawn. In my surgical life in Philadelphia, I was always either in command because of my title or in control because of my knowledge. I had also enjoyed the respect of my crew because of my performance and longevity. In my new life in Washington, until I would be confirmed as Surgeon General, I had to adjust to the relatively powerless position of deputy assistant secretary for health. It was difficult to work in a new situation where I did not have the knowledge to proceed with the things I wanted to do and did not have the authority to act when I knew where I wanted to go.

Some people advised me to go visit Henry Waxman, to try to clear things up in a personal visit. I doubted that it would work but was willing to try almost anything. It did not go well. I did not conduct myself as well as I should have. I felt I was in a bitter struggle and no doubt came across brash, antagonistic, prepared to give no quarter.

It was obvious after our brief exchange that I had not impressed Henry Waxman favorably and that there was going to be no change in our relationship. As we walked to the door he pointed to the scarlet thread that went through the buttonhole of my left lapel signifying that I had been awarded the medal of the French Legion of Honor.

"What's that?" Waxman asked. "Some pro-life ribbon?"

"No, that signifies that I have been awarded the medal of the Legion of Honor by the government of France. And before you ask the next dumb question, recipients are never told why the French government selects them for this honor."

My frustration had given way to rudeness.

I was particularly vexed because I believed that Henry Waxman's support for public health issues was good for the country, and it was ridiculous for someone with his power who shared my concerns for health to keep his distance over the single issue of abortion. Abortion may be the greatest moral issue facing the nation, but that does not necessarily make it the greatest political issue. The competence of elected officials on local, state, and national levels should never be determined by a single issue.

When I first went to Washington in March, I never would have thought my summer would be consumed in a parliamentary shenanigan called a discharge petition. I had never heard of a discharge petition, the rarely used procedure that allows a majority in the House of Representatives to discharge a bill that is being stalled in committee. Republicans in the House started a discharge petition to release from Waxman's committee the legislation changing the age requirement for the Surgeon General. Most Republicans and some pro-life Democrats signed up right away, and we began to approach the magic number of 218 needed to release the bill. But the closer we got to the desired total, the more difficult it became to enlist new supporters. And we began to lose some Democrats who had signed earlier, because signing a discharge petition is very public business. A Congressman had to walk forward to sign the petition, right under the nose of Tip O'Neill. Young Democratic congressmen did not want to displease their party leader.

While we were trying to collect signatures on the petition, O'Neill happened to attend a dinner in Palm Desert hosted by the grandmother of a little boy on whom I had operated several times before he eventually died at the age of nine. O'Neill's hostess made it very clear that she was concerned that I be treated fairly and that the discharge petition proceed in an orderly fashion to permit a vote on my age to be made on the floor of the House. O'Neill promised her that he would do all that he could for me. Instead, he returned to Washington and did just the opposite, calling certain younger members of the House to make it clear to them that their signing the discharge petition had aroused his displeasure. Several Democrats then returned to the podium and crossed out the signatures they had previously affixed to the petition. It took a while before I figured out this was why on some days we had fewer names than the day before. But the total crept toward the needed 218, especially as a grass-roots campaign among evangelical and pro-life voters called several representatives to my aid.

And much to my surprise, in midsummer the first pro-Koop article appeared in *The Washington Post.* Reporter Mary Meehan defended my record, point by point, against the packaged accusations. She enumerated my long history of training women surgeons long before it was popular, the vital link between my surgery on infants and my high regard for the lives of unborn children, the legitimacy of my concerns about the alarming spread of infanticide in American hospital nurseries, and my commitment to improving the health of the handicapped and the aging. The article lifted my spirits and I actually almost enjoyed going to work, at least for the day or two until the next attack, the next political roadblock arose.

Even though those were depressing days, even though I never received a word of support from the White House—did Reagan even know what was going on with his Surgeon General–designate?—nonetheless it was somehow exhilarating to be part of the new Reagan administration. There was a feeling around the White House, in the agencies, and about town that is hard to impart to other people, but if you were in it, you felt it. There was an expectation, an enthusiasm, a knowledge that somehow it was great to be an American once again and that the future looked bright, no matter how many stumbles there might be along the way. That enthusiasm diminished only ever so slowly over the next three years.

As the number of names on the discharge petition grew, shrank, and grew again, suddenly the whole issue was taken behind closed doors. A big deal was being negotiated by Senator Hatch and Congressman Waxman. They were haggling over the various health provisions in the large budget reconciliation compromise between the House and Senate. I never knew what was being traded, what was being protected. I only hoped that no important health legislation would be sacrificed to the sordid political process necessary for my confirmation.

Rumors were born every few minutes, accelerating my roller-coaster ride. First I would hear that the path looked clear for speedy confirmation, then a few minutes later would come hints that a political trade had barred forever my becoming Surgeon General. I speculated that the chances were about fifty-fifty that I would be packing up to go home—wherever that was—in a few days.

Even after the closed-door meetings had adjourned, I had no idea about the crucial wording of the final version of the bill. Two days went by; still no word. I found myself reading volumes into every frown and smile I saw in the corridors. Finally, in the parking garage I bumped into a friend from the HHS Office of Legislation who assured me that the language of the bill had eliminated the age restriction, enabling my formal nomination as Surgeon General.

When I realized that at last this phase was all over, I felt absolutely drained of emotion. The previous eighteen weeks had been a real trial, as I had seen my inner certainty about becoming Surgeon General continually gnawed by doubt and had endured vicious personal attacks without any means of response. Even though I had enjoyed a long and productive medical career, in Washington I had been forced to prove myself to everyone I met. Although painful, humiliating, and infuriating at the time, the ordeal would prove important to my success as Surgeon General. The people I needed to win over in those first nine months would in the years ahead become my allies in joint ventures for the health of the American people.

Getting past the age requirement was not the end of my struggle, however. The actual confirmation hearing still stood ahead of me, and although Republican control of the Senate made ultimate confirmation likely, I was warned to expect trouble along the way from the Democrats and even some Republicans on the Labor and Human Resources Committee. It reminded me of canoeing on a swift New Hampshire river. No sooner would I paddle through one set of dangerous rapids than another obstacle course of rocks and waves would loom around the next bend.

I kept telling myself I didn't have much to worry about because that comfortable Republican Senate majority would not deny Reagan his choice for Surgeon General, even if some of them were not all that wild about me. One columnist had written, "With a Republican Senate, if Ronald Reagan wanted Jack the Ripper for Surgeon General, he'd get him confirmed."

But then I would think about how many "sure things" had not panned out already, and I would start to worry. Either way, I wanted to do the "walk around," the customary courtesy calls at the offices of the sixteen senators on the committee that would deal with my nomination.

My meeting with Connecticut Senator Lowell Weicker—an avowed opponent—started off rather badly, but the atmosphere changed when the conversation turned in a more personal way to the problems of handicapped children, especially those with Down Syndrome. Senator Weicker had a child with Down Syndrome, of whom he seemed very proud. We shared a common concern for these winsome kids with special needs. We ended on a warm note. But he voted against me. A few years later Weicker would prove a valued ally in the war on AIDS, and we would continue to work together on health issues after he returned to the private sector and until his election as governor of Connecticut in 1990.

As I made the rounds of other senators, I was discouraged to learn that each of them had received letters from public health workers in their state, urging my rejection. It was clear evidence of the continuing campaign of the American Public Health Association to cut me off at the hearing. Most of the senators recognized the letters as part of an orchestrated maneuver; only Senator Dan Quayle, who otherwise was pleasant, seemed uncertain.

Only one senator, Don Riegle of Michigan, flatly refused to see me. He told one of our legislative representatives that there was nothing Dr. Koop had ever said, was saying now, or could say in the future that was of any possible interest to him.

My chat with Senator Kennedy—up until then my most outspoken opponent in the Senate—proved to be much more cordial than I had expected. He started off by saying to me, "There are a lot of things that you and I can do together in health." We got down to brass tacks quickly and had an especially productive talk about babies who suffer from respiratory distress syndrome, the disease that had killed his nephew, the little boy born to his brother Jack. I outlined for him the strides we had made at the Children's Hospital of Philadelphia to improve the survival rate of these youngsters, and how we had gone on to set up a system of home care for them that provided the same level of care as a hospital, plus the extra emotional support of the family, at a price tag of $60 per day rather than the $600-per-day cost of hospital care. Kennedy turned to his health advisor and exclaimed, "If Dr. Koop can do this for Pennsylvania and New Jersey, we ought to be able to do it for the whole country as a public health initiative. Make a note of it."

What I had feared would be a contentious encounter with Ted Kennedy instead became the beginning of an affable cooperation in a number of vital health endeavors over the next eight years. But during the Senate debate on my confirmation, his attack on me was bitter enough to upset Betty to the point that Senator Orrin Hatch was moved to climb to the balcony to offer her a word of much-appreciated comfort.

My conversation with Senator Hatch, chairman of the Senate com-

mittee, simply underscored his consistent support for me as we reviewed our common stance on the major issues. Once I became Surgeon General, Orrin and I would work in productive cooperation on
a number of important health initiatives. No one in Washington played
a more important role in my life or Betty's. I was pleased that he was
the first member of Congress to receive the Surgeon General's medallion. He concluded our preconfirmation chat with some practical advice: "It may be a long hearing, Chick. Make sure you go to the john
just before it starts."

As I prepared for the confirmation hearing, I still had to contend
with the everyday business that crossed my desk: bilateral health meetings with the Nigerians, a symposium on the problems of aging,
speeches at the National Institutes of Health, a conference on "What
ever Happened to the Polio Patient?", and no small share of strange
stuff, like the letters from a woman in Tucson who wanted advice
because her goats could not eat molasses. Really.

The testimony at my confirmation hearing before the Committee on
Labor and Human Resources on October 1, 1981, brought nothing
new. Betty and our daughter, Betsy, sat in the audience, taking it all
in. First came the tedious repetition of the summer's charges about my
supposed inadequacy in dealing with the issues of public health. In
addition to listing the newspapers that opposed my nomination, the
testimony also listed groups that had come out against me, among
which were the American Public Health Association, the United Mine
Workers, the United Steelworkers, the International Ladies Garment
Union, the Association of Teachers of Preventive Medicine, the National Gay Health Coalition, National Organization for Women, the
American Association of University Women, and the United Presbyterian Church in the USA. I always wondered who orchestrated the
opposition. I was pleased when eventually some of these groups as well
as the opposing newspapers would number themselves among my most
fervent supporters.

Then, at last, I got a chance to defend my record. I told the senators
that the Surgeon General should come to the job with three kinds of
prior experiences: a professional career in medicine, competence in
dealing with the broad health needs of a cross section of American
society, and knowledge of international health issues. So I described my
career in terms of these issues, first highlighting my thirty-five years as
a pediatric surgeon, which included clinical experiences, the establishment of the nation's first newborn surgical intensive care unit, and my
leadership in the development of the specialty of pediatric surgery.

To reassure them of my requisite background in public health, I reviewed my role in banning the use of X-ray machines for ascertaining the fit of children's shoes, my part in studies at the University of Pennsylvania on hepatitis during the Second World War, and my understanding of the problems of health care for the underserved members of our society, which I had gained first while delivering babies in Harlem and later in the years when the Children's Hospital of Philadelphia was located in a black ghetto.

After reviewing my international health experience in Ghana, Mexico, the Dominican Republic, and with missionary medicine around the world, I concluded by setting out my views of the challenges facing the Surgeon General in the next few years: the need to revitalize the Commissioned Corps of the Public Health Service, the importance of preserving the integrity of the office of Surgeon General, the special health needs of the handicapped and the aging.

I remain ever grateful to those people who came to testify on my behalf: my former surgical mentor Dr. Jonathan Rhoads; Pennsylvania Secretary of Health Arnold Muller, M.D.; Alabama State Health Officer Ira Meyers; three from the Children's Hospital of Philadelphia: cancer expert Dr. Guilio John D'Angio, medical staff president and chief anesthesiologist Dr. John Downes, and board chairman Richard Wood; and representatives from several organizations for the handicapped, especially Sandy Parrino, chairperson of the National Council on Disability.

When the hearing ended, I felt relieved and hopeful. But there was yet another delay. The committee vote and then the final Senate vote would be postponed until mid-November. So I busied myself with some thorny problems in international health, heading first for Paris, then to Marseilles and Madrid to track down a problem concerning contaminated olive oil. Washington politicking remained as close as the nearest phone. It was during haggling in Madrid over the Spanish- and English-language versions of a health document that I was called from the room to be told by a friend that Senator Kennedy said he would not vote for me only because I did not need his vote on the committee to win and politics in his home state Massachusetts constrained him from backing me. That was a friendly gesture on Kennedy's part and made his sixteen-minute diatribe against me before the whole Senate all the more puzzling. Even so, the committee vote was eleven to five in my favor, removing the next-to-last obstacle. Only the final Senate vote remained. And that kept getting postponed, probably by Democrats still scrambling for ways to defeat me.

As the ordeal dragged on, I went to have a physical done by NIH physician Tony Fauci, who later became famous as a leader in AIDS research. Although he was thirty years younger than I, Tony and I had much in common: We were both Brooklyn boys who had graduated from Cornell Medical School across the East River in Manhattan, each dedicated to both clinical practice and research. We loved to swap stories about things we had done with our fathers in Brooklyn. In a private chat before the hearing, Tony turned serious as he talked about my confirmation problems.

"If you don't get confirmed by the Senate, I will have to take a very serious look at the rest of my life, because as a government employee in research, one of the things I might be doing twenty years from now is what you are doing. If providing excellent patient care and taking care of people to the best of your ability does not qualify you for the job you are seeking, then I ought to leave the government now."

Finally, on November 16, 1981, the big day arrived, the day I had expected in March, the day I had looked forward to since then with alternating hope and fear. Thirty-five weeks after I had arrived in Washington, the Senate would get around to voting on my confirmation as the president's nominee to be the Surgeon General of the Public Health Service. I was scheduled to meet with the directors of a Vanderbilt University handicapped program at the same time as the Senate would be voting. However, Betty was able to attend the Senate debate and vote.

In the hour that was allotted to the debate, Senators Hatch, Helms, Hatfield, Jepsen, Denton, Spector, Nickles, Grassley, Thurmond, and Heinz spoke in favor of my confirmation, while speaking in opposition were Senators Kennedy, Mathias, Dodd, Metzenbaum, Levin, Packwood, Cranston, Weicker, Tsongas, Riegle, Moynihan, and Bradley. They all followed Kennedy's lead in attacking my "inexperience" in public health, while Kennedy also offered his view that I "endorsed a cruel, outdated, and patronizing stereotype of women." My opponents—and supporters—were speaking more to their own constituents and pressure groups than to their Senate colleagues, and the vote followed at the close of the hour.

I, of course, did not know what was going on in the Senate chamber, but while I was in my meeting, someone opened the door to tell me the vote had been 68–24, much more heavily in my favor than we had anticipated.

It was hard to believe. I was confirmed. I was sworn in quietly and immediately. After that long wait, that bitter struggle, I really would be the Surgeon General. That evening Betty and I went out to celebrate at an inn in Georgetown. The place boasted an unusually elaborate menu. When the waiter came to our table I placed a complicated order, looking forward to an elegant meal. Nothing came for over an hour, in spite of my repeated inquiries. Nine months of waiting for confirmation had made me a patient man, but I did not want to wait nine more months for our meal. Finally I insisted on seeing the manager, and when she returned from the kitchen she informed me that my order had been too complicated for the new waiter. He had just signed on, and, she guessed, rather than asking for help, he had simply ducked into the men's room and escaped out the window. Betty and I went home and ate Cheerios.

The next day, instead of feeling elated, on cloud nine, I simply felt emotionally drained now that the tension-producing confirmation process had finally come to an end. People at work seemed much friendlier than before, several stopping me in the hall to congratulate me. The end of the morning found me close to nodding off in a dull meeting on something or other, when suddenly a woman with long blond hair bolted through the door, yelling, "Is Chick Koop in this room?"

Several people pointed to me. As she charged over to me, with fire in her eyes, I was certain that she was an enraged opponent about to assassinate me. About half the people in the room feared the same. The other half saw what was coming. She stood right before me and said, "I suppose you are one of those people who gets embarrassed if a girl strips in front of you."

With that she reached down, grabbed the hem of her skirt, pulled her clothes off, and stood there in sequined leotards and a kind of clown suit. She blew a whistle, identified herself as a representative of the Eastern Onion Singing Telegram organization, read a proclamation, got everyone in the room to clap hands in time with her kazoo music, and then sang a little song about my incompetence in public health. After that she gave me a dunce cap and a whistle, blew her whistle again, kissed me on the cheek, and disappeared. The telegram identified the sponsoring culprits as my former surgical associates in Philadelphia.

My official swearing-in ceremony and subsequent dinner at Fort McNair for family and friends who had helped me along the way took place on a soft, snowy evening at the end of January, marking the end of the first chapter of my life in Washington and the start of a new one.

Once I was confirmed, my problems with the press, the cheap

potshots, the snide remarks in gossip columns, all fell like leaves off a tree. My life started afresh. And quickly I knew that I had entered the most exciting period of my life. It had been a long time since I had felt excited to be going to work. Now I realized that my life would change at least once an hour throughout each coming day, perhaps as often as every fifteen minutes. With a sense of excitement and humility, I realized that each day I was doing something that was counting not just for me, not just for now, but for the entire country, and for maybe an endless time ahead. I was grateful to the Lord that the bad days were over and the good days lay ahead.

Chapter 7

Wearing the Uniform

Once confirmed, I was entitled to wear a uniform with all the regalia befitting my rank as vice admiral. I put it on immediately because I felt it would help to reestablish the languishing authority of the Surgeon General and revive the morale of the Commissioned Corps of the United States Public Health Service. There is something about a uniform. I had last worn one in my Boy Scout days in Brooklyn. During the Second World War, my surgery and my wartime research kept me stateside, commissioned but not in uniform. I was too old to serve in Korea and Vietnam. So I didn't wear my second uniform until I was sixty-five, and then only after an act of Congress declared that I was not too old.

I admit that unlike some of my predecessors, I enjoyed wearing my uniform, and I enjoyed being able to enter the service at the top, as vice admiral, the rank assigned to the Surgeon General of the Public Health Service. After the War of 1812, the designation of rank and accompanying insignia were identical with those of the Navy. The Commissioned Corps of the Public Health Service had no enlisted men and women—only officers from one stripe to three stars. I was never quite sure how I could be both a general and an admiral, but I wore my three stars with pride—and with gratitude to all those who made it possible. Actually, Surgeon General is an archaic title—it simply means chief surgeon—and is not used to address the title bearer.

Over the years I accumulated a few decorations for this and for that, and when someone would ask me what my ribbons were for, I would always reply, "The top row is for what the liberals did to me; the bottom row is for what the conservatives did to me!"

The press had some fun with my uniform, calling me sometimes an admiral with no ships, sometimes an admiral in the Ruritanian navy. And there were a couple of times on airplanes when elderly women mistook me for a steward, handed me their luggage, and confidently assumed that I would put it in the overhead compartment. I always complied immediately. But there were reasons for the uniform. Not only did I hope it would give a greater aura of authority to the health messages I wanted the American public to receive, but also it was directly related to an important, if relatively unknown, aspect of the Surgeon General's job.

The congressional legislation officially defining the duties of the Surgeon General contains rather broad—even vague—language about the responsibility of warning the American people about risks to their health. It does, however, contain a specific charge about being the commanding officer of the Commissioned Corps of the Public Health Service.

The Commissioned Corps was created in 1889. By the end of the Second World War, Surgeon General Thomas Parran envisioned a true public health service that would include sanitation, hospital care, medical personnel, and medical research to meet the needs of the entire population. Throughout much of the world, public health is in the hands of health professionals, often with government support but without political interference. In the United States, public health enjoyed much less government support and suffered much more political meddling. Beginning in the sixties, the politics of the Cabinet department responsible for the Public Health Service stymied its effectiveness as secretaries and assistant secretaries for health came and went and one layer of reorganization was piled on another like layers of an onion. The authority of the Surgeon General was shifted to the office of the secretary, and for years at a time the office of Surgeon General stood vacant. While the Public Health Service budget grew to nearly $10 billion, its agencies grew increasingly autonomous and often difficult to administer: the Food and Drug Administration; the Health Resources and Services Administration; the Centers for Disease Control; the National Institutes of Health; the Alcohol, Drug Abuse, and Mental Health Administration; and the Indian Health Service. In the continuing budget wars of the seventies, the Office of Management and Budget continually took aim at what it saw as prime targets: Public Health Service hospitals and the Commissioned Corps of the Public Health Service.

Before I first donned the uniform of the Surgeon General, I, like

With my mother at eighteen
months

In a sailor's suit at five

My father, his mother, her mother, and me

The closest thing to riding a horse in Brooklyn

Grandma and Grandpa
Koop

Grandpa Apel

The day I left for college (1933)

A freshman at Dartmouth, still required to wear a beanie (September 1933)

On skis (1934)

The Flatbush school's undefeated, untied, unscored-upon team
(1932) with five ringers that made it possible

Betty as she looked when I
met her

Betty and I when we were married in 1938

As a brash young surgeon in 1952

FABIAN BACHRAC

Betty and I in the White Mountains (1937)

Our family at our summer home in New Hampshire (1955)

The family in 1959

The family in 1963

With Norman and David on top of Mount Katahdin (1962)

FABIAN BACHRACH

After twenty-five years at the
Children's Hospital of Philadelphia

Preparing to operate at Children's Hospital. Margo Deming giving anesthesia, Erna Goulding in the background

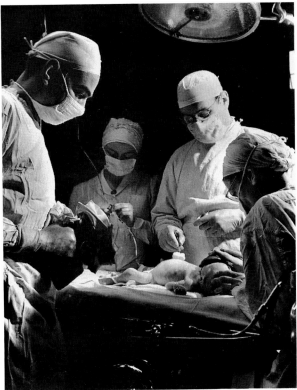

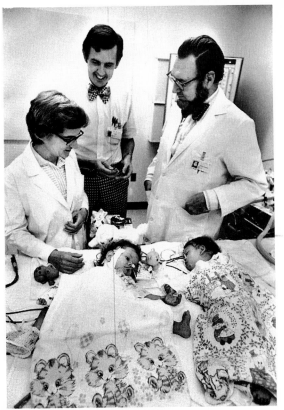

The Rodríguez Siamese twins the day after their successful separation. Louise Schnaufer and Ed Hatch assisted Dr. Koop in the operation.

Gorrell (*Richmond News-Leader*)

Jim Borgman (reprinted with special permission of King Features Syndicate, Inc.)

S. Kelley (Copley News Service)

Brookins (*Richmond Times-Dispatch*)

Senator Orin Hatch, Betty, Secretary Dick Schweiker, just before
the formal swearing-in ceremony as Surgeon General

Norman, Betsy, and Allen, in front
of a picture of David before the
salute to the Surgeon General
(1987)

Betty and I with all the
grandchildren (November
1988)

As referee at the family football game at Thanksgiving (1988)

Dancing with Betty at the Surgeon General's reception (December 1988)

Leading the Coast Guard Band on the hundredth anniversary
of the Commissioned Corps (January 4, 1989)

Placing a wreath on the grave of Luther Terry on the twenty-fifth anniversary of his release of the first Report on Cigarettes and Cancer

With Faye Abdellah at her retirement (September 1989)

Betty and I in the fall of 1990

most Americans, knew very little about the Commissioned Corps, one of the American uniformed services along with the Army, Navy, Marines, Air Force, Coast Guard, National Oceanographic and Atmospheric Administration, and National Park Service. In my forty years as a practicing physician I had rarely dealt with the Commissioned Corps, and—I confess—I may have shared the prejudice of those in academic medicine who looked down on "government doctors." I was wrong. One of the true delights of my service as Surgeon General was my discovery of the excellence, dedication, compassion, and noble service performed by the 6,200 women and men of the Commissioned Corps, which made up about 10 percent of the Public Health Service when I came on board. I know they continue to appreciate the efforts I made on their behalf. I am proud to have been counted among them.

However, when I was sworn in as Surgeon General, I found them to be in a sorry state. They knew they were top notch, they knew they were needed. They also knew they were an endangered species. Once the proud bearers of a tradition of accomplishment stretching back to the presidency of John Adams, the Commissioned Corps of the eighties had begun to jump ship. I found them in the slough of despond, cowering before the budget cutter's ax. A potent little acronym named RIS was responsible.

RIS—"reduction in strength"—is the bureaucratic term for cutting personnel from a uniformed service. One of the first actions of the new Reagan administration was to decide that the Merchant Marine, which since 1798 had had its health care provided by the Public Health Service, would no longer enjoy that largesse at the expense of the government. I was told that someone at the White House had said, "Why don't all of those Merchant Mariners have Blue Cross–Blue Shield like the rest of us?"

In any event, the Office of Management and Budget (OMB), with the blessing of the Reagan White House, eliminated that service to the Merchant Marine. It might have made sense in someone's ledger book, but it had a profound ripple effect, touching the lives and health of thousands. Since the Public Health Service would no longer provide medical care for the Merchant Marine, the Public Health Service hospitals in major seaports on both coasts and the Gulf of Mexico were closed down, and the Commissioned Corps' numbers were cut by 2,600, the number of women and men who staffed those hospitals.

Any "reduction in strength" weakens a force, but the effect on the Commissioned Corps was magnified because the loss of those hospitals meant a loss in medical training and practice; Commissioned Corps health personnel could no longer be rotated through those hospitals for refreshment training in a wide variety of medical fields. This diminished the Corps' ability to discharge its remaining responsibilities to the Coast Guard, migrant workers, native Americans and Alaskan natives, federal prison inmates, and people living in poverty across America. There should be some mechanism in government to assess the long-term impact of OMB's short-term and often myopic budget cutting.

I learned during my first year as Surgeon General that OMB or its equivalent had been trying to get rid of the Commissioned Corps for seventy years. The Commissioned Corps did not enjoy the best reputation, and many people regarded it as a bailiwick of elitism. It bore the brunt of the lingering legacy of the Vietnam years, when it was possible to avoid military service by joining the Public Health Service. The Commissioned Corps swelled with members who were anti–Vietnam war, anti-establishment, anti-government, anti–"lots of things." And in Washington, where avoidance of military service was often branded cowardice, the Commissioned Corps was dubbed the "Yellow Berets." In the years that followed, when the position of Surgeon General declined, the lack of leadership added to the perception that the Commissioned Corps was not what it once had been.

Luther Terry, the former Surgeon General who in 1964 had released the first report on the health hazards of smoking, wrote to me in February 1982 urging me to do what I could as Surgeon General to preserve the position and integrity of the Public Health Service. Terry and I had been on the same faculty at the University of Pennsylvania before he had gone to Washington, and I had known him when he had served as Surgeon General and then also in his postgovernment service. He told me in his letter that many saw me as "a face which has been brought into the current situation to destroy everything for which they have stood." But soon the corps knew that a new wind was blowing when, on July 16, 1982 I wished the Public Health Service a "Happy 184th Anniversary" and assured them I felt honored to be part of the Commissioned Corps of the Public Health Service. As the nearly omnipotent OMB accelerated its plan to dismantle the corps, I realized that I had to do all I could to save this little-known jewel in the American crown.

Effective management always requires an appropriate blend of style and substance. Changes in substance might come slowly, but changes in style can become apparent overnight. I decided the corps needed to assert itself and take pride in its mission. As one of the uniformed services of this republic, it ought to wear the uniform with pride. So, for the first time in many years, the Surgeon General began to appear in uniform, not just for occasional functions where protocol demanded it but whenever he was doing the work of the Surgeon General. In my first major appearance on national television, just after I released my first report on smoking, I made a special point of wearing my uniform. I hoped the navy blue jacket, gold braid, and my little collection of decorations would raise the profile of the Commissioned Corps. From that time on, wearing my uniform became the symbol in my long struggle to revitalize the Commissioned Corps, to make it all it could be. I know some people joked about my wearing my uniform, some teased me to my face, some mocked me behind my back, but I accomplished my purpose.

In March 1982 one of my first official acts was to appoint Faye Abdellah my Deputy Surgeon General. Faye Glenn Abdellah, deriving most of her genes from her Scottish mother, was tall, handsome, and stately, which made her, in uniform, the model of what a commissioned officer should look like. She was the chief nurse of the Public Health Service.

Faye was the first woman to hold the post of Deputy Surgeon General and became the highest-ranking uniformed woman in the United States. She was a gem in both her offices. Faye had already served the Public Health Service for twenty-five years when I came on board. She was the quintessential commissioned officer and aided the career development of every officer whose path she crossed. She was a presence in the nursing profession for a quarter century and was the author of Abdellah's laws, which set new standards for patient comfort. She forced the government to establish criteria for long-term care in nursing homes. She was my guide and mentor through many a mine field, providing wise counsel. Our interests were similar, from the care of handicapped children and their families to the expansion of self-help and mutual aid groups, from the integrity of the Commissioned Corps to innovative opportunities for the elderly, from long-term nursing care to continuing nursing education. She conformed her schedule to mine and saw to it that I was never without her assistance if needed. She prepared me for many a new experience and successfully kept me out of trouble. She embodied the best of service and devotion. She even brought me *The Washington Post* every day. We had some disagreements, but never an argument. From the day I met her Faye Abdellah was a true friend and ally to both Betty and me. Faye would be with me, with us, every step of the way for the next eight years.

Although I can recommend entering the service at the rank of admiral, there were a few drawbacks. Other admirals, having worked their way up through the ranks, know all there is to know about military protocol. I was in the dark about even such basics as when, how, and whom to salute. But I learned that if I stood just slightly behind Faye, I could take my cues from her. Betty frequently said that Faye and I, resplendent in our dress uniforms as we reviewed the troops—or the nurses and the doctors—were a smashing couple.

Wearing the uniform was important both to me and to other officers, and I followed it with more substantive steps. The Indian Health Service needed—and deserved—special attention. There was nothing substantive I could do for the IHS, but there was a lot I could do for its morale. My first inspection tour of a small portion of its facilities opened my eyes and bonded my soul to the IHS, especially to the old-timers in the Commissioned Corps who had cut their teeth in public health by serving in it. Mine was also the first such visit to IHS outposts by a Surgeon General in anyone's memory. My flight to remote facilities in the Southwest included the usual transit nightmare of the Atlanta airport, then we flew to Oklahoma City, concluding with a small plane winging and bumping to Window Rock, Arizona, on a remote Navajo reservation. I was accompanied by Everett Rhoades, the highly regarded director of the Indian Health Service, and by my helpful personal aide, Sol Levy. Tall Sol, crunched in the back of the little plane, finally yielded to the airsickness that had threatened him for hours. Sol quickly whipped a nice Stetson hat that been presented to me as a gift by some commissioned officers out of its bag and then used the empty receptacle as an airsickness bag, not realizing it was perforated on the bottom.

At every Indian Health Service hospital or clinic I visited I saw excellence. Pharmacies and record rooms were on a par with any I had seen in academic medicine. The dedication and integrity of IHS personnel were unsurpassed. At Shiprock, Arizona, for example, Dr. John Provaznik, a superb surgeon who graduated from Harvard Medical School and the surgical training program at Massachusetts General Hospital, was typical of many in the Indian Health Service who share a love for the Indians, a love of the Southwest, a dedication to service, a sense of compassion, and no greed for money. People like this have made the Indian Health Service the professional force it is.

The Indian Health Service often ignores more orthodox limits of specialization. For example, its pharmacists far exceed the role of civilian pharmacists. They act not only as pharmacists, counseling patients about medication, but also in a role that is somewhat between that of a physician's assistant and a nurse practitioner, counseling patients about their life-style, the whole regimen of therapy, and the need to return for follow-up.

While in Window Rock I learned to go to the source. Before undertaking my Navajo inspection trip, I was told that Navajos did not like uniforms, so I should go in civilian clothes. One night I found myself in a room alone with about thirteen Native Americans. One man, obviously their elder, concluded our profitable conversation by saying something like this: "I'm so glad to see you wearing a uniform. There was a time when we didn't know whether those who cared for us were doctors or impostors. They wore anything they pleased, sometimes different shoes on each foot. Thank you for bringing back a sense of decorum to the Public Health Service."

In Alaska I saw more clearly the challenges presented to the Indian Health Service. The cost of providing health care for 77,000 Alaskan natives was high—$121 million per year. The Alaskan economy had divided the native population into the very rich (North Slope oil) and the very poor. In Point Barrow I saw an elderly Alaskan native peel off the necessary $2,700 to buy a large-screen TV from a roll of bills that he could barely fit into his pocket. Not far away other Alaskan natives were struggling in abject poverty. Three-wheel all-terrain-vehicle accidents provided a steady stream of admissions to clinics and emergency rooms. Alcoholism exacts as terrible a toll among Alaskan natives as among other Native Americans; several communities I visited in Alaska had already gone "dry" by local referendum.

The patients under the care of the Indian Health Service are not an easy population to manage. Native Americans reflect an extraordinary diversity of tribal, cultural, educational, and economic status, and their numbers stretch from the tip of Alaska to Key West, Florida, from southern California to northern Maine. The cost of health care per patient therefore appears inordinately high. Multiple agencies and congressional committees share the oversight of Native Americans, so to the cultural and geographic problems are added confusing and competing layers of bureaucracy and administration: tribal chiefs, the Bureau of Indian Affairs, the Department of the Interior, and the health care providers in the communities adjoining the reservations. Considering the daunting problems, I was always deeply impressed and even moved by the medical relationship between the Indian Health Service and its patients.

The IHS proved itself to be unusually innovative, like the time several Native American representatives met with Everett Rhoades and me to discuss their decision to make eight IHS hospitals smoke-free. This was a grass-roots movement coming from the bottom echelon of the hospital administration. The Native Americans working in the hospital insisted on no smoking, not even in private offices, saying that because only doctors had offices such a plan would be discriminatory. They had decided to start the smoke-free policy in late spring so that by the time the cold weather came, the smokers would either have given it up or have become accustomed to smoking outdoors. They also had figured out how to handle patient needs. Any patient whose attending physician felt that he was so addicted to nicotine that he could not go without cigarettes must have them prescribed by time and number on the order sheet. But such patients' charts were to be stamped in red: "Nicotine Addict." Hospitals all over the country could learn a lot from these IHS hospitals.

On a smaller scale, but a more difficult task, is the Public Health Service's responsibility to supply the medical care for the Federal Bureau of Prisons. Both parties benefited from the arrangement: the Bureau of Prisons knew by experience that the medical care provided by the Public Health Service was superior to anything else it had ever been able to obtain, while the Public Health Service enjoyed the opportunity to rotate its officers through the Bureau of Prisons for one more variety of federal health service.

This can be difficult, unsung work, an example of the way the Commissioned Corps can meet the health challenges posed to the country, as when boatloads of Cuban and Haitian refugees, many desperately ill, some with highly communicable diseases, suddenly landed on Florida beaches in 1981. Castro had opened his hospitals, prisons, and insane asylums and allowed those inmates to drift to American shores, where their health problems became ours. Almost every disease known to human beings arrived with those Cubans: tuberculosis, leprosy, hepatitis, cancer, and more. The scope of the problem lay beyond the capabilities of the Florida health officials, and federal civil servants usually responded to requests to assist by saying, "It's not in my job description." But Commissioned Corps health personnel could simply be ordered to report for duty in Florida. They saluted, they went, and they conquered many health problems. For the two years after Florida made its request, the Commissioned Corps provided 268 officers, men and women who spent from two weeks to two years serving those refugees. Their work is one of the unheralded health care accomplishments of this era.

Most of the Cuban refugees found permanent settlement, but some nineteen hundred individuals, classified in Cuba as criminals, were also found to be mentally ill, and were eventually incarcerated in the federal penitentiary in Atlanta, where I visited them in April 1985. Some were indeed criminally insane, some were murderers, others self-mutilators. The Public Health Service provided what care it could through our agreement with the Bureau of Prisons, but there was little that could be done with these men and their problems. On my visit to Atlanta I had to walk under the double-tiered cells carrying an umbrella because as we passed the prisoners spat on us, urinated on us, and ejaculated on us, all the while chanting obscenities in several languages.

Through the good offices of other nations, the United States was finally able to arrange for the return of two hundred prisoners a month by way of Guantanamo, the American naval base in Cuba. I was of two minds about this arrangement because I feared these people were going home to execution. They thought so, too, and they eventually rioted in a detention center in Louisiana as well as in the federal penitentiary in Atlanta.

During the prison riots, Public Health Service officers as well as prison guards were held hostage while the prisoners devastated the buildings. Even while held hostage, Commissioned Corps officers continued to serve both prisoners and guards, and outside the prison walls the corps provided psychiatric care for the families of hostages and prisoners alike. (The entire arrangement of prisoner return was canceled by Cuba in late May 1985 because of Cuban objections to Radio Martí beaming anti-Castro messages from Florida to Cuba.) As I saw this heroic medical effort under the most trying circumstances, I wished the bureaucrats from OMB could see what they had almost destroyed.

The other duties of the Commissioned Corps included providing medical care for other uniformed services, the largest of which was the Coast Guard. Changing times had brought new duties. The families of Coast Guardsmen always knew that Coast Guard search-and-rescue operations were risky, but the drug crisis suddenly put Coast Guardsmen in the front lines of drug interdiction. For the Commissioned Corps, this meant a significant rise in the need for psychiatric consultation with family members of Coast Guardsmen who found themselves exposed to the violence of the drug wars. I was the first Surgeon General to visit the Coast Guard in action, and I developed a great respect for them.

The PHS also provided health care to the National Oceanographic and Atmospheric Administration (NOAA), a little-known uniformed service that involves itself with the issues its title suggests.

I also sought to integrate the Commissioned Corps—logically, it seemed to me—into the Department of Defense's emergency plans. In an era of tightening budgets and personnel shortages in some military units, I introduced MEDSTARR (Medical Staffing and Training to Augment Reserve Readiness), which allowed understaffed Army and Air Force reserve units to be brought up to full strength by having Public Health Service health personnel fill vacant posts as doctors, dentists, operating room nurses, and so on.

In my work with military medicine, my aim was not only to do what I could to make available the skills and resources of the Public Health Service, but also to pursue my larger objective of improving the health of the nation. Improving the health of service men and women, encouraging them in preventive medicine, and promoting healthful living would, I hoped, have a positive ripple effect once they returned to civilian life.

My pursuit of this objective in government and in the private sector was aided by the many other positions held *ex officio* by the Surgeon General: board member of the National Library of Medicine, the Uniformed Services University of the Health Sciences, the Gorgas Memorial Institute of Tropical Medicine, and the National Council for International Health; representative to the House of Delegates of the American Medical Association along with the surgeons general of the Army, Navy, and Air Force and the chief medical officer of the Veterans Administration; and liaison to the Merchant Marine through the Seamen's Health Improvement Project (SHIP).

There were some very small, but very special, places where the Commissioned Corps made big contributions to medicine, such as at the nation's only leprosy hospital. The Hansen's Disease Center in Carville, Louisiana, on a bend of the Mississippi River at the site of an antebellum sugar plantation, maintains a public-sector link with the Armed Forces Institute of Pathology and a private-sector link with the American Leprosy Mission. Although leprosy has almost vanished from the United States (there are at present only about five thousand patients), in Asia seventeen thousand new cases arise each week. Carville's experience in protecting leprosy patients from leg amputations has brought new hope to American diabetics. I became convinced that if every American diabetic threatened with a foot or leg amputation could be treated as we treat leprosy patients at Carville, we would be able to reduce the diabetic amputations from forty thousand per year to four thousand.

But, as successful as we were in these small steps to utilize the talents and skills of the Commissioned Corps, it became obvious to me that a piecemeal approach would not do. In early 1987 I concluded sadly that OMB would not have to kill the Commissioned Corps; it would die by itself. Morale in the corps had continued to languish as its ranks became depleted and as officers in the corps assigned to the various Public Health Service agencies (like the National Institutes of Health) came to view themselves more as agency personnel and less as Commissioned Corps officers, distinguished from their civilian colleagues only by a different pay scale. Recruitment of minorities and women lagged behind. There was little sense of belonging to a uniformed, disciplined, mobile service: The Corps had lost its *esprit.* I determined that it needed revitalization, and I turned to four people who made it happen: Secretary of Health and Human Services Otis Bowen, who shared my vision for the corps; Assistant Secretary for Health Robert Windom, who gave his authority; Bowen's chief of staff, Thomas Burke, whose military background and determination flattened many an obstacle in the path; and my own chief of staff, Edward R. Martin, the quintessential commissioned officer who deserves the major credit. Ed brought superb management skills and innovative thought to my endeavors. He gave valuable counsel and understood the impact of our decisions on the country, the Public Health Service, and me.

We revitalized the Commissioned Corps so that it became a dynamic, flexible, mobile, responsive, professional career system for health professionals who wished to dedicate themselves to the problems and programs of our Public Health Service. We knew we were on the right track when our most consistent antagonist in OMB, David Klineberg, admitted, "How could I be opposed to your revitalization plan when you are doing what I have wanted somebody to do for fourteen years?" I look back on the revitalization of the Commissioned Corps of the United States Public Health Service as one of the most significant accomplishments of my tenure as Surgeon General.

Part IV

Great Issues

Chapter 8

Smoking

As Surgeon General, I took as my mission nothing less than improving the health of the entire nation. I started with smoking. "A thousand people will stop smoking today. Their funerals will be held sometime during the next three or four days."

That is how I would begin my lecture on smoking. It gets people's attention. Why have Americans been so complacent about tobacco, about nicotine addiction? If any other substance, legal or illegal, were killing half a million people a year, the public would be up in arms, demanding action from Congress.

About 45 million Americans still smoke cigarettes, even though health officials have long identified cigarette smoking as the main reason why Americans get sick and die too soon. Cigarette smoking is associated with more death and illness than drugs, alcohol, automobile accidents, and AIDS *combined.*

Smoking is the primary or associated cause of many cancers, not only of the lung but also of the mouth, larynx, esophagus, stomach, and bladder. The cancer statistics are staggering: Male smokers are more than twenty-two times as likely to die of lung cancer than male non-smokers; among women smokers the risk of lung cancer is twelve times greater than among nonsmokers. By 1991, smoking-related cancer deaths climbed to 175,000 annually, or 35 percent of all cancer deaths. These are "excess" or premature deaths, deaths that have tragically cut short the lives of tobacco users.

• Smoking is one of the major risk factors in the development of coronary heart disease and stroke.

• Smoking produces chronic obstructive lung disease, including bronchitis and emphysema. A terrible and debilitating disease, emphysema is found almost exclusively in smokers.

• Smoking is not only dangerous for the smoker, but also dangerous for the nonsmoker who inhales environmental tobacco smoke—sometimes called passive smoking. Passive smoking causes many diseases, including cancer. Simple separation of smoker from nonsmoker in the same room does not protect the nonsmoker from the harmful effects of environmental tobacco smoke. Children who are exposed to passive smoking have a slower start in life. They have more upper respiratory infections, they have more diagnoses of pneumonia, they miss more time in school; some of the effects of their retarded development can be measured for as long as six years after exposure.

• Smoking has been targeted as the primary public health problem in the United States. And, at long last, the battle against smoking is—slowly—being won.

American attitudes toward smoking have changed, especially in recent years. In 1964 over half of the American adult population smoked. When I took office in 1981, 33 percent of adult Americans smoked. When I left office in 1989, a little more than 26 percent of adult Americans smoked. If I had anything to do with the decrease in smoking, it gives me a sense of genuine satisfaction. I tried hard, and I enjoyed the support of a growing army of nonsmokers, anti-smokers, and—best of all—former smokers.

The signs of change are everywhere. I certainly noticed it in my own professional circles. Fifteen years ago at medical meetings—attended by doctors, who should have known better—the air was blue with smoke. Today you rarely see a physician smoking.

The anti-smoking achievements in the United States—the most successful of any country's—reflect the combined efforts of private citizens, private organizations, health professionals, and the government.

The role of the government has been important in both positive and negative ways. On the positive side, the government has raised excise and sales taxes on cigarettes, making cigarettes increasingly a painful pocketbook issue for smokers. Governments—federal, state, and local—have also severely restricted the areas where people can smoke in public. It is now illegal to smoke on most public conveyances, in most retail stores, in virtually all government buildings, in all theaters and sport centers, and in many places where people work. A growing number of restaurants have either banned smoking or set aside nonsmoking areas. The government has also ordered five new and stiffer health warnings to be placed on cigarette packages and in cigarette advertisements in rotation.

But the government, especially the federal government, has also hurt the effort against smoking and tobacco. Those federal taxes on tobacco, though increased, have not kept up with inflation. More serious, federal politicians have excluded tobacco and tobacco products from certain regulatory activities covering hazardous or toxic substances, and from most packaging and labeling restrictions except for the Surgeon General's warning. Tobacco is considered to be neither a food nor a drug nor a cosmetic; therefore it is a unique substance, virtually outside regulatory control.

All Americans concerned about the ill effects of smoking owe a great debt to the efforts of private nonprofit organizations such as the American Lung Association, the American Cancer Society, and the American Heart Association. These groups have been involved not only in educating the public about the hazards of smoking, but also in sponsoring programs to help people stop smoking. Private industry has done more and more—though not yet enough—to help employees to quit smoking (and, incidentally, to quit needing smoking-related health insurance benefits).

My first step in the anti-smoking crusade came with the 1982 *Surgeon General's Report on Smoking and Health,* then the most serious indictment of cigarette smoking the Public Health Service had ever made. During those long months of my confirmation struggle I had heard words here and there about this upcoming report, but no one had thought to include me in its preparation. It was not until the early weeks of 1982 that I began to realize that I would have to present the report at my first major press conference since assuming office.

I looked up Don Shopland to find out what was going on. Don, the acting director of the Office on Smoking and Health, had been on the staff of the original Advisory Committee to the Surgeon General way back in 1963–64, when the first Surgeon General's report on smoking had been released, and he probably had the best memory on smoking of anyone in the government. He was an indefatigable worker, and I knew immediately that I would enjoy working with him in following years, when I would play an active part in the preparation of the

Surgeon General's Report. Eventually he would become one of the first recipients of the Surgeon General's Medallion, the highest award I could give.

As the scheduled date for the press conference, February 22, 1982, drew closer, my tension began to mount. I spent the weekend before the Monday press conference reviewing the report once more, going over my briefing book, and, I admit, dealing with no small amount of nervousness. My concerns were not only for my own reputation, but also for the reputation of the office of the Surgeon General. Maintaining the integrity of the office of the Surgeon General had become one of my objectives from the first time my name was associated with the office. Previous Surgeons General of the Public Health Service had not blundered; I profited from that, and I wanted to uphold the high traditions of the office.

The night before the conference I had the same disturbing dream that had visited me regularly for the previous fifty-five years. I am about to go into German class to take an exam. Already on the dean's list, I have not been required to attend classes; I have not studied, either. When I sit down to take the German exam, I discover to my horror that everything on the page is in French.

Shaking off the same old frightening dream, I awoke long before dawn, reviewed my papers, paused for my customary breakfast and Bible reading with Betty, and left for my office at the Humphrey Building, just a few hundred yards down the Mall from the Capitol.

Sometimes little things make the biggest impression, and when I walked into the auditorium of the Humphrey Building to meet the press for the first time, I noticed that the thirty or so microphones on the podium left no room for my notes. (It would take me three years to get someone to build a little extension onto the podium.)

After a brief introduction by Assistant Secretary of Health Ed Brandt, I explained that the 1982 *Report on Smoking and Health* focused on the clear relationship between smoking and cancer. Thirty percent of all cancer deaths, I said, were attributable to smoking. The 1982 report identified cigarette smoking as a major cause not only of lung cancer, but also of cancers of the larynx, oral cavity, and esophagus and confirmed it as a contributing factor in the development of cancers of the bladder, pancreas, and kidney; new studies also suggested an association between smoking and cancers of the stomach and cervix. The report concluded by pointing to the elevated risk of cancer associated with passive smoking.

Although the report dealt most specifically with smoking and cancer,

I also stressed the public health concerns stemming from the overall responsibility of smoking for nearly 400,000 deaths annually. I explained that smoking exacted $13 billion annually in health care expenses and over $25 billion in lost production and wages. I said then for the first time what I have repeated so often since: "Cigarette smoking is the chief preventable cause of death in our society."

At the question-and-answer session after my report, Brandt and I were asked if we had ever smoked. Brandt admitted that he had smoked until a year before, when he had assumed the position of assistant secretary of health; I said I had given up my occasional pipe a decade earlier. In my most widely reported remark, I said, "If I were a smoker of a pipe, cigars, or cigarettes, and were reasonably intelligent and had read this report, I would long since have quit." My first major exposure on national television came in the wake of the 1982 report on smoking and cancer.

The report, my press conference, and my picture received front-page coverage from most major newspapers, and I began to see the valuable ways in which the Surgeon General's position could be used to advance the health of the nation with moral suasion. I also realized that for the first time since my arrival in Washington, I had begun to earn back the credibility I had possessed in my previous surgical career. This marked the turning point in my relationship with the press. They had arrived at my first press conference displaying their preconfirmation hostility, and they left neutral. The next press conference saw them arrive neutral, and leave favorably impressed. Eventually, the press even became friendly, and in 1986, when I returned to the public eye following neck surgery, some even applauded. I thanked them and wondered if I were blushing—under my beard, of course.

I felt I was off to a great start in the fight against smoking, and I thanked the many people whose work on the 1982 report enabled it to be so well received. I owed an even greater debt of gratitude to the Surgeon General who had started it all, Luther Terry, and to his successors, all of whom had kept up the fight.

While the report on smoking that Dr. Terry had released on January 11, 1964, was a landmark in public education, it was not the initial spur for research linking smoking with major diseases. Indeed, by 1964, there were already seven thousand articles in world biomedical literature dealing with that link. It was after reviewing those research papers that the Surgeon General's advisory committee came to the following conclusions for its landmark 1964 report:

1. Men who smoked had an overall higher mortality rate than men who did not.

2. Smokers had increased mortality rates from coronary heart disease, cerebral vascular disease, and other cardiovascular conditions.

3. Cigarettes were a major cause of chronic bronchitis and contributed to the high mortality of emphysema.

4. Cigarette smoking was the major cause of lung cancer in men and maybe for women also.

5. Smoking, at the very least, was a contributing cause of esophageal, bladder, and pancreatic cancer, and pipe smoking contributed to cancer of the lip and the oral cavity.

6. Cigarette smoking is a health hazard of sufficient importance in the United States to warrant appropriate remedial action.

The committee wanted to be sure the message sunk in, but without premature press leaks or distortions. So when they held the press conference to release the report, after the reporters were seated, they locked the doors, gave the reporters ninety minutes to read the report, answered their questions, and then turned them loose on the country.

The first remedial action was the passage of a law requiring all cigarette packages to carry the following message: "Caution: Cigarette Smoking May Be Hazardous to Your Health." Six years later, Congress enacted a sweeping law that banned cigarette advertising from radio and television. The new law also toughened the health warning on cigarette packages to read, "Warning: The Surgeon General Has Determined that Cigarette Smoking Is Dangerous to Your Health."

Meanwhile, more than nineteen thousand studies confirmed the linkage of cigarette smoking to pancreatic, stomach, kidney, and cervical cancers, as well as identified cigarettes as the chief culprit in arteriosclerosis, peptic ulcer, and complications of pregnancy.

Researchers charted the ways these diseases had reflected the social history of smoking. American men started to smoke in great numbers following World War I, while women started to smoke in similar numbers during and after World War II. By 1990, after more than two decades of warnings about the dangers of smoking, the number of illnesses and deaths due to smoking had leveled off for men, but continued to rise for women. Among women lung cancer had surpassed breast cancer as the leading cancer death. Women will soon make up more than half of all smokers.

Following the lead of the initial reports, Congress demanded that an annual report on smoking and health be submitted by the Surgeon

General. Officially entitled *Health Consequences of Smoking,* each report is made by the Surgeon General, and then as mandated by law, transmitted by the secretary of Health and Human Services to the Speaker of the House of Representatives and the president of the Senate.

These reports have boasted an unassailable data base, tracking more than two million individuals in all fifty states. Each report is prepared by the Office on Smoking and Health working in close collaboration with a wide range of scientists in and out of government in whatever field is the subject for that year. And with each Surgeon General's report has come the grim news that more and more deaths were attributable to smoking.

Cancer and heart disease top the list of the health concerns of most Americans. The public recognized smoking's connection with cancer early on, but the connection between smoking and heart disease was not widely known. That changed, I hope, with the 1983 Surgeon General's report, *Health Consequences of Smoking: Cardiovascular Disease,* which stressed the proven link between smoking and heart disease. Many Americans were surprised to realize that smoking caused even more deaths from heart disease than from cancer. Heart disease kills about 565,000 Americans annually, about 170,000 of whom (30 percent) are smokers. The report indicated that the average smoker had a 70 percent greater chance of dying of heart disease than a nonsmoker. Heavy smokers, those who consume two packs or more a day, suffer a 200 percent higher mortality rate. Unless smoking habits changed, the report said, 24 million Americans, or nearly 10 percent of people currently alive, would die prematurely because of heart disease caused by smoking. The risk was ten times higher for women who both smoked and used contraceptive pills. Warning that the 55 million Americans who smoke thirty or more cigarettes a day mount an incredible assault on the national health, I nonetheless tried to provide some positive reinforcement by noting that since the first Surgeon General's report on smoking in 1964, the percentage of smokers in the general population had declined from 41.7 percent to 32.6 percent. In other words, the decision to stop smoking—or never to start—had saved 290,000 lives.

The 1984 report, *Health Consequences of Smoking: Chronic Obstructive Lung Disease,* presented clear conclusions: Cigarette smoking is the major cause of illness and death from chronic obstructive lung disease in the United States for both men and women. At the report's press conference I tried to inject a touch of humor while making a serious point. I asked for a volunteer, someone who was trying to quit smoking, to come forward for a small "reward." (A California philanthropist, Joseph Shane, with whom I was later to travel to Israel for a private sector anti-smoking campaign, had provided me with some special buttons that I was about to use for the first time.) Bill Hines, a reporter for *The Chicago Sun Times*, pushed forward his wife, Judith Randal, a reporter for *The Daily News* in New York. I gave her one of my newly minted blue buttons with the slogan "The Surgeon General asked me *personally* to stop smoking." Then I promised her one of my red "And I Did" buttons to go along with it if she earned it. A few other reporters came up to me for their own buttons. I was always tickled when I could reward people with the red button of achievement when they stopped smoking. And of course, they felt even better than I did.

I released only one smoking report with some misgivings and uneasiness. The major point of the 1985 report on *Smoking and the Workplace* was that "For the majority of American workers, cigarette smoking represents a greater cause of death and disability than their workplace environment. . . . In those work sites where well-established disease outcomes occur, smoking control and reduction and exposure to hazardous agents are effective, compatible, and occasionally synergistic approaches to the reduction of disease risk for the individual worker." The report was referring to risk factors such as exposure to coal dust, asbestos, and cotton fibers.

The AFL-CIO criticized the report, saying it would make it easier for companies to avoid responsibility for workplace health problems. I countered by saying that the AFL-CIO criticism was based on their misunderstanding the report, and that nowhere along the line had we downplayed the importance of protecting workers from hazardous substances of the work site. I could not understand the opposition of the AFL-CIO to the publication of my final report. I still don't understand it.

I believe this report was leaked. I can't prove it, but I think staffers in the secretary's office bent to pressure from the tobacco lobby. I could never find out whether the White House was involved. I was discouraged to learn about the cozy relationship between tobacco management and labor unions, especially the Bakery, Confectionery and Tobacco Workers International Union, whose jobs, as one reporter put it, "depend upon a society gorged on cookies, cream cakes, and cigarettes."

There was one skirmish in the smoking wars from which I was

relieved to be excluded. It began when Ed Brandt and I, along with other health officials, testified in 1982 before the House of Representatives' Subcommittee on Health, chaired by Congressman Henry Waxman of California, the same committee that had blocked my nomination for four bitter months the year before. The issue before the subcommittee was a bill that would change the current Surgeon General's warning on cigarette labels and advertising—"Warning: The Surgeon General Has Determined That Cigarette Smoking Is Dangerous to Your Health"—to a series of rotating warnings against the specific dangers of smoking (heart disease, cancer, emphysema, the hazard to unborn children of pregnant women who smoke) and the benefits of quitting no matter how long one had smoked. When Brandt and I testified in favor of the bill before a receptive subcommittee, Brandt stated that such legislation was a "high priority" of the administration.

Immediately, and predictably, the tobacco industry, in its testimony before the subcommittee, dusted off its own research alleging the minimal health consequences of smoking. Under questioning from Waxman, however, R. J. Reynolds Tobacco Company's Edward Horrigan, conceded that their industry advertising budget was more than $900 million annually, compared to about $70 million for research.

Down in tobacco country, North Carolina governor Jim Hunt, who was running against Jesse Helms for his Senate seat, called for my resignation, charging that I was "doing worse than [Joseph] Califano," the Carter administration Cabinet secretary who had run a strong anti-smoking campaign. Hunt also criticized Helms for laboring so diligently for my appointment.

People often wondered how Jesse Helms and I got along. We had stood together against abortion for many years, and in the beginning he and Senator Orrin Hatch had been my strongest supporters. I would never have become Surgeon General without them. But I did take on the tobacco industry, so deeply entrenched in North Carolina.

At first, Jesse Helms never seemed to let my opposition to tobacco intrude in our relationship. When *Decision* magazine published a profile on me in 1986, Jesse Helms wrote an affectionate note, and a year later, when a North Carolina newspaper carried an editorial alleging that my strong stand against smoking had cost me Helms' support, Jesse immediately wrote me a letter in which he said, "Nothing could break up the friendship that you and I have." Once, at a Washington reception, not long after a devastating report on the health consequences of smoking, he patted me on the back and said, "Keep up the good work, son; you are doing the Lord's work." We met from time to time at various Washington social functions, and even though I wondered if he opposed my stands on AIDS issues, we remained cordial. Then, in 1988, at about the same time that Helms phoned me to ask a personal medical favor for one of his staffers, he made an official request that I be investigated by the Inspector General to see if I had timed the release of the report on nicotine addiction to coincide with a tobacco company liability trial. It was a ludicrous charge, and I think he knew it. But I never heard from him again.

Just as the administration's commitment to health was winning widespread approval in the press, the powerful Office of Management and Budget caved in to pressure from tobacco state congressmen. The next time Brandt and I went to testify on the Hill, this time before the Senate committee sponsoring a bill similar to the one we had supported the week before in the House, Brandt's testimony made it clear that he had been forced to back down from his earlier support of the legislation proposing the more specific warning labels. Now, he said, the administration's earlier support of the measure had been changed to "no position."

I was as surprised as anyone. When I had arrived in the anteroom of the hearing chamber that morning, I had seen Senator Hatch and Brandt looking very grim. Brandt walked over to me and said very quietly that he had been ordered not to support the bill. I replied, "What do you mean? We've already supported it in our testimony before the House." Brandt informed me that OMB had decided to oppose the bill the night before. So, without even knowing what the White House position was, much less why it was, I walked into the hearing chamber with Brandt. When it became clear to the committee that Brandt had backed off from supporting the bill, Senator Packwood questioned him aggressively, attempting to find out what had caused this abrupt about-face. Brandt squirmed uncomfortably under the questioning. When specifically asked if he had been instructed how to testify, he looked straight ahead and remained silent. Senator Packwood, after three attempts, excused him on the basis that he was playing the role of the good soldier. I was very uncomfortable and relieved I had not been placed in Brandt's position, because I may have chosen to resign.

I did not assume the position of Surgeon General with the clear intention of being such an active opponent of tobacco, but after I studied the incontrovertible truths about the health hazards of smoking, and then became at first dumbfounded and then plainly furious at the tobacco industry for attempting to obfuscate and trivialize this extraordinarily important public health information.

How could the tobacco industry dare to dismiss as unfounded and unproven the absolutely clear connection between smoking and heart disease: between smoking and death from stroke; between smoking and cancer of the lung, the mouth, the esophagus, and the stomach; and between smoking and a dozen or more serious, debilitating, exhausting, expensive, and humiliating diseases?

How could it do that? The answer was—it just did. The tobacco industry is accountable to no one. It flaunts its ability to buy its way into the marketplace of ideas and pollute it with its false and deadly information.

Tobacco has been associated not only with disease and death, but also with money. That is why it has so long enjoyed special treatment. Tobacco was the cash crop that financed much of the American Revolution—those Virginia planters fetched a greater return for tobacco leaves than did the hardy New Englanders for their pumpkins. And Congress has been held hostage ever since.

Despite sinister associations, first with slavery, later with cancer and heart disease, American tobacco has always enjoyed government protection. The tobacco lobby is overwhelmingly powerful. It has seemingly unlimited funding. Somehow or other it impacts on the lives of almost every member of Congress. The tobacco industry contributes to political action committees, pays congressmen for lectures, and lobbies congressmen to support tobacco-related legislation.

One congressman from a tobacco-producing state, whose name I've somewhat contemptuously repressed, called me at home several nights after the release of the 1983 *Surgeon General's Report on Smoking and Health.* Our conversation ended when he said, "I don't give a good goddamn how many people die of cancer or anything else that you say is associated with tobacco. All I want is jobs and prosperity for constituents in my district. Why don't you lay off all this nonsense about smoking and health?"

The tobacco interests have the ability to reach into government and affect decision-making. When the Environmental Protection Agency was pulling together a sixteen-member panel to assure the accuracy and objectivity of two of its yet unpublished studies on passive smoking, tobacco lobbyists pressured the agency to dismiss from the panel Dr. David Burns of the University of California, San Diego, probably the most highly regarded authority on the issue of passive smoking. He was reinstated only after public outcry. But then *The New York Times* reported that of the sixteen members on the panel, six of the scientists had ties with the tobacco industry. Many people wondered how such a panel could deliver an unbiased opinion.

One tobacco company's promotion of its smokeless cigarette infuriated me. In September 1987 I noticed a "Cancer Meeting" on my calendar. I had no idea what this meant, and my secretaries couldn't remember making the strange notation. I could hardly believe it when I was found myself at a meeting where I would be introduced to a smokeless cigarette by R. J. Reynolds. Then I was amazed to discover that two of the people representing the nicotine merchants were former high-ranking officials of the Food and Drug Administration: Peter Barton Hutt and Arthur Hull Hayes, M.D., former commissioner of the FDA. I was dismayed that they would rather switch sides than fight. No amount of money could ever entice me to represent a tobacco company under any circumstances.

Although most people concerned about the health problems associated with tobacco focused—rightly—on smoking, even when there was no smoke there was fire. My efforts against smokeless tobacco (most people call it "chewing tobacco") formed a microcosm of the struggle between health and tobacco.

Smokeless tobacco comes in the form of chewing tobacco, dry snuff, and moist snuff (sometimes packaged in paper like tea bags). Just like smoking tobacco, smokeless tobacco is addictive, is protected by a strong lobby, has its own "institute," is advertised to the most vulnerable people, and is heavily promoted to children despite laws forbidding its sale to minors. In some parts of the country it enjoys cultural approval, as many boys are introduced to smokeless tobacco by fathers, grandfathers, and uncles, who are probably unaware of the risk. Its manufacturers have knowingly sunk to the level of introducing an addictive drug to youngsters. At state fairs they have been known to sponsor tobacco-spitting contests by age groups, with four-year-olds starting off.

In the fall of 1984, someone from Congressman Jack Kemp's office called my secretary, asking if I would meet with a Mr. Nick Buoniconti. I knew Buoniconti had been a professional football player, and I guessed that Kemp probably knew him from his own days with the Buffalo Bills. The caller from Kemp's office told me that Buoniconti was representing the tobacco interests, but that he was a "good guy." Because of Kemp's earlier support for me, I agreed to see the man. Kemp called a little later, leaving a message that although he did not necessarily share all of Buoniconti's views, nonetheless he was a reasonable gentleman whom Kemp knew from their common work with parents for drug-free youths. I wondered if Kemp knew that nicotine is a highly addictive drug. Then I learned that Buoniconti would be accompanied by Lou Bantel, president of the U.S. Tobacco Company.

The next step in the carefully orchestrated pageant was a call from Patty Tyson, special assistant to Secretary of Health Margaret Heckler. (Dick Schweiker had resigned after eighteen months and Representative Heckler was his replacement. She and I never had the same kind of close working relationship I had enjoyed with Schweiker.) I was told that Heckler knew I was meeting with Bantel, a large contributor to the Reagan campaign, so would I handle him in my usual charming manner? The message was clear, but I did not know whether it came from Heckler or the White House.

I wanted to get more information on the visitors and their mission. A few phone calls revealed the real agenda: (1) Kemp seemed to want only that I let Buoniconti know that Kemp had called me on his behalf (the issue to be discussed didn't seem to matter); (2) the topic of conversation would most likely be moist snuff (75 percent of the world supply of moist snuff was made by the U.S. Tobacco Company); (3) the company was a defendant in a $19 million suit in Oklahoma brought by parents of Shawn Marsee, a teenage snuff user who had died of cancer of the mouth.

When I first met with Buoniconti and Bantel, the tobacco president, looking like a courtier of Louis XIV, took an antique sterling silver snuff box out of his pocket and tucked some tobacco between his lower gum and cheek, the very spot of the original site of the cancer that had killed Shawn Marsee. I didn't know which bothered me more; his arrogance or his insensitivity. I listened to the same old spiel, that tobacco was being incorrectly blamed for cancer. I told these two men that they were wrong, that my conclusions were guided by good science, and that I strongly objected to their advertising aimed at young people. As I knew it would, the meeting ended, as it began, in disagreement.

I wanted to fight back against the slippery tactics of the smokeless tobacco industry, but my efforts were being thwarted by Secretary Heckler's obstructive inactivity. We needed an advisory committee to help me in setting up a task force to investigate the health hazards of smokeless tobacco and put the scientific stance against smokeless tobacco on a par with that against smoking. But my repeated requests to Secretary Heckler's staff remained unanswered for more than six weeks. Times like these tried my patience, and I wearied at having to cover for distracted leadership that allowed important public health concerns to languish, possibly for political reasons. I knew that the tobacco industry could be exerting pressure in Heckler's office. After all, Mike Deaver, once a member of the triumvirate surrounding Reagan, was running the public relations firm that handled the Smokeless Tobacco Institute.

So I took matters into my own hands. I met with people from the Federal Trade Commission, found they were on my side, and told them of my plan to announce the appointment of a task force to investigate the health effects of smokeless tobacco. Joe Cullen of the Prevention Division of the National Cancer Institute agreed to become chair of the task force and Jim Wyngaarten, director of NIH, and Vince De Vita, director of the National Cancer Institute, approved NCI's staffing of the project.

Meanwhile, Connecticut senator Lowell Weicker asked me to meet in his Capitol office with Buoniconti and another representative from the U.S. Tobacco Company, which was based in Weicker's state. I had decided to keep as cool as possible, hoping that Buoniconti would lose his composure just as he had shortly before on *60 Minutes*, when he was being interrogated about the health hazards of his product. Sure enough, in Weicker's office, his voice got higher and louder and he seemed almost hysterical as he trotted out the old cliché so dear to the tobacco industry when it is short on scientific information: that the scientific studies that demonstrate the hazards of smoking are "anecdotal." I wondered if Buoniconti had just learned the word, because he used it repeatedly, referring to all the information on smoking used by the government as "anecdotal." The diatribe went on so long that even Weicker, who was supposed to be sympathetic to his constituent, made some remarks favorable to the side of health. Just before our half hour came to an end, Joe Cullen, who was with me, disarmed Buoniconti by making some complimentary remarks about his football exploits. Then Buoniconti started a new subject, relating how his wife had quit smoking easily, proving that nicotine couldn't be addictive. I chose that moment to stand up to leave, pointed right at Buoniconti, and said, "That, sir, is anecdotal." Everyone in the room laughed, except Buoniconti. As I shook Weicker's hand before leaving, his legislative aide smiled at me and said, "You won the first round!"

Even though governmental wheels grind slowly, we finally got our smokeless tobacco committee, congressional hearings, and eventually the Comprehensive Smokeless Tobacco Health Education Act of 1986, which provided for public education concerning the health hazards of smokeless tobacco. The scientific conclusions were clear: A careful examination of the relevant epidemiological, experimental, and clinical data indicated that the oral use of smokeless tobacco represents a significant health risk. It is not a safe substitute for smoking cigarettes. It can cause cancer and a number of noncancerous oral conditions and can lead to nicotine addiction and dependence.

But a convincing report and a law about education did not end the threat to health. I thought I had four questions on tobacco (smoking and smokeless) on the 1990 census form, but then learned that the OMB had axed the four questions from the census form only when it was too late to appeal. I'll never know whether they buckled under tobacco industry pressure. And the U.S. Tobacco Company, looking for new markets abroad, got Connecticut Senators Christopher Dodd and Weicker, along with Senators Bob Kasten and Robert Dole, to attempt to put pressure on the government of Hong Kong to abandon its wise ban on importing smokeless tobacco. I imagine they thought it was more important to save a Connecticut firm's profits than Asian lives.

The fight continued on other fronts. Shawn Marsee's mother lost her suit against the U.S. Tobacco Company, but eventually we were able to get Surgeon General's warnings on smokeless tobacco, in part because Shawn had repeatedly said to his mother, "It couldn't be dangerous or there would be a warning on the package." When Greg Connolly, a Massachusetts dentist and health officer, learned that Shawn (and many other youngsters) said, "It couldn't be dangerous or baseball players wouldn't use it," he made it a personal mission to ask pro baseball players to be better models for kids. There was immediate compliance. Bubble gum was in. Then came the relapses. But the second time around many players quit when they learned what the stakes were for kids.

The deeper I probed into the murky, smoky world of tobacco power, the more I realized how extensive was the grasp of its tentacles. On the board of the American Medical Association sat two men who, it was ferreted out by concerned medical students, owned a tobacco farm. The television networks have knuckled under to tobacco power, as when CBS suddenly refused to show the American Cancer Society's public service announcement that showed a fetus smoking because it was "too graphic." When I heard about it, I thought of all the graphic violence and sex that CBS so willingly airs. And, of course, everywhere there were reminders about the cozy relationship between tobacco and politics. At Republican fund-raiser dinners each table offered free cigarettes, complete with the president's profile embossed in gold. At the

White House mess those free cigarette packages came stamped with the presidential seal.

Fortunately, sometimes the blatant tactics of the tobacco industry backfired. In a not-too-subtle threat to magazines and purchasers of advertising, Philip Morris ran a series of ads noting the "economic force" of American smokers. A few days later the political cartoonist Herblock countered with a cartoon showing how smokers help the economy by giving business to doctors, hospitals, and undertakers.

As Surgeon General I usually enjoyed a good working relationship with the military, but I had a few battles with them. One that I didn't win was about smoking. I hope I didn't lose it altogether. Many Americans thought there was only one Surgeon General, but there were three others, the surgeons general of the armed forces. Each of them was gracious and helpful to me as I learned my job and then discharged my responsibilities; they all had known me in my former surgical incarnation. I tried to do what I could do to help them tackle a problem we shared: the high rate of smoking among military personnel. The armed forces don't have to worry about the health problems of smokers in the long term; those health problems end up much later in the Veterans Administration and in the civilian health care system, where we all pay for them. Too many soldiers, sailors, and airmen were smoking: While in 1984, 36.7 percent of American men in civilian life smoked, 52 percent of military personnel smoked.

I thought I saw an opening in 1984 when General John Wickham, Jr., Army Chief of Staff, decided to ban happy hours with their high consumption of liquor in military facilities. I sent him a congratulatory letter and suggested that "with cigarette smoking the cause of 350,000 deaths per year, isn't it time to change the policy of cheap cigarettes in Army facilities?" I never got an answer.

One aspect of the problem was the availability of cheap cigarettes in PXs and commissaries around the world. They were cheap because they were exempt from federal or state taxes. I felt deeply disappointed when Secretary of Defense Caspar Weinberger announced that commissaries would continue to sell cigarettes at a discount rather than to follow the advice of his own assistant secretary of defense for health affairs, Bud Mayer. When I complained to the Pentagon, I was told that eliminating discount cigarettes "would be perceived by some troops as a reduction of benefits." Many of them would pay dearly for those "benefits" years down the road. Although there was some progress a few years later when military policy changed to allow the commanding officer of a post to establish smoking policy, this usually followed the personal smoking habits of the commandant, strict in some places and lax in others. In general, though, the military continued to put the lives of its troops at risk by making it too easy for them to smoke.

Overall, I knew the anti-smoking campaign was making progress, but I also knew we needed a new vision. I was sure the tobacco companies were regathering for a counteroffensive. I wanted to beat them to the punch. I knew I had more allies than ever before among nonsmokers, in the health community, and in government. So I decided to challenge the country.

Early in 1983 I assessed the nonsmoking United States to be composed of many different types of nonsmokers: those who never thought much about it, those who were former smokers, environmentalists who wanted to rid the atmosphere of tobacco smoke, and that small group who correctly believed that passive smoking was actually dangerous to their health. Organized medicine was increasingly vocal about the health hazards of smoking, and the voluntary organizations (the American Lung Association, the American Cancer Society, and the American Heart Association) had formed the Coalition on Smoking OR Health and could mount a tremendous voluntary effort on demand. The time had come for a bold initiative.

I decided to make a public call for "A Smoke-Free Society by the Year 2000"—with the appropriate logo SFS-2000. After first discussing the idea with Betty, I mentioned it only to my colleagues: Jim Dickson; Ted Cron, my personal assistant; and Matt Meyers, executive officer of the Coalition on Smoking OR Health. Earlier I had raised the idea only very generally with Susan Attis and William McBeath of the American Public Health Association, and I had immediately regretted it, because I knew if my plan leaked to the administration and thence to the tobacco industry, some way would be found to block the effort. That never happened.

Trying to do too many things at once, I spent my spare time at the 1984 World Health Assembly meetings in Geneva closeted away in an Alpine chalet, working on my speech to announce the goal of a smoke-free society by the year 2000. In the usual packets of mail crossing the Atlantic from Washington to Geneva came some words of caution from Ted Cron, who was concerned about my incurring the wrath of the White House and Margaret Heckler for my SFS-2000 initiative. My brief Washington career had made me more sensitive than I might have been to the need for political savvy, but I decided I was not about to be hamstrung by politics, no matter what the risk might be.

For years it had been my custom, when I began to doubt a decision I had made, to pray about it. Often I had been convinced that the Lord had sent me a confirming sign. I certainly felt that way after my day of doubt in Geneva. I went to speak with Dave Wilson, communications officer at our mission in Geneva, and in the course of our conversation about other issues he told me of a recent discussion he had had with Jeane Kirkpatrick, the U.S. ambassador to the United Nations. While she had been in Geneva on U.N. business, the president had made an announcement with which she disagreed. Wilson told me that she had turned to him and said that in government you had to move in the direction you thought was right and let the chips fall where they may.

With neither budget nor line authority, I could do little on my own to implement a plan. But what if I called upon American society itself, the people, to make America smoke-free by the year 2000? With this in mind, I finished penning my "Smoke-Free Society–2000" speech and I arranged for it to be typed and photocopied at the Washington office of the American Lung Association. To my knowledge, Betty, Matt Myers, the typist, and I were the only ones who knew of the existence of the speech. It would never have survived the smoky clearance process.

I had been giving speeches since I was twenty-three years old, but never before had I spent so much effort and concern on a single one. I chose the right year to present it: 1984, a time when the American majority was getting fed up with the smoke in their eyes, the twentieth anniversary of the Surgeon General's first report on smoking. I also chose the right month: May, an interlude in the constant barrage of news about the presidential primaries. And I chose the right audience: a combined meeting in Miami of the American Lung Association and the American Thoracic Society.

My speech made clear that this was not just another job for the Surgeon General, this was a job for America. And I said that when I called for a smoke-free society by the year 2000, I was not advocating totalitarianism, I was not calling for laws. I was calling upon nonsmokers to stand up for their rights. And I was calling upon smokers to respect those rights. When I called for a smoke-free society, I defined "society" as any group of Americans getting together for any purpose. I meant that smokers should not feel free to light up in the presence of other people without their permission.

The audience in Miami who were the first to hear my call for a smoke-free society were on board right away. Then I carried the call to other groups all across the country: the Boy Scouts, the Girl Scouts, the Respiratory Therapists, and many others. Everywhere that I carried the message, the people responded with enthusiasm and dedication.

I heard from citizens all over the country who wanted to be part of the effort. For example, John Capozzi, a Connecticut philanthropist, produced thousands of black enamel little pins shaped like stop signs, with gold SFS-2000 lettering. Each lapel pin was large enough to be seen from across the room, but the letters were small enough so that one had to bend down and then ask, "What does that stand for?" The people who wore the pins were only too glad to answer. There was no doubt about it, SFS-2000 struck a respondent note in American society.

Then I asked the Coalition on Smoking OR Health to take steps to insure that the high school graduating class in the year 2000 was a smoke-free class. They got to work right away and by 1988 had begun to implement a twelve-year curriculum, starting in 1988–89 with first-graders, the next year with grades 1 and 2, the next year with grades 1–3, and so on, until by the time the youngsters who started anti-smoking education in first grade graduated from high school in 2000, they would have received anti-smoking messages throughout each of their school years.

Of all the public appearances I would make, few topped the times I would speak to youngsters at school, explaining the dangers of smoking and asking them to take a pledge never to smoke, to turn their backs on anyone who offered them a cigarette. But I had to make sure that the children got the message straight. In Honolulu I was joined by Governor John Waihee's wife, Lynn—an enthusiastic ally in the SFS-2000 campaign—on a visit to an elementary school where the students had studied the SFS-2000 anti-smoking curriculum. After a few minutes of banter and giggles I said, "I know your teachers have taught you very well about what's going to happen a long time from now when you graduate from high school in the year 2000. Who can tell me what's going to happen in the year 2000?"

A hundred hands went up and I pointed to a little Japanese-American lad in the back row who yelled, "We are all going to die!"

I knew I had to talk fast.

"No, no, you've got that all wrong. There are some people who don't make the promise not to smoke that you have just made. *They* might die many years from now, but you are going to be alive and well if you keep the pledge to turn your back on cigarettes."

That broke the ice. After a few laughs we were on the same level, and we had a great dialogue, not so much on the dangers of smoking as on the privilege of making choices, which in the wisdom of the Coalition on Smoking OR Health is what the first-year curriculum is all about. I would look at the faces of those kids and pray that they would keep that pledge, that those young lives would not be cut short by smoking, as too many lives in their parents' generation would be.

A year or so later, at the press conference where I released my final Report on Smoking and Health, the Great Hall of the Humphrey Building was filled with a hundred children brought in by the local chapter of the American Lung Association. They all stood up, raised their right hand, and repeated the pledge to turn their back on anyone offering them a cigarette. One of my four granddaughters joined the smoke-free class of 2000 as a first-grader in her Georgia elementary school.

My personal messages about smoking seemed to be particularly effective, and I found early on that a personal plea from the Surgeon General might be enough to get a smoker to quit. One night before I gave the banquet speech at the Congressional Country Club, my host introduced me to the two bartenders. At first they were astonished that the Surgeon General was a real person and not just a symbol like, as a cabbie once put it, Betty Crocker. When I learned that each of these fellows smoked more than a pack a day, I begged them to quit for the sake of their health. A few months later I returned to the same club, but with a different speech, and found the same two bartenders: "We ain't smoked since we saw you, Doc!"

People took special pleasure in telling me personally that they had stopped smoking, and I shared their sense of delight and accomplishment. One day someone dressed in a Mr. Potato Head costume came all the way to my office to turn in his pipe, signalling that henceforth the Mr. Potato Heads sold in toy stores would no longer include pipes. (I must admit that when my secretary said that "a Mr. Potato Head" had arrived to see me, I wondered if she were referring to some government official. Several likely candidates went through my mind.)

After the public began to recognize me, people seldom smoked in my presence. When the nonsmoking tables in a Reno restaurant were all occupied, my hostess said, "I'll just seat you in the smoking section; they'll all put their cigarettes out." Sure enough, they did.

The next move in the attack on the tobacco interests brought the controversy home. Early on a humid July morning in 1986, as I walked out of the door of our duplex home on the grounds of NIH, about ten reporters toting cameras and microphones suddenly sprang from the shrubbery and surrounded my car. One obnoxious reporter stuck a microphone into my face and yelled, "Is it true that you have been censored by the White House?" Betty, in the doorway in her bathrobe, was as surprised as I by the ambush. The bungling of Donald Regan, President Reagan's controversy-prone chief of staff, had brought the intruders and inadvertently propelled me to a minor triumph.

I had been scheduled for several weeks to testify again on Capitol Hill on legislation that would ban all cigarette advertising in magazines and newspapers, and on billboards. All congressional testimony is submitted in advance to OMB several days before.

My White House spies told me that Jim Miller, the director of OMB, was annoyed by my testimony because of its economic implications. Miller voiced his displeasure at a White House senior staff meeting, and Regan said I should not be allowed to testify. *The Washington Post*, responding to a tip, called Regan to ask if I had been forbidden to testify. Regan said, "Yes." I knew none of this at the time. Regan never called then or later. I would never have withdrawn my testimony under this kind of pressure. But I realized that postponing it would make things go my way.

It was a pleasure to watch the next events unfold, as the heavy-handed White House tactics boomeranged. Throughout the following day, at least a hundred people spoke to me, encouraging me to stand my ground. Regan had obviously shot himself in the foot, and my position and the crusade against tobacco advertising benefited from favorable press coverage that we could not have come by for a million dollars. Regan's action made front-page and prime-time coverage out of a story that ordinarily might have been lost. The networks carried interviews with Yul Brynner's daughter (Brynner had recently died of cancer caused by his lifelong chain-smoking) and R. J. Reynolds' heir Pat Reynolds, both of whom spoke forcefully against cigarette advertising. Commentators such as *Good Morning America*'s David Hartman summed it all up by concluding that there was a growing groundswell in America to ban cigarette advertising.

When I finally testified, I used the opportunity to say that if the Public Health Service could get equal space in magazines to counter cigarette advertising with the truth about the effects of smoking, the tobacco industry would throw in the towel. I was sure they would prefer not to advertise at all rather than risk having the American people learning the terrible truth about smoking.

Some of the government witnesses made the administration look foolish. A representative of the Justice Department presented the administration's argument that a ban on advertising would lead to a decline in revenue for magazines and thus could lead to a smaller variety of reading material for the public. I was delighted when Congressman Henry Waxman picked right up on this idiocy, saying, "In other words, the Reagan administration is willing to sacrifice 360,000 lives a year in order that the people of this country have a greater variety of reading material in magazines." It was getting easier to make the White House staffers look foolish. They usually accomplished that by themselves.

By 1986 the anti-smoking population had become a militant army. They had a goal. They needed a weapon. When I released the 1986 Surgeon General's report on the dangers of passive smoking, the nonsmokers got the weapon they needed. This marked the real turning of the tide.

The *Health Consequences of Passive Smoking* determined without a doubt that passive smoking—*causes* disease, including cancer. Stipulating that simply separating smokers and nonsmokers in the same airspace did not solve the problem, the report stressed the especially harmful effects of passive smoking on children.

I felt that future historians would consider this report just as important as the original 1964 report. All across the country smokers were in retreat. Lawmakers and regulators on all levels of government began to protect the lungs of nonsmokers. The General Services Administration restricted smoking in its 6,800 federal buildings, affecting 890,000 federal employees. By early 1987, forty states had restricted smoking in public places, thirty-three states had prohibited smoking on public conveyances, and seventeen states had banned smoking in offices and other work sites. On the local level, there were about eight hundred local ordinances against tobacco (fewer than a hundred had been on the books when I called for the smoke-free society plans in 1984). A tough local smoking control ordinance was approved by the voters in Greensboro, North Carolina, in spite of heavy opposition by tobacco companies. If the tobacco companies can be beaten in North Carolina, they can be beaten anywhere.

Next, my colleagues and I went on to the heart of the issue, nicotine addiction. That is what we are really talking about: not smoking, not tobacco, but nicotine addiction. Most smokers are drug addicts. On one hand, we need to show them our understanding and help them break their addiction, and on the other hand, we need stronger societal censure of their persistence in addiction, an addiction whose health consequences are borne not only by the individual, but also by society.

The 1988 Surgeon General's report, based upon years of scientific studies, clearly and unequivocally branded nicotine as an addictive substance. The report presented convincing evidence that the pharmacologic and behavioral processes that determine tobacco (nicotine) addiction are similar to those processes that make cocaine and heroin addictive. Tobacco is an addictive drug, according to the standard definition of drug addiction adopted by the World Health Organization, the American Psychiatric Association, and the American Medical Association. In other words, tobacco is a "mood-altering" substance, as well as a reinforcing substance that rewards the user. The addictive qualities of nicotine make smokers compulsive in their use of tobacco, and their addiction leads them to build up a tolerance to nicotine, requiring them to use increasingly higher doses to get their nicotine "high." As with heroin, cocaine, and other addictive drugs, nicotine produces physical dependence, including a withdrawal syndrome for those who quit. And quitting is difficult, with nicotine users (like heroin and cocaine users) being very likely to relapse and return to the use of the drug. Successful quitters need an average of five attempts before they succeed. The report revealed a surprise to many people: The same percentage of heroin addicts as tobacco users are able to quit on their own.

The cigarette industry feared the term "addiction" more than any other. In the days when legislation to print rotating labels on cigarette packages and advertisements was being discussed, one of the labels that those of us in the Public Health Service wanted most was "Surgeon General's Warning: Tobacco Contains Nicotine, Which is an Addictive Drug." Of course, the tobacco industry fought hard against any labels, but then the four rotating labels on smoking's effects on heart disease, cancer, emphysema, and pregnancy passed Congress relatively easily only because the tobacco industry backed off in trade for dropping the addiction warning.

The addiction report had a strangely blunted effect. People never really took it in. Or they chose not to take it in. If any other commonly consumed substance were labeled addictive, it would be taken off the shelves within a week. Imagine if suddenly ice cream were labeled addictive. Politicians would be stumbling over each other to ban it, to make sure our kids would not be lured into addiction.

Perhaps the public didn't take the report to heart because the stereotyped idea of drug addiction does not include images of nicotine craving. While television might offer graphic images of heroin or cocaine addiction, it doesn't usually show the craving of the nicotine addict who is trying to give up smoking; it is just as devastating. I have been with ex–drug addicts who say something like this: "You know, I kicked heroin, I kicked pot, I kicked cocaine, I kicked morphine; why can't I kick cigarettes?"

We don't take addiction seriously. We don't provide enough treatment programs for cocaine and heroin addicts, and we simply ignore the nicotine addiction that enslaves so many *millions* of Americans. One of the best investments of our health dollars would be in programs to help addicts stop smoking. It doesn't make sense to me for an insurance company to fork over $150,000 for a client's terminal illness with lung cancer, but not be willing to put up $64 or $200 to help him stop smoking and avoid lung cancer in the first place. Insurance executives told me I didn't understand insurance. I'm not sure they do.

My last Surgeon General's report on smoking, in 1989, confirmed that smoking was still the greatest preventable cause of death in the United States (the annual mortality figures were revised upward to 390,000) and for the first time stated that smoking can cause strokes (as opposed to just being associated with them). Men under the age of sixty-five who smoke increase their risk of stroke 3.7 times, while women under the age of sixty-five increase their risk 4.8 times. After the report a consensus developed that the mortality figure is closer to 500,000 annually. I thought it was more graphic to say that as many Americans would die each day from smoking as in a crash of two jumbo jets with no survivors.

The 1989 report was more reflective than earlier reports. It was the Silver Anniversary Report, released twenty-five years after Surgeon General Luther Terry woke up Americans with his 1964 report. Luther Terry, who died in 1985, did not live to read the report that reviewed our progress on the crusade he had started. I count it among my more meaningful accomplishments that I was able to help his family cut through the red tape to enable Terry to be buried at the National Cemetery in Arlington, with full honors. He certainly affected—and saved—more lives than many of the generals buried there.

We had come a long way since the 1964 report, but there was still a long way to go. Any time I spoke about smoking, it was a good news–bad news story.

Cigarette smoking continued to decline, the percentage of smokers falling from over 50 percent of Americans in 1964 to just over 26 percent in 1989—an amazing accomplishment! And the *rate* of decline increased each year. But the progress was uneven. For example, while smoking among male high school students decreased dramatically—

about a 30 percent decline in the late eighties—smoking among senior high school girls remained static and then increased during the same years. Vanity will kill them: Many high school girls told me they smoked because they thought it would keep them from gaining weight. I wish when they looked in the mirror they could see what was happening to their lungs and arteries.

The scientific base supporting the anti-smoking crusade grows daily. The seven thousand scientific studies of 1964 had grown in twenty-five years to nearly sixty thousand, proving conclusively the causal relationship between cigarettes and the three leading killers of Americans: heart disease, cancer, and stroke.

The lives of nonsmokers have improved dramatically. Five years ago most of us nonsmokers still had to spend too much time in smoke-filled rooms. We would not dare ask a smoker to snuff it out. Now, when someone lights up around nonsmokers, at the first whiff they turn their heads, glare at the smoker, and make it clear: "Don't poison my air!"

One of the most important victories in the battle for smoke-free society, for smoke-free air was won, well, in the air. Nonsmokers have always been annoyed when forced to fly in airplanes with smokers. The so-called smoking section was a farce, as the smoke drifted around the cabin or was recycled throughout the cabin by the airplane ventilating system. It did not take a scientific test to make it clear to anyone who flew in commercial aircraft that no place in the plane was safe from environmental smoke. I didn't like traveling in those smoke-filled rooms, and most of my fellow travelers felt the same. But most of all I was concerned about the long-term health effects of environmental smoke on the flight attendants. As I watched them do their jobs while people smoked around them, I was certain that nonsmoking flight attendants were "smoking" the equivalent of several cigarettes a day whether they wanted to or not.

I had a very simple plan. I asked for nonsmoking volunteers to sit in various places throughout the airplane cabin. Then I would test the saliva and urine of the volunteers and the flight crew before, during, and after long flights to see if they were absorbing nicotine into their bodies. We had no trouble finding volunteers, but we could not get an airline to cooperate. In March 1988, while I was trying to arrange these tests, Northwest Airlines announced that it would become the first nonsmoking airline. To my delight, its business increased.

To get the test results I wanted, I had to go north. Canadian Minister of Health Jake Epp, who had become a personal friend, secured the cooperation of Air Canada. The test worked just the way we thought it would. Public Health Service employees sat in various seats in the coach section of planes and along with nonsmoking volunteer flight attendants submitted their saliva and urine for testing before, during, and after five-and-a-half-hour flights from Montreal to Vancouver. We also tested them twenty-four hours later. Sure enough, the tests indicated that they were unwillingly inhaling a significant amount of cigarette smoke each day, no matter where they sat or worked in the airplane. We also discovered that it took them longer to flush the nicotine from their bodies than it did a smoker.

The study was especially pleasing to me because it left the Tobacco Institute on the ropes. They could not claim that the smoke had come from some other source, like jet fuel or diesel fumes on the ground. Nicotine comes from tobacco alone, and the test showed that cotinine, a metabolic product of nicotine, had appeared in the saliva and urine of the volunteers. The studies, eventually published in the *Journal of the American Medical Association,* were all the ammunition Congress needed to ban smoking on all flights under six hours long. Almost every time I fly, grateful airline workers thank me for helping to clear the air. Their lives have been improved and many have been lengthened. As I settle into my airline seat, I tell them how glad I was to be part of the effort, and then I breathe in some clear air with a deep sigh of satisfaction.

We also see good news in the way our educational efforts have changed their focus. For twenty-five years we tried to convince Americans to stop smoking—and never to start. By 1990 it was clear that most smokers—perhaps as high as 90 percent—wanted to stop. They didn't need convincing. They needed—and almost 45 million still need—help in quitting. Schools are taking their anti-smoking curriculums seriously, preparing for the smoke-free class of 2000. Self-help programs as well as support groups in the community and at the work site are helping smokers quit. Physicians are responding—still too slowly—to their great opportunity, for we have learned that nothing is quite as effective to get someone to stop smoking as a doctor looking that patient straight in the eye and saying, "If you continue to smoke, you're going to kill yourself. You need to stop . . . . *now!*" But for all the value of these programs and interventions, we must remember that nicotine addicts must do the quitting themselves. And, to their credit, 85 percent of those who quit . . . just do it. And each one who quits offers hope—and life—to others. They are the real battlefield heroes in the war on drugs.

I do not believe the United States will ever again be a growing market for tobacco products. The curve is going down at an accelerating pace. But the tobacco companies have not given up. There are still battles to be fought: cigarette vending machines, cigarette advertising, and the international power of the tobacco companies.

It is illegal to sell both alcohol and cigarettes to minors, because alcohol and nicotine are the two major legal addictive drugs in our society. We would never tolerate selling alcoholic beverages in vending machines, but somehow we tolerate cigarette vending machines, sad evidence of our failure to take seriously the dangers of selling this addictive substance to minors.

Cigarette advertising is equally pernicious. The tobacco industry spends $4,000 per *minute* on promotion, or $2.5 billion a year. For every dollar spent by the Public Health Service to warn Americans about the dangers of tobacco, the tobacco industry spends $4,000 in advertising to say that our warnings are incorrect. Although cigarette ads have been banned from television, they are sneaking back again through videos. And cigarette advertising still assaults our society in print and on billboards. You cannot watch a sports event on TV without seeing cigarette ads on billboards, clothing, and equipment.

I am particularly disturbed by cigarette advertising that targets vulnerable groups within our population: young people, women, and minorities. Cigarette firms manipulate them because these people have the strongest aspirations to change their status. So these ads associate smoking with making it in the white, Anglo, male, or adult world. These ads associate smoking with a higher economic status, when in reality higher-income groups are now smoking less.

We know that people with more education tend to quit more readily—"The more you know, the less you smoke"—but tobacco advertisers associate smoking—contrary to all evidence—with financial and sexual success, robust activity, athletics, social acceptability, outdoor leisure, and even good health.

One of the more outrageous advertising gimmicks comes from Newport cigarettes (manufactured by Lorillard): their "Alive with Pleasure" theme. This is clearly an effort to undermine the Surgeon General's warning on each pack. Truth in advertising should require those ads to read not "Alive with Pleasure," but "Dying in Agony."

In the advertising wars you hear a lot about proof. The tobacco companies say that it has not been proven that advertising increases cigarette smoking. Of course, the complexity of the issue of human behavior and advertising will probably preclude the establishment of "scientific proof" of a causal link acceptable to the tobacco industry.

Of course, the important causal link is not between advertising and sales; the important causal link is between tobacco and death. I always say that while I don't understand all there is to know about electrons and conductivity, I know that when I flip the switch the light goes on. That's the way it is with smoking and disease. To my mind the burden of proof should be on the tobacco industry to show that advertising does *not* increase consumption of a product that we know leads to death when used as intended.

In the 1850s John Snow ended the cholera epidemic in London by removing the handle of the Broad Street water pump, thirty years before the bacterium causing cholera was discovered. Fortunately, he did not need to contend with a "Cholera Institute" that demanded the pump keep working until it was *proven* that water from the pump was causing the cholera.

At this point the cigarette companies trot out the old line that their advertising is intended only to enforce brand loyalty and to get consumers to switch to their brand. No one really believes that. Brand changers form only a tiny fraction of the market. The real purpose of cigarette advertising is to hold on to those smokers already hooked—addicted— and to attract new ones. It works. Recent studies confirm that increased advertising brings about a higher demand for cigarettes in general, not just for the brands advertised.

We know advertising is effective, and the tobacco firms know it is effective, because of the brief experience with counter-advertising in the sixties. Early in the debate about cigarette advertising on television, the Public Health Service received equal time for counter-advertising about the health problems caused by cigarette smoking. The results were so devastating to the tobacco industry that the cigarette firms decided they would rather have no advertising at all on television than have the true effects of smoking brought before American viewers. That was the reason I advocated counter-advertising in newspapers and magazines.

The tobacco companies talk a lot about freedom, free choice, free speech. Cigarette advertising, far from allowing free choice, actually undermines free choice by encouraging addiction. Nicotine addicts do not enjoy free choice.

Nothing is more hypocritical than the tobacco companies whining about "free speech" as they attempt to justify their advertisements for their addictive substance. The "free speech" argument used by tobacco advertisers is a smoke screen. You do not see these people out in front on other First Amendment issues. Free speech has never been an unlimited right: We all know you cannot yell "Fire" in a crowded theater. Free speech cannot injure the common welfare to serve the commercial interests of a few. The First Amendment was not intended to allow lies to be foisted on the public. And most cigarette advertising is lies. It associates with romance, glamour, athletics, and success substances that instead lead to disability and death. You could say cigarette advertising should be banned because it is deceptive.

Furthermore, First Amendment protection is not extended to speech encouraging illegal activity. Tobacco advertisers depend upon reaching young people. Most of those who smoke began before they were twenty, or even fifteen. In other words, the continued strength of the tobacco market depends on those to whom the products may not be legally sold. You could say cigarette advertising is illegal because it targets underage potential smokers.

For all their talk about "freedom," tobacco interests are great enemies of freedom. Far from believing in free speech, tobacco advertisers use their economic clout to force publishers not to print articles about the real consequences of smoking. Tobacco advertisers blackmail magazine editors. *Harper's Bazaar* rejected an article entitled "Protect Your Man from Cancer," after having requested and paid for it, because, as the editor lamely explained, since they had run three full-page color ads for tobacco they could not publish an article that focused "too much on tobacco." Now that cigarette manufacturers are part of conglomerate corporations with food companies (R. J. Reynolds and Nabisco as RJR-Nabisco) ethical concerns are raised when endeavors such as anti-cholesterol drives by the AMA, the American Heart Association, and the Academy of Family Practice are paid for by Fleischman's margarine, a subsidiary of RJR-Nabisco.

The ten leading women's magazines offer a barrage of health messages for their female clientele—how to treat everything from falling hair to falling arches. But there is rarely even a mild admonition to women to avoid smoking for the sake of their health. The reason is obvious. Up to 22 percent of the income of those magazines is derived from cigarette advertising. Some investigative reporters who turn in accurate articles against cigarettes have had them turned down for publication, and some have been fired for their audacity in submitting such truth.

It is easy to see why cigarette advertisers push so hard. After all, about 90 percent of the people who are hooked on their product would prefer to quit. And of course, the advertisers face a special challenge. They need to replenish the diminishing supply of tobacco users: Remember those one thousand smokers who die every day.

Although we are beating the American tobacco industry on its own turf, it is scouring the globe for other victims. The tobacco industry has moved to make up the profits lost in the United States by wringing money from the misery and death of new customers around the world. While smoking in the United States dropped another 5 percent in 1989, American tobacco exports rose 20 percent that same year. In 1989 American companies manufactured 600 billion cigarettes; 100 billion of those cigarettes went overseas.

The tobacco industry has targeted the less developed and developing countries of the world as their most promising markets for the nineties. The transnational tobacco companies travel from country to country with a great deal of cash—not credits, not promises, but hard, cold cash. Therefore it is very difficult for any government struggling to get its economy in order to turn away such well-paying guests. These companies build factories and employ many people. They spend large sums on advertising and special events. In some areas they virtually subsidize the media. The seven major transnational tobacco companies—four American and three British—operate with the arrogance of a colonial power. These companies ostentatiously pump large amounts of money into the economy of a poor nation, only to extract the physical health of its people. We see the result in the rising morbidity and mortality rates from Western smoking-related diseases. The recent news that in fifteen Asian countries communicable disease was no longer the number one public health menace was not really good news. It just meant that in those Asian countries, the top three causes of death had become the same three smoking-related causes of death that prevail in the United States: heart disease, cancer, and stroke.

This export of disease, disability, and death has been carried out with the support of the U.S. government—our trade representatives, our State Department, our Commerce Department, and our Agriculture Department. They are supporting one of the most disgraceful examples of private enterprise gone amok. The cigarette industry is focusing its high-powered marketing attention on the unprotected people of Asia, Africa, and South America. It is appalling that corporate America should behave this way, but it is even more shocking that our own government would support their actions.

And here is where we deserve to squirm in shame—in ten out of fifteen Asian countries, American cigarettes were the most common kind imported. But those American cigarettes are different overseas: They do not carry the Surgeon General's warning, and many American cigarettes manufactured for export have a higher tar content and are, therefore, even more dangerous than the lower-tar, fully labeled products sold here in the United States. In other words, American cigarette manufacturers *knowingly* produce a more harmful cigarette for export than they produce for domestic consumption.

When tobacco invades a new market, it does so with immense speed and impact. According to the World Health Organization, between 1971 and 1981 cigarette consumption increased in Asia and Latin America at a rate 30 percent ahead of the rate of population increase—in Africa 70 percent ahead of the rise in population. In China, 50 million children running around today will eventually die prematurely from smoking. Our export of tobacco products is not only a moral outrage, it is also foolish. There is no sense in our helping a foreign nation plan for its long-term economic health and providing that society with foreign aid if American tobacco exports are to undermine the physical health of that society.

We may have a balance-of-trade problem, but that does not justify exporting disease, disability, and death to developing and under-developed countries. U.S. trade representatives, responding to petitions from the tobacco industry, threaten smaller nations with trade sanctions if they do not open their doors to the offensive marketing practices of American tobacco companies.

In 1985 Taiwan reduced its smoking by 5 percent, and in 1986, with a tremendous effort, reduced it by another 6 percent. But in 1987, responding to the threat of sanctions by the U.S. trade representative, Taiwan opened its market to American cigarettes. Smoking rose 10 percent that year.

In my last official act as Surgeon General, I was one of more than thirty witnesses at a congressional public hearing on tobacco and trade. I made my point and concluded by saying:

It is the height of hypocrisy for the United States, in our war against drugs, to demand that foreign nations take steps to stop the export of cocaine to our country while at the same time we export nicotine, a drug just as addictive as cocaine, to the rest of the world.

Chapter 9

AIDS

When I was designated as Surgeon General in February 1981, I had never heard of AIDS. No one had heard of AIDS, and the handful of scientists who knew about this immunodeficiency disease did not even know what to call it, much less what it really was. AIDS entered the consciousness of the Public Health Service quietly, gradually, and without fanfare. In June 1981 the Centers for Disease Control (CDC), an agency of the United States Public Health Service, published a report concerning five "previously healthy" homosexuals who had been admitted to Los Angeles hospitals with pneumonia caused by a very rare organism, *Pneumocystis carinii.*

By the time the report was published, two of the men had died. The other three died shortly thereafter. Five cases are not many, but this lethal pneumonia is so rare that a handful of cases in a single year constitutes an epidemic. Soon the reports trickled in of cases in other cities as well.

Then, a month later, the Public Health Service published a report that twenty-six young homosexual men had been recently diagnosed as having Kaposi's sarcoma, an "uncommonly reported" cancerous condition usually found, if at all, among elderly men.

From that small beginning mushroomed the AIDS epidemic of the late eighties. Epidemiologists from the CDC investigated the strange cases and discovered that otherwise healthy, normal people were apparently acquiring some kind of "bug"—a virus, most likely—that attacked and destroyed their natural immune systems. The bug itself was not killing these people; they were succumbing to other extremely virulent diseases called "opportunistic," because this infectious agent—

whatever it was—prevented the body from fighting them off. Since the first cases affected only homosexuals, the Public Health Service dubbed the disease GRID—gay-related immune deficiency. Shortly thereafter, as heterosexuals began to fall victim to it, GRID became the "acquired immunodeficiency syndrome," or A.I.D.S., which was finally shortened to just AIDS.

The Public Health Service had never come upon anything like AIDS before. Some people infected with AIDS might not develop symptoms for many years. (We still don't know what keeps the virus quiescent, or what stimulates it to activity.) Death from AIDS is difficult to endure and unpleasant to observe. Patients with Kaposi's sarcoma are ravaged by the purplish skin lesions that are the hallmark of that condition; those with *Pneumocystis carinii* suffer the gradual failure of their lungs. As the disease progresses, people with AIDS become more and more immunodeficient, leaving them easy prey for diseases and infections healthy people can easily fight off. The specific opportunistic diseases depend on geographical area. Toward the end, people with AIDS become extremely weak and emaciated; in Africa it is called "slim disease." I have seen men dying of AIDS who look like starving kittens, too weak to make a sound. Ultimately unable to perform even the simplest tasks for themselves, AIDS patients slip into a coma and die.

By August 1981 I and others who were paying attention to the unusual news from the CDC learned that there were 108 cases of AIDS reported with 43 dead. I knew we were in big trouble. And there was nothing I could do about it. I was not yet the Surgeon General, and all through the summer and autumn of 1981 I was preoccupied by my long struggle to win confirmation. But I realized that if there ever was a disease made for a Surgeon General, it was AIDS. The Surgeon General is mandated by Congress to inform the American people about the prevention of disease and the promotion of health. If ever there was a public in need of education and straight talk about AIDS, it was the American people.

But for an astonishing five and a half years I was completely cut off from AIDS. I was told by the assistant secretary for health, my immediate boss, that I would not be assigned to cover AIDS. The department took its cue from him. Even though the Centers for Disease Control commissioned the first AIDS task force as early as June 1981, I, as Surgeon General, was not allowed to speak about AIDS publicly until the second Reagan term. Whenever I spoke on a health issue at a press conference or on a network morning TV show, the government public affairs people told the media in advance that I would not answer questions on AIDS, and I was not to be asked any questions on the subject. I have never understood why these peculiar restraints were placed on me. And although I have sought to find the explanation, I still don't know the answer.

Perhaps, in the first months of the AIDS epidemic, when I was still unconfirmed as Surgeon General, my exclusion went along with HHS Secretary Dick Schweiker's advice that I should keep my head down and my mouth shut, keeping a low profile until confirmed. But even after my confirmation, I continued to be excluded from the government's handling of the issue. I had to be content to learn about AIDS on my own, from the newspapers, internal documents of the Public Health Service, what spilled over in staff meetings, reports from the CDC such as *Morbidity and Mortality Weekly Reports (MMWR)*, and discussions with colleagues.

In 1983, Assistant Secretary of Health Ed Brandt had created an Executive Task Force on AIDS, a high-level group drawn from the Public Health Service to deal with the many facets of the growing AIDS epidemic. I was not asked to join the task force. It became increasingly awkward and embarrassing for me, especially when outsiders asked if there were any trouble between Ed Brandt and me. When I brought up the issue with Ed in private, he seemed genuinely surprised at the suggestion, but he never took any concrete measures to end my exclusion from such a burning issue. Maybe it was just Brandt's management style, because after he left our friendship deepened.

At the time, I never considered myself muzzled about AIDS. I really believed initially that my exclusion was simply the result of a division of labor—a very naive belief, I now realize. It was my job as Surgeon General to communicate with the American people in order to protect their health. It sounds simple. But it did not take long for me to discover how difficult it could be to get the word out, because no matter what the issue, there were always forces trying to keep me from communicating health messages to the American people. I had to wage scores of political battles before I could even begin to do my job. Some of them were small, with equally small stakes: petty squabbles within the Department of Health and Human Services, mostly about bruised egos, or interagency skirmishes over turf, which often pitted the FDA against other departmental agencies. I would spend too much time in bureaucratic bushwhacking, trying to find out whether deliberate sabotage or simply ordinary incompetence had caused a delay in printing or broadcasting a health message.

But some political struggles were large, and the stakes were equally high: life-and-death conflict over cigarette advertising that lured people into lives of nicotine addiction, trade policies that made the United States a de facto leader in the drug cartel, and the bitter politics of AIDS. The politics of AIDS poses a threat not only to the health of some Americans but also to our constitutional safeguards of basic rights, to our ethic of care and compassion, to the very fabric of American society.

Within the politics of AIDS lay one enduring, central conflict: AIDS pitted the politics of the gay revolution of the seventies against the politics of the Reagan revolution of the eighties.

There were two reasons why it took a while for public health authorities to get a handle on AIDS. One was the relatively rare nature of the diseases associated with the AIDS virus: *Pneumocystis carinii* pneumonia, cytomegalovirus and *Candida* infections, Kaposi's sarcoma, cryptococcal meningitis, toxoplasmosis, disseminated *Mycobacterium avium-intracellulare*, and so on. In 1981 and 1982 the United States had relatively few trained clinicians and researchers who were familiar with these rare diseases that were suddenly cropping up in Los Angeles, San Francisco, and New York. And in any case, we had no cure for them.

The other was that the first patients with those conditions were in every case homosexual men, who placed themselves where it was unlikely that they would be helped. In the seventies and early eighties, many homosexual and bisexual men chose to patronize physicians and clinics that were more understanding of the so-called "gay life-style." In making that choice, these men effectively placed themselves outside the mainstream of clinical medicine, making them difficult to reach and to help.

Meanwhile, in what was known at the time as the "gay revolution," homosexual and bisexual men were "coming out of the closet" and asserting their civil rights. Unfortunately, most gay activists combined the otherwise separate issues of homosexual health and politics. They then placed this single package of grievances before the general public for redress. Their concerns about AIDS were mixed in with a host of other homosexual issues such as access to jobs and housing as well as protection against social discrimination. The American people did not have the patience to sort out these issues, so the demands of the homosexual community generated more public confusion and anger than they did understanding and sympathy. As a result, the first public health priority—to stop further transmission of the AIDS virus—became needlessly mired in the sexual politics of the early eighties. We lost a great deal of precious time because of this, and I suspect we lost some lives as well.

The Reagan revolution brought into positions of power and influence Americans whose politics and personal beliefs predisposed them to antipathy toward the homosexual community. This influenced the AIDS crisis in two ways. First, it slowed the understanding of AIDS. In the early years of AIDS (also the early years of the Reagan administration), health officials were shocked and dismayed by the link between the spread of AIDS and the promiscuity and perversity of many homosexuals' behavior: AIDS patients admitted to an astounding number of sexual encounters with an equally astounding number of different partners in a single day, and they described such practices as "fisting," where one man inserts his fist into his partner's rectum. Such revelations, along with the high incidence of anal intercourse—sodomy—with multiple anonymous partners provided valuable information about a possible method of AIDS transmission: semen of one to blood of the other. However, even some health officials displayed a profound reluctance to discuss these sensitive (some said abhorrent) issues publicly. So, under directions from more than one White House source, they simply made vague references to "exchanging bodily fluids," thus considerably slowing down the public's understanding of how AIDS can be transmitted.

Second, the conservative politics of the middle and late years of the Reagan administration attempted to thwart my attempts to educate the public about AIDS and tried to stir up hostility toward its victims. I tried to rise above the politics of AIDS, but it would cost me many friendships.

In May 1983, Robert Gallo of the National Institutes of Health and Luc Montagnier of the Pasteur Institute in Paris identified the infectious agent that caused AIDS: a virus dubbed HIV-III, or human immunodeficiency virus. In early 1984, there were over five thousand reported cases of AIDS with about 2,300 deaths. But, in a strange way, except for the homosexual community organizations and segments of the public health community now concerned about persons with AIDS, there seemed to be little outcry from the public or even organized medicine for more and appropriate leadership from the government. In 1985, as the Public Health Service and other branches of the medical community learned more about AIDS, they provided a weapon in the struggle against the strange disease: a test to identify the presence of antibodies to the HIV virus in the blood supply.

Not many criticisms make my blood boil anymore, but there is one that still does. I still hear people complain that "the government dragged its feet" and would not release a blood screening test until 1985. Instead, in spite of the confusion, frustration, anger, and ignorance, the government *did* press forward and made astounding advances in biomedical science and research. We learned as much about AIDS in six years as we had learned about polio in forty. It is a testament to these unflagging efforts that a reliable blood test was discovered and made generally available as early as the fall of 1985.

The stakes were very high. The discovery of the blood test saved many lives. Without it, the nation's blood supply would have become increasingly contaminated; people unknowingly infected with the virus by transfusions could have infected their sexual partners; some mothers could have spread it to newborns; infected people could have become blood donors; and so on. We had a close call. Even so, an estimated twelve thousand transfusion recipients were infected with HIV-contaminated blood.

But the test changed all that. The odds of getting an AIDS-contaminated unit of transfused blood fell to between one in 40,000 and one in 250,000. Compare those odds with, say, death on the highway: one in 5,900. The AIDS blood test is one of the research miracles of this century, because at the time it was developed we were unable to test the human blood supply for the lethal virus itself. Scientists instead discovered a successful way to screen blood for the antibodies, the "footprints" of a virus they otherwise could not find.

By the mid-eighties, we acknowledged that there was much we did not know about AIDS but in comparison to the accumulation of knowledge about most diseases, we had made extraordinary progress in our understanding of the syndrome. We had identified the virus, named it, and renamed it. We had understood the epidemiology among homosexual men and IV drug abusers. We had learned how homosexual practices hitherto barely mentioned could spread it. We had identified antibodies to the AIDS virus and developed a screening test on the basis of the detection of these antibodies, making the blood supply safe for transfusion. We had learned how to kill the virus in blood products and how to make clotting factors safe for hemophiliacs.

Above all we learned about how the disease is transmitted. We learned that although the virus had been identified in several body fluids, it seemed to be transmitted only through blood and semen. Researchers were very cautious. For example, Dr. Tony Fauci, later to direct AIDS research at NIH, insisted we check out any study that did not seem to rule out spread of AIDS by casual contact. But gradually a convincing body of research led us to some important conclusions. The most important thing we knew was the deadliest news: If you had AIDS, your chances of surviving the next two or three years were not very good, and the chances of surviving any longer than that were almost nil.

It was clear that in spite of all kinds of unsubstantiated claims about mosquitos and toilet seats, AIDS could be transmitted in four ways, and only four ways:

- The first way of transmission was sexual intercourse, mostly but not exclusively anal intercourse, which occurred most frequently among homosexuals and bisexual males. This accounted for about two thirds of all cases of AIDS at that time. However, AIDS could also be transmitted through heterosexual intercourse, and even though the statistical incidence of heterosexual transmission was lower, the disease was just as fatal.
- AIDS could also be transmitted into the blood of intravenous drug users who used the needles and syringes of other addicts already infected with the AIDS virus.
- The HIV virus could also be transmitted from an AIDS-infected mother to her infant during pregnancy or at the time of delivery.
- And finally, AIDS could be transmitted through transfused blood or blood products. (The development of the AIDS blood test virtually closed off this avenue of transmission.)

In addition to knowing the four methods of transmission, we stressed four other important conclusions about AIDS:

- It was fatal.
- It was spreading.
- It was transmitted mainly by certain specific behavior involving sex and/or drugs.
- There was no cure.

Understanding the means of AIDS transmission was a long way from finding a vaccine, even though research in that area accelerated. Because of the nature of the AIDS virus, it became very clear very soon that a vaccine lay years in the future, I thought well beyond the year 2000. Virologists were quick to point out that it had taken nineteen years to develop the vaccine against hepatitis B, which was a relatively simple virus compared to the complex AIDS virus.

We also had to acknowledge that although a vaccine might eventually protect Americans, it alone would not rid the planet of AIDS. Although vaccines for the six major communicable diseases of childhood have been generally available in most of the industrialized western world, these very same vaccines have yet to penetrate fully many less developed countries, societies in which AIDS has already spread rapidly.

A cure seemed equally elusive, as the only drugs that seemed to help, such as AZT (zidorudine, formerly azidothymidine), prolonged a person's life for only a few months or a year, if they worked at all. They did not cure anyone of AIDS, nor did they cure anyone of any condition brought on by AIDS.

An aerosol spray, pentamidine, first made available in 1981, proved effective in treating bouts of *Pneumocystis carinii* pneumonia. To some extent it has also proven to be effective prophylactically if administered to people whose blood tests show diminished immune functions. Pentamidine offers only palliative help; it is not a cure for AIDS. A controversy quickly arose about AIDS patients' rights to quicker approval by the Food and Drug Administration (FDA) of drugs to treat AIDS, their right to obtain unapproved medications, and the issue of the adequacy of funding for therapeutic research proportional to the prevalence of the disease.

At about the same time as the blood test was announced, my personal distance from AIDS information and policy came to an end. It was obvious that my silence on AIDS had become increasingly difficult for the public to understand. In midsummer 1985, the HHS secretary's office was inexplicably deluged with telegrams asking why the Surgeon General was being muzzled on AIDS. These were followed by more than five thousand postcards, each demanding that I be unmuzzled. Attached to each postcard was a ballot with four questions: (1) Should it be a felony for an AIDS carrier to donate blood to a blood bank? (2) Should hospital patients be allowed to handpick their own blood donors? (3) Should we enforce strict immigration laws to keep homosexuals from entering the United States? (4) Should legislation be enacted to outlaw homosexuals from working in close contact with children, in the food service industry, in hospitals and clinics? It looked to me like an organized campaign but I couldn't tell who had started it. However, we did begin to identify the agenda hidden behind it.

Meanwhile, the numbers and the concern continued to mount. By July 1985 the CDC had reported 11,737 AIDS cases, with 5,812 deaths. Just a week later the toll for each category had risen by about a hundred. That summer the death of Rock Hudson (the first national figure to die of AIDS) raised further the public concern about the disease. For the first time, because of Reagan's friendship with his fellow actor, AIDS seemed to touch the White House, even if indirectly.

It does not take long for public concern and fear to lead to charges of conspiracy. And conspiracy charges about AIDS grew along with the epidemic. One side accused the government of not leveling with the public, conspiring with the homosexual community to "cover up" the epidemic. How that would have helped the government or the homosexual community was never clear to me. If ever there were an administration that would not conspire with homosexuals, it was Reagan's. On the other side, the homosexuals and their advocates accused the government of a conspiracy to do nothing, to allow the disease to decimate the homosexual community.

I felt caught in the middle but still on the sidelines. Finally, at a July meeting of HHS agency heads, I spoke openly for the first time about the difficulties I was facing concerning the number of requests I had received to say something about AIDS. I had even been forced to decline invitations to provide private briefings on health issues for senators and congressmen. It was embarrassing for the Surgeon General to be unable to discuss a major national health issue with the nation's elected representatives. By this time Ed Brandt had left to go to the University of Maryland as provost on the Baltimore campus and had been succeeded by James O. Mason as acting assistant secretary for health. Since I was no longer the new kid on the block but actually the oldest kid on the block, Mason at last made me a member of the AIDS Task Force. He and I also agreed that AIDS demanded a clear spokesperson and that I could make any statement I thought appropriate. At last I could speak up.

I was finally in the mainstream of AIDS information. Although I was not a part of AIDS research or epidemiology—roles beyond my domain—I could at last use my information and the influence of my office to answer the public's questions about AIDS. But a lot of press conferences and podium time had been wasted. I had already given 202 formal addresses representing the administration, the Department of Health and Human Services, and the Public Health Service before I ever addressed any segment of the American public on the most mysterious and most vexing health issue of the century.

Ironically, after waiting so long to be able to speak to the public on AIDS, my first opportunity to do so on television would not give me the freedom of speech I needed. In October 1985 I was scheduled to appear on a brief segment of NBC's *The Today Show* to discuss interpersonal violence. Before the show the producer asked me if I would discuss AIDS. Because it was too large an issue to discuss credibly in a sound bite, and because I would have fewer future opportunities to address violence than to discuss AIDS, I said that no, I would stick to the violence issue. On the set, after I shared my concerns about family violence, Bryant Gumbel smugly opined that 4 million people injured in family violence wasn't much of a public health issue, and then—contrary to my explicit agreement with his producer—asked me a question on AIDS. I answered it briefly, annoyed by Gumbel's blend of duplicity and discourtesy. So I attempted to make sure that my first printed interview on AIDS, which appeared in the November 1985 issued of *Christianity Today*, stuck to the issues as I saw them. I stated for the first time my oft-repeated conclusion that in preventing AIDS the moralist and the scientist could walk hand in hand.

The American people were getting increasingly frightened about AIDS, but I was convinced they could be warned, they could be assured that you have to make a conscious decision to carry out a specific form of personal behavior before you expose yourself to the AIDS virus. It was clear that the only weapon we had against AIDS was education, education, and more education.

My intense involvement with AIDS came after President Reagan asked me to write a report to the American people about the disease. For the next two years AIDS took over my life.

I had heard the rumors for a week or so. At the end of January 1986, at a dinner hosted by then Treasury Secretary Jim Baker and his wife, Susan, two of the White House staffers present slipped up to me and whispered, "You're in the State of the Union message." They said that the president was going to ask me to write a report on AIDS. I thought this unlikely because about 1,500 issues are suggested for the State of the Union address, and even if the president might finally be ready to talk about AIDS, I knew his advisors were not.

Betty and I watched the 1986 State of the Union speech on television and it was such an upbeat, frothy address that we knew halfway through that Reagan would never mention AIDS. He didn't, and I said to Betty before we went to bed that night, "I guess I'm off the hook on writing that report."

Then, only a few days later, on February 5, President Reagan made an unprecedented visit to the Department of Health and Human Services. The Navy band had shown up to herald his arrival. Having milled around for almost an hour, they played a few bars of "Hail to the Chief" when Reagan appeared, and that was it for the music.

Dr. Otis Bowen, the new secretary for Health and Human Services, who had been sworn in about six weeks earlier, spoke first, then introduced the president. Reagan announced that he wanted AIDS to be a top priority in the department and was looking forward to the day when there would be a vaccine. He then declared that he was asking the Surgeon General to prepare a special report on AIDS. That was it. There was never any formal request. It's a good thing I was there and paying attention.

I started the next day. I knew that telling the truth about AIDS, the truth, the whole truth, and nothing but the truth would not be well received in some places. One of those places would be the White House, at least in those offices where ideology would be the main concern. Several months earlier, I had told a circle of high-echelon White House advisors that a report on AIDS from the Surgeon General was necessary, but that it might bring criticism to the president and his administration. A large portion of the president's constituency was anti-homosexual, anti–drug abuse, anti-promiscuity, and anti–sex education; these people would not respond well to some of the things that would have to be said in a health report on AIDS.

I said then—and I repeated it frequently—that the Surgeon General was the Surgeon General of homosexuals as well as of heterosexuals and of the promiscuous as well as of the moral. I am not sure anyone listened. If they had, they would not have been so surprised that my AIDS report was a health report, not the exercise in moral censure they wanted.

I possessed a mandate from the president to write a report on AIDS to the American people. I assumed it was to be in simple language for the average citizen, that it was to allay the panic that was spreading among people who were in no danger of getting AIDS and to warn those engaged in high-risk behavior of the inevitable outcome if they encountered the AIDS virus.

My first task was to jump the chain of command for clearance. I knew how the normal clearance process sanitized and watered down the message of many a draft document, and I knew my AIDS report would never have the necessary impact if it had to pass through too many hands in the Department of Health and Human Services and the White House. One of my most effective speeches, the one calling for a "Smoke-Free Society by the Year 2000," had been "cleared" only by Betty and several other confidantes. I realized that my success in writing an honest AIDS report depended upon my getting the green light from Secretary Bowen to bypass the normal clearance process.

At first I found it a little difficult to get to Bowen. Like most high officials, he was protected, sometimes too much, by his intimidating chief of staff, Tom Burke. Eventually Burke and I became allies and friends, especially as we worked together to revitalize the Commissioned Corps of the Public Health Service, but when Burke first arrived I was disturbed, to put it mildly. He more or less said there was no need for a Surgeon General: Any pronouncements on health could be made by the secretary, "Doc" Bowen, who was a physician. I had to clear this up. Bowen did it for me in one of our early meetings.

Otis Bowen had already enjoyed careers as a respected family physician and two-term governor of Indiana when he agreed to succeed Margaret Heckler as secretary of Health and Human Services. Serving as head of our department was not viewed as a plum. When Reagan's first secretary of Health and Human Services, Dick Schweiker, had taken office in 1981, Schweiker's father had spent a few minutes wandering around the Humphrey Building and looking at the photos of previous secretaries. Noting that none had served very long, he told Dick that it couldn't be a very good job if people came and went so frequently. But Doc Bowen fooled them all. Although initially regarded as little more than a caretaker, Bowen, a true public servant, would serve with distinction as secretary of HHS longer than anyone else in the history of the department. He certainly ranks at the top of Reagan's Cabinet appointees, even though his quiet and unassuming style did not attract the attention he deserved. I found Bowen to be gentle, kind, a superb politician, honest as the day is long, and wise: "If you tell the truth, Chick, you don't have to have a good memory to recall the lies."

Otis Bowen and I shared a common view of medicine, politics, government, and, well, life. He displayed a unique blend of the highest competence and modesty. One day toward the end of our time in office, I received a letter from the State Department, requesting that I address the United Nations General Assembly on the subject of AIDS. When I learned that other speakers would be the ministers of health from several nations—officials with rank equal to Bowen's but superior to mine—I felt placed in an embarrassing situation. So I sent a copy of the letter to Otis with a note from me stating that it was his privilege and prerogative to address the U.N. and that I thought he should do it. He replied in his own hand, as was frequently his custom in such communications, "Dear Chick, they asked you, they wanted you, you should do it. Besides, you'll do it better than I would. Otis."

At any point in my increasingly independent work as Surgeon General, Otis Bowen could have stopped me in my tracks. Instead, he backed me up every time. I gave him my utmost respect, and I cherished our friendship.

At an early meeting when I remarked that the Surgeon General had neither power nor budget (if you excluded money for travel, paper clips, and renting a word processor), Bowen replied, "When it comes to power, you are the most influential person in this whole department, the best known, and the one with the highest profile."

Otis Bowen gave me the green light I needed on the AIDS report. I told him that I would seek the best scientific advice within and outside the government, and that when the report was ready I assumed he would join me to present it before the Domestic Policy Council (those Cabinet members dealing with domestic affairs).

Like much of my work in Washington, writing the AIDS report amounted to walking a tightrope. I needed to be in touch with all of the national groups that were concerned about AIDS. I wanted to make sure they knew what I was doing, and I wanted none to say, after the report was published, that they had been blindsided or kept in the dark. There would have been no AIDS report without the cooperation of the many groups who traveled to Washington to meet with me.* But at the same time I had to make sure that the report was independent and objective, that it was *my* report. To do that I had to distance myself from the same groups that provided me with information and counsel.

Maintaining control of the report, keeping the circle small, meant that I would have only a very small staff to help me. Dr. Michael Samuels brought with him a broad background in public health endeavors, and he also brought the part-time help of Jim McTigue, a commissioned officer with whom Mike and I had frequently worked on intergovernmental affairs. We were supported by a small team: Assistant Surgeons General Jim Dickson and Edward Martin; my deputy director of the Office of International Health, Hal Thompson; my

*The National Hemophilia Foundation, United States Conference of Local Health Officials, National Association of County Health Officials, American Medical Association, AIDS Action Council, American Red Cross, American Dental Association, Health Insurance Institute, American Council of Life Insurance, United States Catholic Conference, National Council of Churches, Washington Business Group on Health, Association of State and Territorial Health Officials, American Nurses Association, National Coalition of Black Lesbians and Gays, National Minority AIDS Council, National Association of Secondary School Principals, National Association of Elementary School Principals, National Association of State Boards of Education, American Federation of Teachers, National Educational Association, and American Osteopathic Association.

personal assistant, Stephanie Stein; and of course my deputy, Faye Abdellah.

We learned a lot, and we learned fast. Some groups surprised me, usually pleasantly. For instance, I was delighted by the American Medical Association's aggressive action against AIDS and the willingness of the AMA Board of Trustees to expend large sums of money on their AIDS Action Plan, which would include plans for education and projections about the spread of the epidemic. The AMA may earn its share of criticism, but it should be lauded for this private-sector effort of the doctors of America against AIDS. The National Coalition of Black Lesbians and Gays, far from adopting the combative posture many expected, was one of the most articulate and caring groups. I found the people from the Southern Baptist Convention to be delightful, but very naive about AIDS. I think they were shocked by what we had to tell them about how the virus was sexually transmitted. I thought they might be uncomfortable with the mandate for sex education I planned to mention in my report, so I challenged them to write their own sex education curriculum for their 26 million constituents. To their credit, within six months of our chat, they did what I suggested, and I had the pleasure of giving their annual convention's keynote address when they announced their curriculum on human sexuality.

As we met with each group, I made it clear that I would do my best to include in my report a reference to its special concerns. For example, the Red Cross wanted accurate information on the safety of the blood supply; the American Dental Association wanted me to mention that dentists should protect their patients and themselves by wearing rubber gloves.

A few meetings were especially helpful. The information provided by the National Hemophilia Foundation was critical. The experience of hemophiliacs who had become infected with AIDS by a transfusion before the blood test had become available or by injection with clotting factors before heat treatment made them safe made a major contribution to our understanding of the disease. (Tragically, 90 percent of severe hemophiliacs became infected with HIV before the blood supply was made safe.) From hemophiliacs, we also learned about the strength of young people who now had to live with two diseases as well as with the fear of discrimination.

The experience of hemophiliacs nailed down the evidence that AIDS was not spread by nonsexual casual contact. Six hundred families of hemophiliacs were studied. Family members who lived with an HIV-positive male touched each other, used the same utensils, kissed each other, and shared razors without passing the virus. Even the 7 percent who shared toothbrushes (I was surprised by that figure!) did not transmit the virus to their toothbrush partners.

This—and a number of other studies—confirmed that most Americans were not at risk, *if* they did not engage in high-risk behavior with sex and drugs. This also meant that persons with AIDS should not suffer discrimination, that the strident calls to quarantine them or deny them housing, employment, or public schooling were misinformed and wrong. Nevertheless, the calls for taking drastic measures against persons with AIDS were mounting each day.

As I traveled around the country speaking out about AIDS, it was clear that we needed federal, state, and municipal dialogue on three questions: (1) Who would foot the AIDS bill? (2) Where did insurance fit in? (3) Couldn't AIDS patients find terminal care less costly than in hospital intensive care units?

Some California congressmen had come under the sway of a group who despised not only homosexual behavior, but also homosexuals. They perpetuated a number of myths about AIDS transmission and called for unnecessary quarantine and testing. Among these propagandists was Paul Cameron, one of the country's most outspoken anti-homosexuals. California Congressman William Dannemeyer, who had apparently bought into those myths, became increasingly strident about AIDS. Repeatedly during the AIDS crisis he would complain to me, "Dr. Koop, you are so reasonable about everything else, why are you so wrong about AIDS?" Dannemeyer advocated mandatory testing for the entire nation, the quarantine of all those who tested positively, and a law that would make it a felony for people to "exchange body fluids" if they were contaminated with the virus. (How this would be enforced, Dannemeyer never made clear.) Dannemeyer's proposed legislation covering all these outrageous demands never left committee.

One evening he called me at home: "Chick, why won't you get on with mandatory testing of the entire country?"

"I've told you, that's not within the power of the Surgeon General, but for reasons I've also explained over and over, I wouldn't do it if I could. But suppose just for the sake of argument, I could and did. Suppose I called you next week and said I now knew who every seropositive person was in the whole United States. What would you do?"

After a long pause, Dannemeyer, as I recall, replied, "Wipe them off the face of the earth!"

This attitude, I realized as I conducted my interviews on the AIDS report, although not widely voiced, was widely held. I could see where these people were coming from, but I could not agree with them. I strongly disapproved of the forms of behavior responsible for most AIDS transmission: promiscuity, homosexual behavior, sex outside of marriage, and drug use. My Christian faith forms the basis for my moral standards, and I knew that the practice of homosexuality was anathema to most Christians, who believe that it, along with much that we humans do, is sinful.

But I also knew that as a Christian and physician I was under two clear obligations to persons with AIDS, no matter how they might have contracted the virus. As a physician, it was my job to save lives and alleviate suffering. It was not my job to make decisions on accepting or treating a patient based upon how he had incurred the disease or injury. Any doctor who has served her or his time in an emergency room knows that. If two people arrive in an emergency room at the same time, both victims of wounds from a gunfight between them, one a policeman, one a robber, the doctor treats the most severely injured person first, no matter what.

Knowing what Christians believe, I felt I was in a unique position to understand their point of view. I also knew that Christians are taught to separate the sin from the sinner, and treat those in need with compassion, just as Jesus did. Judgment is God's business. As Surgeon General, moved by Christian compassion and the profession of medicine, my course was clear: to do all I could in this report to halt the spread of AIDS by educating the American people accurately and completely.

And education itself, I could see, was going to cause problems. Since AIDS was most often transmitted through sexual contact, my report would have to call for sex education, which in this case was a life-or-death proposition. And I knew that sex education was a buzzword that would drive many conservatives up the wall. But I hoped I could reason with the large conservative pro-life constituency (Roman Catholics, evangelicals, Protestants, and Mormons), people who knew me and had supported my confirmation. I hoped that they would be able to see that we would need very explicit sex education because if kids experimented with sex in the age of AIDS, they could die.

I saw a unique opportunity for these groups to join together to produce a morally based sex education program that would conform to their moral standards and also serve to protect a generation of youngsters from AIDS. I hoped that we could work together after the release of the report to unite morality and science. But while some of them saw it that way, all too many fell back on old fears and prejudices.

I had hoped that the delegation from the Roman Catholic Church would see the need for a health report on AIDS, even if it mentioned condoms for disease control and not for contraception. My early discussions with Roman Catholic representatives offered hints of support. I told them that they would like the stand the report took on monogamy but would find the mention of condoms troublesome. One prelate, Father O'Hehre, said that Roman Catholic philosophy, when faced with a health crisis, might find a way to accommodate that problem. On one occasion when I was discussing the forthcoming report on AIDS with John Cardinal O'Connor, I said, "Before you answer me on the condom issue, let me tell you that you can't have it both ways. Several years ago, in a communication about euthanasia, the Pope made a remarkable statement about the use of morphine in the treatment of intractable pain. The repetitive use of morphine in such a situation might hasten death but alleviate suffering. The Pope said, in reference to the morphine, 'It is not the means used but the intent of the heart.' Therefore it seems to me that under some circumstances even a Roman Catholic should see the use of a condom as a moral act. There ought to be this kind of accommodation for the use of a condom by a married couple where one became infected with the AIDS virus, say, from a transfusion, and the other has only two choices: to risk certain death by continuing a loving relationship or to remain abstinent for the remainder of the marriage. It is not the means used but the intent of the heart that counts."

But then a woman on the Roman Catholic delegation I interviewed made it clear that my report would never get the approval of the Catholic Church. A few days before the report was released, the Pope had issued his strongest ever denunciation of homosexuality, and I concluded that the Catholic Church in the United States, even if it agreed with my position on the health issues, would not be inclined to take a position that might appear to be at odds with the papacy. I sympathized with the church's theological position, but as a health officer I had hoped that they could have accommodated the health crisis, especially where it concerned non-Catholics. I was disappointed but tried to understand the dilemma they must have faced.

I knew of many Catholics' compassion for those with AIDS, including Cardinal O'Connor's selfless concern and care for persons with AIDS at St. Claire's Hospital in New York. But later I would be distressed by his statement: "Sometimes I believe the greatest damage done to persons with AIDS is done by the dishonesty of those health care professionals who refuse to confront the moral dimensions of sexual aberrations or drug abuse." All during the AIDS epidemic I have maintained that this is one disease where the scientist and moralist walk hand in hand because they advocate the same measures, even if for different reasons. When the cardinal said, "Good morality is good medicine," he was quite right. But good medicine is not always simply good morality. We would all have had an easier time if Catholic compassion were expressed not only in care of AIDS patients, but also in supporting broad measures for AIDS prevention.

As these problems nagged me, I thought I could save the American people a lot of confusion if I could get around the low-level White House staffers and invite the president to make a statement about the most pressing health threat of his tenure. I saw a great opportunity at the end of July 1986, when the first lady and the president would be mounting a new initiative against drugs—the famous "Just Say No" campaign. I did not think that "Just Say No" was going to solve our national drug problem, but because the most rapidly expanding group of persons with AIDS was intravenous drug users, I saw a way for the president to address both issues.

I called Jack Svahn, domestic policy advisor to the president, and made my pitch.

"Jack, everyplace I go I am called upon to defend the administration for some perceived mismanagement of AIDS. This is especially true of the president because of his silence on the greatest health threat of the century. If he would tie AIDS in with the first lady's drug initiative about to be launched, he would win tremendous praise not only for speaking out but also for being innovative with the IV drug spread of AIDS. It can only enhance the first lady's program."

"I'll be with the president in forty-five minutes, and I promise I'll convey your message."

Jack was true to his word and called me at home that evening.

"I talked with the president. He has seven questions."

Jack made it clear to me that Reagan had grasped the issues completely and appreciated the implications of tying the two together. I was elated.

But nothing happened. The "Just Say No" program was launched with much fanfare, but not a word about AIDS. One of my White House contacts told me later that Reagan had come to the staff meeting the next morning sold on my idea, but his advisors were simply not interested in the president's doing anything about AIDS. All they cared about were the political gains they could make from having Reagan act against drugs. AIDS was a grim and controversial subject, so they were not going to allow the president to get involved in it. As they said, " 'Just Say No' is win-win; AIDS is 'no-win.' "

In August I began to write the first draft of the AIDS report. I wrote. And I rewrote. And I rewrote some more, usually in the evening at the stand-up desk in my basement. The next day Mike Samuels and I would spend two or three hours going over a few pages word by word. Sometimes Betty gave me advice. About the time I had written the fifteenth draft, Jim Dickson suggested that we get additional female perspectives, so I shared the manuscript with his wife, my wife, and Assistant Secretary of Health Bob Windom's wife. They made a few suggestions, which we included.

After the sixteenth draft, I asked Tony Fauci, chief AIDS researcher at NIH, to read it, and he made some excellent suggestions. A few days later, on September 19, 1987, the forty-eighth anniversary of my marriage, I completed the seventeenth draft, and Mike Samuels took it to the Government Printing Office. My next step would be to present the report before the Domestic Policy Council in a series of meetings. In each meeting I would have to skate fast on thin ice to get by political appointees who placed conservative ideology above saving lives.

Knowing the way some on the Domestic Policy Council thought, I could see them nitpicking the report to pieces, and soon we would have an AIDS report steered by politics, not health—if we ended up with any report at all. I also knew they did not like to spend money. So I decided to take a psychological gamble. It had been our plan to print this report as a thirty-six-page brochure on cheap paper. We would print 2 million copies, enough, we thought, to cover any requests we might get. (Ultimately, we needed over 20 million to fill the demand.) But I also ordered 1,000 copies printed on the best-quality glossy stock, with a cover in the royal blue of the Public Health Service, its seal printed in shining silver, and across the top the title: *The Surgeon General's Report on Acquired Immune Deficiency Syndrome.* I figured that if the Domestic Policy Council were handed a pamphlet shrieking expensive paper and printing, they might be disinclined to make changes because of the cost of reprinting. I think it worked.

As I went to the Domestic Policy Council meeting accompanied by Mike Samuels and Jim McTigue, I was a little nervous but confident it would go smoothly with Ed Meese in the chair. I knew that in Otis Bowen I had a strong ally on the council.

No one but my kitchen cabinet, three wives, and two or three scientists had seen the report, and I wanted to keep it that way. I think my first remark took them by surprise.

"From what I read in the newspapers, this room has great leaks in it, and I would be very unhappy if this report were to reach the press before it was released by me. Therefore, I am handing out numbered copies of *The Surgeon General's Report on Acquired Immune Deficiency Syndrome,* and I hope you will not be insulted if I tell you that I expect to collect each of them at the close of this meeting." A few eyebrows went up.

The report covered signs and symptoms, groups at risk, methods of transmission, and prevention. I reviewed the report page by page, but in a rather superficial manner. There was little discussion. I had the general impression that it was well received, although I knew it had not been absorbed in depth by anyone present. The meeting adjourned with the consensus that I would present the report soon at a press conference. I heaved a sigh of relief, drove home more relaxed than I had been in months, and packed my bags for a visit with our son in New Hampshire and then a government trip to the Soviet Union. AIDS receded from my life for a few days. I knew some controversy might lie ahead, but I did not know how much.

At long last, on October 22, 1986, I called a press conference to release the AIDS report. The report was brief enough for the reporters to read for themselves. Its main points were clear. I reviewed them, answered questions, said good-bye, and hopped a plane for London where I had scheduled several speeches, not realizing what a stir I was leaving behind. The press conference television lights had barely been switched off when I was immediately and witlessly accused of advocating the teaching of sodomy to third-graders and passing out condoms to eight-year-olds. But those personal attacks were not my chief worry. I knew they would have no lasting effect on me. Such attacks never have. Rather, I was annoyed at those critics who attacked me personally in order to compromise the government's ability to deliver the facts about AIDS to the American people. They hated the message, so they decided to discredit the messenger.

ABC caught up with me in London, where I did two interviews for their morning news show, and then from Edinburgh phone calls to Betty and my office indicated that in general the press had reacted favorably to my report. But Betty said that of all the things I had said, only two words seemed to be remembered: sex education. I recalled that someone had asked me a question, one of the less important questions of the day, about at what age I thought sex education should begin. I simply said, "Sex education should begin at the earliest age possible." When I was asked to be more specific, I replied, "the third grade." This one comment would unleash a fire storm that would be continually reignited by shrill self-appointed protectors of the public morality such as Phyllis Schlafly.

"Sex education" has become such a buzzword and red flag that I often refer instead to "human development." But sex education is important to talk about—without buzzwords, red flags, and jargon. Sex education should begin with the child's first question on sex. Until the age of about six, children usually have only two questions: "Where did I come from?" and "Why do I look different from my brother [or sister]?" From the age of six to nine, youngsters generally ask few questions about sex. This lulls their parents into the mistaken belief that their children do not need sex education, and therefore none is given. Parents need to recognize that in our society, children receive constant sex education from siblings, friends, advertisements, and, most of all, television. When children once again begin to ask questions (about age nine), the sophistication of the queries is often embarrassing and baffling to parents, who usually give fuzzy or incomplete replies, inadvertently turning their children back to television, movies, and older kids for advanced sex education.

Recent research at Michigan State University found, for example, that the large number of ninth- and tenth-grade girls who watch between one and two hours of soap operas every day after school see sexual intercourse depicted between unmarried partners or hear it discussed an average of 1.56 times an hour. In the evening, a larger number of ninth- and tenth-graders watch three to four hours of television that in some way portray acts of unmarried intercourse an average of once an hour. The same researchers also found that 60 to 70 percent of those ninth- and tenth-graders had seen the top five "R"-rated films, in which sexual intercourse between unmarried partners occurred between eight and fifteen times per film.

Parents seem to forget that one of their obligations is to find out what their children are learning in school and from their peers. That is when they have the opportunity to correct their children's misconceptions, integrating family ethics, morality, and religion. I firmly believe that if parents accepted their responsibilities in sex education, if they worked with their schools, churches, and civic associations, then sex education curricula would teach kind, loving, considerate, and caring relationships in a family context. We might be able to turn out a generation of teenagers less sexually active—and less at risk—than the present one.

.   .   .

I returned from Great Britain to find that the White House was out to do battle with me. Of course that is not true. The White House is a building. It does not do battle. It does not even make telephone calls. But some people who work there pretend that it does. They telephone the small and the great: "This is the White House calling," and suddenly knees tremble, machinery stops, and plans are changed. The chief White House resident, the president, does not know how often he is misrepresented by those with White House stationery and telephones.

I don't know who in the White House started the campaign against the AIDS report and me. I know that by printing the word "condom" I offended Roman Catholics such as White House aide Carl Anderson (my former political mentor who now worked there), and I know that some White House staffers could not tolerate the mention of sex education. At any rate, my staff informed me that they had been told by the "White House" that printing the AIDS report would have to be "delayed" until "corrections" were made in it.

The ploy of the obstructionists in the White House was to bottle up the report. In an unusual move, White House staffers Gary Bauer and Nancy Risque came to see me and "wondered" if I didn't want to "update" the report. The report, then only a few weeks old, did not need "updating"; it doesn't need "updating" even today. The only updating they sought was to remove the reference to condoms. I refused.

Eventually the presses rolled, the mail trucks ran, and the report went out. The report was sent to anyone who requested it. Congressmen sent it to their constituents, as did many of the groups who had counseled my AIDS staff. The PTA sent out 55,000 copies. The combined circulation of newspapers that reprinted the entire text of the report was over two million. At last the American people knew what was myth and what was fact about the AIDS epidemic, and they knew it in plain English. But they wanted to hear more, and I found myself deluged by requests from all over the country to speak at various meetings and conventions, even to combined sessions of state legislatures. Invitations—some read more like a summons—poured in at a rate of thirty-five a week. America was finally getting mobilized against AIDS. And a new and surprising band of opponents was mobilizing against me.

At first I did not realize what impact the report would have on the public. Suddenly I found myself praised by my former liberal adversaries and condemned by my former conservative allies. Of course, the praise was easy to accept, and it was especially gratifying when those groups and senators who had fought my confirmation now saw that I had done what I had promised to do: anything I could for the health of the American people. But the opposition troubled me, especially because it often came from people whom I considered my friends.

Castigation by the *political* right, although disappointing and unpleasant, did not unduly upset me; after all, castigation seemed to be their business. But I did feel a profound sense of betrayal by those on the *religious* right who took me to task. My position on AIDS was dictated by scientific integrity and Christian compassion. I felt that my Christian opponents had abandoned not only their old friend, but also their own commitment to integrity and compassion.

Everybody, or at least those who did not know me, said that I had changed. Conservatives said I had changed, and they were angry. Liberals said I had changed, and they were pleased. But I had not changed at all. All the fuss surprised me. I just did what I had always done as a doctor. My whole career had been dedicated to prolonging lives, especially the lives of people who were weak and powerless, the disenfranchised who needed an advocate: newborns who needed surgery, handicapped children, unborn children, people with AIDS.

I thought that once I had released my report, AIDS and I would part company for a while, and I could get back to the other issues piling up on my desk. Two more smoking reports were in the pipeline, one on passive smoking and one on nicotine addiction, and the now frightened and still unscrupulous tobacco people were fighting back. And there were severe problems in the Commissioned Corps of the Public Health Service—my direct responsibility—that needed to be addressed yesterday.

Suddenly, when I had more to do than ever, I was sidelined by injury, an old ski-jumping injury. For a frightening twenty-four hours I thought that I might have become quadriplegic. My neck, broken in that spectacular soaring crash in the intramural ski-jumping competition at Dartmouth fifty-one years before, had served me pretty well until I awoke in the middle of a November night in Texas, unable to move either arm, barely able to wiggle my toes. I had gone to San Antonio to accept the presidency of the Association of Military Surgeons of the United States and for some reason, while relaxing on a patio for a few minutes I broke out in a case of hives. Perhaps I had been stung by an insect. Later I figured out that the Benedryl that I took to relieve the hives had put me into a very deep sleep and my head had rolled off the pillow with my neck bent in such a way that my anterior spinal artery was compressed in my spinal canal (narrowed by my ski-jumping injury and arthritis) causing the paralysis. It was a frightening experience, and although I regained all of my neurologic function I willingly underwent spinal surgery to make sure it did not happen again. But it kept me home from work almost every day from early November until early January. Thank God I recovered completely, with a neck stronger than before, even though I had to wear a cervical collar for six weeks. My office wanted to make sure the public knew that I would recover fully, so they released the story, explaining that the problem stemmed from the ski-jumping accident when I was in college. A few press accounts did not specify when the accident had occurred, leaving the impression that the seventy-year-old Surgeon General had been injured in a ski-jumping accident . . . in Texas?

The weeks of postoperative recovery—never before had I suffered/ enjoyed such a long period of forced inactivity—gave me the period of reflection and contemplation I needed. I saw three major challenges ahead of me as far as AIDS was concerned.

First, I needed to capitalize on my new alliance with the moderates and liberals to continue to get the message on AIDS to each American citizen. The report was the first step, to be followed by more speeches than I could count, and eventually an AIDS mailer sent to 107 million American households.

Second, I had to do what I could to align the White House properly in the fight against AIDS. That meant getting around my sniping adversaries to prompt the president to follow his natural instincts of fairness, compassion, and leadership. If I did not succeed, it was not for lack of trying.

Finally, I wanted to mend fences where possible with my critics on the right, even though that seemed impossible. I soon realized that many conservative political columnists and pundits, such as Ronald Evans, Robert Novak, and *National Review* authors, were not about to be inconvenienced by the truth. I am ashamed that in my earliest days in Washington I was pleased when Evans and Novak blasted someone I opposed. If Evans and Novak were as inaccurate about them as they were about me and the facts surrounding me, I should have written letters of condolence to their targets. I was told once that the president read Evans and Novak the first thing each morning. If that is true, he had a warped idea of the Washington world.

In the relatively brief article Evans and Novak wrote about me and AIDS in *The Washington Post* (January 26, 1987) I found seventeen factual errors and twenty omissions that distorted the truth. On a television appearance with the McLaughlin Group, Novak predicted that there would be a confrontation between Secretary of Education William Bennett and me, and one of us would have to leave the administration. When asked which one, he said, "Koop will have to go." How do you mend fences with someone like Novak? Fortunately Novak was as wrong as he was offensive.

Then there was Phyllis Schlafly. Why anyone paid attention to this lady is one of the mysteries of the eighties. Maybe no one really did. She buzzed around me like an angry hornet. Phyllis Schafly made it clear to me that she would rather see promiscuous young people contract and transmit AIDS than expose her own children to the existence of condoms. Schlafly, whose idea of sex education was something like, "Don't let anyone touch you where you wear your swimsuit," attacked me by mail and through the newsletter of her "Eagle Forum." My gut reaction was to pen a point-by-point refutation of all the lies she was circulating about me, but then I decided against dignifying her charges by a specific rebuttal, so I was content to release a general statement, repeating the main points of the AIDS report. She responded by holding a press conference, claiming that my AIDS report "looks and reads like it was edited by the Gay Task Force," and that I advocated teaching "safe sodomy" to third-graders—words that never crossed my lips. My mental image of what she must have imagined about that teaching exercise was mind-shattering. At one point I simply told reporters, "I'm not Surgeon General to make Phyllis Schlafly happy. I'm Surgeon General to save lives." In the middle of all this, she stormed into my office in the Humphrey Building to hand-deliver another angry letter. Schlafly was beneath contempt, and I would not lower myself to respond.

But she was not through with me. Later in the spring, when I was still under daily attack for my forthright stand on AIDS, I was deeply moved when a small group of my faithful conservative supporters decided to boost my spirits by hosting a dinner "Salute to the Surgeon General." A number of political luminaries, including the long list of budding Republican presidential candidates, accepted the invitation to be on the dinner committee. Then Schlafly went to work, in the deceptive way I had seen her work so many times before, to sabotage the salute. At one of her Republican fund-raising meetings, she circulated a piece of paper on which she said people should sign their names if they wanted more information on sex education. (Was she going to send them a picture of a swimsuit?) Then, without the knowledge of those who signed the request form, she instead appended their names to a petition denouncing me and urging a boycott of the dinner in my honor. To my amazement, supposed stalwarts Bob Dole, Jack Kemp, Pete Dupont, and Pat Robertson knuckled under and backed out. Jesse Helms, who had told me a month earlier that he had to be in North Carolina, remained a sponsor. And George Bush, whose schedule did not allow him to attend, sent me a deeply appreciated letter of support. Orrin Hatch, his usual gracious self, attended the salute and spoke movingly.

Although I was stung by the attacks of political conservatives like Schlafly, Evans, and Novak, I realized that their vitriolic behavior was probably only compensation for their lack of real influence. I decided that not only could fences not be mended, but also it was not worth my time to talk with them, because they had long since stopped listening.

But I held out hope that I could reason with the religious right, people with whom I shared the deepest beliefs and values. As I recuperated from my neck surgery, I decided to do something that probably no other government official had ever done: to spend seven weeks speaking only to religious groups.

When I explained my plan to Jerry Falwell, he immediately invited me to speak in his church (to be televised over a broad network) and at Chapel Service at his Liberty University in Lynchburg, Virginia. I wanted to make clear the connection between my Christian faith, my commitment to integrity, and the opportunity AIDS presented the Christian community to demonstrate true compassion. I also wanted to emphasize the role of morality and values in sex education. My speechwriter, Ted Cron, and I spent hours on my address, and then Mike Samuels, Betty, and I went over every word again once we arrived in Lynchburg. In morning church service I gave my personal Christian testimony and then spoke briefly about the challenge of AIDS. In the evening I gave my speech, which I repeated again the next day to more than five thousand students at the university. I made similar use of a speaking invitation from the National Association of Religious Broadcasters and radio interviews on religious networks. Most of these, like my time on WMBI, the radio station of the Moody Bible Institute in Chicago, went very well, and I think did a lot to set thinking straight on AIDS in the Bible Belt. Sometimes, though, these people proved stubbornly uneducable, like the interviewer on CBN (Pat Robertson's network) who obviously disapproved of my efforts and kept asking why I hadn't taken steps to protect the blood supply by rounding up all the people with "bad blood." Nothing I said about statistics or public health principles made any impression, so I asked her how she would go about rounding up people, where she would put them, and how would it be fair? When she said that I had not answered her question, I said she had not answered mine, and until she did, I wouldn't. I got so annoyed with her and with CBN that I walked off the set early.

In general, I think my efforts with the religious right were productive. All of us would have preferred not to need to deal with AIDS. But we could agree on the role of Christian compassion in a secular world. The church still has a long way to go on meeting the challenge of AIDS worldwide, and there are too many Christians moved by prejudice and fear rather than by love and understanding. But some of the most productive, resourceful, and helpful assistance to people with AIDS and their families has come from religious groups all across the country—people who rolled up their sleeves and did what could be done and what ought to be done, without debate or fanfare.

The opposition in the White House would be thornier. I thought the best way to deal with their unrelenting opposition was for all of us to get together and talk through the issues. My convalescence from surgery made that difficult, but one day I was driven to the White House, where I discussed AIDS and sex education with White House aides Carl Anderson, Bob Sweet, Becky Dunlap, and Gary Bauer. At this time I think it was sex education that rankled most with Bauer and Sweet. I had reminded them that before they knew what sex was, I had been on the stump decrying the semi-pornographic type of sex education they opposed. Bauer and Sweet were hostile from the beginning, Anderson seemed sullen, but Dunlap pointed out that the Surgeon General was fulfilling his obligation as a health officer, that the AIDS report had said everything that it had to say, and that anyway, it had been approved unanimously by the Domestic Policy Council. I did not think her co-workers were listening.

A second White House meeting went even worse. Carl Anderson objected to the statement in the AIDS report that "Most Americans are opposed to homosexuality, promiscuity of any kind, and prostitution." He wanted me to say "All Americans . . ." and did not seem to understand that I could not say it because it was not true.

Gary Bauer relayed to me a telling incident that had taken place at his wife's home over Christmas. He said that when the subject of AIDS had come up, some member of the family had said, "Koop wants to give condoms to kids in the third grade." I said to Bauer, "I'm sure no one in your family read the report if that's what they think." He said,

"That's true." The Reagan White House, including the president himself at times, reasoned anecdotally instead of examining the evidence and drawing conclusions. I was dismayed that this was the kind of thinking that was going into White House policy-making.

One of the problems was William Bennett and his allies in the White House. Although I approached sex education from the standpoint of my health responsibilities, Secretary of Education Bennett claimed that it was in his domain. The press thrived on "leaks" from the White House about the feud between Bennett and me, even before he and I had ever spoken to each other about AIDS. During my several meetings with Bill Bennett, we seemed to get along quite well. I think that if he had not held such preconceived notions about the inappropriateness of sex education for grade school children, we might have gotten along just fine. We may have been closer than the public thought.

Things got straightened out as much as possible at a meeting of the Domestic Policy Council on the government's role in sex education. Secretary Bowen opened with a well-balanced speech that stressed the need for compassion for the afflicted and for education for those who might be. I spoke next, explaining that sex education takes place whether parents like it or not, and that the death threat posed by AIDS mandated school-based education. As soon as I finished, Secretary of Energy John Herrington moved that we should do all we can, with haste, in reference to AIDS education. All went well until Gary Bauer had his turn. He dug out his old white notebook containing examples of bad semi-pornographic sex education material. I had seen this book on Carl Anderson's desk and in Bob Sweet's hands; I thought it must have made the rounds of every meeting in the White House. Bauer said that he did not want his five-year-old daughter, his six-year-old daughter, or even his fifteen-year-old girl to hear the lurid details of anal intercourse. No one had ever suggested they should learn this, so I spoke up. I said that there were a lot of things parents did not like to tell their children or have them learn. Parents don't like to tell their children that there are people out there who will offer them candy, take them on rides, and then sexually molest them and perhaps never bring them back. Hundreds of parents who have tried to spare their children this warning have lost those children forever, victims of kidnapping or murder. I thought I had made my point, although the meeting ended with the usual admonitions for Education and Health to get together and iron out their differences.

But the sniping continued, so back I went to the Domestic Policy

Council for round three. I said I would not discuss AIDS or sex education. What more could I say on those subjects for the present? But I would talk about the integrity of my office and how angry I was at the attempt to have me muzzled. When I finished, Ed Meese, who had chaired the meeting, looked completely surprised, claiming that no one in the White House had tried to muzzle me. Then those who had tried to muzzle me pretended they knew nothing about it. In the end we agreed that I was free to speak my mind and that sex education should be done at the local level, with the government providing health consultation to educators but not dispensing education for the country.

It seemed like reason had won the day, but I knew that no one's mind had been changed. Just a short time later another meeting of the working group on health of the Domestic Policy Council left me depressed and angry. Becky Dunlap, who had spoken intelligently earlier and was even a nurse, said that there were many people in the country whose ideas on AIDS differed from those of the government, and perhaps we should hear from them. She meant people who thought AIDS was transmitted by cats, mosquitos, doorknobs, toilet seats, and the like. "Who is to know?" she said. "Maybe they are right and the government is wrong." I replied that it had become obvious to me in my last two meetings with the Domestic Policy Council that some crazies had gotten to some members of the Cabinet. I tried to explain the difference between prejudiced ideas and solid science. The people around the table who had some health background nodded in agreement, but these discussions about AIDS depressed me more than ever about the lack of judgment among some government figures in high places.

Another example of the unreal world in which the president and his advisors were living came when Carl Anderson called me to get some information about the Philadelphia College of Physicians because Reagan planned to speak there on "Challenges for Medicine in the Future." Carl asked me if I thought the president should mention AIDS. I replied, "How can the president speak on medical challenges of the future and never mention the greatest single threat to the health of the nation?" Once again I hung up the phone, shaking my head in disbelief at the strange mentality of the White House staff.

But I still wanted to maintain a personal relationship with Carl. I felt especially saddened about the breach that AIDS had produced with him, who had been my early Washington friend and mentor. One day, after an uneasy lunch at the White House mess, we went back to his office. I turned to him and asked: "You're disappointed with me, aren't you?" Anderson replied, "I wouldn't quite put it that way, but I don't think that sex education should be given to children, and I also think you've been too lenient toward homosexuals in the language you use in your report and in your speeches." I told him that I had not addressed a single word to homosexuals; I had addressed dying people. "If some of them are homosexual, that cannot be an issue of concern for a health officer." Later, a mutual friend who knew how concerned I was about the distance that had grown between Anderson and me arranged a dinner as an opportunity for discussion and possible reconciliation. It was a discouraging occasion. He objected to everything in the AIDS report: sex education, the mention of condoms, the explicit descriptions of the disease and its transmission, and even the inclusion of telephone numbers of homosexual organizations offering help to people with AIDS. He did not buy my argument that an infected homosexual was unlikely to turn to the National Council of Churches or the government to find a place of refuge or a place to die. After that dinner I never heard from Anderson again.

I will not pretend that I was happy with the harshness of the judgment on me by those conservatives whom I had counted as allies and even friends. I also felt stung by the lack of support from the White House. But, as in so many moments of stress in my life, I realized that God was still sovereign, that I was performing a necessary role, that even though I was unable to control the forces around me, I was confident I was right. I admit I do not take lightly to criticism, and I had a strong desire to defend myself against the attacks of my erstwhile friends turned hostile critics. But I knew that the best defense was a good offense, and there was much to do in the offensive against AIDS. So I kept busy.

By this time my travels around the country confirmed that although a few people on the far right still opposed my efforts on AIDS because they were misinformed, misguided, or vindictive, most of the country was behind me. But many people thought the president should be out in front offering the leadership that only he could provide. At least a dozen times I had pleaded with my critics in the White House to set up a meeting between the president and me so he could hear my concerns about America and the AIDS epidemic. And for months I had tried to cover for the embarrassing silence of the Oval Office on the scourge of AIDS. I kept telling myself the president had to speak out soon. As the nation awaited Reagan's penultimate State of the Union address, I was informed that at last he would speak boldly on AIDS. Hopeful and attentive, I tuned in. Reagan covered everything from Afghanistan to defense, but offered not a word about AIDS, as great a threat to the American people as anything on the horizon. I knew that Reagan, like most presidents, cared about his place in history, and I feared that his accomplishments might pale if he were eventually remembered as the president who did nothing about the AIDS epidemic.

After I returned from a trip to California where my AIDS messages were warmly received, I called Gary Bauer to tell him that the West Coast press had intensified its charges that the president was failing the country by his silence on AIDS. Bauer lashed out, saying that Reagan and he (was this a new alliance?) had decided to move further away from me on issues like sex education and condoms. He said the president wanted to say only one thing about AIDS: The nation was facing the problem of AIDS simply because it had abandoned traditional morality, and it would not get out of the situation until we returned to that morality. I said that while I and many Americans might agree with that assessment, the country was not going to accept that as the president's way of addressing a national health threat.

Then, as I talked it all over with Betty, I came to agree with her view that I should not try to reach the president to push him, that I would have to let the White House act in its own way, no matter how misguided it appeared. So I called Bauer back to say that I was not trying to put pressure on Reagan. Bauer then asked if I wanted to set up a meeting with the president to discuss AIDS. I said I would welcome the opportunity. No invitation came.

Finally, on April 1, 1987, the president mentioned AIDS for the first time in public, touching on the epidemic briefly and superficially in his speech at the Philadelphia College of Physicians. Striding by a number of reporters shouting questions about AIDS as he went up the ramp to Air Force One, he turned on the top step and said, "Just Say No." That night, NBC anchorman Tom Brokaw reported that the president had not even read *The Surgeon General's Report on Acquired Immune Deficiency Syndrome*.

At least I was able to talk to the vice president. George Bush and I had met soon after I arrived in Washington. At a reception for some visiting Nigerian dignitaries I had walked up to him, introducing myself as the "controversial Surgeon General–designate." We had an amiable but substantive chat and seemed to get onto the same wavelength quickly. In the next few years we crossed paths several times, and he always made a point to exchange a few personal words. I hoped that a meeting with Bush would accomplish two things: It might lead to ending the White House silence on the AIDS crisis, and it would help prepare the man who might be the next president for the national health crisis of AIDS. We spent an hour and a half together, during which he revealed his basic moral stance, derived, as he said, from the Bible, and committed to fidelity and monogamy. He said he was opposed to homosexual behavior and promiscuity, but it was difficult to speak publicly on these issues. He quickly sized up the different dimensions of the AIDS problem, and we discussed holding an international meeting on AIDS. The presidential primary season had already opened, and I was pleased to hear that in an Iowa primary campaign speech Bush stated that he would not distance himself from AIDS as Reagan had, but he would speak forcefully on the issue. But in the first years of his presidency he was just as silent on AIDS as his predecessor was.

Congress was way ahead of the White House in meeting the challenge of AIDS, and I suddenly found myself the hero of those Democrats who had most strongly opposed my nomination as Surgeon General. And since the Democrats had regained control of the Senate, my new alliance with the influential leaders of the Senate and House committees concerned with health issues allowed us to accomplish a lot in a hurry. When Assistant Secretary of Health Bob Windom and I were called to testify before the Senate Committee on Labor and Human Resources, just before the session was called to order by Chairman Ted Kennedy, someone tapped me on the shoulder. Senator Kennedy—who had spoken so harshly against me in my confirmation hearing before voting a resounding "No!"—said, "I want to tell you how pleased I am with the leadership role you have taken as Surgeon General in the Public Health Service; we're all very proud of you." As he smiled and started to walk away I replied, "Senator, the first thing you said to me when I came to Washington was that you and I could do a lot for health together in this town; now that you're back in the saddle, let's do it." Senators Lowell Weicker and Howard Metzenbaum, both of whom had voted against my confirmation, were embarrassingly effusive at the hearing about my conduct of the office of Surgeon General, very gratifying words, even it four years later.

I enjoyed a similarly warm and appreciative reception by the House committee dealing with health, another group that had enjoyed pillorying me a few years earlier. Chairman Henry Waxman and I had long since smoked the peace pipe—figuratively speaking, of course—because of our joint efforts against smoking. When I was under attack for the report on AIDS, Waxman went on television to say he had been wrong about me: "Dr. Koop is a man of great integrity." I was deeply touched.

But while I had come to like Henry, I did not like what I had to say before his committee. The main subject of one of his committee hearings was condom advertising on television. I did not like having to talk repeatedly about condoms. Many of my critics viewed anal intercourse as a violation of laws both spiritual and temporal. So did I. But that was hardly the compelling public health issue in 1987. The issue then was that anal intercourse was a primary method of transmitting the AIDS virus. We had to recognize that, and then we had to convince men to stop doing it, or at least to minimize their risk by using condoms. It was difficult for an old-timer of seventy, about to celebrate his fiftieth wedding anniversary, to talk about condoms. When Betty heard what I was doing, she said, "I'm glad your mother's not alive to hear you!" I often wondered what my prim and proper mother would have thought. I did not like being called the "condom king." I did not like how the press would often ignore most of what I said, just to focus on a sentence on condoms. Sometimes all the talk about condoms in America in 1987 reminded me of seventh-grade boys suddenly realizing they can get away with saying naughty words. Almost everywhere I spoke, there seemed to be the obligatory condom joke. The most oft-told, and a reflection of the times, was about Tommy and his little brother, who were playing outside on the patio. The younger boy ran inside to tell his parent, "Tommy says he found a condom on the patio . . . What's a patio?" But as people chuckled I found myself deeply saddened by what had happened to America's sexual morality and by the associated grim epidemic.

I was concerned because the preoccupation with condoms obscured my message. I never mentioned the use of condoms as a preventive measure against AIDS without *first* stressing the much better and much safer alternatives of *abstinence* and *monogamy*. I also said that condoms were all we had to offer, but that they were not 100 percent reliable, although they were often more reliable than the people who used them. Often I would spend several minutes of a speech extolling abstinence and monogamy (for social and moral reasons as well as reasons of health), and then at the end I would say that those foolish enough not to practice abstinence or mutually faithful monogamy should, for their protection and their partner's protection, use a latex condom. Usually the press would repeat only the last phrase. That annoyed me.

But, in general, I must commend the press for the way they conveyed the message on AIDS to the American people. We were making progress. There was still too much ignorance, too much fear, too much prejudice, but the American people were learning about AIDS. I felt I was doing all I could. But for all we had accomplished, one major issue loomed large, an issue that would dictate the course of the American response to AIDS and shape official AIDS policy: testing.

At first it made sense to many people: With a killer disease on the loose, just test everybody to see who has it. But a little more thought on the issue revealed the shortcomings of that simplistic solution. First, what would you do with those who tested positive? Of course, I had already heard from those congressmen and others who wanted to get rid of those with the AIDS virus or put them into concentration camps. And there was that little issue of the Constitution, which did not allow you to round up people because they were ill. AIDS became an issue not only of health, but also of civil rights. Widespread AIDS testing could result only in widespread discrimination against people who tested positive. Already the American people, at least those Americans with a sense of justice and compassion, were horrified by the story of Ryan White, the schoolboy who had contracted AIDS from a blood transfusion. Picketed by schoolmates' parents, shunned by his classmates, he had been driven by fear and hatred from his school and town in Indiana. And then there was the Ray family in Florida, whose three little hemophiliac boys—infected with HIV through no decision of their own—not only suffered humiliating discrimination but also saw their house burned down by arsonists, presumably fearful and hate-filled neighbors.

Although health officials continued to stress the vital importance of *voluntary* and *confidential* testing for AIDS, we opposed mandatory testing. Millions of ordinary Americans concerned about civil rights and basic liberties recoiled from what could happen to people who tested positive for AIDS, even those who had not yet displayed any symptoms. They could lose their jobs, their homes, their insurance, their families. And all these calamities could also befall the small percentage of those tested who in those days would register a false positive because of inaccuracies inherent in the test itself.

Above all, mandatory AIDS testing would drive underground, away from help and counseling, the very AIDS-infected people who needed help—not only with their own health care, but in reforming their behavior so they would not infect others. Driven underground, these people would only continue to spread the disease.

Testing advocates then called for premarital testing. This seemed to be a way to get testing in through the back door. Their logic, which likened AIDS testing to the once-mandatory Wassermann test for syphilis for all couples intending to marry was flawed. First, the test for syphilis, although discovered sixteen years before a cure for syphilis was available, was not mandated until the cure was available. What was the point of the premarital AIDS test if there was no cure? Second, times had changed. When the Wassermann test was introduced, there still existed in the United States public censure against premarital cohabitation. In the eighties, about 75 percent of marrying couples had lived together before marriage. A medical test might be a deterrent to marriage, but would do nothing to stop the spread of AIDS.

The most important ten days in the politics of AIDS began on May 21, 1987. Two events loomed on the horizon, and the president was going to have to make a clear policy statement on AIDS. He was slated to make a speech at the American Medical Foundation for AIDS Research (AMFAR) gala featuring Elizabeth Taylor, at which I was to be honored. Ten days later, Washington would host the annual International Congress on AIDS, and the administration could not pretend that the congress and the disease did not exist. So when I received a call from Landon Parvin, Nancy Reagan's speechwriter, I figured he might be preparing the president's speech. I took the opportunity to fill his ear for a half hour, giving him some anecdotes for Reagan to use, hoping to make it clear that the president and I were not of different minds on AIDS.

Later Parvin called back, saying that he had discussed the speech with the president, who said to tell me he knew all too well how the press could make two people appear to be at odds when really they were allies. Then Parvin told me that Reagan had said, "No, I'll tell Dr. Koop that myself." I waited for the president's phone call, but it never came.

However, a couple of days later, when I was speaking after dinner in Salt Lake City, I received a summons to a Domestic Policy Council meeting at 2 P.M. the next day. On almost no sleep, I zipped to the airport early in the morning, jetted to Dulles, and then ducked out the back of the plane onto the tarmac and into a waiting van that took me to a car that sped into Washington on Route 66. I reached the southwest gate of the White House at exactly 2 P.M., was recognized by the guard, and hurried to the Roosevelt Room. Gary Bauer, who ran the meeting, went over a number of options regarding AIDS, including mandatory testing.

Then I had the chance to make my points. First, I said, we should refer to testing as "targeted," not "mandatory," to avoid the authoritarian overtones. I went on to discuss the disruptive impact on families and communities of false-positive tests for AIDS. I was able to cite a hypothetical study done for *The Boston Globe* that estimated that 100,000 tests in Massachusetts would result in 175 true positives and 250 false positives. I pointed out the invalid comparison between the AIDS test and the Wassermann test. I felt that I was heard, and heeded.

But there was still one big hurdle. At last, there would be a full Cabinet meeting devoted primarily to AIDS. As far as I know, it might be the only U.S. Cabinet meeting at which AIDS was discussed, and it would determine the Reagan administration's future plans on AIDS. The few of us from the Department of Health and Human Services who were invited sat around before the meeting, nervously planning our strategy. Then Secretary Bowen arrived, apparently happy with his advance draft of Reagan's embargoed speech for the AMFAR gala. It made us all breathe a little easier. The president was going to follow the path marked by health officers, not by political advisors in the White House. The speech included almost every one of the ideas I had discussed with speechwriter Parvin. But I knew it could all change if the discussion in the Cabinet went the wrong way.

The president came in, took his place at the table flanked by cabinet members, told a joke, and proceeded to a discussion of AIDS. It turned out I had the best seat in the house, in the row of chairs one removed from the table, but directly opposite the president. By looking between the heads of the two men just in front of me, I had eye-to-eye contact with the president. Unobtrusively, I pushed my chair back about six inches, so I was slightly behind the two men seated on either side of me, James Mason and Bob Windom. No one was behind me. No one could see my face easily except the president.

The discussions covered the gamut of AIDS questions, ranging from mandatory testing to discrimination to segregation of HIV-positive prisoners to the testing of aliens and those applying for immigration. Whenever the president had a query that I wanted to answer, or whenever a Cabinet member made a statement I wanted to reinforce or rebut, I raised my right index finger beside my nose and almost imperceptibly nodded toward the president. It was like silent bidding at an auction; no one except Reagan could see me. He acknowledged me on each occasion, saying something like, "I'd like to hear from Dr. Koop on that," or "Would you care to comment on that, Dr. Koop?"

That system worked eight times; there were no misses. Several times Jim Mason spoke up to confirm what I had said. Reagan ended up espousing the precepts of the Public Health Service on AIDS. The integrity of the AMFAR speech was preserved. The president would not follow the advice of his staff and take positions contrary to good public health policy.

The next evening, at the AMFAR gala (held along the Potomac in a sweltering tent), Reagan's excellent speech—the key sentence was that we would *offer* routine testing—laid to rest the danger of mandatory testing and kept the federal government off the wrong road on AIDS. I was so pleased that I barely noticed the picketers, led by anti-homosexual Paul Cameron, who were shouting obscenities as they milled around carrying placards: "Quarantine Manhattan Island," "Burn Koop," and other encouraging messages.

Our position against mandatory premarital testing was eventually vindicated by the states that initially adopted it, Illinois and Louisiana, because they later repealed their testing laws. I inadvertently stopped governor John Sununu from making a similar mistake in New Hampshire. In the spring of 1987, one Bob Wilson, who had been an intern when I had been a resident in Philadelphia years before, got in touch to ask me about the arguments against premarital HIV testing. He told me he was practicing pediatrics in Concord, New Hampshire. He did not say that he was also a member of the state legislature. During the New Hampshire legislature's debate on Sununu's bill mandating premarital HIV testing, Wilson reported that he had just heard from the Surgeon General and went on to summarize my reasons against premarital testing. Sununu's bill was defeated.

A few weeks later, when I attended my fiftieth reunion at Dartmouth, I was introduced to Sununu. By his demeanor I assumed he was still smarting from the defeat of his bill, but I explained my unsuspecting role and added, "But let me tell you, sir, the day will come when you will be grateful that bill did not pass."

The AIDS Cabinet meeting and Reagan's speech kept the government from doing the wrong thing on AIDS. Whether they always did the right things is a different question.

For me, the rest of 1987, as jottings from my appointment ledger indicate, was an AIDS kaleidoscope: Went on ABC with Tim Johnson to discuss AIDS . . . Appeared on PBS on John McLaughlin's "One-on-One". . . . Operating surgeons were getting stuck by needles contaminated with the blood of HIV-positive patients . . . Met with Howard Baker (then White House chief of staff) concerning the composition of the Presidential Commission on AIDS and its charter, discussions he asked not be made public . . . Had lunch with George Bush to discuss his concerns about AIDS and then met with Nick Brady (his eventual Secretary of the Treasury) concerning the need for Bush to take an up-front position on AIDS and to distance himself from the perception the public had about President Reagan and AIDS . . . Helped the AMA House of Delegates get through its large number of AIDS resolutions . . . Discussed in the *American Medical News* the issue of confidential AIDS testing of patients before surgery . . . Spent a week in West and East Berlin on AIDS . . . Met with Benjamin Hooks, executive director of the NAACP, on AIDS, and then spoke briefly with Jesse Jackson . . . Made a public service announcement on AIDS with Ed Koch, Mayor of New York . . . Discussed the issue of providing clean needles to drug addicts, but was discouraged by the claim that drug addicts often want to share used needles as part of their camaraderie . . . All the talk about a national drug strategy seemed pointless without an understanding of the link between drug use and HIV infection . . . Met with representatives of the AMA and the pharmaceutical industry and bounced off them my idea for incentive testing, i.e., get tested and be listed by number to take priority advantage should the day come when a better drug than AZT is available . . . Spoke to Evangelical Christian Publishers about hating the sin but loving the sinner . . . Spoke to 900 recruits and 650 instruction officers at the Army's Fort Leonard Wood in preparing an AIDS video to be seen by all recruits to the U.S. Army . . . Learned that Army personnel who speak to an AIDS counselor at social functions are assumed to be seropositive, thus putting AIDS counselors in social isolation . . . Spoke in Cincinnati to the National Council of Juvenile and Family Court Judges and was concerned that the questions asked revealed how little was understood about AIDS . . . Discussed with teenagers how when you have sex with someone, as far as disease transmittal is concerned you're having sex with everyone they have had sex with, everyone those people have had sex with, and so on . . . Taped an HBO show, "Everything You Wanted to Know about AIDS But Were Afraid to Ask" . . . Met with labor groups about AIDS, telling them that I was the grandson of a letter carrier and a metalworker (their two unions happened to be the first mentioned at the meeting) . . . Health attendants' contact with splashed AIDS blood has become an issue . . . Went with President Reagan and the new members of the AIDS Commission to NIH, where the president and I, alone in an anteroom for security reasons, discussed AIDS briefly but long enough to have a good conversation . . . Participated in a bipartisan briefing on AIDS run by Senator Kennedy . . . Met with Bill Smith from the Academy of Health Education, who has a $118 million contract with WHO to teach about AIDS in the Third World . . . Went to New York, where I visited Dr. Margaret Haggerty, who does AIDS work at Harlem Hospital . . . Visited clinics in Greenwich Village, met with gay and lesbian groups, made rounds on pediatric wards . . . Excellent discussion on *Good Morning America* with four teenagers who are AIDS counselors in their high schools . . . Met when I could for news photos with congressmen who were sending letters and/or the *Surgeon General's Report* to constituents . . . Spoke to 4,500 in Indianapolis at a meeting of the Society of State Legislatures . . . Flurry of announcements defending the president once again because his staff has been slow in declaring October to be AIDS Awareness Month . . . Congress got so impatient that even though Kennedy thought this initiative should come from the president, he and Waxman prepared bills to be brought up when Congress reconvened after Labor Day to force the issue . . . The AIDS virus is being transmitted from female to male although it is easier to do it the other way . . . Although mandatory testing is a bad idea, voluntary testing should be encouraged, especially for people with high-risk behavior in their past who are about to be married, not only for their own sake, but to keep their children from the danger of AIDS . . . The Ray family in Florida, with three hemophiliac children who are HIV-positive, are being harassed; the kids cannot go to school . . . Helped the American Red Cross film *Letter from Brian* (an AIDS teaching film for high schools) . . . Secretary of Education Bennett is critical of HHS and I am asked to adjudicate . . . Appeared on *Good Morning, America* in reference to the Ray children, whose home has now been burned down . . . Bennett returns from England with an incorrect story that condoms are 70 percent ineffective; he's wrong, but I'm the lightning rod . . . Increasing number of letters from the religious right criticizing me for my stand on homosexuality in spite of the fact that I've never taken one (most of these letters also demand no tax money for AIDS research, no terminal care for AIDS victims if they are homosexuals, etc.) . . . An increase in heterosexual transmission reported in Puerto Rico, somewhat as it was in Haiti several years before . . . Taped a good Public Broadcasting System show on AIDS with Susan Dey of *L.A. Law* . . . Testified on September 9 before the Commission on AIDS . . . Had supper at the Bush residence and chatted with the vice president and his wife about the epidemic . . . Spoke with Hollywood producers and directors about the difficulties of getting my AIDS message across when their programs glorify infidelity and promiscuity . . . Breakfast with Morgan Fairchild brought a mutual agreement to support each other in reference to AIDS education . . . Taped a Robert Schuller program at the Crystal Cathedral on AIDS and the need for Christians to show compassion to those dying of AIDS . . . Addressed the Los Angeles World's Affair Council on AIDS . . . Involved for the first time in the FDA's production of a brochure on condoms (eventually to go through unbelievable opposition without resolution until April 1990) . . . In London, Edinburgh, and Glasgow to investigate IV drug abusers' needle exchange programs . . . In Tokyo discussing "ethics, culture, and morals" in reference to AIDS . . . Discussions with the Ministry of Health in Japan concerning the incarceration of those with AIDS . . . Advocated in a syndicated article, published throughout the country, forthright admonitions to physicians about taking charge of the AIDS problem, including recommending condoms and instruction in their proper use to sexually active patients . . . Spoke with 365 CEOs from *Fortune* 1,000 gathered for a symposium on "AIDS at the Work Site" . . . Spoke at the U.N. General Assembly in New York on AIDS and its global challenge . . . Testified before the House on pediatric AIDS . . . Surprised by a note of congratulation for my stance on AIDS from former President Nixon . . . Addressed the Institute of Medicine on AIDS . . . Took a firm position against the recommendation that all universities and high schools seek 100 percent participation in voluntary HIV testing to enable us to learn the percentage of students infected with AIDS . . . *The Washington Post* reported that the Conference of Catholic Bishops granted a qualified acceptance of condoms with the publication of *The Many Faces of AIDS* . . . Involved in a controversy with Ted Weiss, congressman from New York, who wants records of our NIH AIDS patients, including their names (usually deleted to assure anonymity), to give Congress qualified access to private patients' confidential records . . . Met with George Bush, Tony Fauci, and the vice president's former Episcopal priest on a number of ethical and moral issues concerning AIDS. . . .

The AIDS Report had done its job: It had made accurate information on AIDS available to the American people. But we knew from the start that making the information available would not ensure that the people would receive it. Because most people did not engage in the kind of high-risk activities that transmitted AIDS, they were not anxiously seeking more information about it. And, for all its accuracy and simplicity, the AIDS report had been distributed very unevenly. We in the

Public Health Service had discussed several times the idea of mailing a copy of the report to everyone on the IRS mailing list, the largest list in the country. After all, the British government, in an unprecedented public health endeavor, had mailed a brochure on AIDS to every noncommercial address in the United Kingdom. But doing the same in the United States was a much more expensive and complicated production. Congress and certainly the White House did not seem interested. Then push came to shove.

The first push came when Congressman Gary E. Studds of the Tenth Congressional District in Massachusetts ordered 265,000 copies of *The Surgeon General's Report* to send to his constituents. Studds not only wanted everyone in his state to have up-to-date medical information on the causes and prevention of AIDS, but he also sought to pressure the White House to drop its resistance to my original desire to mail the AIDS report to every household in the nation. Studds got his reports and mailed them.

However a few weeks later, when Representative Barbara Boxer of California requested 110,000 copies of *The Surgeon General's Report* to send to some of her constituents, she was told she could have no more than one thousand. She called the White House and asked why a homosexual from Cape Cod who did not support the president could get all the copies he wanted, while she could only have one thousand. It took five months to fill her order and those of other members of Congress. There was talk about a snag in the printing and mailing process, and although an investigation blamed inefficient printing contracting and other forms of bureaucratic bungling, I was never reassured that there were not interventions that impeded the propagation of the AIDS report.

We recognized that the thirty-six-page report, while providing the clearest explanation of the problems of AIDS, was too long to be readily absorbed by most Americans. Yet we knew that the public still needed to hear the truth about AIDS, because it was still being bombarded with false information, like the fuss made when sexologists Virginia Masters and William Johnson, with coauthor Robert Kolodny, released a study, *Heterosexual Behavior in the Age of AIDS*, that claimed both that the incidence of HIV infection was much greater than that admitted by the government and that casual contact could spread the virus. Their findings were wildly inaccurate because they were based on a very small and unusually sexually active sample of only eight hundred people. But public fears were aroused. I was in London when Betty reached me by phone to tell me I had to get on American television to reassure a jittery public, which was being told, once again, that you could get AIDS from toilet seats and drinking glasses. So I set up an interview immediately on *Good Morning America* and did some radio interviews in which I branded Masters and Johnson irresponsible. I also reiterated the findings of *The Surgeon General's Report.* It was clear that we had to put the truth right into the hands of the American people.

So the Public Health Service decided we should send each American household a letter about AIDS. As the number of AIDS cases continued to climb, tripling in the eighteen months after the 1986 AIDS report, my repeated calls for action finally got action. I think Congress was embarrassed, so it seized the initiative from the White House, appropriating $20 million so that an AIDS mailer could be sent out to every American residence as soon as possible. Congress stipulated that the AIDS mailer be cleared by health officers, not by White House officials.

We had learned something from the preparation of the longer AIDS report, so, with the usual common sense and helpful hand of Secretary Bowen, we were able to keep intradepartmental turf bickering to a minimum and to rise above the expected White House muddling. The six-page AIDS mailer "Understanding AIDS: A Message from the Surgeon General" (see Appendix A), told the story of AIDS like it is. It was all set to go by May 1988. It had the largest print order and was the largest mailing in American history: 107,000,000 copies.

There were the usual critics. One man wanted to prosecute me for mailing obscene material. And there were the usual cartoons and jokes about the explicit text. But AIDS is not a joking matter, and since surveys indicated a clear increase in public knowledge of AIDS following the mailer, I can conclude only that it did what we intended: It saved lives that would otherwise have been lost.

There was only one small mistake in the brochure, and it was only in format. The part of the brochure explaining that you could not tell by looking at someone whether or not he or she had AIDS was entitled, "What Does Someone With AIDS Look Like?" Right next to it, we had inadvertently placed a photo of Tony Fauci, Director of the National Institute of Allergy and Infectious Diseases at the National Institutes of Health. But he is still my friend and physician.

In addition to its primary purpose of educating Americans about AIDS, the AIDS mailer brought me closer to the American people. For months after it was mailed, people would walk up to me on the street or in airport waiting rooms and say, "I got your letter the other day. Thanks for writing!" It helped me make the office of Surgeon General even more personal, and it helped me in the other health endeavors that were also claiming my attention. Although I continued to speak on AIDS now and then, the AIDS mailer marked the end of a phase of my work with AIDS. And I think it marked the end of a phase of America's encounter with AIDS.

By December 30, 1988, the CDC had received reports of a cumulative total of 82,764 AIDS cases in the United States; 81,418 of these were adults and adolescents, with children under the age of thirteen accounting for the remaining 1,346 AIDS cases. During the same period, 45,602 adults and adolescents and 742 children had died of AIDS.

The first phase of America and AIDS, from the earliest case until the release of the AIDS report, was marked by mystery, fear, suspicion, judgment, the unknown. The second phase saw health officials overcome considerable opposition—some misguided, some mean-spirited—to at last bring the facts of AIDS before the American people: in the AIDS Report, the AIDS mailer, and the hundreds and even thousands of articles and television programs about AIDS. The American people learned that except for recipients of contaminated blood transfusions, babies who got AIDS from their mothers, and innocent sexual partners of AIDS carriers who took no precaution, the only people who got AIDS were those who engaged in risky behavior, behavior that many Americans also thought illegal or immoral.

And in that second phase of AIDS, Americans sorted through the issues of testing, discrimination, and civil rights. In general they rejected the bad laws and approved the good ones, assuring people who did not practice high-risk behavior that they were protected from the disease and protecting the civil rights of those who had contracted AIDS.

But the epidemic has continued to grow, claiming more victims each month. So we have entered the third phase of America and AIDS, the phase when society, our health care system, and probably each American will have to come to grips with people dying of AIDS. A contagious, fatal disease for which there is neither vaccine nor cure, AIDS will infect 390,000 to 480,000 Americans by the end of 1993, and 285,000 to 340,000 will have died of it. In the beginning AIDS was a remote threat, and many Americans had little sympathy for the homosexuals and intravenous drug abusers who made up the majority of persons with AIDS, feeling that somehow they deserved their illness. We know better now. AIDS claims all kinds of people. Before long, most Americans will know someone, love someone dying of AIDS. More than ever, we are fighting a disease, not people.

And each year we will see the disease reach deeper. At first adolescents were not perceived to be at high risk for AIDS because they did not show up in significant numbers in the AIDS mortality reports. Then, when the twenty- to twenty-nine-year-old age group accounted for 20 percent of all reported AIDS cases and AIDS-related deaths, and surveys of college students indicated a higher-than-expected rate of HIV infection (one in five hundred tested HIV-positive in 1990), we learned that the average latency period for the virus was much longer than originally thought. Therefore, health researchers concluded that many young people contract the virus in their teens but do not become symptomatic until they are in their twenties. This trend points out the disturbing failure of our educational efforts to change teenage behavior.

Education *has* proven effective among some target groups, especially among homosexual and bisexual men. But educational efforts—both universal and specific—have yielded discouraging results in the fourteen- to seventeen-year-old age group. In 1987 we targeted teenagers with clear, explicit, repetitive messages about AIDS and other sexually transmitted diseases, only to find the next year that infectious syphilis and penicillin-resistant gonorrhea among fourteen- to seventeen-year-old teenagers climbed at rates not seen in the previous fifteen years.

Adolescents are extraordinarily optimistic. They believe that nothing bad will ever happen to them, that they are immortal and will never die of anything, much less AIDS. They have a limited ability to conceive of the remote consequences of their actions. We must conclude, sadly, that teenagers do not change their behavior out of fear of its consequences. We need to find a new approach. Perhaps nothing will work except a rekindled emphasis on morality. And I am convinced we must start education at a younger age.

But adolescents are not the youngest AIDS victims. Perhaps the most tragic and challenging aspect of the AIDS crisis is the grim business of pediatric AIDS. In 1991 the number of children with AIDS symptoms reached three thousand, and this figure was probably grossly understated. To make matters even worse, many of these babies also suffer from drug addiction, acquired from their mothers before they were born. Many are abandoned in hospitals at birth.

I fear the effect of AIDS upon the health care system in our country, especially upon the 35 million Americans who exist, often with illness, outside the traditional system of health care provision. For the last year of my tenure as Surgeon General, and very forcefully and repeatedly since then, I have called for a thorough overhaul of our dysfunctional health care system, how it provides care (or doesn't provide it), how it is insured (or isn't). I am deeply concerned about the lack of national planning to deal with the impact of AIDS on a health care system already overburdened and under attack. AIDS could be the straw that breaks the back of America's chaotic health care delivery system.

Americans are still afraid of AIDS. They fear this still mysterious disease. They fear its mortality rate, which is virtually 100 percent. They fear the stigma of the disease, of what other people will conclude about their behavior and their judgment. They fear the consequences of that stigma, which can be loss of a job or housing, expulsion from school, or denial of certain necessary health or social services.

A common response to fear is denial. I am concerned about a growing tendency of the American public to deny the AIDS problem. Although this epidemic is reaching deeper and more broadly into our society every day, I see a dangerous complacency developing toward a problem many people think is "old news." The scope of the problem, which is growing larger all the time, is appreciated less and less.

Soon it will be impossible to deny the statistics, which will become all too personal: AIDS is becoming one of the top ten leading causes of death in the United States and will claim an additional 200,000 lives before the mid-nineties. Blacks and Hispanics are disproportionately harder hit. And globally we have seen but the tip of a very large iceberg. The second decade of AIDS—the nineties—will see worldwide eight to ten times as many adults developing AIDS as developed the disease in the eighties.

AIDS is a mysterious, debilitating, fatal disease, made even worse by its social stigma. The AIDS virus is transmitted by the kind of behavior that most people do not engage in—or approve of. Thus far the American people have been very tolerant of people who get sick or injured because they do something they very likely know is not a smart thing to do. We have relied upon general tax revenues to support sexually transmitted disease clinics, alcoholism and drug treatment centers, diet and nutrition counseling, family planning, emergency medical services for highway trauma, and so on. It is hard to explain this public support in a few words, but I suppose the American people know that the flesh is weak, and they also believe in redemption and are willing to help pay for it: Syphilitics can be cured, alcoholics can be rescued, highway daredevils can be healed and reformed, coronary victims can change their diet and life-style.

But AIDS has arrived on the scene and has become the first serious wedge to be driven into our remarkable public health compact because of general disapproval of the high-risk behavior responsible for most AIDS infection. Care for one AIDS patient runs to $20,000 to $30,000 annually, and the average AIDS patient receives this kind of care for a year or eighteen months. And then that person dies. After a prodigious investment of funds, there is no rescue, no reformation of character, no return to society. Just as nonsmokers chafe at having to pay the medical costs incurred by smokers, Americans may begin to resist paying the cost of caring for AIDS patients, a cost that by the end of the century will run into the billions. This disease therefore presents the toughest challenge yet to the American concept of public health.

Most of all I fear the effects of the AIDS virus on the social compact that has held American society together through periods of profound turmoil as well as tranquillity. The epidemic of AIDS may force on us one of the most serious tests of social and political will that our society has ever undergone. It may be difficult and costly to come through such a test and still preserve our institutions and our ideals.

Chapter 10 .

Baby Doe and the Rights of Handicapped Children

On April 9, 1982, the birth of an infant in Bloomington, Indiana, precipitated a controversy that is perhaps less well understood than smoking or AIDS, but that touches the lives of millions. At 8:19 P.M. that day, Dr. Walter Owens, an obstetrician, delivered a baby boy. The infant was blue and was further diagnosed as having Down syndrome. It is not certain whether the child suffered the heart defect that occurs in 40 percent of babies with this condition. He also had esophageal atresia with tracheo-esophageal fistula.

Baby Doe, as he would forever be known, became a symbol not only for children with birth defects, but also of all handicapped infants. From the plight of this single infant sprang a national awareness of the rights of damaged children and a bitter controversy over the government's right to intervene in doctors' medical practice and in the private lives of families. And these issues collided in the office of the Surgeon General.

Although I felt compassion for every patient with whom I dealt as Surgeon General, I could always separate myself emotionally from the issues themselves. But the case of Baby Doe was different. Having devoted my career to saving the lives of hundreds of such infants, I could not remain detached.

Baby Doe was a story of failure. The system certainly failed Baby Doe. And the system—the legal system, the medical system, the government—failed to live up to its responsibilities and standards. And yet, after it was all over, I think we accomplished something for America's future Baby Does, but at a high cost in terms of human life, professional credibility, and emotion.

When I say "we" I mean, well, it is not always clear who I mean. The Baby Doe case was especially difficult for me because it sometimes brought into conflict elements from my two professional lives, my life as Surgeon General and my life as a physician. As I spoke and wrote on Baby Doe, sometimes I would say "we," meaning the government, and sometimes I would say "we," meaning the medical profession. Baby Doe was my most difficult crisis because of this inner conflict. It made me think through the true nature of my responsibilities as the nation's Surgeon General and in that way contributed much to the way I would deal with other issues such as AIDS. It was not always easy to decide on the right combination of private principles and public service.

According to press accounts, Dr. Owens told the parents in Bloomington that the child would be severely retarded, was a "blob," and that the chances of his surviving surgery to correct the obstruction of the esophagus were only 50 percent. But in sharp opposition to the obstetrician, the pediatrician, Dr. James Schaeffer, and Dr. Paul Windsler, the parents' family practitioner, both thought the baby should undergo surgery and wanted Baby Doe to be referred to the Riley Hospital for Children in Indianapolis for lifesaving treatment. The pediatrician, whose career was focused on the care of children, knew that surgery would allow Baby Doe to survive. Dr. Owens, the obstetrician, whose job was over once the baby was delivered, advised the family to refuse consent for surgery and predicted that the baby would die of pneumonia in a few days.

Such a self-fulfilling prophesy was not difficult to make. Pneumonia is a very early complication of untreated esophageal atresia. The baby cannot swallow his own secretions from the nose and throat because of the obstruction in the esophagus and therefore "inhales" or aspirates those alien secretions into his lungs, causing pneumonia. At the same time, because of the abnormal connection between the windpipe and the esophagus, acid secretions from the stomach make their way upward into the esophagus and spill over into the lungs through the fistula, producing a severe chemical irritation.

According to press accounts, our sole source of information, at 9:30 P.M., an hour and a quarter after the birth, the parents of Baby Doe took time to talk it over. By 10:00 P.M. after only a half hour of discussion, they had decided, "We don't want the baby treated."

The pediatrician, Dr. Schaeffer, asked, "Do you realize what you are doing?" The family acknowledged that they did.

Dr. Owens said, "You have made a wise and courageous decision."

We were told that Dr. Schaeffer then called the Riley Hospital for Children in Indianapolis and made Dr. Owens talk with a pediatric surgeon. The press reported that the surgeon termed Owens' decision not to recommend that Baby Doe be operated on as "infanticide."

On Saturday morning, April 10, Dr. Owens wrote orders for Baby Doe, a task usually expected of the pediatrician or family practitioner. Dr. Owens told the nurses that it was all right to feed the baby, even though feeding him might cause him to choke and die. He ordered the nurses not to administer any intravenous fluids to the baby and to keep him comfortable with sedation. It was clear that all three of these orders could only hasten the infant's death and were therefore improper.

No baby with intestinal obstruction should ever be fed, especially since a baby with this type of obstruction could aspirate food into his lungs. Since he could not be fed orally, Baby Doe would need intravenous feedings to stay hydrated and receive necessary nutrients. Baby Doe was not uncomfortable and required no sedation; indeed, sedation could only diminish the natural reflexes he could muster as a defense against the threat of aspiration.

The hospital administrator pleaded with the family to take the baby home, but they refused. The hospital's attorney asked for a judicial hearing, and Superior Court Judge John Baker complied with a bedside hearing. In his startling opinion, the judge said that there were two medical opinions, that of Dr. Owens and the opposing opinions of the pediatrician and the family practitioner. He said that the parents could therefore choose either one. In other words, he would permit the child to die.

Baby Doe was being cared for in the newborn intensive care unit. On Sunday the nurses revolted against carrying out the obstetrician's instructions because they violated all that nurses knew to be the essence of medical ethics. As a result, Baby Doe was transferred to a private room where he was cared for by private-duty nurses, if you can call what he got "care." The hospital nurses had already administered phenobarbital, a sedative, and morphine sulfate, a painkiller, presumably at the instructions of Dr. Owens. (Again, the only information on this came from the media.) Neither drug would normally have been given to an infant in these circumstances because they would only speed the demise of the patient.

The agencies that society charges with the responsibility of looking after defenseless children were either unable or unwilling to go to the aid of Baby Doe. The Monroe County Child Protection Committee (set up to prevent child abuse and appointed Baby Doe's guardian *ad litem* by Judge Baker) found no fault with the judge's decision. Using a different approach, on Monday, April 12, three attorneys, Barry Brown, Lawrence Brodeur, and Phillip Hill, sought to declare Baby Doe a neglected child under the Indiana "CHINS" statute (Child In Need of Services), but an acting judge, Thomas Spencer, ruled that there had been no violation of the statute.

By this time, more than ninety-six hours after birth, Baby Doe was weak, parched, and spitting blood. At 11:00 P.M. that Monday, attorney Phillip Hill sought a court order so that the child could receive intravenous fluids. This was refused.

Meanwhile, it became very clear that Baby Doe was very much a wanted child. His parents may not have wanted him, but there were several couples who were already trying to adopt the dying youngster. But the parents were unwilling to allow him to live in another family, unwilling to allow him to live at all. On Tuesday, April 13, the fifth day of Baby Doe's life, attorney James Bopp, representing one of several couples who were interested, petitioned the court for the adoption of the child. The judge denied the petition, offering the strange explanation that to grant an adoption would make it look as if the family were abandoning the child rather than wanting it to die.

Meanwhile, attorneys Brodeur and Hill appealed Judge Baker's decision to the Indiana Supreme Court. Although the Indiana Supreme Court did not review the substance of his decision, the court ruled that Judge Baker had acted appropriately and had not exceeded his authority.

Even so, attorneys acting to save Baby Doe did not give up. On Thursday, April 15, Lawrence Brodeur flew to Washington to file an appeal with the United States Supreme Court, where Justice John Paul Stevens was to have heard a request to overrule the Indiana Supreme Court decision. Back in Bloomington, the staff at the hospital was in an uproar. The chief of staff ordered the pediatrician, Dr. Schaeffer, to start an IV to give Baby Doe the fluids he needed. This resulted in an altercation with the obstetrician, Dr. Owens.

At 10:01 P.M. on April 15, 1982, Baby Doe died.

Even after most of the dust had settled, some of us in government were not in complete agreement as to what had really happened, what it all meant, and what we had to do next. Most Americans felt the same way. From the very beginning, the Baby Doe issue had at least *two sides* to almost every question raised—two sides as to *what* the treatment should be, *who* should make such decisions, *how* decisions should be made, and *which* procedures should be followed when there was no consensus. Except for that first bedside hearing in Judge Baker's court, the *substance* of the Baby Doe issue had never been thoroughly adjudicated in Indiana, in Washington, in New York—or anywhere.

Above all, it is important to remember that medical opinion at Baby Doe's hospital had been divided. A recurrent misconception all through the subsequent Baby Doe debate pitted the government against the judgment of physicians. But there was never a single medical position. From everything we now know, had there been a forum for discussion among the hospital's physicians, a majority might well have opposed the parents' decision. There is still so much we do not know, still so much I do not know, hidden away in medical files now locked by judicial order. And the anonymous little baby who was the focus of concern and contempt has taken many of the secrets to his very early grave.

The confusion and controversy began with the initial diagnosis of Baby Doe's condition. Although the obstetrician's diagnosis of Down syndrome was not contested, his diagnosis of severe retardation and his assessment that Baby Doe had only a 50 percent chance of surviving the operation to repair the atresia of the esophagus raised sharp disagreement. While it is true that surgery to repair esophageal atresia in a newborn can be difficult and tricky, it is also true that at the time Baby Doe was born the success rate for such surgery was very high.

There was a touch of irony in the situation. After all, as the Surgeon General called into the Baby Doe crisis, I had been among the first pediatric surgeons to perform corrective surgery for esophageal atresia. My colleagues and I had performed about 475 such procedures in thirty-five years with an ever-improving success rate. As early as the fifties, we were reporting a success rate better than that predicted by Dr. Owens. In my last eight years of active practice, I never lost a full-term baby upon whom I operated to correct esophageal atresia; when operating on premature infants, the survival rate was 88 percent. So Dr. Owens' advice to the parents of Baby Doe was dead wrong.

Equally open to question was the obstetrician's prediction of Baby Doe's quality of life, whatever that may mean. There is simply no way that a physician can predict with any accuracy just what the quality of life will be for a child born with Down syndrome. The child's retardation can range from mild to severe, and his quality of life is intimately affected by his family, the response of the community, and the kind and degree of medical and health services available to him.

Although a child with Down syndrome is undoubtedly a burden on a family, in my experience over the years with these special-needs youngsters and their families, I have seen Down syndrome families who are some of the happiest families I have ever known. Even when a child is severely retarded, the presence of love and care among family members often outweighs the hardship. Sometimes parents with a Down syndrome child adopt another child similarly afflicted. And the milder degrees of retardation have been overcome many times by both youngster and family. One time, at a conference on Down syndrome, I was upstaged completely by a thirteen-year-old boy with Down syndrome who spoke briefly before me. He walked to the podium, and referred to a basic cause of his problem, "In Down syndrome you have an extra chromosome. I have Down syndrome." And then, pausing for effect, "Anyone here want my extra chromosome?"

Some people in Bloomington, as well as some of us in Washington, thought that Baby Doe's parents had not been given totally accurate, unbiased information about the condition of their new baby boy. In addition, we cannot discount the role played by the semantic fog. Words can be used to blur as well as to clarify. It is much easier to talk about withholding fluids and nutrition or nourishment from a handicapped or deformed child than to use the term that describes it more accurately: starvation.

I first learned about Baby Doe the way the rest of America did, through news reports. Those news reports were not too helpful and, I could tell by reading between the lines, not too accurate. The press handled Baby Doe more poorly than any issue in which I was involved during my tenure as Surgeon General. What happened to the normal press interest in victims? What happened to their usual questioning of the powerful mishandling the weak? Was the press really so blind to the issue? Could they not see through the hospital setting and perceive that what had happened to Baby Doe would have been considered at the least child abuse, if not criminal negligence or even murder, if it had taken place in the home? Could they not have been enlightened by substituting the word "black" or "female" for "handicapped" in the description of the victim?

I did not become officially or even unofficially involved in the Baby Doe issue until a day or two after Baby Doe hit the headlines; it was not until after Baby Doe had died that the government became officially involved in the controversy. And I became involved only reluctantly. My years in surgery had made me all too familiar with the wrenching discussions associated with the diagnosis and prognosis of infants such as Baby Doe. I was barraged with requests from the press

and physicians around the country to do some long-distance hypothe-
sizing about Baby Doe's chances, but I refused. I believed then—and
I grew to believe it more intensely later—that those kinds of questions
can be answered best by the people who are right there on the scene,
if they think clearly and *if* they act responsibly. Furthermore, we in
the government were handicapped all through the Baby Doe crisis (and
the later Baby Jane Doe affair) by inadequate information. In both
cases, the medical records were sealed by the courts, cutting us off from
pertinent information.

When Baby Doe died a week after birth, the death certificate indicated "multiple congenital birth defects." But what did this mean?
Were the "multiple defects" only the two discussed publicly, Down
syndrome and esophageal atresia? Or were there others? Did Baby Doe
have an uncorrectable heart defect? The mortality rate for such a
condition can be very high. In any case, during Baby Doe's brief life,
the public was denied this vital information. We did not have it then,
and we still do not have it now.

The medical profession was doubly frustrated in this case. First, of
course, there was the lack of medical data. In times when the medical
profession is often criticized for ordering too many tests, for taking too
many X rays, for wanting to know too much, in this case we in the
medical community were theorizing in the dark. Many physicians were
trying to form an opinion about Baby Doe's chances with only the
barest information at hand.

The second frustration reflected the double-edged sword of modern
medicine, the ability of high-tech medicine to extend human life, for
better or for worse. During the last twenty years, the dramatic develop-
ments in medicine and surgery have made us accustomed to cures.
Even though eventually we all must die of something, we have high
expectations that medicine can cure most problems, especially problems of children and young adults. People become bewildered, frustrated, even angry when confronted by a condition that cannot be
cured, such as Down syndrome.

Baby Doe touched that raw nerve. Baby Doe reminded us that
although medicine had provided a readily available and successful cure
for his life-threatening acute problem of esophageal atresia, medicine
held no cure for his other, chronic problem of Down syndrome.

But American medicine and American ethics cannot use "no cure"
as an excuse for "no care." We can offer an incurable patient something just as valuable; we can offer genuine care. Incurable patients still
need us as people, even though as physicians we cannot do as much for

them as we would like to. That is an important message, and it is a demanding message. It demands that we lay aside our medical texts and instead work through those questions, the answers to which are spun out of the depths of our consciences.

As I have already said, in my pediatric surgical practice, I had come upon this kind of situation many times before. Those experiences are engraved in my mind forever: a tragically disabled child; parents who were confused, angry, grieving; a divided medical staff. What then?

My considered judgment, worked out over some years, tells me that we ought to do things to give a person all the life to which he or she is entitled, but not to do anything that would lengthen that person's act of dying. And there is a real difference between the two.

On the basis of what I could learn about Baby Doe, there seemed to be little doubt that the decision had been made not to give Baby Doe all the life that was his, but actually to accelerate the process of his dying. Once people became concerned about that, the legal system came into the issue.

Those who wished to defend Baby Doe attempted to do so under the laws designed to protect defenseless children. But Baby Doe did not fit neatly into the Indiana state law regarding child abuse and neglect. This was not a straightforward case of child abuse and neglect, in which a normal, healthy child is the victim of parental violence. No one did anything "violent" to Baby Doe, in the usual sense of violent child abuse, although the obstetrician's orders had a violent effect upon the infant's digestive and respiratory systems, so much so that if the same violence had been done to a "normal" baby, there would have been a demand to protect him and perhaps to punish the perpetrators.

Obviously, then, the central issue of the Baby Doe case was the little boy's handicap, Down syndrome. This is what drew the federal government into the case, because it seemed very clear that Baby Doe was a victim not only of abuse and neglect (a matter for Indiana child abuse law), but also of discrimination (a matter for federal concern).

If Baby Doe had been born only with Down syndrome, he would have been nourished and cared for. If he had been born only with esophageal atresia, he would have been operated on and cured. But because he had both Down syndrome and esophageal atresia, he was denied the operation that would have saved his life.

When President Reagan learned about the plight of Baby Doe, he instructed then–HHS Secretary Richard Schweiker to make certain that such a thing never happened again. (Typically, his compassion went out to a single individual much more readily than to an issue in general.) What started out as an emotional response from the president turned into a morass of bureaucracy, regulations, and recriminations. HHS churned out one set of regulations and then another, which were successively challenged in the courts. As Surgeon General, I got blamed for things over which I had no control. As a pediatric surgeon, I was never asked to do things I could have done.

Eventually the argument centered around a federal regulation, section No. 504 of the Rehabilitation Act of 1973, which said, "No otherwise qualified handicapped individual shall, solely by reason of his handicap, be excluded from participation in, be denied the benefits of, or be subjected to discrimination under any program or activity receiving federal financial assistance." As a recipient of federal aid, Bloomington Hospital had to follow this federal law.

Baby Doe was not born into a vacuum. For several years ethicists, medicine, the law, and government had been groping toward resolution of similar issues. Two years earlier, in March 1980, Philip Becker, a thirteen-year-old California boy with Down syndrome, made the headlines because his parents refused consent for the heart surgery he needed to save his life and the United States Supreme Court refused to hear an appeal on the boy's behalf. The youngster survived only because he was adopted by another couple who enabled him to have his lifesaving heart surgery. But concern for what might have happened under the travesty of "care" offered by his natural parents led to the nation's first conference on infanticide. (No "official" conclusion came out of the conference, but a consensus grew that children born with handicaps must not be neglected.)

Then, in May 1981, newborn Siamese twins technically known as a triapus (joined at the trunk, but missing one of four legs) were taken into custody by an agency of the State of Illinois because of reports that they were being starved to death. The parents of Jeff and Scott Mueller were eventually charged with attempted murder, along with the children's doctor, but a judge dismissed the charges. So-called medical expertise said that the children could not survive a separation operation, but in 1982 they were successfully separated.

Part of the furor arose because two months before Baby Doe's case arose, a presidential commission on ethical problems in medicine, appointed by Jimmy Carter, had prepared a draft report suggesting that some damaged infants might not be worth saving. When commission chairman Morris Abram asked for my comment on the report, I replied, "Suppose you, Mr. Abram, left work one morning for lunch, were struck by a car, and taken to a hospital room. Suppose you heard some disturbing conversation between the doctors taking care of you: 'With his back injury and the diminished motor power in his legs, he may never walk without braces, and with a head injury like that he will be able to function, but maybe not quite at the level he did before, and with that low back injury and the loss of motion in his legs, I wouldn't be surprised if he were at least partially incontinent of urine. Should we feed Morris Abram?' What would you think?"

What I was describing to Abram were the problems of a newborn with spina bifida, or cleft spine, a defect in the lower back that can cause several different types of neurological damage, but I was phrasing them in terms of an adult, and that adult was Morris Abram. When the final report appeared, just about the same time as the Baby Doe case hit the news, it had this to say under the heading of *Seriously Ill Newborns:*

> Within constraints of equity and availability, infants should receive all therapies that are clearly beneficial to them. For example, an otherwise healthy Down syndrome child whose life is threatened by a surgically correctable complication should receive the surgery because he or she would clearly benefit from it.

That was Baby Doe.

The Reagan administration decided to move ahead with the enforcement regulations required by Section 504. The issue was simple: Does the state have the right and the obligation to step into a matter affecting a newborn child and go over the heads of the parents?

When the Baby Doe case first hit the newspapers, a number of people claimed the government had no right to interfere in matters of parental responsibility. But, of course, the right of government to supersede the rights of parents has been upheld in a number of areas: truancy laws, child abuse laws, immunization laws, and court orders mandating medical treatment for children whose parents attempt to use their religious convictions to deny such treatment.

Not long after Baby Doe's death, a distraught mother in the West took her newborn baby home to a life of squalor. She just could not cope, and, through neglect, the baby died. She was arrested and charged not only with child abuse, but also with manslaughter. Mothers may not kill their children at home, but apparently parents and doctors can get away with it in hospitals.

I have never advocated "life at any cost." There are times when the most reasonable action a physician can take is to step back and let nature take its course. But healers should never be killers. And the state has a legitimate role in protecting the life of an infant even if its parents disagree because they find the situation too difficult to handle.

There is no constitutional definition of how old someone must be in order to receive the protection of the state. There is no minimum age requirement for native-born citizenship. An American-born child does not have to remain in the United States for a month, two weeks, or even one hour in order to qualify, thirty-five years later, to run for president. The child merely has to be born as an American. I do not find that difficult to understand. I never did, and, following the same logic, I believe that a newborn infant whose life is put at risk by a parent, guardian, or physician, is an American and deserves to be accorded the full protection of the state.

Baby Doe's life began with many tragic complications, but none of those handicaps put him outside the protection of the law. None of them relieved the state of its obligation to protect him. None of them permitted anyone to jeopardize further his health or his life. None of them.

I have always been surprised by the stance of most American liberals in the Baby Doe affair, that the government has no right to intervene in the parents' decision, even if it means death for a viable infant—a position they support less as the patient grows older. Usually liberals have rushed to aid the weak, the disenfranchised members of American society. But in the case of Baby Doe, that same liberal faction moved against defenseless handicapped infants. If the country's Baby Does were thirty-five years old, they would have a national advocacy organization and a strong congressional lobby. Unfortunately, they are too small, too weak, and too poor.

At least one prominent liberal voice, however, saw the issue clearly. In the middle of the ongoing Baby Doe controversy, when I was feeling particularly misunderstood, someone sent me a clipping about Baby Doe from *The Village Voice*'s Nat Hentoff, a prominent civil libertarian, a national officer of the American Civil Liberties Union, and a fascinating fellow.

Reaching him with great difficulty through the *Voice*, I asked him if the name Koop meant anything to him.

"You're calling about the piece in the *Voice?*"

"I rather wish I'd written it myself."

"You've written some books in this field? I'd like you to send along anything you have."

I did that immediately, so pleased was I to find someone with

Hentoff's very liberal ideology who could be so logical in his defense of the rights of Baby Doe. On my next trip to New York, I met him. He spoke first.

"I read your stuff and I'm beginning to hate you!"

"Why, for heaven's sake?"

"Because your arguments are going to force me to reexamine my considered position on abortion."

Politics aside, I found Nat Hentoff and I were on the same wavelength. We were both pro-life, not in the political sense, but in the personal and practical sense, pro-life for the unborn, the handicapped, the elderly, persons with AIDS, sexually abused children, beaten wives, the sick, and the injured. We both held the strong conviction that no one's civil liberties should be abrogated.

So Baby Doe and his successors moved from the realm of physicians and parents into the realm of journalists and politicians, and then into the realm of lawyers and bureaucrats. Three sets of regulations later, three judicial countermanding orders later, several lawsuits later, three secretaries of Health and Human Services later, two years later, one Baby Jane Doe later . . . Congress, medicine, and the Department of Health and Human Services finally came together on the treatment of handicapped children. But getting there was not half the fun; getting there was bitter.

My position in all this was never very comfortable. First I was on the sidelines, then I was the lightning rod, then I, as a physician within the government, was caught in the middle.

The government wanted to protect the lives of handicapped infants. The medical profession opposed government interference. After the complex and often rancorous bureaucratic maneuvering over the way the regulations were framed, finally the law would stand on the side of handicapped children.

The final push to a law, not regulations, governing the treatment of handicapped infants stemmed from a groundswell of concern in Congress and in the public. Two episodes fueled the concern. The first, academically laundered but chilling enough, was the publication in the journal *Pediatrics* of what was simply a euthanasia program for babies born with spina bifida, camouflaged in some fancy figuring. The article reported a program in Oklahoma City that used a mathematical formula to compute the "quality of life" of spina bifida patients to determine which would be allowed to die. Infants whose numbers did not add up right were starved to death.

This was documented in a Cable News Network three-part television series by Carleton Sherwood, who had already produced a five-part series on Baby Doe for another network. Sherwood's new series depicted the selection of infants at the Children's Hospital of Oklahoma City by the quality-of-life formula. If they did not "pass," they were transferred to an inadequate nursing home in an adjacent building where their care was euthanasia, but not always by the most direct and painless means; Sherwood's film documented some infants dying of malnutrition, others of infection, some choking to death on feedings poured down their throats. Unfortunately for the Oklahoma physicians, one of their selectees for death did not die. Instead, as sometimes happens with spina bifida patients, in spite of the lack of therapy and some direct action designed to shorten her life, her back healed over spontaneously and her head grew to enormous proportions, poignantly revealed in Sherwood's series.

The Oklahoma tragedy finally got Congress moving, and on February 2, 1984, the U.S. House of Representatives, considering the renewal of the child abuse law, passed legislation extending the definition of child abuse to include the denial of care and treatment to handicapped newborns. The legislation further required that procedures be adopted by state agencies for reporting and investigating such medical neglect. None of this would have been achieved without the unflagging efforts of Madeline Will.

After losing most of the battles, we had won the war. The definition of child abuse was expanded—by congressional statute—to include the withholding of fluids, nutrition, and medically indicated treatment for disabled infants. On October 9, 1984, the Baby Doe amendment became part of Public Law 98-475 when it was signed by President Reagan.

But even with laws protecting newborns with handicaps, even with a renewed general commitment to their rights, there are times when tough medical cases combine with misinformation and professional pride to cause a tragedy. That's what happened in another case, the case of Baby Jane Doe. Her tragic story underscored the need for the new law, and her life was damaged irreparably because the law was not yet on the books when she needed it.

On October 11, 1983, Baby Jane Doe, a baby born with spina bifida, entered this world in the St. Charles Hospital in Port Jefferson, Long Island, New York. Shortly after her birth, Baby Jane was seen by a neurosurgeon, Dr. P. Arjen Keuskamp, not only because of her spina bifida, but also because she seemed to have an abnormally small head as well as hydrocephalus, or "water on the brain," a rare combination. From the beginning Baby Jane was plagued by wrong diagnoses and inaccurate coverage in the press. The two apparently contradictory signs were misinterpreted. A child who has both a small head and hydrocephalus will usually have the best possible brain function because the fluid accumulating within the ventricles of the brain has not squeezed the brain against the surrounding skull, thereby altering its function. Instead of understanding the medical situation, apparently the physicians, and certainly the press, incorrectly assumed that the child had microcephaly, a congenitally small head, and that she would probably be mentally retarded. So, from that initial faulty premise, many problems were compounded as the sad history of Baby Jane unfolded.

Dr. Keuskamp thought that the baby's spina bifida should be closed surgically and a shunt inserted into a ventricle of her brain to drain the accumulating spinal fluid in order to prevent further pressure on the brain. In those judgments, he was correct. Dr. Keuskamp referred the baby to the nearest major facility for such surgery, the University Hospital of the State University of New York at Stony Brook.

No one in the federal government knew that Baby Jane existed from the time of her birth on October 11, 1983, until October 19. I was unprepared for the telephone call from the Office of Civil Rights saying that they had received a hot-line complaint that a baby in the University Hospital at Stony Brook was being discriminated against on the basis of handicap.

As I was drawn into the Baby Jane controversy, I was struck by ironic twists from my own past. I had worked summers during college and medical school at the hospital where she was born. Her serious condition had prompted her transfer to the University Hospital of the State University of New York at Stony Brook, the little Long Island village where as a twelve-year-old I had learned to swim, boat, and fish. And Baby Jane's parents lived in Mt. Sinai, where my parents had spent summers from the time I was thirteen until I left medical school.

I was convinced that this country did not need another Baby Doe controversy. I was also convinced that if there were anything that I could do unofficially, behind the scenes, that could lessen the impact of this new Baby Doe, I was morally bound to do it. And of course, if the child had been discriminated against, that wrong should be righted.

Without discussion with anyone else, I made a personal telephone call to a friend who was a pediatric surgeon on the staff of the University Hospital in Stony Brook. I started off my conversation by saying, "If you wish, this conversation has never taken place." Then I told him about the complaint we had received and that I had some suggestions to make that had nothing at all to do with directing the hospital's management of the patient but to which they should listen because it could save a tremendous amount of grief in the future if Baby Jane became a cause célèbre as her predecessor, Baby Doe, had.

I asked if the neurosurgeon, Dr. Frank Butler, would call me personally and unofficially. When my friend called back and said that Butler was in the operating room. I called him there. Dr. Butler was not in the actual operating room but was in the suite, and he refused to speak with me.

This was Baby Doe in Bloomington all over again. Once again, physicians who could not really assess a child's future quality of life were nevertheless making a prophecy about it, convincing the parents that they would end up raising a very difficult child. And I have to believe the physicians coerced the parents into a decision, into the wrong decision. They elected not to allow their daughter to undergo surgery.

At one time a neurologist from Stony Brook, George Newman, said, "It would be unkind to have this kind of surgery," because "Baby Jane has only limited ability to experience comfort and more ability to experience pain." What an extraordinary assessment from a neurologist! One of the few good things about some of the tragic problems associated with spina bifida is that the difficulties per se do not cause pain.

The Baby Jane affair went from bad to worse. I do not know of any other surgical problem where so much energy was spent, where so much acrimonious debate took place at all levels of government and in the private sector, where so much error and misinformation was presented as absolute truth, where apparently right decisions were made for wrong reasons and wrong decisions were made for apparently right reasons, and where such tragedy ensued.

I believe that the press, the medical profession, and the burgeoning number of so-called ethicists were still smarting in the aftermath of Baby Doe. Therefore, determined that no government would interfere, that no parent would be denied the right to withhold treatment from his or her child, they had an utter disregard for fact, and without the slightest sense of a need for inquisitive and investigative reporting, the juggernaut rolled on with error compounding error.

On October 16, Lawrence Washburn, Jr., a pro-life advocate, arranged with Justice Frank P. DeLuca of the State Supreme Court in

New York to begin a proceeding. At a hearing on October 20, Justice Melvin Tannenbaum presided. Judge Tannenbaum ruled that the infant was in need of immediate surgery to preserve her life and authorized William E. Webber, a Suffolk County attorney, to be guardian *ad litem* to consent to the surgery.

I believe that the summary statement of Judge Tannenbaum was correct when he said: "I find from the totality of the evidence that the infant is in imminent danger, and that the infant has an independent right to survive; that right must be protected by the state acting *in parents patriae* where a life is in jeopardy and the parents have elected to provide no surgical care, this court will order such care."

At this point, those involved in any decision-making process were functioning on the medical misinformation that the child had both microcephaly and hydrocephaly at the same time. Prognostications were made about the future quality of Baby Jane's life by people who were not pediatric experts and did not even know the facts in this case. Not only did the principals involved in the litigation reverse their positions from time to time, but also each accused the other side of lying.

From the very first court session, one tenuous supposition became gospel truth, perhaps only by virtue of endless repetition. Almost every news article written about Baby Jane concluded with something like, "If Baby Jane is not operated upon, she will live two years. If she is operated upon, she will live twenty years." No one on God's earth could make that determination. That nonsense came about this way, in court:

"If Baby Jane is not operated on, how long will she live?" asked the judge.

"I don't know," replied the neurologist.

"Two years?"

"Maybe."

"How long will she live if she is operated on?"

"I don't know."

"Twenty years?"

"Maybe."

Maybe is a long way from certain.

The matter became a self-fulfilling prophecy. It became clear to me that eventually all the doctors at Stony Brook maintained the same party line, but a careful review of their initial statements would indicate that early on there had been some difference of opinion. Nevertheless, these prophets of doom and gloom happened to be on safe ground. They said that if Baby Jane were not operated upon, which was their recommendation, she would grow up to be retarded and the family would have to bear the burden of raising her. But not operating on her set in motion a chain of events that *guaranteed* the fulfillment of those prophecies. It was clear from reports in the press that Baby Jane's spine did become infected, that the infection did ascend into her brain, causing her to develop ventriculitis, an inflammation of the normal cavities in the brain, and that although a shunt was eventually placed in her brain to drain it, the operation was performed much too late to do the good it could have accomplished if it been done earlier. So the prophets could say, "See, we were right." They were—because ventriculitis is always followed by mental retardation.

Baby Jane needed someone to stand up for her and say to all those who wanted her to die, "No, you were wrong. If you had done the right thing, operating right away to relieve the pressure on the child's brain, she would have grown up in the upper 10 percent of those afflicted with this problem." That was the opinion of one of the country's most experienced physicians in the field and the only outside expert who had eventual access to the records, the physicians, and Baby Jane.

On October 21, 1983, a court of appeals reversed the judgment imposed by Tannenbaum's decision and vacated the order appointing the guardian *ad litem.* This reversal was upheld by the New York State Court of Appeals on October 28.

Shortly after the New York Court of Appeals ruling permitted Baby Jane's parents to refuse surgery, the Justice Department sued the hospital in the U.S. District Court for the Southern District of New York claiming the right to see Baby Jane's hospital records so they could determine if Baby Jane's rights had been violated under Section 504. This request was denied. An appeal by the Justice Department to the United States Court of Appeals for the Second Circuit was also denied.

My role thus far had been behind the scenes, answering questions about spina bifida and its prognosis, with or without treatment, from members of both the Department of Justice and the Office of Civil Rights of HHS. I was not a spokesman for the government, nor was I involved in any suit. But once again, because of my previous experience and high profile, the press assumed—incorrectly—that I was responsible for the so-called intrusion of the federal government into the Stony Brook hospital and the family of Baby Jane.

There was a big difference between the government's involvements with Baby Doe and Baby Jane. The government had not intervened with Baby Doe while the child lived. The government became involved subsequently only to prevent a repetition of that tragedy without the safeguards of expert opinion and due process. Baby Doe's case made clear the need for government intervention. With Baby Jane, however, the government became involved with a living child, taking action to make sure she received treatment to ensure the highest quality of life possible.

I advised both the Office of Civil Rights and the Justice Department that the federal government had a right to see the records based on the testimony of the doctors involved, which indicated that Baby Jane's hydrocephalus was getting worse by the day, increasing the risk of further brain damage. My decision was based on the sole known medical fact in medical testimony, after which the records were sealed. Baby Jane was in increasing jeopardy, but those who cared for her were in violation of Section 504 because they were using the presence of a handicap (spina bifida or microcephaly) to deny the necessary shunting procedure to correct the hydrocephalus.

Pride and arrogance deprived Baby Jane of the treatment that would have improved her life dramatically. The pride of physicians kept them from seeking higher consultations (there were expert *pediatric* neuro-surgeons nearby); the arrogance of the court kept it from proper inquiry and disclosure (the court asked no experts for their opinions and asked the wrong questions of the wrong people). Pride and arrogance denied Baby Jane not life, but the ability to live it as best she could.

The cases of Baby Doe and Baby Jane alerted the entire nation that handicapped newborns have rights. But ensuring that they receive the immediate treatment they require is but the first step in a lifelong commitment to the proper care of handicapped children.

Not all babies are born perfect. Many of the operations I had performed on infants corrected congenital defects that, left uncorrected, would have cut short the baby's life. There were times, however, when we saved a precious life but ended up with a less-than-perfect child. Some would remain that way, handicapped for life.

Society terms such a result a tragedy, but that may be too harsh a judgment. It is society that transforms disabilities into handicaps, and I know from thirty-five years of hands-on experience that often the people we too easily label as "handicapped" become super-achievers. As I watched the heroic achievements of so many children with paralyzed lower extremities, I became convinced that Franklin D. Roosevelt probably became a remarkable leader because of his disability rather than in spite of it. Paul Sweeney, my most-operated-on patient— he underwent over fifty surgical procedures—overcame what many of us might call handicaps and became president of his high school class and a college graduate. But, as magnificent as their achievements might be, I realized there was much more we could do for handicapped children and their families to make them more independent.

When I first entered pediatric surgery, children who entered a hospital either were cured or died. Over the years we dramatically reduced the numbers of those who died, but we created a new category of survivor: children who did not go home, children who did not die, but who remained dependent on respirators or ventilators. This situation arose not because doctors believed that leaving a child on a ventilator forever was an acceptable alternative to dying, but because out of the many ventilator-dependent children whose lives were saved and who were then rehabilitated to normal living, there were always a few who slipped back or who could not be weaned from a ventilator until their airways were developed sufficiently. We need to protect the rights of those children and do all we can to ensure their quality of life.

As Surgeon General, I wanted to continue the efforts I had begun in my last years as a surgeon to move ventilator-dependent children out of hospitals and into their homes. This not only freed them from exposure to hospital infections, but also restored them to their family, where they belong, nurturing the natural bond between parent and child, which is difficult to maintain in the hospital setting. And the financial savings were enormous.

I organized a Surgeon General's Workshop on the problems of such children and four years later, the detailed report of what had been done to ease the lives of ventilator-dependent children—nationally, regionally, and locally—filled a book as thick as the Washington phone book.

In all my work for the handicapped, I wanted to involve President Reagan, because I truly believed it was an issue close to his heart. But I was continually frustrated by White House staffers, who kept him at arm's length. They seemed to live in a world of happy photo opportunities and sound bites and did not want to associate the president with anything as serious and "unappealing" as the plight of the handicapped. Once again, it was a personal anecdote that finally got Reagan involved. He had heard about Katie Beckett, a youngster whose difficult problems would soon claim national attention.

Katie Beckett was a ventilator-dependent youngster who was being maintained by Medicaid in an institution far from her family's home in Cedar Rapids, Iowa. Her parents talked to Congressman Thomas J. Tauke, who got to Vice President George Bush, who told the president, and then things began to move. Reagan sent instructions back down the chain, asking Secretary Schweiker to see that people like Katie Beckett obtained waivers so they could receive Medicaid support for respirator care in their homes, surrounded by a loving family, rather than in a distant institution. Medicaid had never paid for home care, even though the cost of home care was often a small fraction of that of hospital care. I became chairman of the "Katie Beckett Board," which granted similar waivers to youngsters all over the country until Congress eventually made the waiver system into law.

Next, I wanted to provide all the help possible to the two groups of people most concerned with handicapped children: parents and pediatricians. In this large, rich, diverse nation, there are programs and self-help groups for every conceivable problem, but it is difficult if not impossible to keep abreast of what is out there. I cherished the hope that someday I might be able to provide instant, computerized service to physicians concerning the hows, whens, and wheres of repairing congenital defects, especially those that threaten life immediately after birth, and provide families with the support they so desperately need.

I was convinced that the Baby Doe story would have had a different ending if his pediatrician could have produced for the opposing obstetrician all there was to know about surgery and rehabilitation of the newborn's handicap. No physician can be expected to know everything about the latest breakthroughs for all problems presented in his practice. It is conceivable that a pediatrician could know a great deal about cystic fibrosis and cerebral palsy but almost nothing about hemophilia or spina bifida. I wanted an easily accessible system where a parent or pediatrician could call one number, state the problem, and then get the necessary information about every community resource, every government and private program, every doctor, every nurse practitioner, and above all every parents' support group having an interest in the child's problem. So I began to work with those who could set up a computer network to make that information available. With funds supplied by the Division of Maternal and Child Health of the Public Health Service, we encouraged and financed the University of South Carolina to proceed with the development of computerized access systems already well along the way for both the profession and parents. By the time I left government the network had spread to thirty-seven states. In all of this work with special-needs children, I am indebted to Dr. Vince Hutchins and his associate, Dr. Merle McPherson, of the Public Health Service division of Maternal and Child Health, as well as to two people outside of government who have a heart for children and were magnificently generous in supporting everything that I did: Dr. Phyllis MaGrab of Georgetown University and Dr. Earl Brewer of Baylor University.

From the Baby Doe saga, the first extended issue of my service as Surgeon General, I think we all had the opportunity to learn something. I hope Americans learned about the pernicious practice of infanticide, which had been growing unnoticed in hospital nurseries across the country.

I hope Americans learned anew the value of a single human life, no matter how small, no matter how handicapped. I hope Americans learned how easy and how wrong it is to ignore or deny the needs of the handicapped. A child does not deserve to die just because it is retarded, or worse, *might be* retarded.

I think American physicians learned that their life-and-death decisions involve a great degree of accountability, not always recognized before. Neither the care of Baby Doe nor of Baby Jane Doe revolved about medical questions alone. More than a medical response, Baby Doe demanded an ethical response and a social response. Medicine's ethical response, the statement called "Principles of Treatment of Disabled Infants" (see Appendix B), came too late to save the child's life. But I think that government officials learned that medicine operates best when there is trust between doctor and patient.

I think that the various individuals and groups holding differing views about the treatment of handicapped infants realized that they could accomplish much by talking with each other—for the sake of the children.

I know I learned a lot from Baby Doe. I learned more about how the government works—and doesn't work. I learned even more about the limits of the law when it comes to medicine.

I also learned from Baby Doe a lot about how to be Surgeon General. When I first heard about how Baby Doe was being denied that lifesaving operation for atresia of the esophagus, I became exceedingly frustrated. As the nation's Surgeon General, no less, I could not do for him what I had done for hundreds of other babies with the same condition.

My first instinct was to speak out loud and clear on behalf of Baby Doe. But then I also realized that I was not only Baby Doe's Surgeon General, I was also Surgeon General for his parents, and, like it or not, I was Surgeon General for those physicians in Bloomington, no matter how poorly I thought some of them were discharging their responsibilities.

Baby Doe needed help, but so did his parents. Like many other parents, they may have simply lacked the resources—material, social, or economic . . . or emotional, moral, or psychological—to care for a disabled child in their own family. I was their Surgeon General, too, and I had a responsibility to them. The parents of all the Baby Janes, Katie Becketts, and other handicapped children demand and deserve our support.

All during my life as a pediatric surgeon and in the succeeding years as a Surgeon General, I took the position that you cannot urge parents to fight for the lives of their disabled or handicapped children and then just walk away when the fight is won. I had learned that lesson many times over, but with the arrival of Baby Doe it suddenly had a great deal more meaning for me.

I did not agree with Baby Doe's attending physicians, but I knew that there were many in the profession who did and that somehow I would have to reconcile with them as well—that is, if I really wanted to prevent the deaths of any more Baby Does. And I did. After a bitter struggle, many people worked together to save the lives of other Baby Does, and to give their families and their country more of what is needed to care for them.

American medicine has not moved to one opinion on the treatment of Baby Does. American medicine and the American government have not come to an agreement about the role of government regulation in medicine. And American medicine and American law have not come to terms on the many issues that divide them. But Baby Doe may have taught us all something about fragility, the fragility of a handicapped infant, the fragility of our preconceptions, the fragility of ethical consensus, the fragility of conscience, the fragility of life itself. Baby Doe also taught us something about resilience, the resilience of life, even of handicapped infants given the chance they deserve to live the lives they have.

Chapter 11
Abortion

For the first fifty years of my life, "abortion" was a word I rarely heard. And when people talked about abortion, they usually whispered. The American society in which I grew up, and the American medical community I joined fifty years ago, stood firmly against abortion. The consensus was clear: The fetus was an unborn child; abortion took a human life. Abortion was illegal because abortion was immoral. All that changed with dramatic speed. Future historians, indeed all Americans alive today, may puzzle over the rapidity with which a society and legal system reversed itself on such a basic moral issue. Abortion has become not only a subject of everyday conversation and everyday practice, but also the most divisive public issue in American history since slavery.

Abortion became my thorniest problem as Surgeon General. As abortion dominated my first nine months in Washington, it also clouded my exit from government service. The issue revolved around me, almost literally. While I stood still, my position on abortion unchanged, my allies and adversaries circled around me, with those who at first had stood behind me on the abortion issue moving around to oppose me, while those who at first had confronted me ended up standing behind me in support. And I was always caught in the vicious crossfire.

I found myself repeatedly misunderstood on the subject of abortion. Many people—critics and admirers alike—claimed that abortion created a conflict between my public and private views. I was both praised and condemned for adopting a public stance on abortion that differed from my private views. But I did not do that. It was never that simple. I do not divide myself into a public self and a private self. My personal religious and ethical convictions are interwoven with my public performance. My beliefs formed the basis for my public actions, calling me not to adopt positions or postures, but to do what needed to be done to discharge faithfully the job that was mine to do, the office I had taken an oath to uphold.

As I have already written, neither my detractors nor my supporters really grasped the origins and basis for my views on abortion. I have always been predisposed against abortion, but my professional position on the issue matured only slowly. And although it was my stance on abortion that attracted the attention of Ronald Reagan and his advisors, my views did not come as part of a prepackaged conservative political philosophy. My opposition to abortion had little to do with politics.

And although I played a major role in the pro-life movement of evangelical Protestants and Catholics, my Christian faith did not blindly dictate my feelings on abortion. True, my convictions about the sanctity of life were buttressed by my study of the Bible and the theological issues. I became convinced that the Bible viewed life within the womb as fully human life. And since God viewed human life as having sanctity, abortion amounted to taking a sacrosanct human life. It seemed clear to me, but I recognized that the issue of abortion might not be addressed as clearly in Scripture as other Christian doctrines. And some pro-life Christians equivocate on issues that seem clear to me.

It all crystallized for me one Saturday in 1976. My residents and I had spent the entire day operating on three newborn babies with defects that were incompatible with life, but were nevertheless amenable to surgical correction. Surgery on newborns is time-consuming, and although we started at 8:00 A.M., we did not have the third youngster safely in his incubator with his immediate future assured until early evening. As the three of us sat in the dimly lit corner of the cafeteria having a meal that had been held for us while it grew cold, I said to my two colleagues: "You know, we have given over two hundreds years of life to three individuals who together barely weighed ten pounds."

One of my residents answered, "And while we were doing that, right next door in the university hospital they were cutting up perfectly formed babies of the same size just because their mothers didn't want them." I knew then that as a surgeon of the newborn, I had to do something about the slaughter of the unborn.

I rose early the next morning and began to write. By Monday evening I had completed *The Right to Live, The Right to Die,* setting

down my concerns about abortion, infanticide, and euthanasia. The
120-page paperback, published by Tyndale, sold over one hundred
thousand copies in its first year, with another hundred thousand sold
in the following years. It continues to be a resource for those concerned
about the connection between abortion, infanticide, and euthanasia.

I aimed the book primarily at Christian readers, as I sought to
awaken the evangelical community to a vital moral issue they were
choosing to ignore. I wrote as a physician, and also as a Christian, about
the inexorable progression from abortion to infanticide to euthanasia.

I began by tracing briefly my own pilgrimage on the issue. It always
seemed clear to me that life begins at conception. After the twenty-
three chromosomes of the sperm are united with the twenty-three
chromosomes of the egg to become a one-celled living organism containing the entire genetic code that will eventually become a you or a
me, that single cell requires nothing except nutrition to become a baby
nine months later. Biologists seem to have no trouble believing that life
begins at the time of fertilization when they talk about lizards, doves,
or baboons; it is only when the argument turns to the highest form of
animal life, a human being, that there enters a lot of fuzzy thinking
about conception and life. For years I had maintained a firm opposition
to abortion but had allowed my belief in my Christian compassion to
make room for abortion in certain "hard cases." But then a Christian
nurse spoke to me, affirming her belief that the "hard cases" were just
as much in the sovereignty of God as any other event in our lives. Her
statement, along with the slow pressure of what I had been reading in
the Bible about the sanctity of life, brought clarity to the issue. I found
I could not justify abortion in any case, except to save the life of the
mother. I always had the greatest sympathy for women who were
pregnant and did not want to be. Sometimes the stakes were high:
continuation of marriage, education, relationship with one's parents,
income, and career plans. But the stakes were higher for the unborn
child.

The issue had become clearer, but that did not make it easier. I
realized that the decision to have an abortion—or not to have an
abortion—could be agonizing and painful, and carry lifelong consequences. The real problem, of course, was that too many women have
unwanted pregnancies, and making the decision to abort the child or
carry it to term is an inadequate solution to a problem that could have
been avoided.

My concerns, though, went beyond the issue of abortion. I became
concerned about what abortion would do not only to unborn children,

but also to American medicine and American society. Abortion would bring along with it deadly consequences that, I felt, even those who favored abortion would not wish to see in our society. My immediate fear was that the 1973 *Roe* v. *Wade* Supreme Court decision legalizing abortion, thereby denying any rights to the unborn child, would soon be extended to newborn children, especially those with handicaps. I did not think the court would rule directly on this issue. I thought instead that the denial of proper treatment to the handicapped newborn—infanticide—would follow abortion, but it would happen slowly, quietly, in the privacy of the neonatal units of our most respected hospitals. Sure enough, soon after abortion became commonplace, some physicians began to refer to a severely defective newborn—the kind I was able to operate on successfully—as a *fetus ex utero*. It was a strange way to refer to a baby. Reality masked by fancy words. The Supreme Court had denied human rights to a fetus, so branding a defective newborn a *fetus ex utero* served to deny human rights to a newborn human.

I was disturbed by the schizophrenic attitude toward identical fetuses. One, a prematurely delivered baby, is admitted to an intensive care unit for superlative care at a thousand dollars a day, while another of identical size and weight is torn from its mother's womb and dropped into the garbage. The only difference is wantedness. Should that standard apply also to four-year-olds, teenagers, old folks—many of whom are undesirable?

I became convinced that the cheapening of newborn life was a result of the large number of abortions each year. After all, a newborn is more like a fetus in appearance and dependency in the first month after birth than it is like an older baby. Physicians know that the actual moment of birth changes but little in the condition of the baby. If abortion is allowed a few days before birth, how is that different from killing a few days after? Abortion, I saw, was leading to infanticide. And infanticide was euthanasia. What would keep it from extending to older people?

Six months after the 1973 Supreme Court decision that opened the way to abortion on demand, I gave the commencement address at Wheaton College in Illinois, predicting a dangerous domino effect of *Roe* v. *Wade* on life-and-death ethics and medicine in the United States. Many of my listeners, even those who agreed with me, thought I had gone too far out on a limb. I predicted that the law would become increasingly ridiculous, requiring, for instance, parental consent for teenage ear piercing, but not for teenage abortions. I predicted that we would see a rapid increase in demands for "mercy killing," demands not

only by the patient, but also by the family. I predicted a dramatic
increase in the number of abortions, as many as one million each year.
(They exceeded 1.22 million in 1990.) I cautioned that abortion would
accelerate our changing sexual morality, with social and health consequences. (Of course, no one knew about AIDS at that time.) I wondered if legal abortion would not allow exploitation of women under
stress by a burgeoning abortion industry. And I warned that defective
newborn infants would be the next to be declared "without meaningful
life." Within three or four years, most of what I had foretold in *The
Right to Live, The Right to Die* and in my commencement speech had
occurred.

The next step in my involvement with abortion took me at the same
time back to the past and forward to a new phase of my career. I was
at York University in Toronto, lecturing to a group of Canadian theolo-
gians on the issues of abortion, infanticide, and euthanasia. After the
question-and-answer session at the close of my talk, a young man arose
and said, "Do you know that Francis Schaeffer is discussing these same
issues at the other end of this campus? Why don't you two get together? He is talking in the abstract and you have all the examples."

Francis Schaeffer was an old friend from my days as a newborn
Christian. Francis and his wife, Edith, later ran a unique Christian
ministry to intellectuals. Named *L'Abri* (the shelter), his home and
adjoining campus in the Swiss Alps above Lake Geneva had become
a refuge for disenchanted intellectuals, searching students, and any
others drawn to his philosophical and artistic approach to the role of
Christianity in twentieth-century culture. His many books formed the
glue that held together the intellectual framework of a new generation
of thoughtful young evangelical students in America and around the
world. When the Schaeffers first moved to Switzerland in the fifties,
I had done what I could to arrange medical care for their children,
especially their young son Frankie, a polio victim. Francis Schaeffer and
I had been through a lot together, and he had become a strong friend,
although our paths had not crossed for about fifteen years.

I walked across the York University campus to the auditorium where
Francis was speaking and caught him just before he was about to begin
his final lecture. He spotted me walking down the center aisle and
leaned down from the platform so that we could embrace. I repeated
what the student said and proposed that we get together on my next
trip to Switzerland. Little did I realize that I had taken the first steps
on the path to Washington, to the job of Surgeon General . . . and to
the continuing controversy over abortion.

A few months later I drove my rented car from Geneva up the steep, winding mountain road to the tiny village of Huemoz-sur-Ollon. As I walked up to the L'Abri auditorium, an elegantly mustached young man standing at the door introduced himself to me as Frankie. I could hardly believe that my patient from long ago, the little boy whose foot had been so seriously hobbled by polio, had become a young man with barely a trace of his earlier disability. He said something rather cryptic, which I did not appreciate at the time: "If you can talk as well as you can write, I think there are some things we can do together."

After I addressed the students Frankie and I walked up the Alpine paths to the next village and then back to Huemoz, stopping briefly for hot chocolate at a roadside stand, discussing all the while the possibilities of doing something significant about the issues of abortion, infanticide, and euthanasia. Late that evening we sat in front of his fireplace and scribbled down the scenario for five motion pictures and the outline for a book, the entire project to be known as *Whatever Happened to the Human Race?* Together, the Schaeffers—father and son—and I determined to awaken the evangelical world—and anyone else who would listen—to the Christian imperative to do something to reverse the perilous realignment of American values on these life-and-death issues.

The entire project, including writing the book, filming the five movies, and holding seminars demanded most of my time for a year and a half. I continued to carry a full load at the hospital when I was there, but I referred the tough cases that required close and long-term follow-up to my colleagues. I realized that my concern about these issues had brought me to a crossroads in my life, that if I altered my surgical practice for that long, I probably would never return to surgery in the same full sense I had enjoyed before. I was right.

We started filming a sequence about the frail elderly and euthanasia in a cemetery in Queens, only a few miles from where I had grown up, then moved on to sites throughout America, Europe, and the Middle East, wherever art, history, or dramatic sequence could enhance our effort. There were several episodes associated with the filming that will live forever in my mind. In one scene, I stood on a little island in the Dead Sea surrounded by a thousand dolls floating in that very buoyant salty water, each doll representing a thousand abortions of unborn babies, to illustrate the enormity of the problem in the United States. We chose the site of Sodom and Gomorrah in the Dead Sea as a place of destruction. I thought it fit in well in the context of the films. But that would be the one clip excerpted years later by opponents to my confirmation as Surgeon General who tried to portray me as a religious zealot.

We opened the first seminar in Philadelphia in September 1979 at the famed Academy of Music, following the format we would use in all the seminars: films, lectures, and discussions spread over two or three days. In the next four months, Schaeffer and I took the seminars to twenty cities in the United States, finishing in Nashville's Grand Ole Opry House in mid-December 1979. Sometimes we were joined by visiting lecturers who shared our concerns. We also took an international swing with seminars in Canada, the United Kingdom, Hong Kong, and Japan. We typically opened a seminar in a convention center or orchestra hall with the first film on abortion and a lecture by both Schaeffer and me followed by a question-and-answer session. The second day included films on infanticide, euthanasia, and changing philosophical values. The third day included workshops, lectures, question-and-answer session, and the final film on Christian alternatives and solutions to the pressing problems.

The book and the films spoke for themselves. The book sold 50,000 copies and appeared in British and Dutch editions. Thousands more people saw the films and subsequent videos as they circulated throughout churches, schools, and homes for more than a decade. About 45,000 people attended our seminars in the United States and abroad. I think the films and the book had a major influence on the thinking of the people who attended, especially the evangelicals in the English-speaking world. I was continually reminded of their impact years later as I traveled around the nation and the world as Surgeon General. Many places I went, strangers would come up to me and start one of the three conversations that always delighted me: First, "Thank you for what you are doing for public health"; second, "You operated on me when I was two days old"; and third, "I never understood the sanctity of life until you made it clear in those seminars built around *Whatever Happened to The Human Race?*"

Soon I had become drawn into the organized pro-life movement. At that time the movement was largely Roman Catholic. Then, with Roman Catholic seed money, a Protestant evangelical pro-life organization was formed, calling itself the Christian Action Council. I was not, as is often reported, one of the founders of the Christian Action Council, but I was in on the organization from its earliest days.

I never unraveled the exact relationships among the various pro-life groups. I did learn that the Ad Hoc Committee for Life, which publishes an unbelievable rag called *Life Letter,* and the Human Life Foundation are closely allied. They are also allied with other Roman Catholic causes, and once you are on the mailing list for one you are apt to get solicitations from the others. There seemed to be a tie with William Buckley, the editor of the *National Review:* editorial comment appearing in one publication appeared in others, true or false, and sometimes without very much scholarship.

In 1977 *The Human Life Review,* published by the Human Life Foundation, ran my essay "The Slide to Auschwitz," in which I continued the argument and evidence about the alarming increase in infanticide in the neonatal units of American hospitals. They liked this so much that they ran it a second time during the Baby Doe controversy in 1982. Both were taken from my 1976 speech to the American Academy of Pediatrics on the occasion of being awarded their Ladd Gold Medal. Although we were allies in the struggle, even in those early days of the pro-life movement I was disturbed by the attitude and activities of some of the people who shared my views. I found their strident tone and vindictive rhetoric offensive. I was even more disturbed by the lack of integrity and absence of scholarship in some pro-life publications. Later, when some of these people turned on me, as they did after *The Surgeon General's Report on Acquired Immune Deficiency Syndrome,* their sleazy and dishonest "journalism" would disturb even some of their own constituents. The pro-life forces, claiming to hold the moral high ground, often employed questionable ethics. I saw this early in the Reagan presidency, while I was still the darling of the pro-life movement. Even before my appointment as Surgeon General I felt a little tension in my relationships within the pro-life movement, although at that time they probably had more to do with style than with substance.

Abortion poisoned my confirmation process, even though I had made clear to Secretary Schweiker that I had nothing more to say publicly on the subject. As the struggle over my confirmation revealed, either no one believed me or they wanted to take me to task for my earlier statements. My attempts to clear the air, to put the controversy to rest, accomplished little, and my first nine months in Washington were dominated by a rehash of the abortion issue under the guise of the confirmation struggle. I remained hostage to the issue. Committee hearings about other issues lapsed into abortion rhetoric, as when representatives from the American Public Health Association, the United Mine Workers, the Women and Health Roundtable, and the National Gay Health Coalition testified against me, ostensibly on the age question. But really their intent was to harass the administration and me because of philosophical differences on the issue of abortion.

When the confirmation struggle was all over, I kept my voluntary promise to Schweiker not to use my post as a pro-life pulpit, even though the administration was seeking to use me as its link to the pro-life movement. I probably remained the most visible pro-life symbol within the administration, except, perhaps, for the president himself.

I do not know how many presidents have written and published a book while they were in office, but Ronald Reagan did. His book was entitled *Abortion and the Conscience of a Nation.* It contained an essay by the president and two essays by other authors, neither of whom was mentioned on the cover. One was my twice-published "The Slide to Auschwitz," and the other was "The Human Holocaust" by Malcolm Muggeridge. I was surprised when I saw the book, because neither the publisher, Nelson, nor the publishers of *The Human Life Review,* nor anyone associated with President Reagan ever discussed the publication with me, let alone asked my permission to publish my essay.

It was common for my opponents on health issues, especially the tobacco people, to drag out the abortion issue as a red herring. For example, when I was testifying before Representative Waxman's Subcommittee on Health and the Environment, I rebutted some misleading (dishonest) testimony by several tobacco state congressmen. In response, one of them, Thomas Blyly, Jr., from Virginia, asked me if I thought that abortion or smoking was the greater public health hazard. I answered him by saying that I presumed he asked me that question only because of my known stand against abortion, but inasmuch as the Supreme Court had taken action on that issue, and in spite of my feeling that the fetus was an extraordinarily important being, I felt as a public health officer that the number of deaths each year from smoking made it the number one public health problem. I gave him that answer because I knew he was merely trying to discredit my anti-smoking efforts by stirring up the abortion advocates against me. I was saddened to realize that abortion had become so politicized that one's stand on the issue could render any other work unproductive. Time proved that a candidate's stand on this single issue either way could result in defeat or election regardless of other qualifications. And although the law of the land had placed the issue of abortion beyond the realm of public health, it remained true that the annual deaths from smoking (then 380,000) fell far short of the number of unborn children then aborted each year: well over 1,000,000.

In little ways I continued quietly to affirm my pro-life stance. For example, on one afternoon I met with three boys from Janesville, Wisconsin, who were doing interviews in Washington for a month as part of a high school project. At their request, I ended up spending over an hour with them discussing abortion because I felt that the opportunity to present the truth to three young minds was certainly worth the time.

And while I made no official pronouncements on abortion, I received over six hundred invitations a year to speak to pro-life and evangelical groups. When some people at Health and Human Services suggested that I automatically decline all of them, I bristled. After all, these people formed a major part of the president's constituency, as well as my constituency, and I felt obliged to accept some of their speaking invitations, even if I focused my remarks on health issues other than those of the pro-life movement.

Meanwhile, the organized pro-life movement was getting restless. They had assumed that the election of pro-life Ronald Reagan would automatically lead to administration efforts to restrict abortion and to overturn *Roe* v. *Wade*. These people were long on symbolism and posturing, short on political savvy. They and others who supported Reagan primarily for his "social agenda"—anti-abortion, prayer in schools, and so on—were disappointed when he took no immediate action on these issues. Economic matters, defense, and foreign policy dominated Reagan's first term.

Okay, they thought, he's saving it for his second term. But even then the Oval Office did almost nothing on the abortion issue, except to make the usual gestures. Occasionally I was asked to make some remarks on relevant health issues to pro-life groups. I would also be called upon to participate in the president's meeting with pro-life representatives in the White House after the annual January 20 March for Life in the capital, a demonstration protesting *Roe* v. *Wade*. Once I was summoned on short notice to the White House to address this group of about thirty people. The White House staff had asked me to speak just before the president was scheduled to make a few remarks. Since this was during the drawn-out Baby Doe controversy, I welcomed the opportunity to allay some of the Baby Doe concerns many pro-lifers aired, usually in a hostile manner. Just as I was finishing, Ronald Reagan walked in and made a brief statement about his personal commitment to the protection of unborn children. He later emphasized that commitment by appearing on the White House balcony before the pro-life marchers, probably the first time a president had ever greeted protesters. I was impressed and moved.

I was much less than pleased with the conduct of some of the people in the pro-life group, their bizarre behavior a foretaste of how they would inexplicably turn against me three years later. After the president's polite remarks, pro-life zealot Nellie Gray berated the president for his inactivity in a manner that was abrasive, brash, irritating, and embarrassing to me and some others present. Increasingly I was dismayed and distressed by the strident, insensitive, and politically self-defeating character of the pro-life movement, which would further limit its role in national politics. At the same gathering, another pro-life leader interrupted a speaker to hand Reagan a brochure, inviting him to an all-day meeting about reversing *Roe* v. *Wade*, still another example of political and personal insensitivity, as well as wasting precious time with the president.

I expected things to go along routinely, with the pro-life movement going its own way, while I, maintaining my support for their causes, removed myself from their tactics. Anyway, my agenda was filling up: smoking, handicapped children, violence, and of course, AIDS.

It was AIDS that once again heated up the abortion controversy around me. It was all based on an awkwardly phrased sentence that the press scooped up and then ran away with. Ironically, I had been trying to make things clearer and calmer. I had planned a speech to clarify the growing national confusion and turmoil about AIDS. At the end of March 1987, I had the honor of addressing the National Press Club. Things started out smoothly. The audience seemed very attentive and receptive to my speech, in which I stressed the manner in which AIDS is transmitted and how it is not.

After I answered a question about the inappropriateness of compulsory premarital testing, I was asked whether a pregnant woman carrying the AIDS virus should have an abortion. I made it very clear that I would never recommend an abortion because of my personal stand against it, but that a pregnant woman whose unborn child had a 50 percent chance of mortality because of AIDS (as we thought then; now it is as low as 30 percent) was entitled to consultation about abortion if she desired.

I answered the question too quickly. I wanted to make clear that although *Roe* v. *Wade* made abortion a legal option for any pregnant woman, it was an option I believed although legal was wrong.

Betty heard my address on the radio and was very much concerned about the effect of my answer to the question. As usual, she anticipated things correctly when she warned that the one remark would cause me a lot of problems. Sure enough, the next day newspaper headlines blared, "Koop Supports Abortion."

I became very upset as the news rippled across the country, its effects multiplied as most press accounts distorted my answer. Predictably, I was taken to task by the far-right pro-lifers. The most blatant attacks came from the stridently conservative *Washington Times.* Although 80 percent of the flap took place inside the Beltway, I wished I could have set the record straight. When I discussed it with Secretary of Health and Human Services Otis Bowen, he counseled, "Look, Chick, look at it this way: Number one, they spelled your name right. Number two, you are getting a lot of publicity. Number three, it may give you the chance to make your position even clearer." I appreciated his attempts to cheer me up, but I realized that I faced a long uphill struggle to undo the damage. I never really did.

Many individuals and groups on the far right had already turned against me because of my efforts to stem the AIDS epidemic. Here, too, they based their feelings on distortions of my pronouncements or even on outright lies written about me. They should have known better. I was hurt, and then angry, having carried water for the pro-life forces for so long, to be attacked by people who should have known better and who should have helped make my position—which was the same as theirs—clear.

Then, as the controversy swirled around me, the knees began to jerk. As a longtime Republican, I had often heard about knee-jerk liberals. It did not take long in Washington for me to see that conservative knees jerk as readily as liberal ones, maybe even faster and less thoughtfully. The controversy over my remark at the National Press Club not only set some conservatives against me but also it brought more liberals to my side. And the very fact that some liberals now cheered me on—correctly for my position on smoking and AIDS, incorrectly for abortion—made the conservative pro-lifers oppose me even more. After all, they thought, if the liberals liked me, I must be doing something wrong.

I decided to meet privately with some pro-life leaders and pro-life congressmen. I gently, and sometimes firmly, remonstrated them for thinking that I could so readily abandon my commitment to the unborn, to the newborn, a commitment based upon both years of surgery and years of faith. I think some understood. Many, like Senator Gordon Humphrey, simply chose not to. The public can be fickle.

· · ·

My last chapter in the abortion saga started when Reagan asked me to write a report on the health effects of abortion on women. Well, he didn't really ask me. He just made an offhand remark in a speech to some pro-life groups that he had asked the Surgeon General to prepare such a report. It was, in somewhat typical Reagan style, a strange way to be asked to do something. There never was a direct order, and I knew there never would be. I, like the rest of the country, learned from the news reports that Reagan had asked me to prepare a comprehensive medical report on the health effects—mental and physical—of abortion on women. It was all White House politics, all pretty detached from reality.

It began with a personnel squabble and a silly idea. The personnel squabble involved Joanne Gaspar, a pro-life appointee in HHS who was dismissed because of insubordination. Pro-life issues were not a factor in her dismissal, although the press portrayed a procedural matter as one involving pro-life principles. The far right was miffed about the Gaspar affair, reading into it a pro-abortion bias. It was clear to me that by calling for the abortion report, the president was seeking to mollify them. Reagan had also embraced a silly idea touted by one of the neophyte right-wingers on the White House staff that the evidence of adverse health effects (presumably mental) of abortion on women that the Surgeon General could pull together would be sufficient to overturn *Roe* v. *Wade.* Anyone with even a smattering of information—and an idea of how the Supreme Court works—would know this idea was foolish. But the young campus-conservative ideologues heady with what they thought was power did not always live in the real world.

From the beginning I felt there was something sinister behind this nonrequest. I wondered if my sniping adversaries in the White House had called for the report not only to placate the far right, but also to distract me from my blunt and realistic approach to AIDS. Later, some friends who understood the often arcane workings of the White House assured me that there was no hidden motive in the request and that my stock at the White House was higher than I assumed. The president, I was told, simply had said there was only one person in the country who could write the abortion report, and he happened to be the Surgeon General.

I did not like the political atmosphere in which this report was conceived. I thought the White House was misguided or even manipulative if it attempted to deal with the issue of abortion in this backhand way. Abortion was more a moral issue than a medical issue. The pro-life movement had always focused—rightly, I thought—on the impact of abortion on the fetus. They lost their bearings when they approached the issue on the grounds of the health effects on the mother.

I also felt from the beginning that this was a no-win situation, that the scientific data that underlay the AIDS report would simply not be available for this one. The AIDS report has remained unassailable and correct in every word, even five years after I released it, because the science on which it was based was unimpeachable. The question of abortion and its health effects on the mother could not draw on the same kind of data and interpretation.

I intended to assume the same control of the report as I had done with AIDS. Assured of Otis Bowen's complete backing, I began to lay plans for the gathering of data. I asked Mike Samuels, whose assistance had been so valuable to me in preparing the AIDS report, to join me. When Mike left the government for academia, he was replaced by George Walter. We had to make do with a tiny staff. For the AIDS report, we had met with twenty-six groups, but as we planned the abortion report 150 groups requested a hearing. It looked as if it would take thirty weeks just for the interviews. Meanwhile, my schedule was already full with other issues and commitments.

There was much anecdotal information, but anecdotes do not make statistics. Most of the scientific papers had an experimental design that betrayed the author's own bias on abortion. On the first day of my interviews, the polarization of positions was clearly evident as I met first with a delegation from Planned Parenthood and then with a group from the National Right to Life Committee. A similar climate prevailed throughout the rest of the interviews with representatives from groups such as the Christian Life Commission of the Southern Baptist Convention, state health officers who dealt with maternal and child health, the American Nursing Association, the Religious Coalition on Abortion Rights, the Alan Gutmacher Institute, the AMA, the American Council on Science and Health, the National Youth Pro-Life Coalition, the National Organization for Women, the American Public Health Association, and the American Psychiatric Association.

So I met with White House aide Gary Bauer to explain that every bit of literature I had read on abortion reflected the sociological or moral bias of the authors. There was as much evidence of positive effects of abortion on women as negative. I told Bauer that a proper study of the issue would cost between $10 million and $100 million, and that this did not seem to be an issue on which Reagan or his party were going to have any political gains. I suggested that either I meet with the president to explain the problems or put them in a letter. Bauer said he wanted some time to think it over. He eventually got back to me, saying I had to go ahead with the report. A White House staffer told me, "The president never changes his mind."

But my commitment to good science made it clearer with each slanted interview I held, with each biased study I perused, that I could never write the kind of report the White House originally had envisioned. By autumn, after I had torn up seven drafts, I had come to the conclusion that the only honest way to proceed was simply to write a letter to the president, explaining why no current studies could reach a defensible conclusion, one way or the other, on the health effects of abortion on women. (Later, an American Psychological Association committee would confirm my assessment.)

I knew this would disappoint or even anger groups on both sides of the issue who wanted my report to fight their battle. I even began to get some opposition from my own staff. Although most of the people who worked with me agreed with my conclusion, a few, prompted more by bureaucratic momentum than anything else, wanted a report published. After all, they said, we've done all this work, so why not write the report? They were not bothered by its methodological flaws.

By December, I decided I had no recourse but to write a letter to the president. I did not want to deliver it in the middle of the holiday crush, but I did feel the responsibility to report to Reagan before he left office. So I decided to send a letter in early January 1989.

The language of my letter was straightforward: "I believe that the issue of abortion is so emotionally charged that it is possible that many who might read this letter would not understand it because I have not arrived at conclusions they can accept. But I have concluded in my review of this issue that, at this time, the available scientific evidence about the psychological sequelae of abortion simply cannot support either the preconceived beliefs of those pro-life or of those pro-choice."

I had hoped to deal with the issue in as dispassionate an atmosphere as possible, but that was not to be. Just as my staff and I were preparing the letter to the president, the Supreme Court announced its *Webster* decision, which put the right to an abortion more or less in the hands of individual states, thereby bringing the abortion issue to center stage in national and state politics.

Because of the volatile political implications, I did not want the president to be blindsided by the report, and I also thought it important—and courteous—to inform president-elect Bush, since he would have to deal with the fallout. As Christmas approached, I repeatedly attempted to reach John Sununu, Bush's newly selected chief of staff, to fill him in on the abortion report situation. I left a message inviting him to join Secretary Bowen and me when we presented the letter to Reagan. No one returned my calls.

It was hard for me to conclude which group was in greater disarray, the departing Reagan crew or the incoming Bush team. As Otis Bowen and I approached the White House late that cold, clear January afternoon eleven days before Reagan was to leave office, I had that now-all-too-familiar feeling that I was walking a tightrope.

Although I thought the matter of sufficient magnitude to warrant a meeting with the president, or at least his chief of staff, Otis and I had been met only by M. B. Oglesby and Nancy Risque of the White House staff. I handed Oglesby the letter, and then Otis and I explained it. Oglesby said that he would deliver my letter to the president, and that he thought he would be interested in my recommendations. He promised to hold it close. We left, feeling elated that it had gone so smoothly.

When I got home, Betty told me that the TV networks, reporting on a distorted wire service story, had announced that I had issued a report confirming that abortion produced no evidence of negative health effects on women. Of course, my letter to the president had said no such thing. It was the National Press Club fracas all over again. Betty pressed me to do something right away, and at her urging I spent the rest of the evening on damage control. More than my feelings were at stake. The real victim was truth.

There were two problems. First, I thought I had been promised that Reagan would respond before the letter was made public. Second, United Press International (UPI) fumbled the reporting. A novice UPI reporter, on her first day covering HHS, had either misread the letter or put an incorrect story on the UPI wire, and the TV networks had taken it from there.

Finally I reached Michael Spector at *The Washington Post* and then Marlene Cimons at *The Los Angeles Times;* each later correctly reported the incident. My most helpful call was to Dr. Tim Johnson of ABC, who was equally distressed about the distortion of health information and promised to do what he could to get me on *Good Morning America* to clear up the mess.

The next morning I could not wait for the first questions from Charles Gibson and Joan Lunden. I welcomed the chance to set the record straight, and I think that in the few minutes available to me I made it clear that I had not wavered at all in my personal pro-life stance, but that as Surgeon General I had always attempted to separate science from my personal views. In the case of abortion, the science was simply not conclusive either way.

As effective as I hoped my few minutes on *Good Morning America* had been, I did not let the matter rest there. I wrote a letter to all the organizations I had interviewed about abortion, making clear to them that the initial TV and press reports they might have heard did not reflect my conclusions and that I would continue to set the record straight as opportunities on national television presented themselves.

No one in the administration responded to my letter to Reagan. The president himself, of course, said nothing. Not surprisingly, the pro-life movement railed against me. I was told that one pro-life leader had complained that I had buried the pro-life movement. If that were true, I thought, they must be in pretty bad shape. I reminded people of what I had said many times: The issue of abortion is not to be decided in terms of its effect upon the mother, but in terms of its effect upon the unborn child. The effect upon the mother is unclear; the effect upon the unborn child is clear—and fatal. I was, of course, disturbed that they were disturbed, but I consoled myself by remembering that this misguided focus of the pro-life movement was not new. These were the same people who saw nothing strange about being against both abortion and contraception.

I was angry about the untrue allegations about me churned out by the pro-life people. And on a deeply personal level I was saddened and hurt, especially by the unkind attacks leveled at me by fellow evangelicals. Once again evangelical editors and columnists denounced me as a man who had abandoned his principles.

Church leaders, people I had worked alongside in the early days of the pro-life movement, were quick to condemn me. Ironically, many of them had been awakened to the issues by the lectures and books I had written as probably the most outspoken American physician against abortion. Now they did not even give me a hearing. No doubt many decided to oppose me only because, once again, liberals and pro-abortion people applauded me since they were equally misinformed about my letter to the president.

I tried responding to my critics, making it as clear as possible that my position against abortion had not changed at all, but that the issue had to be faced on moral, not medical, grounds. I told them that indeed my own research had yielded considerable anecdotal information about the negative effects of abortion on women; I had personally counseled women who were in deep depression because of the remorse and guilt they felt after an abortion. But I had also encountered women who said that their abortion had saved their marriage or job. The worst thing I could have done for the pro-life movement would have been to write a report that could have been scientifically torn apart.

I admit I have been stung by some of these personal attacks. I have been outraged to see my words distorted, my beliefs doubted, my integrity questioned in public by those claiming to be fellow Christians—people who should know better, people who knew that Jesus commanded our love for one another. And it takes more than just saying it. The authors of one evangelical periodical wrote, "we still love you, Dr. Koop, but we find it hard to forgive you." As though I had somehow sinned against *them*. My feelings of sorrow and disappointment increased because I was convinced that my fellow evangelicals had not only failed to understand my position, but also had refused to muster the intelligence and scholarship to try. I believed, however, that no matter how they reacted, I had done the right thing.

As the *Webster* decision caused abortion to become more politicized than ever, I marveled at the inability or even ineptitude of the three branches of government to deal with the problem. The latest court decisions had drawn Congress into the act, and that in turn involved the White House. I took my customary seat in the crossfire. Congressman Ted Weiss (D.-N.Y.) decided to investigate the preparation of the abortion letter. As I collected the material he requested, I got the word from the Office of Management and Budget that I should delete any reference to the White House, delete any reference to a prospective study—the whole point of the report—even delete any reference to the fetus. The White House staffers seemed insane, but what else was new? This supposedly anti-abortion administration did not want me to mention that during an abortion the fetus was killed. In the end, all the dither and apprehension in the preparation for the Weiss hearing in March 1989 came, as I expected, to nothing.

There will always be abortions, law or no law. There are back-alley abortions even now, when abortions are legal. When the time comes— if ever—that abortions are illegal again—say in some states—there will still be illegal abortions, but they will be done with the same equipment now used safely.

By the time I left the office of Surgeon General, I had become convinced that both sides in the abortion debate had reached a dead end. *Webster* might move the site of the debate to the states, but it would not alter the issues, nor would it decrease the intensity or lessen the acrimony. Nor, did I think, would it allow a solution, one way or the other.

I saw two possible resolutions of the abortion issue, each at extreme ends of the spectrum. Far away, but not outside the realm of possibility, lay progress in prenatal care that would allow a fetus to live and develop outside the uterus from the earliest weeks of its life. This would allow abortion without the death of the fetus. It would allow children conceived but unwanted by their natural parents to be "brought to term" artificially and then raised by adoptive parents desperately seeking children. Although enormous technical and even ethical problems loom in this, it would offer a choice that our society might have to face before long. And it would bring into sharp focus the question of whether an abortion means the termination of pregnancy or the destruction of the child-to-be.

At the other end of the realm of possibilities lay the greater likelihood of widespread use of abortifacient drugs such as RU486. This would have the effect of removing abortion from the public arena (although not from the ethical arena). Abortion would become nothing but an issue between a woman and her pharmacist, beyond the reach of a society concerned about the fate of the fetus. We will need "truth in advertising," however, so that the public understands that RU486 is an abortifacient, *not* a contraceptive. At present, we have no idea of the long-term effects of repeated use of this drug.

For the time being, however, it seemed that the standoff would continue. The rhetoric comes straight from the days of World War II. Both sides, pro-life, pro-abortion, are fond of using terms like "battleground," "combat," "war," and "battle." Neither side seems to be winning any converts to its position. Sometimes I think that both sides have forgotten why they are fighting. They care simply about winning: winning each court case, each legislative battle, each electoral contest, each rally. They glare and shout at each other over an unbridgeable chasm. They whoop at their victories, snarl in defeat. I wonder if each side has not forgotten the human element that originally prompted the debate: the innocent unborn child, the agonized pregnant woman.

Many of those who have been opposed to abortion have been notoriously unhelpful to unwed pregnant women. Some religious schools and colleges, very much opposed to abortion, expel a young woman who becomes pregnant, just when she needs all the support she can get to carry her child. Anti-abortion people must be more forthcoming with their time and money to assist pregnant women in hardship. Anti-abortionists cannot simply rail against abortion; they must press for whatever legal, social, and economic changes are necessary to make childbearing equitable and fair. They should be willing to do anything they can to bring conceived children to birth.

And those who call themselves "pro-choice" ought to make more of adoption as a clear choice. Pro-abortionists have often justified the abortion of babies who are "not wanted." But that is a misleading term. Most children conceived are wanted, if not by their natural parents then by the thousands of couples yearning to adopt newborn babies. Lost in the vicious debate over abortion are the hopes of childless couples who cannot have the babies they want. They would love the ability to choose to raise the children of women who do not want the babies they have. The so-called pro-choice faction needs to do more to make these choices possible.

I began to search for a compromise. I had not altered my opposition to abortion, my belief that it violates our basic ethical tradition of preserving human life, of defending the weakest members of our society. Ethical compromise was impossible. But I did see the possibility for a practical compromise that would at least lower the number of abortions, lower the number of unborn children whose death was sanctioned by our laws and society.

Abortion was not the problem. The problem was unwanted pregnancy. If the number of unwanted pregnancies could be reduced, the number of abortions could be reduced. If unwanted pregnancies could be eliminated, abortions could be eliminated. It was as simple as that.

Of course, there were some soldiers in the abortion wars who did not—or would not—see it that way. There were some liberals and conservatives who saw abortion as a plank in their political platform, something to stand on as they attacked the other side or something to pick up to bash the other side.

Even after eight years in Washington, eight years in the center of the storm, I never understood this political approach to abortion. Liberalism and conservatism are political–economic philosophies; abortion is primarily a moral issue that should defy political categorization. I have always been surprised that liberals, usually so concerned about the underdog and the disenfranchised, have failed to champion the rights of unborn children. Nor did I understand some ardent feminists who see abortion as a weapon in the feminist struggle, a tool to oppose those traditionalist males determined to keep women in their place by denying them "control over their own bodies." These extremists of both sides, I realized, did not seek compromise; perhaps they did not even seek resolution. They were in it for the battle.

But there were many others who were weary of confrontation and who might listen to a better way, who would welcome concentration on the root of the problem. For example, a growing number in the pro-abortion group Planned Parenthood began to see that their deep involvement in the abortion controversy had diverted them from their original mission: planning parenthood, rather than eliminating it. On the other side, a number of pro-lifers remembered their original concern—the killing of unborn children—and saw the wisdom of at least reducing the number killed.

Two problems in particular stood in the way of pro-life people trying to reduce the number of abortions. One was their absolutist frame of mind, their all-or-nothing mentality. They were more concerned with the purity of their position than with the actual results of their resolution. I had encountered this attitude in the Baby Doe controversy when a number of pro-life leaders denounced the regulations governing the treatment of handicapped newborns because the regulations promised protection for only 97 percent of such babies. They wanted 100 percent or nothing. In a pluralist society, political compromise does not equal ethical compromise.

Similarly, more than ten years earlier, in the years of the abortion debate before *Roe* v. *Wade,* a political compromise by the pro-life forces could have averted millions of abortions. In the late sixties and first two years of the seventies, as pro-abortion sentiment was growing in an increasingly unfettered society, there was nonetheless little widespread desire for unlimited abortion, abortion on demand. Even abortion advocates knew this. If the pro-life forces had come to a political compromise, firmly denouncing abortion except in the cases of a defection baby, rape, or incest or to save the life of the mother, the pro-abortion side would have jumped to agree, and the subsequent bitter struggle and the more than one million abortions a year since *Roe* v. *Wade* would have been avoided or at least postponed.

In the years since the Supreme Court acted, the anti-abortion movement has made a very large tactical error by concentrating on legal and constitutional issues, when the issue is really moral or ethical. That mistake became increasingly evident as legal abortion became more deeply entrenched in American society. As we have seen with alcohol and tobacco, moral suasion can work better than prohibition. True, we need to tap a different emotion, since we would not be arguing for self-preservation, as in anti-smoking and anti-drinking campaigns. Instead we need to stress our deeply ingrained ethic of caring for the weaker or defenseless members of society, the same arguments we use to combat child abuse or even those subjected to passive smoking.

I am even more concerned about the wider effects of abortion on American medicine and on social and health problems as well as the larger life-and-death issues of infanticide and euthanasia. Changes in sexual behavior have paralleled the growth of abortions, so that 1.2 million teenagers get pregnant every year and 400,000 of them have abortions. We are facing epidemics of sexually transmitted diseases that we have not seen for decades. And of course we all now face the scourge of AIDS. I fear that the cheapening of human life, in combination with economic pressures and the mounting death toll from AIDS, could spawn a movement toward euthanasia in the nineties.

For all the words written, said, and shouted during the abortion controversy, the issue has become no clearer. Indeed, the most commonly used words distort rather than clarify. Each side has chosen a label to improve its popular appeal, a label that obscures the issue. The "pro-choice" people demonstrate no greater concern about free choice in the other issues that plague our society. For example, most of them would not support the right of a husband to choose to threaten a wife in the privacy of the home. Similarly, the "pro-life" camp has not been vocal in its support of other issues affecting human life, from the environment to the death penalty. The issue is not "pro-life" versus "pro-choice." The issue is abortion. The issue is pro-abortion versus anti-abortion. But that is not really accurate either. Even the "pro-abortion" people do not favor abortions, they do not want abortions to occur. And the "anti-abortion" people are not as absolute as their rhetoric indicates.

There have always been some shades of gray in the debate. Even the most extreme pro-abortionists would not condone abortion for any reason whatsoever. I would be surprised if pro-abortion advocates would approve of a woman choosing an abortion because her child's likely birthdate would conflict with a planned Super Bowl Sunday party or because that child happened to be of the wrong sex. Even pro-choice people have limits to choice. And on the other side, even the Roman Catholic Church allows abortion to save the life of the mother. True, those cases are very rare now, but the Catholic position does provide for abortion in some cases where a judgment is required. In other words, the issue is not whether or not abortion shall be allowed, but under which circumstances abortion should be allowed. I bring this up only to point out that discussion on the practical level is possible.

A large obstacle to practical compromise, to focusing on unwanted pregnancies rather than fighting over abortion, lies in the Roman Catholic stance not only against abortion but also against contraception. Again, as a practical matter, I could never understand the opposition to both at once.

Perhaps the problem could be approached by more clearly defining the role of religious ethics in a pluralist society. This poses a problem for all religious groups in the United States. In some cases (for instance, life-and-death issues) we want our religion-based ethical principles to extend throughout society; in other cases (as with holy days and sexual ethics), we limit them to our adherents. I ran into this issue in discussions with Catholic leaders about the AIDS epidemic and the use of condoms. It made sense to me if Catholic leaders opposed the use of condoms by Catholics. That, after all, was their business. Furthermore, as far as AIDS was concerned, Catholic morality should protect Catholics from the consequences of nonmonogamous sexual intercourse or sharing IV drug paraphernalia. So there is no reason for true Catholics to use prophylactic condoms. For Catholics, therefore, the issue of using condoms to prevent the spread of AIDS is moot. And Catholics do not claim the right to determine sexual ethics for non-Catholics.

So, if Catholic opposition to some forms of contraception could be limited to Catholics alone, we could remove a major obstacle to the cooperation needed to reduce the number of abortions in our country. It would allow energy—and government funding—to go into contraceptive research and education, areas in which American science and society lag behind.

In Sweden the teenage pregnancy rate in 1982 was 13.7 per 1,000 women, while in New Jersey in 1985 it was 113 per 1,000. I do not believe that New Jersey girls are eight times as promiscuous as those in Sweden. Education about contraception can work, but Americans need more education and a national commitment. We also need to focus on contraception research. There may be answers no one has thought of, perhaps ones that are acceptable to Americans of all ethical and religious convictions. It is an area of investigation too much ignored.

We already know more than we practice. There are many ways to practice contraception. All Americans agree that pregnancy can be avoided, but they differ on which means of contraception should be used. In public health terms, we must see contraception, not abortion, as the "treatment" for the problem of unwanted pregnancy. Those who oppose contraception as well as abortion present no solution to the abortion issue because they have removed the means of prevention. Every group, every subculture in our society has its approved method of contraception, of avoiding pregnancy. The leaders of those groups, whether they are Roman Catholic bishops or gang leaders, need to exercise this aspect of their influence to avoid unwanted pregnancies in their culture.

I am enough of a realist to know that the abortion controversy in the United States will never offer an easy or popular solution. I wish no abortions were performed. I think most Americans agree with me on that. Even pro-abortionists will admit that every abortion is a failure: a failure to practice contraception, a failure of our institutions, whether family, economic, or social. Abortions are tragic failures. And for the most part, they are preventable failures. I would like to see both sides of the abortion controversy agree on this: It is one of the few points on which they can agree. And then they could take steps to avoid the failure that raises the issue of abortion.

The longest journeys start with a single step. In one city, maybe in a dozen, anti-abortion groups and abortion rights activists, while agreeing to disagree on the "right" to have an abortion, could cooperate, could work together to reduce the number of unwanted pregnancies.

A small step, but also a giant one.

Part V

The Surgeon General Reports

When I was Surgeon General, in addition to discharging my official duties, I also tried to serve the public in a much more intimate way as I answered their health questions and dispensed advice. Here are my views on some of the major health questions facing the American public. I do not suggest they are definitive; they are conclusions from a lifetime of practice.

Prevention

George Bernard Shaw once asked why we pay doctors to take a leg *off*, but we don't pay them to keep a leg *on*. Now, almost eighty years have passed and we still have not come up with a good answer.

Unfortunately, our technology-driven health care system is still predicated on taking the leg off. But some of us are trying to challenge that thinking. We are attempting a new American Revolution—a revolution in everyday individual behavior: preventive health care. In some small ways, preventive health care has been around for a long time. We vaccinate our children and fluoridate our drinking water, and many of us have regular medical checks. But the overall perception among the American people is still the old-fashioned notion that the health care community is there to patch you up if you get hurt or to cure you if you get sick. Too many people think their role as patient is to be passive and simply "follow doctor's orders." Health care is not synonymous with doctors and hospitals. Health care also means prevention. Among the most frequent causes of premature death are smoking, drinking too much, and not wearing a seat belt—habits each of us can control.

We need to make a national commitment to health education that is far greater than the routine and merely ceremonial attention we usually give it. We need to take seriously the obligation of our schools and colleges to deliver to their students a clear, coherent, and consistent public health message. We also need to nurture the self-help and group support networks that have arisen spontaneously and profusely among the general public over the past decade or so. When the goal of education is the accumulation of knowledge, we in public health do quite well. But when the goal is getting people to change their behavior, we have a long way to go. The answer does not lie in finding new teaching techniques; instead, we have to begin far earlier, even before school starts. We need to teach youngsters that they must take charge of their health—all of their lives. We should start this health education the day we teach them to pick up a toothbrush. And we must do more than teach—we must set an example in the way we live.

Preventive health care should become popular because it makes people feel better and saves money. As employers and employees, we have come to realize that healthy workers save everyone money. I am pleased to see an increasing number of companies sponsoring "wellness" programs that reward their employees for adopting healthful life-styles. The American people are getting the message. For example, we have measured a decrease in the consumption of hard liquor and a corresponding dramatic decrease in deaths from chronic liver disease and cirrhosis. And in the last ten years Americans have achieved a decline in deaths from heart disease and stroke because more people have quit smoking and are eating less fat. When we convince ourselves to eat a proper diet, to say "No!" to drugs such as alcohol and nicotine, we take charge of our health. We must not rely completely on high-cost, high-tech medicine to prolong our lives. As I remind people, "You *can* afford prevention even if you *cannot* affort a quadruple bypass."

You can start to take care of yourself now. The prescription is simple:

• Don't smoke.
• If you drink alcohol, do so only in moderation.
• Exercise and diet as appropriate to your age.
• Buckle up. It does not make sense to drive to the health food store without fastening your seat belt.
• Check your blood pressure and cholesterol. See your doctor if they are abnormal; then follow his or her advice.

Fortunately, some of us older folks must have been blessed with good genes, because we have lived so many years even without these helpful health warnings. We have eaten far too much lard and never jogged unless we were late for a trolley car. For years we thought fiber was part of our clothing, not our diet. And we have made it to old age. Of course, if we had known we would live so long, we would have taken better care of ourselves.

Aging

The prevention ethic will keep more of us healthier longer, even though we will get older. And getting older does not mean getting sicker.

There are many myths about aging. One of the worst is that you cling to your health until your sixty-fifth birthday, and then you suddenly slide downhill. That simply is not true. Today, the average sixty-five-year-old can look forward to living another seventeen years. There are more of us oldsters every day. By the year 2010, close to 20 percent of the American population will be over sixty-five. Within that group, the fastest-growing segment will be persons who are eighty-five or older. Older Americans are a great natural resource of common sense and wisdom, a resource we should protect. We must not rob the years after sixty-five of their value. You do not need to give up on living at sixty-five and snooze in a rocking chair. Too many older Americans withdraw into inactivity. Then they find themselves depressed and plagued with poor health.

Now we understand that often we can enjoy disease-free aging. We know how to prevent many of the diseases and disabilities that once denied older people their independence. For example, there are two common one-way tickets to a nursing home: broken hips and urinary incontinence. Both of these conditions are degrading to the patient, and the combined cost to the government was recently estimated at $8 billion annually. But in many cases these problems can be avoided, giving older citizens many more years of independent living.

We frequently hear about elderly folks who become partially disabled because they "fall and break a hip." But what often happens is that they break a hip, and *then* they fall. The neck of the thigh bone where it attaches to the hip joint is relatively narrow, and when subjected to a particular pressure and torque—the kind you apply when you struggle to get out of a deep easy chair or car—it snaps. Many hip injuries could be prevented if doctors simply took the time to educate their elderly patients about how to select the proper chair and how to get out of it safely, and how to get out of bed or out of an automobile. Elderly people need to learn all they can about the role of exercise and calcium (and, for women, the role of estrogens on calcium absorption) in strengthening bones, another way to prevent fractures.

Adult urinary incontinence is an embarrassing and common condition. Few Americans realize that most urinary incontinence is easy to treat, even cure. Far too many adults are in diapers. Although there are many causes of urinary incontinence, the most common cause in women is the weakening of vaginal and pelvic floor muscles. Numerous studies—including a major one I commissioned as Surgeon General—have demonstrated that biofeedback techniques, which combine pelvic floor exercises and a heightened awareness of one's bodily signals, effectively eliminated incontinence in about 70 percent of mentally alert, ambulatory patients. With proper instruction, adults who suffer from urinary incontinence can return to normal, active life, not bothering with diapers—except on their grandchildren or great-grandchildren.

The public health information concerning prevention of hip fractures and incontinence is easy to understand and simple to convey, but it does not get to enough of the people who need it. I am sorry to say that physicians, to their discredit, are not known for their willingness to take the time to teach their elderly patients about these vital issues. But nurses are. As Surgeon General, I made arrangements for the Public Health Service to train a cadre of nurses who could teach these techniques across the nation. I hope that the spread of this information will help to put an end to these needlessly debilitating conditions and restore more dignity and good health to older Americans. With common sense, most of us can live in good health and comfort until the day we die.

But we need to remember that the day we die will come. Sometimes I think Americans have forgotten that they have to die—of something. The miracles of modern medicine may tempt us to worship at the altar of "life at all cost." But now I believe the public wonders if medical technology might be a mixed blessing. Both the lay public and the medical profession are debating the wisdom of using so-called "extraordinary" measures to save or prolong the lives of persons who are profoundly traumatized or terminally ill. For many people who must decide the fate of loved ones, high-tech medicine can be both a friend and an enemy. Therefore, some are turning to legal instruments such as the "living will" and the "durable power of attorney" to protect themselves from runaway medical technology in the event they one day have a terminal illness or incapacitating injury. In our society, we shy away even from talking about death. We need to be more realistic; part of living is preparing for death. As the author of Ecclesiastes wrote, "There is a time to be born; there is a time to die."

But we must be wary of those who are too willing to end the lives of the elderly and the ill. If we ever decide that a poor quality of life justifies ending that life, we have taken a step down a slippery slope that places all of us in danger. There is a difference between allowing nature to take its course and actively assisting death. The call for euthanasia surfaces in our society periodically, as it is doing now under the guise of "death with dignity" or assisted suicide. Euthanasia is a concept, it seems to me, that is in direct conflict with a religious and ethical tradition in which the human race is presented with "a blessing and a curse, life and death," and we are instructed ". . . therefore, to choose life." I believe "euthanasia" lies outside the commonly held life-centered values of the West and cannot be allowed without incurring great social and personal tragedy. This is not merely an intellectual conundrum. This issue involves actual human beings at risk. The most celebrated example of euthanasia in recent years, of course, was the "Baby Doe" incident I discussed at length in an earlier chapter.

While the terror of state-sponsored euthanasia may never grip America as it once did Germany, it is possible that the terror of the euthanasia ethic—tolerated by medicine and an indifferent public and practiced by a few physicians—may grip many invisible and vulnerable Americans. Over fifty years ago, German doctors and courts collaborated to identify millions of people who were labeled "devoid of value." Some Americans are labeled the same today: members of a racial or ethnic "underclass," a sidewalk screamer . . . an illegal alien . . . a nursing home resident with Alzheimer's disease . . . an abandoned migrant worker . . . or anyone too old or weak or poor to help himself or herself. For two millennia the Hippocratic tradition has stood for the "sanctity" of human life. We can alleviate the unbearable in life better than ever before. We can do that and not eliminate life itself. As I have said many times, medicine cannot be both our healer and our killer.

Nutrition and Food Safety

Americans are zany about food and diet. No other country gorges itself on junk food the way we do, and no other country has as many "experts" on health diets. We have become more concerned about what we should not eat than what we should.

Food fads come and go, but the basics of a good diet are actually very simple. An adult's balanced diet every day should be something like this:

1) Four to five servings of fruits, vegetables, and grains (this will give you vitamins A and C, folic acid, minerals, and fiber)

2) Four servings of bread, pasta, rice, or cereal (for carbohydrates, fiber, the B vitamins, and minerals)

3) Two servings of milk, cheese, ice cream, or yogurt (for protein, calcium, vitamin B_2, and minerals)

4) Two servings of meat, fowl, eggs, fish, nuts, or legumes (for protein, iron, vitamin B_1, and niacin)

Naturally, if you eat a balanced diet every day, you will be getting excellent nutrition. But remember that the human body is remarkably adaptable. Don't be afraid of junk food once in a while.

I am a little dismayed by the way the cholesterol issue has confused the public. The cholesterol balloon seems to undergo cycles of inflation and deflation. True, cholesterol is a risk factor for coronary heart disease. It is, however, only one of several risk factors, and most scientists think the others, such as smoking and high blood pressure, are more important and easier to control. And since cholesterol is manufactured in the body naturally, the cholesterol in one's diet does not have the direct relationship to the cholesterol level in one's blood as many misled laymen assume. Then, too, the stated relationship between coronary heart disease and cholesterol blood levels does not apply with reliable longevity correlation to women over fifty-five and men over sixty.

I think officialdom has been at fault by sounding the cholesterol alarm for too large an audience. It may be true that 25 percent of the population could benefit significantly by lowering their blood cholesterol and thereby protecting themselves against heart disease. However, to broadcast this information as though everyone had high blood cholesterol, and especially to distribute this information to elderly people, whose dietary changes may not affect their cholesterol levels to any great degree and whose cholesterol levels do not have any real scientific statistical association with their longevity, is, I think, poor public health policy. I feel sorry for the elderly folks I see in supermarkets, bent low over the food labels, worrying so much about something that plays such a small part in the risk factors of people their age. The cholesterol issue is more complex than Americans initially presumed. For all our study of heart disease, we must admit that we still cannot say for sure what precisely causes this illness. Cholesterol, as important a factor as it may be for some people, cannot be singled out as the single provocative agent for heart disease.

If your cholesterol level is 200 milligrams or less, have your doctor check your level again in two or three years and eat a normal diet. (The American Heart Association recommends that no more than 30 percent of the calories you eat come from fat.) If your cholesterol level is between 200 and 240 and you smoke, have high blood pressure, lead a very stressful life, or have any of the other risk factors for cardiovascular disease, you should control these factors immediately and perhaps reduce your cholesterol intake. If your cholesterol level is higher than 240, then you ought to talk to your doctor about changing many things you do. Your doctor may put you on a low-cholesterol diet but should not do so without also cutting down on your other risk factors. It makes no sense to go on a low-cholesterol diet and continue to smoke. For those who enjoy low blood cholesterol, I see no reason at all why a more liberal diet including some high-cholesterol foods is not perfectly satisfactory. I myself eat that way.

I think the public needs as much education about food safety as about nutrition. Some people believe that all man-made substances should be removed from our food supply and that everything that occurs naturally is beneficial. These people demand that we banish all pesticides. Fortunately, the large chain stores have not jumped on this bandwagon, although some small stores have pledged to sell nothing except foods untreated by pesticides. Not only will this leave them with rotting food, but also they will fail to protect the consumer against natural molds such as aflatoxin, which can be lethal and which occurs, for example, on untreated corn and peanuts.

People who are worried about the health risks from pesticides fail to realize that cancer rates have dropped over the last forty years: Stomach cancer has dropped more than 75 percent, while rectal cancer has dropped more than 65 percent. These encouraging statistics belie the claims that our food supply is laden with carcinogens in pesticides. The cancer rates that are increasing are cigarette-induced lung cancer in women and sun-induced skin cancer.

The World Health Organization and the Food and Agriculture Organization, both United Nations agencies, estimate that legal pesticides used on American produce result in the ingestion of ¼ to 1 percent of the allowable residues, even if consumed every day for a lifetime. The FDA is correct in saying that the average American consumes 45 micrograms of possibly carcinogenic man-made pesticide residues every day. But that is practically nothing compared with the 500 micrograms of naturally occurring carcinogens in one cup of coffee, or the 185 micrograms of natural carcinogens in one slice of bread. Some people insist that no amount of chemicals or pesticide residue in our food is acceptable. Public health officials, however (with abundant evidence), operate on the principle that mere exposure to a substance does not necessarily constitute a hazard. It is the combination of *toxicity* and *exposure* that creates the risk. We still have a long way to go in educating the American people about this difference between exposure and risk.

We do need to be concerned about eating a sensible diet, because this is a fundamental area in which we can take charge of our own health. Indeed, according to the American Council on Science and Health, two thirds of all deaths in America are directly or indirectly related to diet—but not to pesticides. Public health officials become frustrated when concern about diet leads to confusion about the safety of the food supply. Americans enjoy the safest food supply in the world, but it takes only an isolated incident or rumor to spread a national panic about the safety of our entire food supply. During the Alar apple scare of 1989, schools banned "apples for the teachers," housewives pitched out jars of applesauce, and one frantic mother in upstate New York insisted that the state police intercept her daughter's school bus because she had packed an apple in the little girl's lunch box before hearing the reports about Alar. The country was held hostage, apple crops destroyed, farmers impoverished by ill-prepared "experts" supported by Hollywood celebrities who terrorized the nation over nothing. An individual could have consumed the Alar in sixteen thousand apples without harm. Sometimes being too concerned about diet can be counterproductive. Worrying about traces of chemicals in a few foods may be keeping many Americans from eating the well-rounded and nutritious diets they need.

Press reports often confuse Americans about the scientific facts concerning substances such as Alar, saccharine, ethyl dibromide, and cyclamates. The press fails to explain that many scientific reports are based upon high-dose animal tests. Attempting to predict cancer risk in humans based upon these studies amounts more to scare tactics than science. If the Food and Drug Administration had its own way, it would not be as overly cautious as it appears to be, but it is hamstrung by the Delaney clause, a thirty-year-old congressional act that orders *any* additive that causes *any* cancer in *any* animal in *any* dose to be banned from food intended for human consumption. Even when the Delaney clause was passed in 1958, it rested upon very incomplete knowledge. The law failed to distinguish the size of the dose, the toxicity of the substance in question, the form of cancer, or the kind of animal upon which the substance was tested. Since then, the research community has become more sophisticated, determining that some carcinogens in animals do not have the same effect in humans. Further studies have indicated that the damage done to cells in some animals in some tests is due not to the carcinogenic substances themselves, but to the sheer toxicity of the *size* of the dose. Giving a laboratory rat a dose equivalent to my drinking a bathtub full of the same substance has been questioned as a valid scientific experiment. I think the Delaney clause needs to be amended to reflect current science. Of course, it is the height of hypocrisy to become worried about red dye in maraschino cherries while we allow the tobacco companies to peddle disease, disability, and death.

Drugs, Alcohol, and Drunk Driving

The problem of drugs in America is so large and so often discussed that I need not add my voice to all those who point out the urgency of doing something about the drug crisis; I would need another book to do that adequately. It is a complicated problem that touches not only upon public health, but also on law and politics. But I will make one medical comparison. Not too long ago, the medical community spent a good deal of time and effort trying to decide which was the best treatment for cancer: surgery, radiation, or chemotherapy. People divided themselves into camps, each championing its own solution. Eventually it became clear that the smartest strategy was a multiple one that employed all these solutions, emphasizing one or the other as appropriate to the problem at hand. In the same way, I think Americans have spent too much time trying to find the best way to fight drugs: eliminate the supply, reduce the demand, use interdiction or incarceration, or solve basic social problems. We need *all* these solutions and the wisdom to decide which to emphasize when. To raise the money to pay for the war on drugs, we could raise the excise tax on the two legal drugs, nicotine and alcohol. The higher price might put cigarettes out of the range of thousands of teenage purchasers, saving them from a lifetime of nicotine addiction.

If we are going to wage a war on drugs, we must not forget to wage it on alcohol. Alcohol is a toxic, potentially addictive drug, the greatest killer of America's youth between the ages of sixteen and twenty-four. Alcohol abuse causes one hundred thousand deaths annually and $136 billion in economic losses. An estimated 18 million adult Americans have medical, social, and personal problems related to the use of alcohol, as do several million adolescents, for whom alcohol is an illegal drug. Tens of millions of other adults and youths are affected by the alcohol problems of family members, friends, and work associates. These figures do not include the costs of grief and human suffering. How many deficits of this kind can our country afford?

Perhaps the most devastating consequence of alcohol use in this country is drunk driving. Someone is killed by a drunk driver every twenty-two minutes, and over 560,000 people are injured in alcohol-related traffic accidents each year. When the vehicular wreckage is towed away, the human wreckage is left behind—the permanent brain damage, spinal cord injuries, lost or permanently deformed limbs, blindness, impotence—lifetimes crippled with disability. It is easy to be numbed by the statistics, but each one represents a real person, a real human life. Unfortunately, a disproportionate number of highway victims are young people, young men and women between the ages of fifteen and twenty-four, who account for about of a third of all alcohol-related fatalities every year.

My final Surgeon General's Workshop focused on drunk driving and made several recommendations directed at vested interests, including:

• Reduce the permissible blood alcohol concentration (BAC) of drivers from its present level of 0.10 percent to 0.08 percent immediately, and to a level of 0.04 percent by the year 2000. And reduce the permissible BAC level for drivers under twenty-one to zero.
• Increase the federal excise tax or user fee on alcoholic beverages.
• Earmark the revenues from the federal excise tax increase to fund prevention programs.
• Encourage state and local governments to eliminate policies that increase the availability of alcoholic beverages.
• Pass administratively imposed driver's license sanctions separate from other criminal sanctions imposed by the courts.
• Authorize and fund federal agencies to purchase advertising time for pro-health and pro-safety messages if substantially increased public service time and space do not become available.

• Confiscate drivers' licenses on the spot for those found to be above the legal BAC.

• Restrict advertising and marketing practices targeted at underage youth.

• Expand the use of sobriety checkpoints, chemical breath test devices, drug recognition experts, and standardized field sobriety testing.

Alcohol-impaired driving must be seen as a public health and safety problem rather than as an economic and moral issue. Our primary concern must be with preserving human lives. Our goal must be the *total unacceptability* of driving after using alcohol or other drugs.

Domestic Violence

American society harbors an epidemic that infects over a million homes every year: domestic violence. As many as 15 million adult women have been victims of battery, rape, and other forms of physical and sexual assault in the home. Each year a million or more women will be added to that total. Each year an estimated 4 million children are victims of abuse and neglect. And nearly a million elderly persons—most of them women—are abused or neglected as well. Behind these cold numbers are real people: our family members, our neighbors, our fellow citizens. If anything, these statistics are much too low, since they do not take into account the number of unreported cases of abuse. This is an overwhelming moral, economic, and public health burden that our society can no longer bear.

The consequences of battering are enormous: loss of self-esteem, inability to work productively and to care for children, psychiatric problems, alcohol and drug dependence. Studies have shown that battered women are four to five times more likely than nonbattered women to require psychiatric treatment. Many suffer from anxiety, increased levels of hostility, obsessive-compulsive symptoms, and agoraphobia. Some commit suicide. Moreover, studies have shown that women who are abused are eight times more likely to abuse their children than women who are not abused. These abused children often become abusers themselves. We must break this vicious cycle.

Help is available from the law and the courts, and from community and social service organizations such as local and state alliances against domestic violence. Yet it is stunning to realize how ambivalent Americans remain about sex, violence, and power. For example, while rape is a felony crime, fewer than thirty states recognize marital rape as a crime. And while we have strong federal and state laws mandating persons to report actual or suspected cases of child abuse, experts point out that child abuse remains one of the most underreported crimes in our society. For our most vulnerable citizens, family and the home do not represent safety and nurturing—they stand for violence and victimization. No person has the right to abuse another person, and no institution—including "the home" and "the family"—can be allowed to shield such criminal behavior.

At last society is demanding certain kinds of behavior from its families—or it will intervene and effectively break up those families. We will place an abused child in protective custody and arrest the abusing parent, and we will provide shelter for an abused woman and her children, if necessary. As Surgeon General I supported the shelter movement because it was part of the public health system needed to prevent domestic violence and care for its victims. Frankly, this was not been an easy position for me to take, since I have always been ardently "pro-family." I wish I could say, according to my personal ethics, that families should take care of their own, but too often they don't.

Hearing

One of my Surgeon General's initiatives stemmed from a personal physical problem, one I shared with many Americans. After several years in Washington, something strange began to happen to me. I no longer found congressional hearings dull; I was actually enjoying committee meetings at the White House; staff meetings at the Department of Health and Human Services seemed less frustrating. Suddenly I realized why: I could not hear what the others were saying.

Although hearing loss can be a natural part of the aging process, too many people fail to come to terms with it. No one seems to object too strenuously to getting eyeglasses for vision loss, but there is a strange reluctance or shame about getting a hearing aid. Like vision loss, hearing loss often comes slowly. You find yourself asking others to repeat what they have just said to you, in crowded gatherings you tilt your head to try to catch the sound better, and then, as I did, you begin to make inappropriate responses in conversation because you cannot follow what is being said. Finally, I decided it was foolish to live like that when technology offered a simple solution.

Just before I received my hearing aids, I attended one of those

Washington receptions at the Hotel Willard. I had come to feel uncomfortable at receptions, and this one was typically difficult. I had the distinct feeling that I was missing more than I was receiving. The next morning, I got my hearing aids and that evening I hosted our annual Christmas party, where there was as much background noise as at the Willard the night before.

But my world had changed. Once again I was in touch with most of what was being said around me. From that day forward, I carried my head high in crowded rooms. Best of all, I could enjoy the full range of music once again. Shortly after I received my own hearing aids, I was interviewed on National Public Radio to urge other Americans having hearing problems to take the same step. To demonstrate how hearing aids had helped me, the interviewer played an excerpt from a Brandenburg concerto as I would hear it without my hearing aids: most of the high notes and some of the background notes were missing, and the piece sounded muted and flat. Then he played the same piece as my new hearing aids rendered it—and as Bach had written it. That was real music to my ears. Many listeners called or wrote that both versions sounded the same to them. They were referred to audiologists.

Hearing loss is not limited to the elderly: 1 out of 1000 American infants suffers impaired hearing. All too often, their problem goes undiagnosed and they are considered retarded, a classification that can cause them lifelong setbacks that could easily have been avoided. Parents, pediatricians, and the public at large must all be better educated to avoid this real tragedy.

Teenagers are also at risk of hearing loss. Most of them just ignore us when we tell them about the dangers of loud music, whether it blasts from stereo speakers or from portable stereo headphones. But it has been proven that exposure to a single rock concert can produce measurable—and irreparable—hearing loss. Once again, we need to educate parents, doctors, and the public about the problem so that teenagers can enjoy listening to their favorite music without doing permanent damage to their ears.

To eliminate correctable hearing loss, we need to be more aggressive both as a society and in the health professions. Technology is coming very close to the place where inexpensive and effective hearing aids will be within the reach of all Americans who need them. We need to encourage people who would benefit from hearing aids to get them. I am delighted by the way they have helped me. My wife has become accustomed to my changing the battery in my hearing aids even if we are in a fancy restaurant. As I tell her, it should be no different from

cleaning your eyeglasses, and after all, I enjoy making a public statement for hearing aids.

Health Care

Many Americans are critical about our health care system. But not
nearly as many are knowledgeable about it. Maybe I should call it our
health *scare* system, or our health care *non*-system. Unfortunately,
there is no system in the way Americans scramble for health care.

We have very high expectations for medicine and health. We routinely expect miracles to happen—even though the real world of medicine cannot always deliver. And it is becoming clear that our high
expectations are outrunning our ability to pay for them.

Everyone complains about the soaring cost of health care in the
United States. In 1990 we spent more than five times the federal deficit
on health care—$661 billion. That is more than we spent on education
and defense *combined.* There is something terribly wrong with a system of health care that spends more and more money to serve fewer
and fewer people.

In the past, most Americans turned confidently to their insurance
to pay the health care bill. But those days are over and we now have
three groups in this country: the insured, the uninsured, and the uninsurable.

The largest group, fortunately, is still the 160 million Americans
whose health insurance is provided through employers and the small
fraction who purchase their own insurance. These people usually enjoy
access to the best medicine in the world, as long as their insurance holds
out or their premiums are not raised beyond reach. But each year these
privately insured Americans seem to be paying more and more for
insurance that buys them less and less in health care, and employers
are now asking employees to assume more of the cost of health care
through higher deductibles and copayment. But employees are digging
in their heels and refusing, causing health care benefits to be the major
issue for 78 percent of striking workers in 1990. As more money goes
into employee health benefits, those increased costs come down to all
of us as higher prices for goods, services, and utilities. In other words,
our vast system of health insurance and employee health benefit plans
has become little more than a "pass-along" mechanism by which dollars taken from the American people in the open marketplace are
passed along and put into the pockets and treasuries of our ravenous
health care system.

Since 1984 the average premiums for employer-provided insurance have approximately doubled—to over $3,000 in 1989—and have risen from 8 percent of business payroll costs to 13.6 percent in 1990. Businesses cannot absorb these costs and expect to remain competitive.

All over the nation—in Cleveland, Pittsburgh, Denver, northern Wisconsin, central Minnesota, Connecticut, and Ohio—there are promising experiments. Businesses that purchase insurance are demanding—and getting—higher efficiency and higher quality in health care. These businesses are reaping the dividends of health care costs that are actually going *down*. And the efficient providers are being rewarded for their efforts—not with more dollars, but with more patients, who migrate to them from other plans of lower quality and less efficiency. This puts more pressure on inefficient providers to shape up or give up.

Private insurance is not the only institution in crisis. Government insurance—Medicare for the elderly, Medicaid for the poor—no longer fits the bill.

The graying of America carries a price tag. Medicare costs will double by 2020, and as the baby boomers reach their seventies in 2040, nursing home costs will reach astronomical levels. Medicare is not what most people think. It is not a system that provides health care for all the elderly. Older American citizens must first spend their own money before Medicare kicks in, and even then the system will not provide the drugs many need to stay alive. Most critical, Medicare makes no provision for long-term care in hospitals or nursing homes. Elderly people and their grown children are often shocked when they discover that when the aging parent needs nursing home care, it is not covered by Medicare. Furthermore, Medicare makes no attempt to avoid or postpone nursing home costs by providing services to the elderly in their own homes—for example, the cost of someone stopping by once a day to spend an hour on the health and household chores that need to be accomplished to keep an elderly person out of an institution. Medicare is one of the most decent things this country has done to remove much of the fear and uncertainty from elderly life, but it leaves much to be desired.

If Medicare is a disappointment, Medicaid, the federal insurance program designed for the poor, is even worse because it excludes most of the poor . . . by calling them too rich. Medicaid today covers only half of the nation's poor. Medicaid is administered by the individual state, and consequently allows terrible disparities between state systems of coverage and payment. A patient qualifying for an organ transplant in one state might not receive even basic medical services as a resident in an adjoining state. Furthermore, since state officials set the maximum income level needed to qualify for Medicaid, we see shameful standards. In 1990, in Alabama, a family with an annual income of $1,416 was too *rich* to qualify for Medicaid. Medicaid needs to be standardized, expanded, and reformed. Medicaid needs to embrace families rather than exclude them.

Then there are the uninsured, the 12 to 15 percent of our population—33 to 37 million Americans—who are uninsured, underinsured, or only seasonally insured. They are not old enough for Medicare and not poor enough for Medicaid. Their incomes are too low to live on but too high to qualify for Medicaid. These folks could go on welfare, get the dentures, eyeglasses, shoes, and food stamps they need for free, but their dignity keeps them struggling along, fearful of an illness that might claim all of the little they have.

The uninsured derive very little or nothing at all from our health care system. And they are suffering the consequences. There is a strong correlation between having no medical insurance and having serious health problems. All of us will suffer the consequences too, because the health problems of the uninsured, if ignored by society now, will be borne by society later.

Finally, and tragically, are the uninsurable: the 2½ million Americans with serious medical problems who cannot even buy insurance because they are considered to be bad risks. These are the very people for whom insurance should be intended. In addition to those who are denied the right to buy any insurance are the increasing number of patients who have their insurance premiums raised out of sight right in the middle of a serious illness. The disruption to society caused by the escalating costs of health care is simply unconscionable, with thousands of American families each year literally impoverished by the American health care system.

Above all, as a society and as individual citizens we need to eradicate poverty from this country. American health problems stem from diseases not only of the body, but also of society, especially the disease of poverty, which lies at the root of most of our public health problems: drug abuse, AIDS, alcohol abuse, malnutrition, smoking, and communicable diseases. Everything we do to eliminate poverty—whether with our checkbook or with our ballot—confronts our health care problems head on.

And we need leadership to get health care costs under control. It is not the present leadership—they are the ones who got us into our current problems of profligacy and poor care. And it is not a coalition of business and labor, as has been suggested. The coalition that needs to be formed combines business, organized health care, and, of course, the consumer. But until the purchasing public "buys right," the situation will not change.

I do not favor scrapping the system we have now. Its diversity makes it potentially the best in the world. But we need to make big changes. Several groups need to be shaken up: government, consumers, physicians, hospitals, third-party payers, lawyers, and the medical-industrial complex. Each must be willing to accept reform, swallowing some short-term discomfort so we can achieve a more efficient and fairer system for everybody.

We need to cut fat from the system. People fume when they read that health care administration now consumes about 22 percent of health care spending. I believe that 30 percent of what is done diagnostically and therapeutically is unnecessary. Cut the fat alone, and we will have saved $200 billion to pay for what we lack. It seems logical to say that employers should be required to provide health insurance for every employee along with health education and fitness programs. But the economic impact on small businesses must be buffered so they will not be forced to cut their payrolls.

Some of the states are way ahead of the federal government in dealing with the insurance crisis. Massachusetts has initiated a plan requiring employers to choose between providing employee insurance coverage or paying a tax to provide it. In Hawaii, the only state requiring employers to provide health care insurance, 95 percent of the state's population enjoys insured access to health care. Consequently, even though more people are insured, preventive medicine and timely treatment have brought health insurance premiums *below* the national average.

We can lower health care costs and insurance costs by linking insurance coverage to behavior. Insurance coverage should cost more for people who practice high-risk behavior such as not wearing motorcycle helmets, not buckling seat belts, driving after drinking, and, yes, continuing to smoke. On the positive side, we need insurance programs that encourage preventive health care, such as paying for smoking cessation programs.

To make sure we all get more for our health care dollar and for our insurance coverage, we need more open communication about the quality and efficiency of health care. We are developing tools to measure medical necessity, appropriateness, effectiveness, and, of course, outcomes. We are now comparing, for example, the cardiac surgery outcomes of all the hospitals in a state to see which hospitals—and which physicians—have produced mortality rates above normal, after allowing for variation in patient risk factors. After the appropriate adjustments are made, this information is shared with the public, who will know the batting averages—so to speak—of hospitals and physicians. Hospitals and doctors do not like this invasion of privacy, but this scrutiny and public accountability are here to stay. And I have noticed that the doctors who squawk the loudest at first are also the first to bring their outcomes to the normal range.

There are other areas in which we need changes in law and public policy. We must reform the malpractice mess, the tortured tort system that forces doctors and patients to view each other as legal adversaries. We cannot have doctors wondering if they will next see their patients in court, flanked by their lawyers.

In a legal climate in which anything short of perfection is grounds for a suit, some patients have gone to the hospital with their lawyers in tow. Malpractice suits corrupt the basic emotional climate of medicine, making the doctor fear the person she or he wants to help. Between 1981 and 1986, the number of malpractice suits tripled, and the average jury award quadrupled from $400,000 to $1.76 million. No wonder costly malpractice insurance forces doctors to make their insurance premiums, not the cost of medical care, the basis of their fee structure.

Malpractice does exist, and where there is malpractice—bad or negligent practice—restitution and compensation are in order. Medicine must rid itself of the bad apples that bring justified criticism to the profession. Yet too many malpractice suits are brought because a tragedy has occurred in spite of the doctor's best efforts.

We need to distinguish between negligent malpractice and tragic maloccurrence. Our current system does not serve the patient well. Every inappropriate malpractice suit drives up the cost of medicine for all patients and doctors alike, while negligent doctors continue to practice and some very good doctors leave their profession.

Malpractice reform is difficult because lawyers and the law are deeply entrenched, and they are not likely to reform easily. But we must demand reform. Perhaps an adjudicating board could decide which alleged malpractice cases are valid enough to be referred to the courts. We must eliminate awards for alleged pain and suffering. And we must do away with contingency fees, which clog the courts, blackmail physicians, and prompt insurance companies to spend our money out of court just to end the process.

I am sure that both the doctor and the patient would prefer to have the relationship of trust they once had, a relationship that is unfortunately becoming one of provider and consumer. Having to pay a high price for being ill makes it even more unpleasant, but we must subordinate the economic aspect of the relationship to the climate of trust between doctor and patient.

If the patient thinks of himself primarily as a consumer who wants to get the most for his money and shops around for a doctor who will charge five dollars less for an office visit, he automatically puts the doctor in the role of the seller, who wants to get the most for his services. If the doctor is primarily concerned about collecting his fee, he automatically arouses the consumer mentality in his patient. We cannot have patients wondering if their treatment is determined by their doctor's finances. The doctor–patient relationship can be restored. But it will take commitment by people on both ends of the stethoscope.

Epilogue

I was always proud to wear the uniform of the Surgeon General of the United States. But I also had to look ahead to the day when I would hang it in the closet for good. Because my original confirmation as Surgeon General had dragged on for almost a year, my two four-year terms stretched out longer than those of the president who had appointed me. As the election of 1988 drew near, I began to wonder if I would choose to serve with the new administration, either Dukakis or Bush. At no time did anyone in the Bush camp ever approach me to ask whether I would be interested in serving in any capacity if he were elected. Nor did any other Republican candidate for president indicate any such interest. On the other hand, when Democratic candidate Jesse Jackson and I were both addressing a meeting of the NAACP at the New York Hilton in 1988, he stopped me in the hall and said that if he were ever elected president, he would like to work with me. Presidential candidate Al Gore told me the same thing in the Washington Hilton. Boston physicians working for Dukakis made it very clear that if Dukakis were elected president there would be a post for me in his administration.

George Bush was always complimentary, but never gave me a hint about the future. I had met with him repeatedly on health issues, especially AIDS, and felt privileged to advise him. My discussions with George Bush confirmed what I had always believed from a distance: His preparation for the presidency was better than that of anyone who ever ran for the office.

In late 1988, as I entered what would be the last year of my second term as Surgeon General, I realized that I would never have time to accomplish all I wished to do, especially in the larger area of making major reforms in the health care system in the United States. But I realized I could do that just as well out of uniform. The future began to beckon to me, as I began to see all I might accomplish as a concerned citizen, one who had fought hard to earn the right to be heard. I more or less decided that I would leave my position before my term officially expired in November 1989.

But no sooner had I made my decision to leave, just after the Bush election, when a new opportunity, a new temptation—a new red herring—crossed my path. From all across the country, from within the medical profession, from ordinary citizens, and from many in public health, came the suggestion that I serve the new administration as secretary of Health and Human Services. My trusted friend and mentor, Assistant Surgeon General, Rear Admiral Jim Dickson, said that he would change his retirement plans and instead serve with me for two years if I were appointed. The offer gave me pause.

Of course, I had already thought about this job from time to time. No matter where you work, sometimes you think about what it would be like to be the boss. And, as Surgeon General, three levels down from cabinet rank, I had wondered what it would be like to be secretary of my department. There were many things I thought I could do with the position. As secretary of Health and Human Services, I would have the opportunity to try to convince the president and the Cabinet that health ought to assume a higher priority than it had ever been given in this country. The departments of State, Treasury, and Defense understandably were at the top (as in most nations), but why did health need to be at the bottom?

As attractive as the idea was, I recoiled from the apparent necessity to play politics. I quickly decided I did not want the job. But then, as so many urged me to reconsider, I gave it some serious thought.

A few days after the Bush election, I learned that many people were interceding on my behalf, and although I found myself wondering about the outcome, I had a sense of peace about it all. I realized that the heady atmosphere of the Cabinet could be quite enticing, but the more rational side of me said I had better things to do. If it worked out for me to be designated secretary, that would be fine, but the challenges of life out of government seemed inviting.

In the middle of all the rumors about new Bush Cabinet appointees, Betty and I were invited to a dinner hosted by secretary of state–designate Jim Baker and his wife, Susan. We had come to know Susan through administration social affairs and Fellowship House, a headquarters for Christian ministries in Washington. She came right up to us and said, "Jimmy gets lots of letters from people to make sure that you are kept on as Surgeon General." I felt I had to say something, so I boldly took Susan aside and told her that although I liked the Surgeon General's job, I had come to the conclusion that I could best help the president and the nation if I were the secretary of Health and Human Services. I simply stated that I had understudied the job for eight years, that I could hit the ground running and accomplish a lot very quickly. Susan Baker's eyes lit up, and she said, "Of course, you'd be just wonderful in that job." I replied that if she felt that way, she should get the word to Jim that I was available. (I thought it would be improper to approach Jim Baker myself. I am a poor politician.) I explained that I would not approach him myself, but that I would be interested in serving in that job, and I feared that most people in the new inner circle simply assumed I would like to continue as Surgeon General (although no overture had been made to me). I then reviewed briefly with her my general concerns about the future health of the nation, especially the clash between our aspirations for health care and our diminishing resources to pay for them. I said I had a number of ideas that would help the American people as they coped with the looming health crises. I told Susan, "I can say to you that you and I know that the Lord knows who is going to get the job of secretary, and that I am at peace about it no matter how it turns out. But I did feel that I should make known my availability to serve the new administration in a position for which I felt as well qualified as anyone in the country."

Once again I was a name on the Washington rumor roller coaster. This time, it was not nearly as important to me to be named as secretary of Health and Human Services as it had been to be confirmed as Surgeon General. As I said frequently during those weeks of wondering, if I were not nominated, I would be disappointed for three or four days, and then relieved the rest of my life. That is the way it turned out, but not before a few more times around the roller coaster.

Associates called me with "inside information" about the upcoming appointment. I never put complete stock in what they told me, including the statement that the AMA had never lobbied harder for any appointment and that I had unbelievable support in the White House, or that I was still under serious consideration but would have to assure George Bush and his team that I would not be as active and independent as a Cabinet member as I had been as Surgeon General. I knew I would not want the job with those constraints. In the atmosphere of speculation about Cabinet positions under George Bush, I felt I could readily go before Congress and make a plea for increased aid to mothers and children and honestly say, "This is what is needed; I have no idea where the money will come from." But I could never help solve the budget problem by lying, saying something like, "There is no need for further support of mothers and children," or "The states can handle it." In spite of his repeated statements that he wanted Cabinet members who spoke their minds, George Bush, like most presidents, required team players. I think my independence had earned me plaudits, but was anathema to the Bush administration.

In the midst of all the rumors we were invited to a Christmas brunch at the Bushes', and found that Dr. Louis Sullivan, his wife, Ginger, and two of his children had arrived just before us. I had been in Washington circles long enough to recognize the difference in an approach to someone you are thanking for a job well done as compared to someone with whom you are planning an ongoing relationship. Although George and Barbara were extremely cordial, I whispered in Betty's ear about twenty minutes later: "It's all over, the appointment is made. I've made the diagnosis on the basis of ambience and body language."

The brunch was a pleasant occasion, and I felt very privileged to attend the gathering, obviously arranged primarily for close friends of the Bush family and a few they admired, such as Sandra Day O'Connor and Tony Fauci. George Bush walked Betty and me to the door when we left about an hour and a half later, and said good-bye. It was not good-bye for Sunday afternoon, nor for Christmas, it was—sprinkled with sincere words of gratitude—GOOD-BYE.

Once Lou Sullivan was named secretary of Health and Human Services, I felt what I had predicted: a brief disappointment, followed by prolonged relief. The memories of my own wretched experience came back when Sullivan ran into confirmation delays stemming from his flip-flop on abortion and questions about his insistence that he continue to receive money from his former employer, even after he assumed the Cabinet position. If I had tried something like that in my first year, I would have been run out of town.

I thought that the public announcement of Sullivan's nomination was handled without tact. It was one of the last appointments. In his previous appointments of Cabinet members, the president had made it clear that he had selected the best man for the job. I never read that he said this about Sullivan, and I think the press made too much of his color and his friendship with the First Lady. I felt hurt for Lou Sullivan. I was sad that the department of Health and Human Services and the

American people were not off to a better start in health. It was, unfortunately, all too real a picture of the low priority health has in American politics. When will some administration recognize the importance of health of the American people and create a post of prominence for health in the cabinet?

That sense of relief I felt when I knew I would not be secretary was, however, tainted with one regret. I sincerely desired to have the opportunity to influence the president and the Cabinet to bring about a presidential commission to restudy health care delivery in America, to straighten out the chaotic system with which we all struggle. I thought I had earned the credibility with organized medicine and with the public to bring about some of the necessary rapproachment in the health care and insurance communities so we could at last provide health insurance to the 37 million Americans who live in that fearful world of the uninsured. But I soon realized that because of the low priority suffered by health policy in our politics and government, I could work even more effectively for my objectives outside the government.

The day the announcement of Sullivan's designation became official, I called his office at Moorehouse School of Medicine in Atlanta and left a message that of all the people who were standing in line to advise him, I was one who had no personal agenda, no axe to grind. I said that I would be more than pleased to brief him then or at any time, to warn him where the land mines were, and to offer any advice I could to make him a successful secretary. Would he please return my call? He never did.

Eventually, I did get an appointment for a conversation with Lou Sullivan more than two months after my first call. I tried to give him advice that would be helpful to him as he dealt with the problems that were bound to arise, emphasizing the importance of clear communication with those above him, especially with the White House and the OMB, and—even more important—with those below him. But his subsequent actions gave no clue that he had heeded anything I said.

In the last few months of my tenure, Lou Sullivan had the opportunity to introduce me on several occasions when I was about to give a speech or receive an award. He always spoke in complimentary and friendly terms. On two occasions, I made it clear to the public that there was no rancor between us, and that he had my total support. He did, and I only wished he had done more, so I could have had more to support. There were so many issues that cried out for his attention and action and yet seemed ignored: Assurances of understanding and support to the PHS and its agencies, reform of Medicare and Medicaid payments under the Health Care Financing Administration, the appropriate (and rapid) movement of paper through his office, and recognition that we at least need to study the situation of the many Americans without health insurance.

But that seemed to be a problem in the entire government in those first months of the Bush administration. The election of Vice President Bush to succeed President Reagan might have augured a smooth, enthusiastic transition, but instead the period between election and inauguration—and even beyond—was a time of missed opportunities and mistakes. I did not know whether to laugh or cry when I received a letter from the White House, addressed to "Mr. Koop," thanking me for my willingness to serve in the new administration and asking me for my "department, position, and expertise."

The business of government ground to a halt, as people awaited leadership or even instructions from the new team. Eight years earlier, I had arrived in Washington with other Reagan appointees to find a great air of expectancy and enthusiasm in the city, the government, and the Department of Health and Human Services. January 1989 was a different story; morale was low and people carried on in a desultory way. For most of the people I worked with, that period came to an abrupt end. My boss and good friend, Otis Bowen, a man who had served as secretary of Health and Human Services longer than anyone in the department's history, received a telephone call from a White House staffer, ordering him to clear out his desk and vacate his office in three days. In spite of such rude treatment by the Bush people, Bowen's farewell talk to the department was typically graceful and moving.

On George Bush's inauguration day I felt depressed. The people I had worked with for the past eight years were gone, and the new administration was keeping its distance from me. As Betty said, it was like a high school graduation when everyone else was going on vacation and I had to go to summer school.

I had not yet decided on the date of my resignation when I wrote President Bush in February to inform him that it was my intention to resign before my second term as Surgeon General officially ended in November 1989. I had hoped to arrange a proper change of command from me to my successor, as is the practice in the other uniformed services. But the White House seemed uninterested, and, either playing politics or simply being indecisive or indolent, would delay naming my successor for months after I left.

As time went on, I began to wonder if any future I might have contemplated in government service had been spiked by pro-lifers in January 1989, just days after Bush assumed office. After the annual march in Washington to protest *Roe* v. *Wade,* pro-life leaders met with the newly elected Bush. Many in the pro-life crowd thought, erroneously, that I had betrayed them because I had refused to falsify my findings in the letter on the health effects of abortion on women I had sent to Reagan just before he left office. I had made several attempts to explain the situation to the incoming president, because I thought he might have to take some heat from the angered pro-life people. But neither Bush nor Sununu nor their staffs returned my calls. Although Bush claimed an anti-abortion stance, he had done nothing to please the pro-life people. If they had asked him to refuse to keep me on, it would have been a bone he could toss to them. If it did happen that way, there would be a certain irony because it would have meant that my exit from government had been assured by the president and the pro-life leaders, just the way my entry into government had been assured by that same bunch and a different president in the same room eight years earlier. I will never know.

I became increasingly anxious to move on. The Sullivan crew had taken away my personal assistant, leaving me with only my two excellent secretaries, Michelle Trotter and Joyce Lally. I found it more difficult to hack through the everyday details, to pursue larger initiatives. And the sense of drift and malaise that permeated the Department of Health and Human Services took the joy out of going to work.

I wanted my actual resignation to come with as little fuss and with as few questions as possible. So I planned to deliver notice of my decision to resign just before I left for the two-week World Health Assembly in Geneva in May 1989. Since I did not want to be baited by the press into criticizing Sullivan or Bush, I hoped the public announcement of my resignation would not occur until I was winging my way across the Atlantic. Instead, after my letter was delivered to the White House mailroom at 8 A.M., the announcement interrupted the morning news programs, and my office and home telephones were swamped with calls. I was still frantically packing my suitcase for Geneva. I did an end run around reporters at the airport and settled into my seat on the plane, leaving a lot of stories floating around alleging that I left in a huff.

Weeks earlier I had discussed with Chase Untermeyer of White House Personnel how I should go about resigning from the Commissioned Corps. He suggested that I send a letter to the president, stating my intent but inasmuch as the date was not yet settled to wait until all dates were firm and send a second message. My first letter received a lot of publicity, but its full text was never published. So, there was some misinterpretation when I sent my second letter. It was, being a follow-up to the first, merely a statement that I would leave office formally on October 1, 1989, but would go on terminal leave status beginning July 13. Because the letter was short and factual, some reporters interpreted it as being "terse" because I was "miffed." That was not true. George Bush and I remain good friends.

As I contemplated the outlines of my third career—after being a pediatric surgeon for thirty-five years and then Surgeon General for nearly eight years—I wondered if I should be making so many plans. After all, I was then seventy-two, seven years past the age when so many of my colleagues had retired. Once in a while I wondered what it would be like actually to retire, to do all those leisure-time activities that my life had excluded. I had always wanted to mosey through a New England village, look at the town records, poke around the cemetery, talk to the old-timers, get a sense of the history of one little place. Or— another wish going as far back as my days as a college zoology student— to get a bucket of water from a pond, and spend as long as it took to find and classify all the microscopic life that thrived in that invisible world. But I knew that these were fleeting thoughts, that the contemplative life was not my style, that there was more work to do. Betty often said that I had many talents, but that retirement was not one of them. I have always believed that the best way to remain active and alert is to be certain that society expects something of you.

It had dawned on me only slowly that I had moved into a favored place in the public eye. It began when I noticed passersby catching my eye with that look that said, "Where do I know you from?" Then they would say, "Didn't I see you on TV?" By 1988 it seemed that almost everyone who walked by me in an airport or on the street smiled, nodded a greeting, or said hello. I was most surprised—and pleased— when people would crowd around and start conversations, on the New York subway, on street corners, in airport waiting lounges. I was deeply moved by the personal nature of what they had to say: "You made my mother stop smoking, thank you." Or "My son died of AIDS. God bless you." They would ask questions about their mother's broken hip, a son's epilepsy, a nightmare of a problem with medical insurance, or they would ask me to look at a sore elbow. More than any other comment was, "Thank you for a job well done," or "Thank you for what you did for the country."

All this surprised me because for many years people had told me, only after they got to know me, that I had initially seemed austere, intimidating, even frightening. That always had bothered me, since I never tried to scare anyone. I think I am shy. But suddenly total strangers felt at ease with me, willing to share their personal problems. My son Allen said that the content and style of my health messages to the nation had fostered an image of "approachable authority." Maybe so. But I began to feel like the Surgeon General of all the people. As Betty repeatedly said, I had become family doctor to the nation. As I came to the end of my Surgeon General years, I felt that I had gained the public's trust and that I should do something with it.

First, I wanted to make sure I did not use that trust only for private gain. Like many Americans, I was disgusted with the way retired politicians—even presidents—cashed in on their celebrity status. There was no shortage of companies that wanted to make a quick and big buck off me. Offers inviting me to endorse everything from condoms to cereals poured into my office as soon as my intention to resign became known. In one week I turned down more than $8 million. It was a little frightening, since as yet I had no job for the future. And with three children in not-so-profitable careers (history professor, minister, and wife of an officer of a nonprofit organization), there were big education bills ahead for seven grandchildren. But I was not about to sell or rent my integrity and the public trust.

Sometimes when people would ask me what I planned to do next, I would just joke with them, "I'll join a circus." They would look quizzically, and I would say, "The thing I know best is how to walk a tightrope!" But then I would add, pretty weakly, "You'll hear from me." But as questions persisted, "But what are you going to do?" I filled in the answers: "About the same thing I've been doing—only without government portfolio and government constraint. I hope to continue my delivery of health messages to the American people through the written word, the spoken word, and through whatever radio and television outlets are made available to me."

It took me a while to put into words exactly what I intended to do. As so often happens, the right words came to me at a press conference, my final one as Surgeon General. Reporter Jerry Brazda asked how I would like to be remembered. I had never given much thought to a question like that, but the words that came out captured my hopes:

"Sometime five years or more from now I'd like one of you to say, 'You know, after he ceased to be Surgeon General, he continued to be the health conscience of America.' "

I had some idea of what I wanted to do. Like many other people,

I knew the entire health care system in the United States had become desperately ill. It had grown inefficient, wasteful, and, even immoral. It seemed to me that we had a small window of time, maybe five or ten years, to avoid either the imposition of a tyrannical and insensitive government-run health system or the outright exploitation of the American people by a system of private medicine run amok. I knew there was no easy solution, no quick fix. I knew it would take a judicious and delicate balance of public and private reform. I knew that the American people, the American government, and American medicine could do it. But not without effort, discipline, pain, and leadership. I wanted to do what I could do to continue my work in health promotion and disease prevention. I wanted to do what I could do to bring to all Americans reasonable health care at reasonable cost. I did not know if I could make a difference, but I knew I had to try.

By the time I left the government I had gathered around me a little team who would help me. The Children's Hospital National Medical Center appointed me chair of the National "Safe Kids" Campaign, and that gave me a base of operations: an office and a secretary to handle the requests that came in for me to do something in medicine or public health, requests that poured in at a rate of forty to fifty each day (much of the public still seemed to view me as a public servant). Longtime surgical colleagues and close friends Paul Gorsuch, from San Antonio, and Steve Gans, from Los Angeles began to work with me to plan a series of prime-time television health specials. My son Allen split his time between teaching history at Dartmouth College and assisting me with my memoirs and in speechwriting. And of course Betty continued in her role of more than a half century as my chief consultant and partner.

No one had attempted what I sought to do. It reminded me of starting out as an untried pediatric surgeon, starting out as an untried Surgeon General. I knew my endeavors to revamp the American health care system would bring out opponents, people who were too entrenched and too comfortable in the current system to brook change. Once again, I knew I would face some opposition, but perhaps not outright hostility. This time there was a big difference. I did not feel alone. I felt I had at my side the millions of Americans who had reached out to support me as I sought to serve them as their Surgeon General. And, of course, I rested in the firm faith that my future, like my past, was shaped by the sovereignty of God.

Appendix A

Understanding AIDS:
A Message from the Surgeon General

This brochure has been sent to you by the Government of the United States. In preparing it, we have consulted with the top health experts in the country.

I feel it is important that you have the best information now available for fighting the AIDS virus, a health problem that the President has called "Public Enemy Number One."

Stopping AIDS is up to you, your family, and your loved ones.

Some of the issues involved in this brochure may not be things you are used to discussing openly. I can easily understand that. But now you must discuss them. We all must know about AIDS. Read this brochure and talk about it with those you love. Get involved. Many schools, churches, synagogues, and community groups offer AIDS education activities.

I encourage you to practice responsible behavior based on understanding and strong personal values. This is what you can do to stop AIDS.

What AIDS Means to You

AIDS is one of the most serious health problems that has ever faced the American public. It is important that we all, regardless of who we are, understand this disease.

AIDS stands for *acquired immunodeficiency syndrome.* It is a disease caused by the Human Immunodeficiency Virus, HIV—the AIDS virus.

The AIDS virus may live in the human body for years before actual symptoms appear. It primarily affects you by making you unable to fight other diseases. These other diseases can kill you.

Many people feel that only certain "high risk groups" of people are infected by the AIDS virus. This is untrue. *Who you are has nothing to do with whether you are in danger of being infected with the AIDS virus. What matters is what you do.*

People are worried about getting AIDS. Some should be worried and need to take some serious precautions. But many are not in danger of contracting AIDS.

The purpose of this brochure is to tell you how you can, and just as important, how you can't become infected with the AIDS virus.

Your children need to know about AIDS. Discuss it with them as you would any health concern.

How Do You Get AIDS?

There are two main ways you can get AIDS. First, you can become infected by having sex—oral, anal, or vaginal—with someone who is infected with the AIDS virus.

Second, you can be infected by sharing drug needles and syringes with an infected person.

Babies of women who have been infected with the AIDS virus may be born with the infection because it can be transmitted from the mother to the baby before or during birth.

In addition, some persons with hemophilia and others have been infected by receiving blood.

Can You Become Infected?

Yes, if you engage in risky behavior.

The male homosexual population was the first in this country to feel the effects of the disease. But in spite of what you may have heard, the number of heterosexual cases is growing.

People who have died of AIDS in the U.S. have been male and female, rich and poor, white, Black, Hispanic, Asian, and American Indian.

How Do You Get AIDS from Sex?

The AIDS virus can be spread by sexual intercourse whether you are male or female, heterosexual, bisexual, or homosexual.

This happens because a person infected with the AIDS virus may have the virus in semen or vaginal fluids. The virus can enter the body through the vagina, penis, rectum, or mouth.

Anal intercourse, with or without a condom, is risky. The rectum is easily injured during anal intercourse.

Remember, AIDS is sexually transmitted, and the AIDS virus is not the only infection that is passed through intimate sexual contact.

Other sexually transmitted diseases, such as gonorrhea, syphilis, herpes, and chlamydia, can also be contracted through oral, anal, and vaginal intercourse. If you are infected with one of these diseases and engage in risky behavior, you are at greater risk of getting AIDS.

You Won't Get AIDS from Insects—Or a Kiss

No matter what you may have heard, the AIDS virus is hard to get and is easily avoided.

You won't just "catch" AIDS like a cold or flu because the virus is a different type. The AIDS virus is transmitted through sexual intercourse, the sharing of drug needles, or to babies of infected mothers before or during birth.

You won't get the AIDS virus through everyday contact with the people around you in school, in the workplace, at parties, child care centers, or stores. You won't get it by swimming in a pool, even if someone in the pool is infected with the AIDS virus. Students attending school with someone infected with the AIDS virus are not in danger from casual contact.

You won't get AIDS from a mosquito bite. The AIDS virus is not transmitted through a mosquito's salivary glands like other diseases such as malaria or yellow fever. You won't get it from bed bugs, lice, flies, or other insects, either.

You won't get AIDS from saliva, sweat, tears, urine, or a bowel movement.

You won't get AIDS from a kiss.

You won't get AIDS from clothes, a telephone, or from a toilet seat. It can't be passed by using a glass or eating utensils that someone else has used. You won't get the virus by being on a bus, train, or crowded elevator with a person who is infected with the virus, or who has AIDS.

The Difference Between Giving and Receiving Blood

1. Giving blood. You are not now, nor have you ever been in danger of getting AIDS from giving blood at a blood bank. The needles that are used for blood donations are brand-new. Once they are used, they are destroyed. There is no way you can come into contact with the AIDS virus by donating blood.

2. Receiving blood. The risk of getting AIDS from a blood transfusion has been greatly reduced. In the interest of making the blood supply as safe as possible, donors are screened for risk factors and donated blood is tested for the AIDS antibody. Call your local blood bank if you have questions.

What Behavior Puts You at Risk?

You are at risk of being infected with the AIDS virus if you have sex with someone who is infected, or if you share drug needles and syringes with someone who is infected.

Since you can't be sure who is infected, your chances of coming into contact with the virus increase with the number of sex partners you have. Any exchange of infected blood, semen, or vaginal fluids can spread the virus and place you at great risk.

The following behaviors are risky when performed with an infected person. You can't tell by looking if a person is infected.

RISKY BEHAVIOR

Sharing drug needles and syringes.
Anal sex, with or without a condom.
Vaginal or oral sex with someone who shoots drugs or engages in anal sex.
Sex with someone you don't know well (a pickup or prostitute) or with someone you know has several sex partners.
Unprotected sex (without a condom) with an infected person.

SAFE BEHAVIOR

Not having sex.
Sex with one mutually faithful, uninfected partner.
Not shooting drugs.

What About Dating?

Dating and getting to know other people is a normal part of life. Dating doesn't mean the same thing as having sex. Sexual intercourse as a part of dating can be risky. One of the risks is AIDS.

How can you tell if someone you're dating or would like to date has been exposed to the AIDS virus? The bad news is, you can't. But the good news is, as long as sexual activity and sharing drug needles are avoided, it doesn't matter.

You are going to have to be careful about the person you become sexually involved with, making your own decision based on your own best judgment. That can be difficult.

Has this person had any sexually transmitted diseases? How many people have they been to bed with? Have they experimented with drugs? All these are sensitive, but important, questions. But you have a personal responsibility to ask.

Think of it this way. If you know someone well enough to have sex, then you should be able to talk about AIDS. If someone is unwilling to talk, you shouldn't have sex.

Do Married People Get AIDS?

Married people who are uninfected, faithful, and don't shoot drugs are not at risk. But if they engage in risky behavior, they can become infected with the AIDS virus and infect their partners. If you feel your spouse may be putting you at risk, talk to him or her. It's your life.

What Is All the Talk About Condoms?

Not so very long ago, condoms (rubbers or prophylactics) were things we didn't talk about very much.

Now, they're discussed on the evening news and on the front page of your newspaper, and displayed out in the open in your local drugstore, grocery, and convenience store.

For those who are sexually active and not limiting their sexual activity to one partner, condoms have been shown to help prevent the spread of sexually transmitted diseases. That is why the use of condoms is recommended to help reduce the spread of AIDS.

Condoms are the best preventive measure against AIDS besides not having sex and practicing safe behavior.

But condoms are far from being foolproof. You have to use them properly. And you have to use them every time you have sex, from start to finish. If you use a condom, you should remember these guidelines:

(1) Use condoms made of latex rubber. Latex serves as a barrier to the virus. "Lambskin" or "natural membrane" condoms are not as good because of the pores in the material. Look for the word "latex" on the package.

(2) A condom with a spermicide may provide additional protection. Spermicides have been shown in laboratory tests to kill the virus. Use the spermicide in the tip and outside the condom.

(3) Condom use is safer with a lubricant. Check the list of ingredients on the back of the lubricant package to make sure the lubricant is water-based. Do not use petroleum-based jelly, cold cream, baby oil, or cooking shortening. These can weaken the condom and cause it to break.

What Does Someone with AIDS Look Like?

It is very important that everyone understands that a person can be infected with the AIDS virus without showing any symptoms at all.

It is possible to be infected for years, feel fine, look fine, and have no way of knowing you are infected unless you have a test for the AIDS virus.

During this period, however, people infected with the AIDS virus can pass the virus to sexual partners, to people with whom drug needles are shared, and to children before or during birth. That is one of the most disturbing things about AIDS.

Once symptoms do appear, they are similar to the symptoms of some other diseases. As the disease progresses, they become more serious. That is because the AIDS virus keeps your body's natural defenses from operating correctly.

If you are concerned whether you might be infected, consider your own behavior and its effects on others. If you feel you need to be tested for the AIDS virus, talk to a doctor or an AIDS counselor for more information. *(See below.)*

Is There a Cure for AIDS?

There is presently no cure for AIDS.

Medicines such as AZT have prolonged the lives of some people with AIDS. There is hope that additional treatments will be found.

There is also no vaccine to prevent uninfected people from getting the infection. Researchers believe it may take years for an effective, safe vaccine to be found.

The most effective way to prevent AIDS is avoiding exposure to the virus, which you can control by your own behavior.

Should You Get an AIDS Test?

You have probably heard about the "AIDS Test." The test doesn't actually tell you if you have AIDS. It shows if you have been infected with the virus. It looks for changes in blood that occur after you have been infected.

The Public Health Service recommends you be confidentially counseled and tested if you have had any sexually transmitted disease or shared needles; if you are a man who has had sex with another man; or if you have had sex with a prostitute, male or female. You should be tested if you have had sex with anyone who has done any of these things.

If you are a woman who has been engaging in risky behavior and you plan to have a baby or are not using birth control, you should be tested.

Your doctor may advise you to be counseled and tested if you are a hemophiliac, or have received a blood transfusion between 1978 and 1985.

If you test positive, and find you have been infected with the AIDS virus, you must take steps to protect your partner.

People who have always practiced safe behavior do not need to be tested.

There's been a great deal in the press about problems with the test. It is very reliable if it is done by a good laboratory and the results are checked by a physician or counselor.

If you have engaged in risky behavior, speak frankly to a doctor who understands the AIDS problem, or to an AIDS counselor.

For more information, call your local public health agency. They're listed in the government section of your phone book. Or, call your local AIDS hotline. If you can't find the number, call 1-800-342-AIDS.

The Problem of Drugs and AIDS

Today, in some cities, the sharing of drug needles and syringes by those who shoot drugs is the fastest growing way that the virus is being spread.

No one should shoot drugs. It can result in addiction, poor health, family disruption, emotional disturbances, and death. Many drug users are addicted and need to enter a drug treatment program as quickly as possible.

In the meantime, these people must avoid AIDS by not sharing any of the equipment used to prepare and inject illegal drugs.

Sharing drug needles, even once, is an extremely easy way to be infected with the AIDS virus. Blood from an infected person can be trapped in the needle or syringe, and then injected directly into the bloodstream of the next person who uses the needle.

Other kinds of drugs, including alcohol, can also cause problems. Under their influence, your judgment becomes impaired. You could be exposed to the AIDS virus while doing things you wouldn't otherwise do.

Teenagers are at an age when trying different things is especially inviting. They must understand how serious the drug problem is and how to avoid it.

Drugs are also one of the main ways in which prostitutes become infected. They may share needles themselves or have sex with people who do. They then can pass the AIDS virus to others.

For information about drug abuse treatment programs, contact your physician, local public health agency, or community AIDS or drug assistance group.

AIDS and Babies

An infected woman can give the AIDS virus to her baby before it is born, or during birth. If a woman is infected, her child has about one chance in two of being born with the virus.

If you are considering having a baby, and think you might have been at risk of being infected with the AIDS virus, even if it was years ago, you should receive counseling and be tested before you get pregnant.

You must have a long talk with the person with whom you're planning to have a child. Even if you have known this person for a long time, there's no way to be sure he or she hasn't been infected in the past, possibly without realizing it. That person needs to think hard and decide if an AIDS test might be a good idea. So should you.

Talking with Kids About AIDS

Children hear about AIDS, just as we all do. But they don't understand it, so they become frightened. They are worried they or their friends might get sick and die.

Children need to be told they can't get AIDS from everyday contact in the classroom, cafeteria, or bathrooms. They don't have to worry about getting AIDS even if one of their schoolmates is infected.

Basic health education should be started as early as possible, in keeping with parental and community standards. Local schools have the responsibility to see that their students know the facts about AIDS. It is very important that middle school students—those entering their teens—learn to protect themselves from the AIDS virus.

Children must also be taught values and responsibility, as well as skills to help them resist peer pressure that might lead to risky behavior. These skills can be reinforced by religious and community groups. However, final responsibility rests with the parents. As a parent, you should read and discuss this brochure with your children.

Helping a Person with AIDS

If you are one of the growing number of people who know someone who is infected, you need to have a special understanding of the problem.

No one will require more support and more love than your friend with AIDS. Feel free to offer what you can, without fear of becoming infected.

Don't worry about getting AIDS from everyday contact with a person with AIDS. You need to take precautions such as wearing rubber gloves only when blood is present.

If you don't know anyone with AIDS, but you'd still like to offer a helping hand, become a volunteer. You can be sure your help will be appreciated by a person with AIDS.

This might mean dropping by the supermarket to pick up groceries, sitting with the person a while, or just being there to talk. You may even want to enroll in a support group for caregivers. These are available around the country. If you are interested, contact any local AIDS-related organization.

Above all, keep an upbeat attitude. It will help you and everyone face the disease more comfortably.

Do You Know Enough to Talk About AIDS? Try This Quiz

It's important for each of us to share what we know about AIDS with family members and others we love. Knowledge and understanding are the best weapons we have against the disease. Check the boxes. Answers below.

1. If you are not in a "high risk group," you still need to be concerned about AIDS.
    ☐ True   ☐ False

2. The AIDS virus is not spread through
    ☐ A. insect bites.
    ☐ B. casual contact.
    ☐ C. sharing drug needles.
    ☐ D. sexual intercourse.

3. Condoms are an effective, but not foolproof, way to prevent the spread of the AIDS virus.
    ☐ True   ☐ False

4. You can't tell by looking that someone has the AIDS virus.
    ☐ True   ☐ False

5. If you think you've been exposed to the AIDS virus, you should get an AIDS test.
    ☐ True   ☐ False

6. People who provide help for someone with AIDS are not personally at risk for getting the disease.
    ☐ True   ☐ False

ANSWERS

1. True. It is risky *behavior* that puts you at risk for AIDS, regardless of any "group" you belong to. *See pages* 320-321.
2. A & B. The AIDS virus is not spread by insects, kissing, tears, or casual contact. *See page* 321.
3. True. However, the most effective preventive measure against AIDS is

not having sex or shooting drugs. *Condoms are discussed in detail on pages 323-324.*

4. True. You cannot tell by looking if someone is infected. The virus by itself is completely invisible. Symptoms may first appear years after you have been infected. *See page 324.*

5. True. You should be counseled about getting an AIDS test if you have been engaging in risky behavior or think you have been exposed to the virus. There is no reason to be tested if you don't engage in this behavior. *See page 325.*

6. True. You won't get AIDS by helping someone who has the disease. *See page 327.*

Appendix B
Principles of Treatment
of Disabled Infants

Discrimination of any type against any individual with a disability/ disabilities, regardless of the nature or severity of the disability, is morally and legally indefensible.

Throughout their lives, all disabled individuals have the same rights as other citizens, including access to such major societal activities as health care, education, and employment. These rights for all disabled persons must be recognized at birth.

Need for Information

There is need for professional education and dissemination of updated information which will improve decision-making about disabled individuals, especially newborns. To this end, it is imperative to educate all persons involved in the decision-making process. Parents should be given information on available resources to assist in the care of their disabled infant. Society should be informed about the value and worth of disabled persons. Professional organizations, advocacy groups, the government, and individual care givers should educate and inform the general public on the care, need, value, and worth of disabled infants.

Medical Care

When medical care is clearly beneficial, it should always be provided. When appropriate medical care is not available, arrangements should be made to transfer the infant to an appropriate medical facility. Consideration such as anticipated or actual limited potential of an individual and present or future lack of available community resources are irrelevant and must not determine the decisions concerning medical care. The individual's medical condition should be the sole focus of the decision. These are very strict standards.

It is ethically and legally justified to withhold medical or surgical procedures which are clearly futile and will only prolong the act of dying. However, supportive care should be provided including sustenance as medically indicated and relief of pain and suffering. The needs of the dying person should be respected. The family also should be supported in its grieving.

In cases where it is uncertain whether medical treatment will be beneficial, a person's disability must not be the basis for a decision to withhold treatment. At all times during the process when decisions are being made about the benefit or futility of medical treatment, the person should be cared for in the medically most appropriate ways. When doubt exists at any time about whether to treat, a presumption always should be in favor of treatment.

Government and Community Support

Once a decision to treat an infant has been made, government and private agencies must be prepared to allocate adequate resources for appropriate services as needed to child and family for as long as needed. Services should be individualized, community-based, and coordinated.

The federal government has a historical and legitimate role in protecting the rights of its citizens. Among these rights is the enforcement of all applicable federal statutes established to prevent and remedy discrimination against individuals with disabilities, including those afforded by Section 504 of the Rehabilitation Act. States also have legitimate roles in protecting the rights of their citizens and an obligation to enforce all applicable state laws.

Index